DAUGHTER
OF THE
EAST

BY

BENAZIR BHUTTO

HAMISH HAMILTON · LONDON

HAMISH HAMILTON LTD

Published by the Penguin Group
27 Wrights Lane, London W8 5TZ, England
Viking Penguin Inc, 40 West 23rd Street, New York, New York 10010, U.S.A.
Penguin Books Australia Ltd, Ringwood, Victoria, Australia
Penguin Books Canada Ltd, 2801 John Street, Markham, Ontario, Canada L3R 1B4
Penguin Books (N.Z.) Ltd, 182–190 Wairau Road, Auckland 10, New Zealand

Penguin Books Ltd, Registered Offices: Harmondsworth, Middlesex, England

First published in Great Britain 1988 by
Hamish Hamilton Ltd

Copyright © 1988 by Benazir Bhutto

1 3 5 7 9 10 8 6 4 2

British Library Cataloguing in Publication Data

Bhutto, Benazir
    Daughter of the East.
    1. Bhutto, Benazir 2. Politicians
    —— Pakistan —— Biography
    I. Title
    954.9'105'0924   DS385.B4/

ISBN: 0241 123984

Typeset in 11/12pt Palatino
Printed and bound in Great Britain by
Richard Clay Ltd, Bungay, Suffolk

In loving memory of my father, my brother, and
all those who lost their lives in opposing General
Zia's Martial Law in Pakistan

CONTENTS

LIST OF ILLUSTRATIONS

EDITOR'S NOTE

Hours before this book went to press, General Mohammed Zia ul-Haq and thirty-one others were killed when their C-130 Hercules transport plane exploded shortly after take-off from Bahawalpur in the eastern part of Pakistan. Also killed in the crash on August 17, 1988, was the United States Ambassador to Pakistan, Arnold Raphel, and ten senior officers of the Pakistan armed forces, including the Chairman of the joint Chiefs-of-Staff and the Vice-Chief-of-Army-Staff.

Under provisions of the Pakistan Constitution, the Chairman of the Senate, Ghulam Ishaq Khan, became acting President. Stating that 'sabotage cannot be ruled out', he launched an investigation into the accident and declared a state of national emergency.

Acting President Khan also declared that the general elections set for November 16, 1988, by his predecessor were to be held as scheduled. At the time of writing it is not known whether the elections will actually take place or, if so, whether political parties will be allowed to participate.

In Karachi immediately after the accident, Benazir Bhutto endorsed the civil transition of power. Speaking for the Pakistan People's Party, she told the press, 'We think that it is a positive development that the constitutional path has been followed.' She did not hide her shock at General Zia's death. 'It is unbelievable that this entire shadow of death and threat we have lived under for so long is actually gone,' she said. 'I would have preferred to defeat Zia at the polls, but life and death are in God's hands.'

INTRODUCTION

I have always believed in the importance of historical record. When the government of my father, Zulfikar Ali Bhutto, was overthrown in 1977, I encouraged many of those who had worked closely with him to write about the Bhutto period. But in the difficult years of Martial Law that followed in Pakistan many from my father's government were busy fighting the persecution and the false cases brought against them by the military regime. Others had fled into exile, and had no access to their personal papers. My own involvement in the struggle to return democracy to Pakistan, and the years I consequently spent imprisoned without charge, made it impossible for me to write a book on my father's government myself.

More than a million of my countrymen came out to greet me when I returned to Pakistan after two years of exile in April, 1986, catapulting me into the glare of international publicity. Suddenly I received several offers to write not my father's story, but my own. I hesitated. It was one matter to write about my father who had become the democratically elected Prime Minister of Pakistan and had lasting achievements to his name, and quite another to write about myself, whose most important political battles were still to be fought. It seemed presumptuous. I thought autobiographies were written in the autumn of one's life, looking back.

A friend's chance remark changed my mind. 'What is not recorded is not remembered,' she told me. I saw her point. Like many in Pakistan, I had experienced the dark years of Martial Law. Unlike many, I had the opportunity to put those experiences on record. It is important that the world remember the repression we in Pakistan have had to bear following General Zia's coup d'état.

Writing the book has been difficult. It has meant reliving the pain of the past. But it has also been cathartic, forcing me for the first time to come to terms with memories I had been trying to escape.

This is my story: events as I saw them, felt them, reacted to them. It is

1

not an in-depth study of Pakistan, but a glance into the transformation of a society from democracy to dictatorship. Let it also be a call for freedom.

BENAZIR BHUTTO
June 21, 1988
Karachi, Pakistan

1

THE ASSASSINATION OF MY FATHER

They killed my father in the early morning hours of April 4, 1979, inside Rawalpindi Central Jail. Imprisoned with my mother a few miles away in a deserted police training camp at Sihala, I felt the moment of my father's death. Despite the Valiums my mother had given me to try and get through the agonising night, I suddenly sat bolt-upright in bed at 2.00 am. 'No!' the scream burst through the knots in my throat. 'No!' I couldn't breathe, didn't want to breathe. Papa! Papa! I felt cold, so cold, in spite of the heat, and couldn't stop shaking. There was nothing my mother and I could say to console each other. Somehow the hours passed as we huddled together in the bare police quarters. We were ready at dawn to accompany my father's body to our ancestral family graveyard.

'I am in *Iddat* and can't receive outsiders. You talk to him,' my mother said dully when the jailer arrived. She was beginning a widow's four months and ten days of seclusion from strangers.

I walked into the cracked cement-floored front room that was supposed to serve as our sitting room. It stank of mildew and rot.

'We are ready to leave with the Prime Minister,' I told the junior jailer standing nervously before me.

'They have already taken him to be buried,' he said.

I felt as if he had struck me. 'Without his family?' I asked bitterly. 'Even the criminals in the military regime know that it is our family's religious obligation to accompany his body, to recite the prayers for the dead, to see his face before burial. We applied to the jail superintendent . . .'

'They have taken him,' he interrupted.

'Taken him where?'

The jailer was silent.

'It was very peaceful,' he finally replied. 'I have brought what was left.'

He handed me one by one the pitiful items from my father's death cell: my father's *shalwar khameez*, the long shirt and loose trousers he'd worn to the end, refusing as a political prisoner to wear the uniform of a condemned criminal; the tiffin box for food that he had refused for the last ten days; the roll of bedding they had allowed him only after the broken wires of his cot had lacerated his back; his drinking cup . . .

'Where is his ring?' I managed to ask the jailer.

'Did he have a ring?'

I watched him make a great show of fishing through his bag, through his pockets. Finally he handed me my father's ring, which towards the end had regularly slipped off his emaciated fingers.

'Peaceful. It was very peaceful,' he kept muttering.

How could a hanging be peaceful?

Basheer and Ibrahim, our family bearers who had come to prison with us because the authorities did not provide us with food, came into the room. Basheer's face went white when he recognised my father's clothes.

'Ya Allah! Ya Allah! They've killed Sahib! They've killed him!' he screamed. Before we could stop him, Basheer grabbed a can of petrol and doused himself with it, preparing to set himself aflame. My mother had to rush out to prevent his self-immolation.

I stood in a daze, not believing what had happened to my father, not wanting to. It was just not possible that Zulfikar Ali Bhutto, the first Prime Minister of Pakistan to be elected directly by the people, was dead. Where there had been repression under the Generals who had ruled Pakistan since its birth in 1947, my father had been the first to bring democracy. Where the people had lived as they had for centuries at the mercy of their tribal chiefs and landlords, he had installed Pakistan's first constitution to guarantee legal protection and civil rights. Where the people had had to resort to violence and bloodshed to unseat the Generals, he had guaranteed a Parliamentary system of civilian government and elections every five years.

No. It was not possible. 'Jiye Bhutto! Long live Bhutto!' millions had cheered when he became the first politician ever to visit the most forlorn and remote villages of Pakistan. When his Pakistan People's Party was voted into office, my father had started his modernisation programmes, redistributing the land held for generations by the feudal few among the many poor, educating the millions held down by ignorance, nationalising the country's major industries, guaranteeing minimum wages, job security, and forbidding discrimination against women and minorities. The six years of his government had brought light to a country steeped in stagnant darkness – until the dawn of July 5, 1977.

Zia ul-Haq. My father's supposedly loyal army Chief-of-Staff. The General who had sent his soldiers in the middle of the night to overthrow my father and take over the country by force. Zia ul-Haq, the military dictator who had subsequently failed to crush my father's following in spite of all his guns and tear gas and Martial Law regulations, who had failed to break my father's spirit despite his isolation in a death cell. Zia ul-Haq, the desperate General who had just sent my father to his death. Zia ul-Haq. The General who would ruthlessly rule Pakistan for the next nine years.

I stood numbly in front of the junior jailer, holding the small bundle that was all that was left of my father. The scent of his cologne was still on his clothes, the scent of Shalimar. I hugged his *shalwar* to me, suddenly remembering Kathleen Kennedy who had worn her father's parka at Radcliffe long after the Senator had been killed. Our two families had always been compared in terms of politics. Now, we had a new and dreadful bond. That night, and for many other nights, I too tried to keep my father near me by sleeping with his shirt under my pillow.

I felt completely empty, that my life had shattered. For almost two years, I had done nothing but fight the trumped-up charges brought against my father by Zia's military regime. I had worked with the Pakistan People's Party towards the elections Zia had promised at the time of the coup, then cancelled in the face of our impending victory. I had been arrested six times by the military regime and repeatedly forbidden by the Martial Law authorities to set foot in Karachi and Lahore. So had my mother. As acting chairperson of the PPP during my father's imprisonment, she had been detained eight times. We had spent the last six weeks under detention in Sihala, the six months before that under detention in Rawalpindi. Yet not until yesterday had I allowed myself to believe that General Zia would actually assassinate my father.

Who would break the news to my younger brothers who were fighting my father's death sentence from political exile in London? And who would tell my sister Sanam who was just finishing her final year at Harvard? I was especially worried about Sanam. She had never been political. Yet she had been dragged into the tragedy with all of us. Was she alone now? I prayed she wouldn't do anything foolish.

I felt as if my body was literally being torn apart. How could I go on? In spite of our efforts, we had failed to keep my father alive. I felt so alone. I just felt so alone. 'What will I do without you to help me?' I had asked him in his death cell. I needed his political advice. For all that I held degrees in government from Harvard and Oxford, I was not a politician. But what could he say? He had shrugged helplessly.

I had seen my father for the last time the day before. The pain of that meeting was close to unbearable. No one had told him he was to be executed early the next morning. No one had told the world leaders who had officially asked the military regime for clemency, among them Jimmy Carter, Margaret Thatcher, Leonid Brezhnev, Pope John Paul II, Indira Gandhi, and many others from the entire Muslim spectrum, Saudi Arabia, the Emirates, Syria. Certainly none of the cowards in Zia's regime had announced the date of my father's execution to the country, for they feared the people's reaction to their Prime Minister's murder. Only my mother and I knew. And that, by accident and deduction.

I had been lying on my army cot in the early morning of April 2 when

5

my mother suddenly came into the room. 'Pinkie,' she said, calling me by my family nickname, but in a tone that immediately made my body go rigid. 'There are army officers outside saying that *both* of us should go to see your father today. What does that mean?'

I knew exactly what it meant. So did she. But neither of us could bear to admit it. This was my mother's visiting day, allowed her once a week. Mine was scheduled for later in the week. That they wanted both of us to go could only mean that this was to be the last visit. Zia was about to kill my father.

My mind raced. We had to get the word out, to send a last call to the international community and to the people. Time had run out. 'Tell them I'm not well,' I said to my mother hastily. 'Say that if it is the last meeting then, of course, I will come, but if it is not, we will go tomorrow.' While my mother went to speak to the guards, I quickly broke open a message I had already wrapped. I wrote a new one. 'I think they are calling us for our last meeting,' I scribbled furiously to a friend on the outside, hoping she would alert the party's leaders, who in turn would inform the diplomatic corps and mobilise the people. The people were our last hope.

'Take this immediately to Yasmin,' I told Ibrahim, our loyal servant, knowing we were taking a great risk. There wasn't time for him to wait for a sympathetic or lackadaisical guard to come on duty. He could be searched and followed. He wouldn't be able to take the normal precautions. The danger was enormous, but so were the stakes. 'Go, Ibrahim, go!' I urged him. 'Tell the guards you're fetching medicine for me!' And off he ran.

I looked out of the window to see the Martial Law contingent consulting with each other, then transmitting the message that I was ill on their wireless set and waiting to receive information back. In the confusion, Ibrahim reached the gate. 'I have to get medicine for Benazir Sahiba quickly. Quickly!' he said to the guards who had overheard the talk of my bad health. Miraculously, they let Ibrahim through, barely five minutes after my mother had first come to me in the bedroom. My hands would not stop trembling. I had no idea if the message would be safely delivered.

Outside the window, the wireless sets crackled. 'Because your daughter is not feeling well, you can make the visit tomorrow,' the authorities finally told my mother. We had gained another twenty-four hours of life for my father. But when the compound gates were sealed immediately after Ibrahim had fled, we knew something terribly ominous was about to occur.

Fight. We had to fight. But how? I felt so powerless, locked inside the stockade while the moments towards my father's death ticked by. Would the message get through? Would the people rise up in spite of the guns and bayonets they had faced since the coup? And who would lead them? Many of the leaders of the Pakistan People's Party were in jail. So were thousands of our supporters, including, for the first time in Pakistan's history, women. Countless others had been tear-gassed and flogged just for mentioning my father's name, the numbers of lashes to be administered painted on their half-naked bodies. Would the people heed this last desperate call? Would they even hear it?

At 8.15 pm my mother and I tuned in to the BBC Asia report on our radio. Every muscle in my body was rigid. I sat expectantly forward as the BBC reported that I had sent a message from prison that tomorrow, April 3, was to be the last meeting with my father. The message had got through! I waited for the BBC announcement of our call to the people to rise in protest. There was none. Instead, the BBC went on to report that there was no confirmation of the news from the jail superintendent. 'She's panicked,' it quoted one of my father's former ministers as saying. My mother and I couldn't even look at each other. Our last hope had died.

A speeding jeep. Crowds frozen in fear behind security forces, not knowing the fate of their Prime Minister. Prison gates hastily opened and closed. My mother and I being searched again by jail matrons, first leaving our own prison in Sihala, then again when we arrived at the jail in Rawalpindi.

'Why are you both here?' my father says from inside the inferno of his cell.

My mother doesn't answer.

'Is this the last meeting?' he asks.

My mother cannot bear to answer.

'I think so,' I say.

He calls for the jail superintendent who is standing by. They never leave us alone with Papa.

'Is this the last meeting?' my father asks him.

'Yes,' comes the reply. The jail superintendent seems ashamed to be the bearer of the regime's plans.

'Has the date been fixed?'

'Tomorrow morning,' the superintendent says.

'At what time?'

'At five o'clock, accordng to jail regulations.'

'When did you receive this information?'

'Last night,' he says reluctantly.

My father looks at him.

7

'How much time do I have with my family?'

'Half an hour.'

'Under jail regulations, we are entitled to an hour,' he says.

'Half an hour,' the superintendent repeats. 'Those are my orders.'

'Make arrangements for me to have a bath and a shave,' my father tells him. 'The world is beautiful and I want to leave it clean.'

Half an hour. Half an hour to say good-bye to the person I love more than any other in my life. The pain in my chest tightens into a vice. I must not cry. I must not break down and make my father's ordeal any more difficult.

He is sitting on the floor on a mattress, the only furniture left in his cell. They have taken away his table and his chair. They have taken away his bed.

'Take these,' he says, handing me the magazines and books I had brought him before. 'I don't want them touching my things.'

He hands me the few cigars his lawyers have brought him. 'I'll keep one for tonight,' he says. He also keeps his bottle of Shalimar cologne.

He starts to hand me his ring, but my mother tells him to keep it on. 'I'll keep it for now, but afterwards I want it to go to Benazir,' he tells her.

'I have managed to send out a message,' I whisper to him as the jail authorities strain to hear. I outline the details and he looks satisfied. 'She's almost learned the ropes of politics,' his expression reads.

The light inside the death cell is dim. I cannot see him clearly. Every other visit they have allowed us to sit together inside his cell. But not today. My mother and I squeeze together at the bars of his cell door, talking to him in whispers.

'Give my love to the other children,' he says to Mummy. 'Tell Mir and Sunny and Shah that I have tried to be a good father and wish I could have said good-bye to them.' She nods, but cannot speak.

'You have both suffered a lot,' he says. 'Now that they are going to kill me tonight, I want to free you as well. If you want to, you can leave Pakistan while the Constitution is suspended and Martial Law imposed. If you want peace of mind and to pick up your lives again, then you might want to go to Europe. I give you my permission. You can go.'

Our hearts are breaking. 'No, no,' Mummy says. 'We can't go. We'll never go. The Generals must not think they have won. Zia has scheduled elections again, though who knows if he will dare to hold them? If we leave, there will be no one to lead the party, the party you built.'

'And you, Pinkie?' my father asks.

'I could never go,' I say.

He smiles. 'I'm so glad. You don't know how much I love you, how much I've always loved you. You are my jewel. You always have been.'

'Time is up,' the superintendent says. 'Time is up.'

I grip the bars.

'Please open up the cell,' I ask him. 'I want to say good-bye to my father.'

The superintendent refuses.

'*Please*,' I say. 'My father is the elected Prime Minister of Pakistan. I am his daughter. This is our last meeting. I want to hold him.'

The superintendent refuses.

I try to reach my father through the bars. He is so thin, almost wasted away from malaria, dysentery, starvation. But he pulls himself erect, and touches my hand.

'Tonight I will be free,' he says, a glow suffusing his face. 'I will be joining my mother, my father. I am going back to the land of my ancestors in Larkana to become part of its soil, its scent, its air. There will be songs about me. I will become part of its legend.' He smiles. 'But it is very hot in Larkana.'

'I'll build a shade,' I manage to say.

The prison authorities move in.

'Good-bye, Papa,' I call to my father as Mummy reaches through the bars to touch him. We both move down the dusty courtyard. I want to look back, but I can't. I know I can't control myself.

'Until we meet again,' I hear him call.

Somehow my legs move. I cannot feel them. I have turned to stone. But still I move. The jail authorities lead us back through the jail ward, the courtyard filled with army tents. I move in a trance, conscious only of my head. High. I must keep it high. They are all watching.

The car is waiting inside the locked gates so the crowds outside won't see us. My body is so heavy I have difficulty getting in. The car speeds forward through the gate. At its sight the crowds surge towards us but are shoved back roughly by the security forces. I suddenly glimpse my friend Yasmin at the edge of the crowd, waiting to deliver my father's food. 'Yasmin! They are going to kill him tonight!' I try and shout from the window. Did she hear me? Did I make any sound at all?

5.00 came and went. 6.00. Each breath I took reminded me of the last breaths of my father. 'God, let there be a miracle,' my mother and I prayed together. 'Let something happen.' Even my little cat Chun-Chun whom I had smuggled into detention with me felt the tension. She had abandoned her kittens. We couldn't find them anywhere.

Yet we clung to hope. The Supreme Court had unanimously recommended that my father's death sentence be commuted to life imprisonment. Moreover, under Pakistani law, the date of any execution must be announced at least a week before its implementation. There had been no such announcement.

9

PPP leaders on the outside had also sent word that Zia had promised Saudia Arabia, the Emirates, and others in confidence that he would commute my father's death sentence. But Zia's record was filled with broken promises and disregard for the law. In the face of our persistent fears, the Foreign Minister of Saudi Arabia and the Prime Minister of Libya had promised to fly in should a date for execution be announced. Had they heard my message on the BBC? Was there time for them to fly in now?

A Chinese delegation was in Islamabad. My father had pioneered Pakistan's friendship with China. Would they sway Zia on his behalf?

My mother and I sat motionless in the white heat at Sihala, unable to speak. Zia had also let it be known that he would entertain a plea for clemency only from my father, or from us, his immediate family. My father had forbidden it.

How do such moments pass in the countdown towards death? My mother and I just sat. Sometimes we cried. When we lost the strength to sit up, we fell onto the pillows on the bed. They'll snuff out his life, I kept thinking. They'll just snuff out his life. How alone he must be feeling in that cell, with no one near him. He didn't keep any books. He didn't keep anything. He has just that one cigar. My throat tightened until I wanted to rip it open. But I didn't want the guards who were always laughing and talking right outside our window to have the pleasure of hearing me scream. 'I can't bear it, Mummy, I can't,' I finally broke down at 1.30. She brought me some Valium. 'Try to sleep,' she said.

Half an hour later I shot up in bed, feeling my father's noose around my neck.

The skies rained tears of ice that night, pelting our family lands in Larkana with hail. At our family graveyard in the nearby ancestral Bhutto village of Garhi Khuda Bakhsh, the people were awakened by the commotion of a military convoy. While my mother and I were passing the agonising night in prison, my father's body was being secretly flown to Garhi for burial. The advance party of Martial Law administrators made their grim arrangements with Nazar Mohammed, a villager who oversees our lands and whose family has worked with ours for generations.

Nazar Mohammed:

I was sleeping in my house at about 3.00 am on April 4 when I woke to notice strong lights of fifty to sixty military vehicles on the outskirts of the village. At first I thought they were rehearsing again for the actions they were to take after Mr Bhutto was to be hanged as they had two days earlier, claiming they were normal military exercises. The people were quite terrorised then, especially after the police entered the Bhutto grave-yard to take a careful look around. When the police summoned me out of my house at such an early hour, all the village folk — old, young, men and women — came out of their houses. All feared that Mr Bhutto had either already been hanged or was soon to be. There was wailing and crying and desperation in their faces.

'We must arrange for the burial of Mr Bhutto,' the large number of army and police personnel said to me at their temporary headquarters. 'Show us where the grave is to be.' I was weeping. 'Why should we point out the place of burial to you?' I asked them. 'We will perform the final rites by ourselves. Mr Bhutto belongs to us.'

I asked that I be allowed to bring our people to dig the grave, fetch the unbaked bricks to line it, cut the wooden planks to put on top of it, and perform our religious recitations. They permitted me only eight men to help.

While we got busy with this sad task, military and police vehicles not only surrounded the entire village but blockaded every small street. No one from the village could go out and no one from outside the village could enter. We were completely cut off.

At 8.00 am two helicopters landed close to the village on the road where an ambulance was waiting. I watched the coffin being transferred to the ambulance and followed it to the graveyard. 'Evacuate this house,' the Army Colonel said to me, pointing to the small dwelling place in the south corner of the graveyard where the prayer leader who tends the graves lives with his wife and small children. I protested at the cruelty and inconvenience this would be to the Pesh Imam and his family, but the Colonel insisted. Twenty armed uniformed men then took up positions on the roof with their rifles pointed into the graveyard.

Near relatives must have a last look at the face of the departed. There were Bhutto cousins living in Garhi right next to the graveyard. Mr Bhutto's first wife also lived in the nearby village of Naudero, and after great argument the authorities allowed me to fetch her. When she arrived we opened the coffin and transferred the body onto a rope cot I had brought from my house before carrying it into the walled home. The family lived in *purdah* and kept their women protected from the eyes of strangers. No males outside the family were allowed in. But the army people forced their way into the house against all norms of decency.

When the body was brought out half an hour later, I asked the Colonel, on oath, if the bath in accordance with religious rules and the traditional burial ceremony had been given. He swore that it had. I checked to see if the *kaffan*, the unstitched cotton shroud, had been put on the body. It was there.

We were too perturbed and grief-stricken to look at the rest of the body. I'm not sure they would have allowed it as their doings would have been exposed. But his face was the face of a pearl. It shone like a pearl. He looked the way he had at sixteen. His skin was not of several colours, nor did his eyes or tongue bulge out like the pictures I'd seen of the men that Zia had hanged in public. As ritual demands, I turned Bhutto Sahib's face to the West, towards Mecca. His head did not fall to the side. His neck was not broken. There were strange red and black dots on his throat, however, like an official stamp.

The Colonel became very angry. 1,400 to 1,500 people from the village were forcing their way near the coffin and looking at the glow from the martyr's face. Their wailing was heart-rending. The Colonel threatened to baton-charge the people if they didn't leave.

'The burial must take place at once,' he said. 'If we have to, we will do it with the help of the rod.'

'They are mourning and heart-broken,' I told him.

At gunpoint, we hurried through the last prayers for the dead and then, with ceremony befitting the departed soul, we lowered the body into the grave. The recitation of the Holy Book mingled with the wailing of the women rising from the houses.

For days at Sihala, after my father's death, I couldn't eat or drink. I would take sips of water, but then I'd have to spit it out. I couldn't swallow at all. Nor could I sleep. Every time I closed my eyes I had the same dream. I was standing in front of the district jail. The gates were open. I saw a figure walking towards me. Papa! I rushed to him. 'You've come out! You've come out! I thought they had killed you! But you're alive!' Just before I reached him, I would wake up and have to realise once again that he was gone.

'You must eat, Pinkie, you must,' my mother said, bringing me some soup. 'You will need all your strength when we get out of here to prepare for the elections. If you want to keep fighting for your father's principles, to fight the way he fought, then eat. You must.' And I ate a little.

I forced myself to read the messages of condolence that were slipped in to us. 'My dear Auntie and Benazir,' wrote a family friend from Lahore on April 5. 'I have no words to describe my sorrow and grief. The whole nation is responsible to you for what has happened. We are all culprits . . . Every Pakistani is sad, demoralised and insecure. We are all guilty and burdened with sin.'

On the same day, ten thousand people gathered in Rawalpindi on Liaquat Bagh Common, where a year and a half before my mother had drawn huge crowds, standing in for my imprisoned father in the first election campaign. Seeing the overwhelming popularity of the PPP, Zia had cancelled the elections and sentenced my father to death. Now, while offering funeral prayers and eulogies for my father, his followers were once again tear-gassed by the police. The people ran, hurling bricks and stones at the police who moved in with batons and started making arrests. Yasmin, her two sisters and her mother attended the prayer meeting. So did Amina Piracha, a friend who had helped the lawyers working on my father's Supreme Court case, Amina's two sisters, her nieces and their old *ayah* of seventy. All ten women were arrested, along with hundreds of others, and imprisoned for two weeks.

Rumours quickly began to circulate about my father's death. The hangman had gone mad. The pilot who had flown my father's body to Garhi had become so agitated when he'd learned the identity of his cargo that he'd had to land his plane and have another pilot called in. The papers were full of other lurid details about my father's end. He had been tortured almost to death and, with only the barest flicker of a pulse, had been carried on a stretcher to his hanging. Another persistent report claimed that my father had died during a fight in his cell. Military officers had tried to force him to sign a 'confession' that he had orchestrated the coup himself and invited Zia to take over the country. My father had refused to sign the lies the regime needed to give it legitimacy.

In this version one of the officers had given my father a violent push. He had fallen, striking his head on the wall of his cell, and had never regained consciousness. A doctor had been summoned to revive him, giving him a heart massage and a tracheotomy which would explain the marks Nazar Mohammed had seen on his neck. But it had been to no avail.

I tended to believe this story. Why else had my father's body shown no physical signs of a hanging? Why else had I woken up at 2.00 am, a full three hours before his scheduled execution? Another political prisoner, General Babar, told me he, too, had woken in a sudden chill at 2.00. So did other friends and political supporters scattered around the world. It was as if my father's soul was passing among those who had loved him.

And the rumours persisted.

'Exhume the body and order a post-mortem,' my father's cousin and then People's Party leader Mumtaz Bhutto urged me during a condolence call at Sihala. 'It could be to our political advantage.' Political advantage? My father was dead. Exhuming his body was not going to bring him back to life.

'They did not let him live in his death cell even before they killed him,' I told Uncle Mumtaz. 'Now he's free. Let him rest in peace.'

'You don't understand what historical importance this could have,'

Uncle Mumtaz persisted.

I shook my head. 'History will judge him on his life. The details of his death do not matter,' I said. 'I will not have him exhumed. He needs his rest.'

My mother's niece, Fakhri, was permitted to come to Sihala to mourn with us, as was my childhood friend, Samiya Waheed. They were relieved to find that, although we were grief-stricken, we had not fallen apart. 'We had heard you were so depressed you were going to commit suicide,' said Samiya, recounting another rumour the regime was spreading.

Fakhri, who is quite emotional, rushed to embrace my mother, consoling her in Persian. 'Nusrat *joon*, I wish I had died. I wish I had never seen this day,' she cried. 'People are saying hanging is too good for Zia.'

Fakhri hugged me too. She had been the one to bring me the news of my father's death sentence a year before, slipping through the police guard at our house in Karachi where I was being held in detention. I had been sitting in the living room when she suddenly burst through the front door and prostrated herself in the entrance hall, howling in grief and hitting her forehead on the floor. Within half an hour the military authorities had brought a detention order for Fakhri herself, a woman who didn't have a political bone in her body but who spent her days playing mah-jongg and bridge. She had been imprisoned with me for the next week, unable to return to her husband and small children.

Now we wept together. Hundreds of people, she told us — factory workers, taxi drivers, street pedlars — were gathering in our garden in Karachi in preparation for the *soyem*, our religious ceremony on the third day following death. Every night for weeks before, women had come to the house by the busload to pray for my father through the night, holding their Holy Qurans over their heads.

The uniforms of the army, which had always been a source of national pride, were now the objects of derision, Fakhri also told us. On the plane flight from Karachi, she and Samiya had refused to sit next to any man in army uniform. 'Murderers!' they had screamed. The other travellers had lowered their heads in a mark of respect towards those who were grieving. Nobody said a word. There were tears in everyone's eyes.

We had applied to the authorities to visit my father's grave on the *soyem*, and at 7.00 am on April 7 we were told we had five minutes to get ready. We didn't have black mourning clothes to wear and went in what we had brought with us to prison. 'Hurry! Hurry!' a Martial Law officer insisted as we packed into the car to drive to the airport. They were always hurrying us, frightened that the people would catch a glimpse of us, wave, cheer, or in any way demonstrate their sympathy for us and by implication their antipathy for Martial Law.

But not all the military had turned into inhuman machines. At the airport, members of the crew of the military plane were standing like a guard of honour when we arrived, their heads lowered. When my mother got out of the car, they saluted her. It was a fitting gesture for the widow of the man who had brought over ninety thousand of their fellow soldiers safely back from the prison camps of India. Not everyone had forgotten. During the short flight they offered us tea, coffee and sandwiches, their faces showing their shock and sorrow. The crime of the few had become the guilt of the many.

The plane didn't land at Moenjodaro, the airport nearest to Garhi Khuda Bakhsh, but at Jacobabad an hour away. Nor did the local military authorities choose a direct route from the airfield to the village over the modern roads my father had built. Instead, the car bumped and lurched along unpaved lanes, the driver going out of his way to avoid the possibility of our being seen through the heavily curtained windows. We were covered in sweat and dust when we finally arrived at the entrance to our family graveyard.

As I moved towards the narrow portal, an army officer moved with me. I stopped.

'No. You can't enter. None of you can enter,' I said. 'This is our graveyard. You don't belong here.'

'We are under orders not to let you out of our sight,' he told me.

'I cannot permit you to come in here and violate its sanctity,' I told him. 'You killed my father. You sent him here. If we mourn him now, we will mourn him alone.'

'We have been ordered to be with you at all times,' he insisted.

'Then we won't visit the grave. Take us back,' my mother said, moving towards the car. He stepped back, and we entered the walled graveyard, leaving our shoes at the entrance as a sign of respect.

How peaceful it seemed. And how familiar. Generations of Bhuttos whose lives were sweeter lay there: my grandfather, Sir Shah Nawaz Khan Bhutto, former Prime Minister of Junagadh State, knighted by the British for his services to the Bombay presidency before the partition of India; his wife, Lady Khurshid; my uncle, Sikander Bhutto, and his legendary brother, Imdad Ali, so handsome, it is said, that when he drove his carriage down Elphinstone Street, Karachi's main shopping area, the English ladies ran out of their shops to stare at him. Many other relatives also lay there, in the soil which had given us birth and to which we return when we die.

My father had brought me here just before I had left Pakistan to go to

Harvard University in 1969. 'You are going far away to America,' he had told me as we stood among the graves of our forebears. 'You will see many things that amaze you and travel to places you've never heard of. But remember, whatever happens to you, you will ultimately return here. Your place is here. Your roots are here. The dust and mud and heat of Larkana are in your bones. And it is here that you will be buried.'

Through my tears now, I looked for his grave. I didn't even know where they had buried him. I almost didn't recognise his grave when I saw it. It was just a mound of mud. Raw mud sprinkled with flower petals. Mummy and I sat at the foot of the grave. I couldn't believe my father was under it. I dropped down and kissed the part of the mud where I imagined his feet to be.

'Forgive me, father, if I ever caused you any unhappiness,' I whispered.

Alone. I felt so alone. Like all children, I had taken my father for granted. Now that I had lost him, I felt an emptiness that could never be filled. But I did not weep, believing as a Muslim that tears pull a spirit earthward and won't let it be free.

My father had earned his freedom, had paid dearly for his peace. His suffering had ended. 'Glory be to Him who has control over all things,' I read from the Ya Sin *surah* of the Holy Quran. 'To Him, you shall all return.' My father's soul was with God in Paradise.

They hurried us back to the airport over a different and even more tortuous route. But the same crew again stood at attention. There was no difference either in our searches at the gates to Sihala, no difference in the grimy rooms we were being held in. But a sense of peace and a new certainty had settled over me.

Stand up to challenge. Fight against overwhelming odds. Overcome the enemy. In the stories my father had told us over and over as children, good always triumphed over evil.

'Whether you grasp an opportunity or let it slip away, whether you are impetuous or thoughtful, whether you have unsinkable nerves or are timid, all of these choices are up to you,' he had always impressed upon us. 'What you make of your destinies is up to you.'

Now, in the nightmare that had engulfed Pakistan, his cause had become my own. I had felt it as I stood by my father's grave, felt the strength and conviction of his soul replenishing me. At that moment I pledged to myself that I would not rest until democracy returned to Pakistan. I promised that the light of hope that he had kindled would be kept alive. He had been the first leader of Pakistan to speak for all the people, not just for the military and the élite. It was up to us to continue.

As my mother and I were being taken back to Sihala after my father's

16

soyem, soldiers were lobbing tear gas shells among the hundreds packed into our garden at 70 Clifton to read and reread prayers for my father's soul. The barrage of shells was so intense that the canopy over the patio was set on fire. Clutching their Holy Qurans, the grieving people dispersed, choking.

THE YEARS OF
DETENTION

2

IMPRISONED IN MY OWN HOME

My mother and I were released from Sihala at the end of May, 1979, seven weeks after my father's death. We returned to 70 Clifton, our family home in Karachi.

Everything was the same. But nothing was the same. 'Zulfikar Ali Bhutto, Bar-at-Law' read the brass nameplate beside the gate to 70 Clifton. Above it was another brass plate, faded with time, inscribed with my grandfather's name, Sir Shah Nawaz Bhutto. My grandmother built this two-storey sprawling bungalow shortly after I was born in 1953 and my brothers, sister and I grew up here in the cooling breezes from the Arabian Sea just a quarter of a mile away. Who could have foreseen the tragedy and violence that would overtake this peaceful family compound?

Every day hundreds of wailing mourners mass in the garden of coconut palms, mangoes, and red and yellow flowering trees coaxed from the desert of Karachi. Hundreds more wait patiently outside the gates to pay condolence calls to their leader's family. My mother is still in *Iddat* and can't receive outsiders. She sends me to greet them instead.

The familiarity of being at home makes our nightmare seem even more unreal. Two nights before my father was hanged, the staff tell us, the army raided 70 Clifton for the second time, searching the roof and the garden, opening my mother's safe, rifling through the clothes in my father's cupboards. 'Do you have a search warrant?' one of the staff had asked, still clinging to the concept of civil law. 'I am with the search party, so there is no need for a warrant,' claimed the army officer who had come with the police. For ten hours they had torn the house apart, taking many of my personal letters from my bedroom and two black briefcases containing bank orders and cancelled cheques, evidence I had collected to refute the regime's trumped up charges of corruption against my father.

'There are secret cupboards and passages here. Show them to us!' the army officers commanded the staff, then beat them when they said there were none. As the search wore on, the servants were taken to the reception room and locked in. When the milkman came early in the morning, he was locked in with them. So was the man who came with the newspapers. The army was getting desperate. 'Sign this paper,' an officer said to one of our staff. He refused. 'You've seen what happened to your Sahib,' the officer threatened him. 'If you don't sign, imagine what will happen to you.' The man was so frightened that he signed.

When the search turned out to be fruitless, a truck rumbled through the gate. The soldiers unloaded a red carpet, covered it with documents that also came from the truck, and then brought in the press to photograph the new 'evidence' against my father. Many assumed the regime was trying to build another case against my father in view of the Supreme Court's unanimous recommendation to commute the death sentence against him to life imprisonment. When the raiding party left in the late afternoon, they took their 'evidence' with them as well as many of our personal possessions, among them my father's collection of antique maps.

At 70 Clifton now, I make preparations to go to Larkana to pay my respects at my father's grave. The regime learns of my plan and cancels the scheduled flights, so I take the train. Massive crowds meet me at every station. Where there are no stations they lie across the track, forcing the train to halt. 'Revenge! Revenge!' the crowds shout. 'We must turn our grief to strength to beat Zia at the polls,' I tell them, encouraged by the huge turnout. The crowds are the best answer to our political opponents who had publicly declared that 'Bhutto's strength has been buried in his grave, and along with it that of the PPP.'

Back in Karachi, I meet PPP leaders and supporters at ten-minute intervals from nine in the morning until nine at night. Every few hours I take a break to greet my father's mourners in the garden. Their eyes brighten when they see me – and my mother as well, after her period of seclusion is over. The people did not expect either of us to survive our periods of detention or my father's death. We have lived a softer, more privileged life than their harsh ones. But seeing us with their own eyes seems to fill them with new hope. As one group leaves the garden, another enters.

At night I immerse myself in organisational matters, policy matters, complaints, and political arrests, having summaries prepared for my mother to read. I feel I'll never catch up and probably wouldn't have without the help of my schoolfriend Samiya and also of Amina and Yasmin, two young women who had become my friends and aides during the fight to appeal against my father's death sentence. The Western press dubs Samiya, Amina and Yasmin 'Charlie's Angels', though I'm sure the real Charlie's Angels would have given up under the workload. One night I fall asleep with a report in my lap. The next night I move my toothbrush and toothpaste into my study.

To calm the people before he ordered my father's death, General Zia had again promised elections that would return the country from his military dictatorship to civilian rule. But was he going to let the PPP win? He had publicly declared that he would 'not hand power to those he had taken it from', and that only elections with 'positive results' would be acceptable to him.

Zia had been in this predicament before, when he scheduled elections shortly after he overthrew my father in 1977. Faced with the PPP's certain victory at the polls, his answer then had been to cancel the elections and arrest all the party leaders instead. What would he do this time?

The local elections come first, in September. The PPP sweeps them. The national elections are to come next, the elections Zia desperately needs to win to gain legitimacy. Knowing that the rules are likely to be rigged against the PPP, our own party officials meet at 70 Clifton to debate whether or not to enter the national elections or boycott them instead. 'Electoral fields should never be left open,' I argue, remembering what my father had told me. No matter how heavy the odds, no matter how crooked the rules, always mount an opposition. And the rules certainly are crooked. Just as we expect, Zia changes them as soon as the PPP decision to participate is announced.

'Register as a political party or you can't participate,' the regime informs us.

We refuse. To register is to recognise Zia's military regime.

'We'll run as Independents,' we counter, though we realise the loss of our party emblem on the ballots is a great risk in a society with an official literacy rate of 27 per cent, and an actual rate closer to 8 per cent.

The regime raises the stakes. 'Independent candidates must secure 51 per cent of the popular vote,' the new rule says.

'Fine,' we say. 'We'll carry it.'

But on October 15, 1979, a month before the elections are scheduled to take place, the PPP reconvenes at the request of some high-ranking party officials. The question of fighting the elections is reopened, and the party splits down the middle. 'Boycott! Boycott!' several of the party officials urge my mother in the dining room of 70 Clifton now serving as a conference room. Some of them, I know, have called me 'a silly little girl' in private, but I speak up again. 'By continually changing the rules, Zia has lost his confidence,' I argue. 'We must not lose ours. We swept the Local Bodies elections and we will sweep the general election too.' It is late at night before the PPP decides by a narrow margin to uphold the decision to contest.

When Zia hears of our intention the next day, his nerves crack. The Chief Martial Law Administrator repeats the pattern of 1977, cancelling the elections altogether and once again sending his soldiers to 70 Clifton.

'The house is surrounded,' one of the staff tells me in the middle of the night. Quickly I gather all the political papers I had laboriously collected – party papers, membership lists, letters, lists of those in jail – throw them in the bath, and burn them. I don't want to make the regime's persecution easier. Minutes later the soldiers enter the house to take my mother and me at gunpoint to Al-Murtaza, our country home in Larkana. We will be imprisoned there for six months.

I pace the corridors of Al-Murtaza. Though this is my mother's ninth political detention and my seventh since the coup two years ago, I still can't adjust to the forced isolation. Each incarceration is just adding another layer of anger. Perhaps at twenty-six, it is my age. But I don't think I would feel differently at any age, especially being detained at Al-Murtaza.

Al-Murtaza was the heart of our family, the house to which we always returned from the four corners of the earth to pass our winter vacations, to celebrate *Eid* at the end of the holy month of Ramazan as well as my father's birthday, to attend family weddings or pay condolences to our many relatives living on the lands that had been in the family for hundreds of years. Now the regime has declared Al-Murtaza a sub-jail for my mother and me.

The Western press is being told by the regime that we are under 'house arrest'. But that is inaccurate. 'House arrest' in Pakistan is quite informal, the detained person being allowed visits from friends and family, press interviews, local and long distance telephone calls, books, and sometimes even a quick drive or outside meetings. Under sub-jail rules, Al-Murtaza has been deemed a prison where the Jail Manual Regulations prevail. Our telephone is disconnected. My mother and I are confined to the compound and allowed no visitors except for an occasional visit from Sanam.

The house both inside and outside the walls is surrounded by soldiers from the Frontier Force, a paramilitary group of Pathan tribesmen from the Northwest Frontier Province. In my father's time, special commandos were posted at Al-Murtaza to keep intruders out. The Frontier Force is here now for the sole purpose of keeping his widow and his daughter in. Zia wants the country, even the world, to forget that there was ever a family named Bhutto.

In Pakistan, the papers hardly even mention our names. From October 16, 1979, the day Zia cancelled the second elections and arrested my mother and me, he added to his burgeoning list of Martial Law regulations by imposing total censorship on the press. Under Martial Law Order No. 49, the editor of any publication deemed dangerous to the 'sovereignty, integrity and security of Pakistan, or morality and maintenance of public order', is now subject to ten lashes and twenty-five years of rigorous imprisonment.

Our party newspaper, *Musawaat*, with a circulation of over 100,000 in the city of Lahore alone, has been closed down, and its presses seized. Other newspapers are being threatened with closure or the cut-off of government controlled newsprint and advertising if they do not comply. For the next six years, pictures of my father, mother or me will rarely appear in any newspaper. Nor will there be any favourable mention of our names. If the military censors find any story even slightly sympathetic, they will cut it out of the galleys each newspaper is required to submit for approval. At times, whole newspaper columns will run blank, the journalists' method of letting the reading public know that news worthy of being printed has been removed by the censors.

The strength of the PPP has also forced Zia to tighten his already oppressive political restrictions. Since the imposition of Martial Law in 1977, anyone participating in political activity had been subject to imprisonment and whipping. But from October 16, 1979, the military regime decreed that political parties themselves were illegal, a clear attempt to kill popular support for my father's policies once and for all. 'All political parties in Pakistan with all their groups, branches and factions . . . shall cease to exist,' General Zia's Martial Law Order No. 48 stated bluntly. Any member of a political party, or anyone who even calls himself one in private conversation, is now subject to fourteen years rigorous imprisonment, the loss of his property, and twenty-five lashes. From that moment on, any mention of the PPP in the press will be preceded by the word 'defunct'. My mother and I are thus reduced to the 'defunct' leaders of a 'defunct' party in a defunct democracy.

Photographs of my grandfather at the 1931 Indian Round Table Conference in London. Photographs of my father's annual birthday celebrations. So much of our family history is rooted in Al-Murtaza. My father and his three sisters were born here, the midwife from the nearby village of Larkana coming to the women's quarters built by my grandfather to deliver them. Though the old house has been replaced by a more modern one, the sense of Al-Murtaza as the true home of the Bhuttos remains.

Blue and white tiles flank the front door depicting the men and women of Moenjodaro, a nearby ruin of a highly advanced Indus civilisation dating from 2500 BC. As a small child I thought the ancient city was called 'Munj Jo Dero', which in Sindhi means 'my place'. My brothers, sister and I took great pride that we had been raised in the shadow of Moenjodaro, that we lived on the bank of the Indus which had been bringing life to the land since the beginnings of time. In no other place did we feel such continuity with the past, for our ancestors were directly traceable to the Muslim invasion of India in 712 AD. The diaries of one of our ancestors giving details about the family were washed away in a great flood in my great-grandfather's time. But as children we were told that we were either descended from the Rajputs, the Hindu warrior class in India which converted to Islam at the time of the Muslim invasion, or from the conquering Arabs who entered India through our home province of Sindh, giving it the name 'The Gateway to Islam'.

Hundreds of thousands throughout India and Pakistan belonged to the Bhutto tribe, one of the largest in Sindh, whose members ranged from farmers to landowners. Our branch of the family was directly descended from the famous tribal chief of the Bhuttos, Sardar Dodo Khan. Several villages in Upper Sindh – Mirpur Bhutto where uncle Mumtaz's family live, Garhi Khuda Bakhsh Bhutto where my own family graveyard is located – are named after our ancestors, who had owned much of the land in the province and dominated its politics for hundreds of years. My immediate family retained a house near Garhi Khuda Bakhsh Bhutto in Naudero, where my father and brothers used to go on *Eid* days to offer guests the traditional holiday fare of rice cooked with sugar cane and water flavoured with flower petals. But since my grandfather's time the true centre of the family had been in Larkana, at Al-Murtaza.

Before the first land reforms in 1958, the Bhuttos were among the largest employers of agricultural workers in the province. Our lands like those of other landowners in Sindh were measured in square miles, not acres. As children we loved to hear the story of the amazement of Charles Napier, the British conqueror of Sindh in 1843. 'Whose lands are these?' he repeatedly asked his driver as he toured the province. 'Bhutto's lands,' came the inevitable response. 'Wake me up when we are off Bhutto's lands,' he ordered. He was surprised when some time later he woke up on his own. 'Who owns this land?' he asked. 'Bhutto,' the driver repeated. Napier became famous for his dispatch in Latin to the British military command after he conquered the province: *'Peccavi* – I have sinned.' As children we thought it a confession, not a pun.

My father loved to recount other family stories. 'Your great-grand-father, Mir Ghulam Murtaza Bhutto, was a handsome and dashing man of around twenty-one,' my father would begin one of our favourite stories. 'All the women in Sindh were in love with him, including a young British woman. In those days, it was *haram* – forbidden – to marry a foreigner but he couldn't prevent her feelings for him. A certain British army officer Colonel Mayhew heard about this forbidden relationship and sent for your great-grandfather.

26

'It did not matter to the British officer that he was in Larkana, the hometown of the Bhuttos. It did not matter to him that the Bhutto land stretched farther than the eye could see. The British had little respect for our family heritage. All they saw was our brown skin.

'"How dare you encourage the affections of a British woman!" the Colonel warned Ghulam Murtaza when your great-grandfather stood before him. "I am going to have to teach you a lesson." And the Colonel picked up a whip. But, as the Colonel raised his hand to lash Ghulam Murtaza, your great-grandfather seized the whip and lashed the officer instead. Screaming for help, the Colonel sought refuge under a table until Ghulam Murtaza strode out of the office. "You must escape," Ghulam Murtaza's family and friends urged him. "The British will kill you." So your great-grandfather left Larkana, accompanied by some companions and the British woman who insisted on leaving with him.

'The British were soon in hot pursuit. "Split up," Ghulam Murtaza ordered his companions. "One group come with me. The rest of you go with the English woman. But on no account let her be taken by the British. It is a matter of honour." And off they galloped in different directions, crisscrossing the river Indus to deceive the pursuing British. The British moved perilously close to the party with the British woman, for she could not travel with the speed of your great-grandfather. To fool them the men dug a tunnel to hide in and covered the entrance with leaves. When the British found the tunnel, your great-grandfather's friends became desperate. They had promised Ghulam Murtaza they would not hand the girl over to the British. They could not face the dishonour of surrendering her to the enemy. Just before the British reached the woman, your great-grandfather's retinue killed her.'

Our eyes were wide by this point, but the story had just begun. Our great-grandfather had escaped into the independent state of Bahwalpur. But after the British threatened to seize the state my great-grandfather thanked the Nawab for his hospitality and crossed the Indus again to gain sanctuary in the kingdom of Afghanistan where he was a guest of the Royal family. In fury, the British had seized all his lands. Our family home was auctioned. Our silk carpets were auctioned. Our sofas made of the imported silks, satins and velvets of the old days, our plates made of pure gold and silver, the huge cooking pots used to cook for the thousands of family followers on religious holidays, the embroidered tents set up for celebrations were all sold. Ghulam Murtaza had to be punished and punished severely, for it was unthinkable for anyone to defy the British. They were like gods. In parts of India natives were not allowed to walk the same streets; they could not answer back to a British person, let alone strike one.

Finally a compromise was worked out with the British and Ghulam

Murtaza returned to Larkana. But his days were numbered. He became ill and began to lose weight. The *hakims*, or village doctors, suspected poison though no one could find the source. Your great-grandfather had tasters to test his food and drinking water, but the poisoning continued until it killed him at the early age of twenty-seven. Afterwards, the source was found to be his *hookah*, the water pipe he used to smoke tobacco after dinner.

I loved hearing these family stories, as did my brothers Mir Murtaza and Shah Nawaz, who naturally identified with their namesakes. The adversities faced by our ancestors formed our own moral code, just as my father had intended. Loyalty. Honour. Principle.

Ghulam Murtaza Bhutto's son, my grandfather, Sir Shah Nawaz, was the first to start breaking the Bhuttos away from the feudal ethos that was stifling a whole segment of society. Until his time, the Bhuttos had only married other Bhuttos, first cousins or possibly, second. Islam entitled women to inherit property and the only way to keep the land within the family was through marriage. Such a 'business' marriage had been arranged between my father and his cousin Amir when he was only twelve and she eight or nine years older. He had resisted until my grandfather tempted him with a cricket set from England. After their marriage, Amir had returned to live with her family and my father had returned to school, leaving him with a lasting impression of the inequity, especially as far as women were concerned, of forced, family marriages.

At least Amir had married. When there was no suitable cousin in the family, the Bhutto women did not marry at all. For this reason my aunts, my grandfather's daughters from his first marriage, had remained single all their lives. Despite great opposition from the family, my grandfather had allowed his daughters from his second marriage to marry outside the Bhutto circle, though they were not love matches, but strictly arranged affairs. A generation later, my sister Sanam would become the first Bhutto woman to make her own decision. Contrary to my expectations, I would follow the traditional path and have an arranged marriage myself.

Still, my grandfather was considered very progressive. He educated his children, even sending his daughters to school, an act that was considered scandalous by the other landowners. Many feudal landowners did not even bother to educate their sons. 'My sons have land. They have a guaranteed income, and will never become employees or work for anyone else. My daughters will inherit land, and be looked after by their husbands or their brothers. So why bother with education?' ran the feudal ethos.

My grandfather, however, had seen at first hand the advances being made by the educated Hindus and urban Muslims in Bombay where he served in the government during the rule of the British Raj. By educating his own children, Sir Shah Nawaz tried to set an example for the other Sindhi landowners so that after the partition of India in 1947 and the establishment of independent Pakistan, our society would not stagnate. Despite the raised eyebrows of his peers, he sent my father abroad to study. My father had not disappointed him, graduating with honours from the University of California at Berkeley and then going on to read law at Christ Church, Oxford, and being called to the Bar at Lincoln's Inn before returning to Pakistan to practise law.

My mother, on the other hand, came from the new class of urban industrialists whose views were more cosmopolitan than those of the landowning class. While the Bhutto women still lived in *purdah*, rarely allowed to leave the four walls of their compounds and then completely covered in black *burqas*, my mother and her sisters went around Karachi without veils and drove their own cars. The daughters of an Iranian businessman, they had gone to college and after the birth of Pakistan, even served as officers in the National Guard, a paramilitary force of women. Such public exposure would have been impossible for the Bhutto women.

After my mother and father married in 1951, my mother entered *purdah* with the other Bhutto women, and at first was allowed to leave the compound only once a week to visit her family. But the old ways were getting tiresome to everyone. When my grandmother wanted to leave the family compound in Karachi and there was no driver available, she often asked my mother to drive her. When the family went to Al-Murtaza, my father insisted on staying with my mother in the women's wing instead of returning to the men's quarters. And when 70 Clifton was built there were no separate quarters provided for the women, though my grandfather bought a house opposite to meet his male visitors. A new and more enlightened generation was taking root in Pakistan.

In our male-dominated culture, boys had always been favoured over girls and were not only more often given an education, but in extreme instances were given food first while the mother and daughters waited. In our family, however, there was no discrimination at all. If anything, I received the most attention. The oldest of four, I was born in Karachi on June 21, 1953, my skin evidently so rosy that I was immediately nicknamed 'Pinkie'. My brother Mir Murtaza was born a year after me, Sanam in 1957 and the baby, Shah Nawaz, in 1958. As the first born, I held a special and sometimes lonely place in the family from the beginning.

I was only four and my father twenty-eight when he was first sent to the United Nations by the President, Iskander Mirza. My father's subsequent government posts as Commerce Minister under President Ayub Khan, then as Minister of Energy, Foreign Minister and leader of Pakistan's delegation to the United Nations off and on for seven years, kept him and my mother away from home much of the time.

I saw my father as much on the front pages of the newspapers as in person – arguing for Pakistan and other Third World Countries at the United Nations, negotiating financial and technical assistance agreements with the Soviet Union in 1960, returning from forbidden Peking in 1963 with a border treaty peacefully ceding 750 square miles of disputed territory to Pakistan. My mother usually travelled with him, leaving the children at home with the household staff – and me. 'Look after the other children,' my parents would charge me. 'You are the oldest.'

I was only eight or so when I was left nominally in charge of the house when my parents were away. My mother would give me the money for food and household supplies which I hid under my pillow. Though I was just learning my sums at school, every night in her absence I would climb on a stool in the kitchen and pretend to go over the accounts with Babu, our long-time, loyal major-domo. Whether the figures tallied, I have no recollection. Luckily very small sums were involved. At that time, rupees ten, about two dollars, bought food for the whole household.

In our house education was top-priority. Like his father before him, my father wanted to make examples out of us, the next generation of educated and progressive Pakistanis. At three I was sent to Lady Jennings' nursery school, then at five to one of the top schools in Karachi, the Convent of Jesus and Mary. Instruction at CJM was in English, the language we spoke at home more often than my parents' native languages of Sindhi or Persian or the national language of Urdu. And though the Irish nuns who taught there divided the older students into houses with inspirational names like 'Discipline', 'Courtesy', 'Endeavour' and 'Service', they made no effort to convert us to Christianity. The school was too good a source of income for the missionaries who ran it to risk alienating the small numbers of Muslim families rich enough and far-sighted enough to educate their children.

'I ask only one thing of you, that you do well in your studies,' my father told us time and again. As we grew older he hired tutors to instruct us in Maths and English in the afternoons after school, and he kept track of our school reports by phone from wherever he was in the world. Luckily I was a good student, for he had great plans for me to be the first woman in the Bhutto family to study abroad.

'You will all pack your suitcases and I will take you to the airport to see you off,' he started saying to the four of us as early as I can remember. 'Pinkie will leave as a scruffy little kid and come back a beautiful young lady in a sari. Shah Nawaz will pack so many clothes his suitcase won't close. We will have to call Babu and ask him to sit on it.'

There was no question in my family that my sister and I would be given the same opportunities in life as my brothers. Nor was there in Islam. We learned at an early age that it was men's interpretation of our

30

religion that restricted women's opportunities, not our religion itself. Islam in fact had been quite progressive towards women from its inception: the Prophet Mohammed (PBUH)* had forbidden the killing of female infants common among the Arabs of the time, and called for education for women and their right to inherit long before these privileges were granted to them in the West.

Bibi Khadijah, the first convert to Islam, was a widow who ran her own business, employed the Prophet Mohammed (PBUH) when he was a young boy and later married him. Umm e-Umara fought alongside the men in the Muslims' early battles against their enemies, her powerful sword-arm saving the life of the Prophet (PBUH). Chand Bibi, the female ruler of the South Indian state of Ahmadnagar, defeated the Mogul Emperor Akbar and forced him to enter into a peace treaty with her. Noor-Jehan, the wife of Emperor Jehangir and the virtual ruler of India, was famous for her skill in the field of administration. Muslim history was full of women who had taken a public role and performed every bit as successfully as men. Nothing in Islam discouraged them, or me, from pursuing that course. 'I have found a woman ruling over them. And she has been given abundance of all things and hers is a mighty throne,' reads the *surah* of the Ant in the Holy Quran. 'To men is allotted what they earn, and to women what they earn,' reads the Women *surah*.

Every afternoon we read these and other *surah*s from our Holy Book with the *maulvi* who came to the house after our academic tutoring to give us religious instruction. Reading the Holy Quran in Arabic and understanding its lessons was the most important subject of all. We spent hours struggling over the difficult Arabic, whose alphabet was similar to the one we used in Urdu, but which had totally different grammar and meanings, like the differences between English and French.

'Paradise lies at the feet of the mother,' our *maulvi* taught us during those afternoons, citing the Quranic injunction always to be kind to one's parents and to obey them. Not surprisingly, it was an instruction my mother would often use to keep us in line. The *maulvi* taught us too, that our actions on earth would determine our destiny in the afterlife. 'You will have to cross above a valley of fire and the bridge will be a hair. Do you know how thin a hair is?' he said with great drama. 'Those who have committed sin will fall into the fire of hell and burn, whereas those who have been good will cross into Paradise where milk and honey flow like water.'

It was my mother, however, who taught me the rituals of prayer. She took her faith very seriously. No matter where she was in the world, or what she was doing, she prostrated herself five times a day in prayer. When I was nine years old, she began to include me, slipping into my

*Peace Be Upon Him.

31

bedroom to lead me in the morning prayer. Together we would perform the *wuzoo*, the washing of our hands, feet and faces so that we would be pure before God, then prostrate ourselves facing west towards Mecca.

My mother was a Shiite Muslim, as are most Iranians, while the rest of the family was Sunni. But that was never a problem. Shiites and Sunnis had lived side by side and intermarried for over a thousand years and our differences were far fewer than our similarities. What was fundamental was that all Muslims, regardless of their sects, surrender to the will of God, and believe that there is no God but Allah and Mohammed is his last Prophet. That is the Quranic definition of a Muslim and, in our family, what mattered most.

During *muharram*, the month commemorating the massacre of the Prophet's grandson Imam Hussein at Karbala in Iraq, I would sometimes dress all in black and go with my mother to join other women in the Shiite rituals. 'Follow closely,' Mummy would say to me, for the Shiite ceremonies were more elaborate than those of the Sunnis. I never took my eyes off the speaker who dramatically recaptured the tragedy that befell Imam Hussein and his small band of followers at Karbala, where they were ambushed and brutally slaughtered by the troops of the usurper Yazid. No one was spared, not even the little children who fell under Yazid's knives. Imam Hussein was beheaded, and his sister Zeinab was made to walk bareheaded to Yazid's court where she watched the tyrant play with the head of her brother. But instead of allowing her spirit to be broken, Bibi Zeinab became filled with resolve, as did the other followers of Imam Hussein. Their descendants, known today as the Shiites, never let themselves forget the tragedy at Karbala.

'Hear the little baby cry for water,' the speaker called out, her voice filled with emotion. 'Feel the heart of the mother, hearing the cry of her child. Look at the handsome man on his horse, going for the water. He bends by the river. We see him bending. Look! Look! Men are attacking them with swords . . .' As she spoke some of the women performed the *matam*, striking their chests in anguish. The vivid recounting of the story was very moving, and I often cried.

My father was determined to bring his country – and his children – into the twentieth century. 'Will the children marry into the family?' I overheard my mother ask my father one day. I held my breath for his answer. 'I don't want the boys to marry their cousins and leave them behind our compound walls any more than I want my daughters buried alive behind some other relative's compound walls,' he said to my great relief. 'Let them finish their education first. Then they can decide what to do with their lives.'

His reaction was just as welcome the day my mother covered me in a *burqa* for the first time. We had been on the train from Karachi to Larkana when my mother took the black, gauzy cloth out of her bag and draped it over me. 'You are no longer a child,' she told me with a tinge of regret. As she performed this age-old rite of passage for the daughters of conservative land-owning families, I passed from childhood into the world of the adult. But what a disappointing world it turned out to be. The colours of the sky, the grass, the flowers were gone, muted and greyish. Everything was blurred by the pattern over my eyes. As I got off the train, the fabric which covered me from head to toe made it difficult to walk. Shut off from whatever breeze there might be, the sweat began to pour down my face.

'Pinkie wore her *burqa* for the first time today,' my mother told my father when we reached Al-Murtaza. There was a long pause. 'She doesn't need to wear it,' my father finally said. 'The Prophet himself said that the best veil is the veil behind the eyes. Let her be judged by her character and her mind, not by her clothing.' And I became the first Bhutto woman to be released from a life spent in perpetual twilight.

My father always encouraged me to feel part of the greater world, though sometimes his lessons went over my head. I was travelling with him in the Foreign Minister's private railway carriage in the autumn of 1963 when he shook me awake. 'This is no time to sleep,' he said urgently. 'There has been a great tragedy. The young President of the United States has been shot.' Though I was only ten and had heard only vaguely of the US president, he made me stay by his side while he received the latest bulletins on the condition of President John F. Kennedy, a man whom he'd met several times at the White House and whom he admired for his liberal social views.

Occasionally, he took my brothers, sister and me to meet the foreign delegations visiting Pakistan. When he told us one day that we were to meet 'some important men from China', I was very excited. My father had often spoken highly of the Chinese Revolution and its leader Mao Tse Tung who had led his army through the mountains and deserts to throw out the old order. I was sure one of the men was going to be Mao, whose cap, a personal gift from the Chinese revolutionary, was hung up in my father's dressing room. For once I didn't mind being dressed up in the outfits my father brought back every year from Saks Fifth Avenue in New York where the saleslady kept our measurements. But I was quite disappointed when the 'important Chinese men' did not include Mao, but the Premier of China, Chou En-lai, and two of his Ministers, Chen-Yi, and Liu-Shao Chi who would subsequently die in jail during the Cultural Revolution.

Chou En-lai wasn't the only 'important guest' in Karachi who didn't match up to my expectations. But we didn't actually meet this one. We knew a VIP must be coming to dinner because the outside of the house was covered with strings of lights. When a limousine drove through the gates, we peered from the upstairs window to see President Ayub Khan and an American gentleman entering 70 Clifton. I recognised the American immediately from the films we had seen in town. 'Did you enjoy meeting Bob Hope?' I nonchalantly asked my mother the next morning. 'Who?' my mother asked. 'Bob Hope,' I said. 'You silly,' she said to me. 'That was the Vice President of the United States, Hubert Humphrey.' Later I found out that Hubert Humphrey was trying to elicit Pakistan's support for America in Vietnam in the mild form of supplying badminton rackets for the US troops. But my father refused even that gesture, being morally opposed to any foreign involvement in Vietnam's civil war.

When I was ten and Sanam seven, we were sent north to boarding school in the pine-covered former British hill station of Murree. Our governess had given very short notice and was returning to England. Boarding school seemed the quick solution and my father was in favour of it, thinking the experience would toughen us up. For the first time I had to make my own bed, polish my shoes, carry water for bathing and tooth-brushing back and forth from the water taps in the corridors. 'Treat my children like the others,' my father had told the nuns. And they certainly did, laying the brush on Sunny and me for any infringement of the strict rules.

At Murree my father continued our political education by mail. Shortly after he returned from the Summit of Non-Aligned Countries in Jakarta, he wrote us a long letter elaborating on the self-interest of the Super-powers in the United Nations and the resulting neglect of Third World countries. One of the nuns sat Sanam and me down on a bench in the school garden and read the letter to us in its entirety, though we under-stood little of its content.

During our second and last year at Murree, Sanam and I learned some political lessons at first hand. On September 6, 1965, India and Pakistan went to war over Kashmir. While my father flew off to the United Nations to argue for the right of self-determination for the people of Kashmir and against the aggression of India, the nuns at the Convent of Jesus and Mary prepared their students for the possibility of an Indian invasion. The road to Kashmir ran right through Murree, a clear invitation most people thought, for Indian troops to use it to march into Pakistan.

Where once we had played 'jacks' with goat bones after dinner, or read Enid Blyton books, now suddenly we had air raid practices and blackouts. The nuns made older girls responsible for getting their younger sisters into the shelters, and I made Sunny tie her slippers to her feet at night so she wouldn't lose time in looking for them. Many of our schoolmates were daughters of prominent government officials or army officers, and with excitement we gave each other false names and practised them in case we fell into the hands of our enemies. In the flush of adolescence, we were all quite dramatic about the possibility of being kidnapped and carried off into the hills. But for the seventeen days of the war, the threat of invasion was quite real and frightening.

The United States was making the situation in Pakistan even more difficult. Alarmed to find that the arms they had provided Pakistan against a Communist threat were being used instead against India, the Johnson administration imposed an arms embargo on the entire sub-continent. But India was also getting arms from the Soviet Union, and Pakistan wasn't. Despite this handicap, our soldiers fought successfully right up to the time of the cease-fire called by the United Nations on September 23. The country felt triumphant. Not only had we repulsed the Indian attack, but we had taken more of their territory than they had of ours.

Our elation was short-lived. During the peace negotiations held in the southern Russian city of Tashkent, President Ayub Khan lost everything we had gained on the battlefield. Under the Tashkent Agreement, both countries agreed to pull their troops back to their pre-war positions. My father was disgusted, and tendered his resignation as Foreign Minister. When the Indian Foreign Minister Lal Bahadur Shastri died of a heart attack the day after the agreement was signed, my father acidly remarked that he must have died from happiness.

As the terms of the settlement were disclosed to the people, massive demonstrations erupted in the provinces of Punjab and Sindh, amidst reports of police brutality. Still, the demonstrations continued. And the lives of the Bhuttos were changed forever.

In June 1966, Ayub finally accepted my father's resignation. The differences between Ayub and my father were now in the open and the groundswell of popular support for my father as a political leader soared. On our last ride home to Larkana in the Foreign Minister's private railway carriage, the crowds were frenzied, running alongside the train, hurling themselves towards the handrails to try and ride along with us. 'Fakhr-e-Asia-Zindabad! Long Live the Pride of Asia!' the crowd roared, climbing on top of the train and running along the tops of buildings by the track. 'Bhutto Zindabad! Long live Bhutto!'

I was terrified in Lahore where my father left the train to have a luncheon meeting with the Governor of Punjab. 'There is blood on Mr Bhutto's shirt,' someone cried out. My heart froze until I saw my father return through the crowds, smiling and waving. His shirt was torn and he had a small scratch, but nothing more. His tie was gone, as well. I heard later that it was auctioned for thousands of rupees. When he got back into the Foreign Minister's carriage, the crowd started rocking the train, the momentum growing until I thought we would come off the rails.

Safely back at home, the talk turned to politics even more. Terms such as 'cold war' and 'arms embargo' had already become part of our dimly understood vocabulary as small children. We were as familiar with hearing the results of roundtable conferences and summit meetings as other children were with World Cup Cricket scores. But after my father broke with Ayub Khan in 1966, the words 'civil liberties' and 'democracy' were the ones that came up most, words which were mythical to most Pakistanis, who had only experienced restricted political participation under Ayub. Until my father formed his own political party in 1967, the Pakistan People's Party.

Roti. Kapra. Makan. Bread. Clothing. Shelter. These simple promises became the rallying cry for the Pakistan People's Party, fundamentals which the millions of poor in Pakistan did not have. Whereas all Muslims prostrated themselves before Allah, the poor in our country still prostrated themselves before the rich. 'Stand up! Do not grovel before others! You are human beings and have rights!' my father exhorted the crowds in the most remote and forlorn villages of Pakistan where no politician had travelled before. 'Call for democracy, where the vote of the poorest carries the same weight as the vote of the richest.'

Who is Bhutto? What is Bhutto? Why do people say that everyone is coming to hear him when only *tonga* drivers, rickshaw drivers and *rehri* drivers are at his public meetings, Ayub Khan's Governor questioned in the government-controlled press. As an idealist, I was shocked. Though we were living sheltered lives and attending privileged schools, I had seen people without shoes, without shirts, young girls with matted hair and thin babies. Did the poor not even count as people? We knew from our Quranic studies that everyone in Islam was equal in the eyes of God. We had also been taught by our parents to treat everyone with respect and not to allow anyone to prostrate himself before us to touch our feet, or to back out of our presence.

'There is no law of God that we here in Pakistan alone should be poor,' my father continued to argue to the masses of poor and increasingly, to the groups of women standing shyly on the edges of the crowds. 'Our country is rich. It has many resources. Why then should there be poverty, hunger and disease?' It was a question people could readily understand. Ayub's promised economic restructuring of Pakistan's economy had failed while his family and a handful of others had become rich. In the eleven years of Ayub's rule, a group known familiarly as Pakistan's 'Twenty-Two Families' had established practically every bank, insurance company and major industry in Pakistan. The outrage drew hundreds, then thousands of people to hear my father's call for social and economic reform.

The first floor of our house at 70 Clifton, Karachi, began to serve as a branch office of the PPP. At eleven and fourteen my sister and I enthusiastically paid the four anna dues to join the party so that we, too, could help our major-domo Babu sign up the increasing numbers of people who lined up at the gates every day. But in the midst of our normal recountings of our days – who had won at netball or cricket – we also began to hear my father's accounts of the bribes offered him by the Ayub regime. 'You are young, with your whole life ahead of you. Let Ayub have his turn and later you will have yours. Work with us, rather than against us and we will make things very ease for you,' Ayub and his colleagues were telling my father, exactly the same words I would hear later from the envoys of another dictator. When Ayub's offers of bribery failed to silence my father, death threats began.

The world of violence was unknown to me then. There was the world of politics in which my father lived, and there was the world of the children: schools and games, laughter at the beach. But the two worlds collided when news of armed attacks against my father began to come in. Ayub supporters fired on him at Rahimyarkhan, Sanghar and other stops on his tour to popularise the PPP. Thankfully, the assassins missed. At Sanghar, my father's life had been saved by his supporters, who threw themselves over him and suffered injuries from the bullets themselves.

Our house became filled with tension, but I tried not to show my fear. What good would it have done? This was the stuff of political life in Pakistan, and therefore the life we led. Death threats. Corruption. Violence. What was, was. I didn't even allow myself to feel frightened. I tried, in fact, not to feel anything at all, even when eleven months after the founding of the Pakistan People's Party, Ayub arrested my father and the other senior party leaders and threw them in jail. That was the way of dictators. Where there is protest, crush it. Where there are dissenters, arrest them. Under what law? We are the law.

The violent events of 1968 were not restricted to Pakistan. A revolutionary fever was sweeping the world, students rioting on campuses in Paris, Tokyo, Mexico City, Berkeley as well as Rawalpindi. In Pakistan, the rioting against Ayub spread with the news that my father had been arrested and taken to Mianwali, one of the worst prisons in Pakistan. It continued when he was transferred to Sahiwal, where his cell was infested with rats. In an effort to quell the disturbances, the regime closed down all schools and universities.

Meanwhile, I was facing the most critical time of my academic life, preparing for my O-level exams which covered the last three years of my studies, as well as for my SATs, Achievements and my entrance exam for possible admission to Radcliffe. I had begged my father to let me apply to Berkeley where he had gone, but he wouldn't let me. 'The weather in

California is too nice,' he had explained. 'The snow and ice in Massachusetts will force you to study.'

There was no question of my not taking the exams, since they were sent from England only once a year in December. 'You stay in Karachi and study,' my mother said, taking the younger children with her to Lahore to file a petition of habeas corpus in the High Court against my father's detention. I was left alone at 70 Clifton, confined to the immediate area, a long way from the commercial centre where the rioting was taking place.

To distract myself from worrying about my father in prison I buried myself in my work, going over and over my subjects with the tutors who came to the house every day. In the evenings I sometimes joined my friends Fifi, Thamineh, Fatima and Samiya at the nearby Sindh Club, once a British enclave where 'natives and dogs' were not allowed, and now a sporting club for well-to-do Pakistanis. We played squash and swam in the pool, though we all knew things were not as carefree as they seemed. Ever since my father started challenging Ayub, some of my friends' relatives and 'well-wishers' had begun cautioning them that friendship with the Bhuttos was dangerous, an invitation to reprisal by Ayub's regime. Samiya's father had been warned by the Inspector General himself that his daughter's friendship with me could bring trouble to his family. Samiya and my other friends bravely stuck by me, though I noticed other schoolmates beginning to distance themselves.

'I am praying for your success in your O-level examinations,' my father wrote from Sahiwal prison on November 28. 'I am really proud to have a daughter who is so bright that she is doing O-levels at the young age of fifteen, three years before I did them. At this rate, you might become the president.'

Though he was being held in solitary confinement, my father led me to believe that his major concern continued to be my education. 'I know you read a great deal, but you should read a little more literature and history,' his letter continued. 'You have all the books you need. Read about Napoleon Bonaparte, the most complete man of modern history. Read about the American revolution and about Abraham Lincoln. Read *Ten Days That Shook the World* by John Reed. Read about Bismarck and Lenin, Ataturk and Mao Tse-Tung. Read the history of India from ancient times. And above all read the history of Islam.' The prison form was signed 'Zulfikar Ali Bhutto'.

I wanted more than anything to be in Lahore with my family, but I couldn't. Sanam rang to tell me that my mother was leading women in protest marches against my father's imprisonment every two or three days, making sure each demonstrator carried a wet towel in a plastic bag in case Ayub's riot police fired tear gas. Several times the police broke up the processions with bamboo *lathis,* yet the demonstrations were continuing to grow. Ayub ordered the military out to arrest the protesters. But the soldiers refused to arrest the women, waving at them instead. Even under Ayub, women were still considered sacrosanct.

When the time for the O-level exams finally came in December, the Convent of Jesus and Mary arranged for us to take the tests at the Vatican Embassy, also in Clifton. Its sanctity and its distance from the commercial centre of Karachi made it the safest choice. While students in Britain sat their several days of exams in tidy classrooms, we were slipped in and out of Pakistan's headquarters of the Church of Rome.

Meanwhile the rioting continued, the anger against Ayub mounting after the police fired on the demonstrators, killing several. Now rioters all over Pakistan began calling for Ayub's resignation as well as the release of my father and the other political prisoners.

Three months after my father's arrest, the chaos in Pakistan forced Ayub Khan to let the PPP leaders go. Amidst rumours that the plane that was to bring my father home to Larkana from Lahore would be sabotaged and my father killed, supposedly by accident, my mother held a press conference to expose the possible plot before it could be carried out. My father was brought to Larkana by train instead. I have never been so happy to see anyone in my life. But the struggle against Ayub was far from over.

'Get down!' my father shouted at Sanam and me during a victory march in Larkana soon after his release. While our open car moved slowly through the mobs cheering *'Jiye* Bhutto!' and *'Girti Houi Deewar Ko Aakhri Dhaka Dow'* – Give the falling wall a final push – an Ayub agent fired pointblank at my father. Miraculously, the pistol jammed, but the crowd was unforgiving.

I peeked out from under my father's hand to see a young man literally being torn apart. His neck, his head, his arms and legs were being pulled in different directions, as was his mouth, which was bleeding heavily. 'Don't look!' my father said sharply, pushing me down harder. I hunched down over my knees while my father shouted at the crowd to let his would-be assassin live. Reluctantly they did so, but the sight stayed with me for months.

So did the sight of my father wasting away on a hunger-strike in his continuing protest against Ayub's dictatorship and powers of arbitrary arrest. For days after his release from prison he sat under a *shamiana* at Al-Murtaza with other PPP leaders, in full view of the street. All Larkana watched and grew frightened as he got thinner and thinner. 'Please give in to Papa,' I silently willed Ayub Khan, wondering why the men sitting with my father looked so well. 'They order food when they are in their rooms at night,' one of the staff confided to me. 'Don't tell your father.'

Like mushrooms, hunger-strike groups sprang up in front of the Bar associations and the busy streets of cities all across Pakistan. Large crowds gathered every day to give the hunger-strikers moral support and call for Ayub's resignation. Realising that even his police could not control the situation, Ayub finally stepped down on March 25, 1969. But the victory was hollow. Instead of passing power to the Speaker of the National Assembly as laid down in his own constitution, Ayub designated his Army Chief-of-Staff Yahya Khan the new leader of Pakistan. Once again Pakistan was under the grip of a military dictator who promptly suspended all civil law and imposed martial rule.

'You have a letter from Radcliffe,' my mother told me in April. I took the envelope from her with misgivings. Did I really want to go? The college had cautioned my father that at sixteen, I would be too young to enter Radcliffe, and had suggested that I wait a year. But my father saw no reason to hold me back. Instead he had asked the help of his friend John Kenneth Galbraith, a professor of Economics at Harvard and the former US Ambassador to India. I opened the envelope. I had been accepted for the autumn of 1969.

My father gave me a beautiful volume of the Holy Quran bound in mother-of-pearl as a going-away present. 'You will see many things that surprise you in America and some that may shock you,' he said. 'But I know you have the ability to adapt. Above all you must study hard. Very few in Pakistan have the opportunity you now have and you must take advantage of it. Never forget that the money it is costing to send you comes from the land, from the people who sweat and toil on those lands. You will owe a debt to them, a debt you can repay with God's blessing by using your education to better their lives.'

In late August, I stood in the carved wooden doorway of 70 Clifton while my mother passed my new Holy Quran over my head. I kissed it. And together we left for the airport to fly to the United States.

3

REFLECTIONS FROM AL-MURTAZA:
MY FIRST TASTE OF DEMOCRACY

As my mother and I enter our second month of detention at Al-Murtaza, the gardens are dying. Before my father's imprisonment and death we had needed a staff of ten to maintain the large gardens and tend to the grounds. But since Al-Murtaza has been turned into a sub-jail for my mother and me, Zia's military regime has permitted only three gardeners to enter. I join in the struggle to keep the gardens alive.

I cannot bear to watch the flowers wither, especially my father's roses. Every time he had travelled abroad, he'd brought back new and exotic varieties to plant in our garden – violet roses, tangerine roses, roses that didn't even look like roses but were so perfectly sculpted that they looked as though they had been fashioned out of clay. His favourite was a blue rose called the 'rose of peace'. Now the rose bushes begin to shrivel and turn brown out of neglect.

Every morning in the lingering summer heat I'm in the garden by seven, helping the gardeners haul the heavy canvas hoses from one bed to the next. From the corners of the house the Frontier Forces watch me. It used to take the staff three days to water the garden. It takes us eight. By the time we reach the last rose bushes, the first have already begun to wilt. I will them to survive, seeing in their struggle to live denied adequate water and nourishment my own struggle to survive denied freedom.

The happiest hours of my life have been spent among the roses and the cool shade of the fruit trees at Al-Murtaza. During the day the air carried the scent of the *Din ka Raja*, the King of the Day, the sweet white flowers which my mother, like many Pakistani women, used to weave into her hair. At sunset, the air filled with the scent of *Raat ki Raani*, the Queen of the Night, which sweetened the evenings we spent as a family on the terrace.

More hoses. More water. I sweep the leaves from the patio, rake the lawn until my arms ache. My palms become raw and blister. 'Why are you doing this to yourself?' my mother asks in concern when I slump, exhausted, by midday. It is something to do, I tell her. But it is something more. If I work so hard that every bone in my body is tired, then I am too tired even to think. And I don't want to think of our lives wasting away under Martial Law.

I dig a new flower bed and plant rose cuttings, but they do not survive. My mother is more successful with her plantings of ladyfingers, chillies and mint. In the evenings, I whistle to a pair of tamed cranes and am gratified when they rush towards me, wings flapping, to take a piece of bread. Calling an animal and it coming, planting something and it growing, become essential. It is proof that I exist.

When I am not working in the garden, time becomes something merely to get through. I read and re-read my grandfather's Erle Stanley Gardner books, though the electricity is often turned off, leaving my mother and me to spend days and nights in darkness. There is a television set, but even when the electricity is working there's nothing to watch. In my father's time, there were plays, films, even soap operas on television, as well as talk shows and literacy programmes to teach the people to read. When I turn on the television now, there is almost nothing but Zia: Zia giving another speech, discussions of Zia's speeches, censored news programmes reporting who Zia has had meetings with.

At 8.15 every night my mother and I tune in without fail to the BBC Urdu report on the radio. Only on the BBC do we learn in November that the American Embassy in Islamabad has been burned to the ground by angry mobs believing that the United States was behind the takeover of the Grand Mosque in Mecca. As the story unfolds, my mother and I are astonished to learn that in security-conscious and Martial-Law-regulated Islamabad buses had been permitted to gather, pick up fundamentalist students, and deliver them to the American Embassy which they then set on fire. The Embassy had burned for hours before the authorities who had always turned up at the blink of an eye for a PPP demonstration made an appearance. The American Embassy was gutted, and one person killed. A contrite Zia went on television to make a public apology to the Americans and offer to pay damages. But what was he playing at? It remains a mystery to this day.

The news on the BBC a month later is even more provocative.

On December 27, 1979, Russian troops move into Afghanistan. My mother and I stare at each other when we hear the news on the BBC, knowing that the political implications are enormous. The battle between the Superpowers is now right on Pakistan's doorstep. If the US wants a country which is internally strong to meet the Soviet presence, they will move quickly to restore democracy to Pakistan. If they decide to wait and see what happens in Afghanistan, Zia's dictatorship will be strengthened.

America. It was in America that I had experienced democracy for the first time, and where I spent four of the happiest years of my life. I could close my eyes now and visualise the Harvard-Radcliffe campus, the crimsons and yellows of the trees in the autumn, the soft blanket of snow in the winter, the excitement we all felt at the first shoots of green in the spring. As a student at Radcliffe, however, I had also learned first hand the powerlessness of Third World countries in face of the self-interest of the Superpowers.

'Pak-i-*stan*? Where's Pak-i-*stan*?' my new classmates asked me when I first arrived at Radcliffe. The answer was simpler then.

'Pakistan is the largest Muslim country in the world,' I replied, sounding like an embassy hand-out. 'There are two wings of Pakistan separated by India.'

'Oh, India,' came the relieved response. 'You're next to India.'

I smarted every time I heard the reference to India with whom we had had two bitter wars. Pakistan was supposed to be one of America's strongest allies, a geographical buffer against the Soviet influence in India, and our other border countries of Communist China, Afghanistan and Iran. The United States used our airbases in northern Pakistan for their U-2 reconnaissance flights, including the ill-fated flight of Gary Powers in 1960. Henry Kissinger's secret flight from Islamabad to China in 1971 was more successful, paving the way for President Nixon's historic visit the next year. Yet Americans seemed completely unaware even of the existence of my country.

They were also understandably unaware of the Bhuttos and I relished the first anonymity I had had in my life. In Pakistan, the Bhutto name always brought recognition and with it a sense of shyness for me. I never knew whether people were approaching me on my own merit – or for my family's name. At Harvard, I was on my own for the first time.

My mother had stayed with me for the first few weeks, settling me into my room at Eliot Hall and calculating the location of Mecca so I would know in which direction to pray. When she departed, she left behind warm woollen *shalwar khameez* she had gone to great lengths to have made for me, lined with silk so the wool wouldn't scratch.

I was attentive to her directions for prayer, but not to her wardrobe which was impractical in the rain and snow and set me apart from the other students. I quickly shed the *shalwar khameez* and re-emerged in jeans and sweatshirts from the Harvard Co-op. I let my hair grow long and straight and was flattered when my friends in Eliot Hall told me I looked like Joan Baez. I drank gallons of apple cider, ate unconscionable numbers of peppermint-stick ice cream cones sprinkled with 'jimmies' from Brigham's ice cream parlour, and regularly attended rock concerts in Boston as well as the garden parties at Professor and Mrs Galbraith's, my 'parents-in-residence'. I loved the novelty of America.

The anti-war movement was at its peak and I marched with thousands of other students from Harvard in a Moratorium Day rally on the Boston Common and in a huge rally in Washington, DC, where, ironically, I caught my first whiff of tear gas. I was nervous as I pinned on my 'Bring the Boys Home Now' badge for the first time. As a foreigner I risked deportation if I was caught taking part in any political rally. But I had opposed the Vietnam war at home and was becoming even more radicalised by the anti-war fever in America. The motives of my fellow marchers and mine were strangely the same: Americans should not be involved in an Asian civil war.

Having been to six different branches of four schools in Pakistan, I relished the continuity of four years at Harvard. And there was so much going on. The momentum of the Women's Movement was building and the Harvard bookshop was filled with books and magazines about women, including the campus bible, Kate Millett's *Sexual Politics* and the first issues of *Ms* magazine. Night after night my friends and I gathered to talk about our aspirations for the future and what kind of new rules would govern our relationships with the people we married – if indeed we chose to get married at all. In Pakistan I had been among the minority who didn't view marriage and family as their primary goal. At Harvard I was amongst a sea of women who felt as unimpeded by their gender as I did. My fledgling confidence soared and I got over the shyness that had plagued my earlier years.

In Pakistan, my sister, brothers and I moved within a small circle of friends and relatives. As a result, I was uneasy in front of people I didn't know. At Harvard, I knew no one, except for Peter Galbraith, to whom I'd been introduced at his parents' house just before college began. To my sheltered and conservative eye, Peter Galbraith seemed shocking. His hair was long, he was dressed in old and untidy clothes and he smoked cigarettes in front of his parents. He looked more like a waif the former Ambassador to India had brought home with him, rather than the son of a senior diplomat and respected professor. Little did I know then the role Peter, who became a good friend, would play in my release from detention in Pakistan fifteen years later.

But Peter was just one among thousands of students at Harvard. I had to go up to strangers and ask directions to the Library, to the lecture halls, the dorms. I couldn't afford to be tongue-tied. I had been thrown in at the deep end of a strange and foreign pool. If I were to get to the surface, I had to get there by myself.

I settled in quickly, becoming Social Secretary of Eliot Hall during my first year and later going on to try out for the Harvard newspaper, *The Crimson*, and to give guided tours of the campus for the Crimson Key Society. 'The official name of this building is the Center of International Affairs, but we all know what CIA really stands for,' I would say conspiratorially to the new students, perpetuating the irreverent campus spirit that had so delighted me on my own first tour. Harvard's controversial visual-arts building designed by the French architect Le Corbusier fared no better. 'The prevailing opinion is that the builder read the plans upside-down,' was the standard wisecrack.

There were certain culture clashes, however, that I found difficult to overcome. I never did adjust to living in such close quarters to young men, especially after Eliot Hall went co-ed in my junior year. Even finding a male undergraduate in the laundry room was enough to cause me to postpone doing my own laundry. The problem was solved by moving to Eliot House on the Harvard campus where my roommate Yolanda Kodrzycki and I had our own suite of rooms and bathroom, and the communal laundry room was much larger.

I had thought I wanted to study psychology. But, when I discovered that the major entailed courses in medical sciences and the dissection of animals, I turned squeamish and chose comparative government instead. My father was delighted; he had secretly written to Mary Bunting, the president of Radcliffe, asking her to try and steer me towards political courses. Instead, Mrs Bunting had kindly asked me what I wanted to do with my life, never letting on that she'd had a letter from my father. Comparative government certainly turned out to be a wise choice.

By studying government at Harvard I began to understand more about Pakistan than I ever had by living there. 'When a policeman holds up his hand in the street and says "Stop!", everybody stops. But when you or I hold up our hands and say "stop", nobody stops. Why?' Professor John Womack asked the small group of us in his freshman seminar on 'revolution'. 'Because the policeman is authorised by the constitution, by the government, to enforce laws. He has the mandate, the legitimacy to say "stop" and you and I don't.'

I remember sitting spellbound in Professor Womack's study where I was probably the only student who actually lived in a dictatorship. With one example, Professor Womack had pinpointed the state of lawlessness and contempt in Pakistan under Ayub and Yahya Khan, and later, Zia ul-Haq. The authority of these dictators to govern was self-imposed, not a mandate from the people. I saw clearly for the first time why the people in Pakistan saw no reason to obey this sort of regime, no reason to 'stop'. Where there was no legitimate government, there was anarchy.

I was half-way through my sophomore year when legitimate government came closer to reality in Pakistan. On December 7, 1970, Yahya Khan finally held elections, the first in thirteen years. On the other side of the world in Cambridge, I studied all night with the telephone beside me. When my mother called me to say that my father and the PPP had unexpectedly swept West Pakistan, capturing 82 of 138 seats in the National Assembly, I was exultant. In East Pakistan, where Sheikh Mujib ur-Rahman, the leader of the Awami League had run unopposed, Mujib had won an even greater majority. 'Congratulations,' people I had never met said to me the next day, having read of my father's victory in the *New York Times*.

My elation, however, was short lived. Instead of working with my father and the representatives of West Pakistan to write a new constitution acceptable to both wings of Pakistan, Mujib instigated an independence movement to sever East Pakistan, or East Bengal, from the western federation completely. Time and again my father appealed to Sheikh Mujib to keep Pakistan intact, to work together with him, a fellow civilian, to oust the military rule of Yahya. But instead of showing flexibility and agreeing to what was a political necessity, Mujib showed an obstinacy the logic of which to this day defies me. East Bengali rebels heeded his call for independence by seizing the airports. Bengali citizens refused to pay their taxes. Bengali employees of the central government went on strike. By March, civil war was imminent.

My father continued to negotiate with Mujib, hoping to keep Pakistan intact, hoping to spare East Pakistan the military reprisal so easily available to a military regime. On March 27, 1971, he was actually in East Pakistan's capital city of Dacca for another round of talks with Mujib when his worst fears were realised: Yahya Khan ordered in the army to quell the insurrection. Alone in his hotel room, my father watched Dacca go up in flames, sick at heart at the Generals' inevitable solution of force. And six thousand miles away in Cambridge, I learned a bitter lesson.

Looting. Rape. Kidnappings. Murder. Where no one had cared about Pakistan when I arrived at Harvard, now everyone did. And the condemnation of my country was universal. At first, I refused to believe the accounts in the Western press of atrocities being committed by our army in what the East Bengal rebels were now calling Bangladesh. According to the government-controlled Pakistani papers my parents sent me every week, the brief rebellion had been quelled. What were these charges then that Dacca had been burned to the ground and firing squads sent into the university to execute students, teachers, poets, novelists, doctors and lawyers? I shook my head in disbelief. Refugees were reportedly fleeing by the thousands, so many of them strafed and killed by Pakistani planes that their bodies were being used to erect road blocks.

The stories were so extreme I didn't know what to think. The lecture we'd been given about the dangers of rape during freshman orientation week at Radcliffe had initially seemed as unbelievable. I had never even heard of rape until I came to America and the very possibility of it kept me from going out alone at night for the next four years. After the lecture, the possibility of rape at Harvard was real to me. The rape of East Bengal was not. I found security in the official jingoistic line in our part of the world that the reports in the Western press were 'exaggerated' and a

'Zionist plot' against an Islamic state.

My classmates at Harvard were harder to convince. 'Your army is barbaric,' the accusations would come. 'You're slaughtering the Bengalis.' 'We are not killing the Bengalis,' I would counter, my face turning blue with indignation. 'Do you believe everything you read in the newspapers?' Everyone was turning against West Pakistan, even the people with whom I had gone door to door earlier in the year, collecting money for the victims of a devastating cyclone in East Pakistan. The charges mounted. 'You people are fascist dictators.' I wouldn't even try to bite my tongue, especially when I read that India was training thousands of Bengali refugees in guerrilla warfare, then slipping them back over the border. 'We are fighting an Indian-backed insurgency,' I'd lash back. 'We are fighting to hold our country together, just as you did during your own Civil War.'

There was no place to avoid condemnation, even when it was unfounded. 'Pakistan has denied the people of Bangladesh the right of self-determination,' thundered Professor Walzer in a public lecture on 'War and Morality' in the autumn of my junior year. I shot to my feet in front of the 200 other students in the lecture hall and delivered my first political speech. 'That's completely wrong, Professor,' I corrected him, my voice quivering. 'The people of Bengal exercised the right to self-determination in 1947 when they opted for Pakistan.' There was a stunned silence. But my point was historically correct. The sadder truth which I was refusing to face lay in the disillusionment that had followed the creation of East Pakistan.

How many times since have I asked God to forgive me for my ignorance? I didn't see then that the democratic mandate for Pakistan had been grossly violated. The majority province of East Pakistan was basically being treated as a colony by the minority West. From revenues of more than thirty-one billion rupees from East Pakistan's exports, the minority in West Pakistan had built roads, schools, universities and hospitals for themselves, but had developed little in the East. The army, the largest employer in our very poor country, drew 90 per cent of its forces from West Pakistan. 80 per cent of government jobs were filled by people from the West. The central government had even declared Urdu our national language, a language few in East Pakistan understood, thus further handicapping the Bengalis in competing for jobs in government or education. No wonder they felt excluded and exploited.

I was also too young and naïve at Harvard to understand that the Pakistani army was capable of commiting the same atrocities as any army let loose in a civilian population. The psychology can be deadly as it was when US forces massacred innocent civilians in Mylai in 1968. Years later, Zia's suppression of my home province of Sindh would be no different. Members of the armed forces can lose control and wreak havoc among civilians. They look upon them as 'the enemy' to be shot or looted or raped. Yet, during that terrible spring of 1971, I clung to my childish image of the heroic Pakistani soldiers who had fought so valiantly during the 1965 war against India. It was an image that was to die slowly and painfully.

'Pakistan is passing through a terrible ordeal,' my father wrote in a long letter to me which was later published as a book called *The Great Tragedy*. 'The nightmare of Pakistanis killing Pakistanis is not yet over. Blood is still being spilled. The situation has become greatly complicated by the aggressive involvement of India. Pakistan will live purposefully forever if we survive the turmoil of today; otherwise catastrophic convulsions will lead to total ruin.'

The catastrophic convulsions came on the morning of December 3, 1971. 'No!' I cried in Eliot Hall, throwing down the newspaper. Under the guise of establishing order so that the steady stream of refugees pouring into India could be reversed, the Indian army invaded East Pakistan and struck at West Pakistan as well. Sophisticated Soviet-made missiles were sinking our warships at their moorings in Karachi Harbour. Indian planes were strafing the city's vital installations. Our weapons were so outdated, we couldn't even fight back. Now the very existence of my country was being threatened.

'You are lucky not to be here,' Samiya wrote to me from Karachi. 'There are air strikes every night and we have had to put black paper on the windows to block out any light. The schools and universities are closed, so there is nothing to do all day but worry. As usual, the newspapers are telling us nothing. We didn't even know India had invaded East Pakistan until somebody knocked on our gate and yelled "There's war! There's war!" Now the 7.00 news says we are winning, but the BBC Asia broadcast says we are being crushed. The BBC is also reporting terrible crimes committed by the army in East Pakistan. Have you heard anything about that?

'Your brother Shah Nawaz is the most excited thirteen-year-old in Karachi. He has joined the Civil Defence and patrols the neighbourhood every night on his motorbike, telling everyone to put out their lights. The rest of us are terrified. I was at your house with Sanam during one strike, and your mother took us into the downstairs dining room where there are no windows. At home, I'm sleeping with my mother we're both so nervous. Three bombs have fallen just across the street from our house but luckily they didn't explode. Our garden is full of glass.

'The Indian planes fly so close to the windows that you can actually see the pilots! But none of our air force seems to be striking back. Three nights ago the explosions were so loud I thought they'd bombed our neighbour's house. I went up on the roof and the whole sky was pink. I found out the next morning that the oil terminals in Karachi harbour had been hit by missiles. The fires are still burning. We are waiting for help from the Americans.'

Military help from America never arrived. Though Pakistan had a defence treaty with the United States, the arrangement suffered from mistaken identity. The Americans were prepared to defend us from their enemy, the Soviet Union. But Pakistan's real threat had always been India. Even now, much of the military aid designated for use by the Afghan rebels against the Soviets is going into the Pakistani army arsenal for potential use against India.

In the crisis of 1971, President Nixon eschewed military intervention in favour of safer diplomatic manoeuvres, ordering what came to be called America's 'tilt' towards Pakistan. On December 4, the second day of what turned out to be a thirteen-day war, the US State Department placed the blame for the hostilities squarely on India's shoulders. On December 5 the United States sponsored a cease-fire resolution in the United Nations Security Council. On December 6, the Nixon administration suspended more than eighty-five million dollars worth of development loans promised to India.

But these manoeuvres would prove to be insufficient. A week after India's invasion, Dacca, our last stronghold, was about to fall. Indian troops had crossed the border into West Pakistan. Facing total defeat on the battlefield and the overrunning of our country, Yahya Khan turned to the one elected leader in Pakistan who, as such, had the authority and credibility to save Pakistan: my father.

'I am coming to the United Nations. Meet me in New York at the Pierre Hotel on December 9,' the message read from my father.

'Do you think Pakistan will get a fair hearing at the United Nations?' my father asked me when I met him in New York.

'Of course, Papa,' I said with the certainty of an eighteen-year-old. 'No one can deny that India, in violation of international law, has invaded and occupied another country.'

'And do you think the Security Council will condemn India and insist on a withdrawal of her forces?'

'How can they not?' I answered incredulously. 'It would be a travesty of their mandate as an international peace-keeping organisation to sit by while thousands are being slaughtered and a country dismembered.'

'You may be a good student of international law, Pinkie, and I hesitate to disagree with a Harvard undergraduate,' he said mildly. 'But you don't know anything about power politics.'

Images from the four futile days my father tried to save a united Pakistan still stand clearly in my mind.

I am sitting two rows behind him in the Security Council. 104 countries in the General Assembly as well as the United States and China have voted to condemn India but, under the threat of a Soviet veto, the five permanent members of the Security Council can't even agree on a cease-fire. After seven sessions on the Indian-Pakistan conflict and a dozen draft resolutions, the Security Council has not adopted one. Everything that my father has taught me about the manipulation of Third World countries by the Superpowers is being played out in this one room. Pakistan is defenceless in the face of Superpower self-interest.

'December 11. 5.40. Our army is fighting heroically but without air and naval support and facing a 6:1 ratio, it cannot last longer than 36 hours from yesterday,' read the notes I scribble on Hotel Pierre stationery. My notes the next day are just as devastating. '6.30 am Ambassador Shah Nawaz called to say situation grim. Only answer is Chinese intervention with Americans putting screws on the Russians to prevent them from intervening. Papa sent telegram to Islamabad saying hold on for 72, not 36, hours. General Niazi (the commander of our army in East Pakistan) says will go forward to the last man.'

On December 12, my father calls on the Security Council for a cease-fire, the withdrawal of Indian forces from Pakistani territory, the stationing of UN forces and the means to ensure that no reprisals take place in East Pakistan. But his pleas fall on deaf ears. Instead I listen in disbelief to an hour-long debate on whether the Security Council should convene the next morning at 9.30 or at the more leisurely hour of 11.00. Meanwhile, Pakistan as we know it is dying.

'We must get Yahya to open the western front,' my father says urgently to the Pakistani delegation in our hotel room. 'An offensive in the West will draw the concentration of Indian troops from the East and relieve pressure there. Without that pressure, we are in great danger of losing all of Pakistan.' I place a call to Yahya Khan in Pakistan for my father, but Yahya's military aide tells me the President is sleeping and can't be disturbed. My father grabs the phone. 'There's a war going on! Wake up the President!' he shouts. 'He must open the western front. We must relieve pressure on the East immediately.'

A Western journalist reports that General Niazi has surrendered to the Indians in East Pakistan. My father loses his temper with Yahya altogether. 'Rescind the rumours!' my father shouts over the phone to Pakistan to Yahya's military secretary because Yahya is still unavailable. 'How can I negotiate a favourable settlement if I have nothing to bargain with?'

The telephones at the Pierre ring non-stop. One afternoon I take a call from US Secretary of State Henry Kissinger on one line, and one from Huang Hua, chairman of the delegation from the People's Republic of China, on another. Henry Kissinger is very worried that the Chinese will intervene militarily on the side of Pakistan. My father is worried that the

Chinese won't. While Papa is planning to ask Yahya to fly to Peking as a last resort, Henry Kissinger, I read later, is having meetings with the Chinese in CIA 'safe houses' all over New York.

The Soviet delegation comes and goes from my father's suite. The Chinese come and go. So does the United States delegation, headed by George Bush. 'My son is up at Harvard, too. Call me if you ever need anything,' Ambassador Bush tells me, handing me his card. Through it all I sit by the phone in the bedroom, taking down real messages, relaying false ones.

'Interrupt the meetings,' my father tells me. 'If the Soviets are here, tell me the Chinese are calling. If the Americans are here, tell me that the Russians are on the line or the Indians. And don't tell anyone who really is here. One of the fundamental lessons of diplomacy is to create doubt: never lay all your cards on the table.' I follow his instructions but not his lesson. I always lay my cards on the table.

The diplomatic card-playing in New York, however, all comes to an abrupt end. Yahya does not open the western front; the military regime has already psychologically conceded the loss of East Pakistan and lost heart. The Chinese do not intervene, in spite of their statements of military support. And the rumour of our premature surrender leaves a damaging legacy, even after the error is corrected. The Indians now know our military commanders in East Pakistan want to give up the fight. So do the Permanent Members of the Security Council. Dacca is about to fall.

On December 15 I take my accustomed seat behind my father in the Security Council when his patience with the do-nothing strategy of the members wears out. 'There is no such thing as a neutral animal. You take positions,' he charges them, pointing a finger especially at Britain and France who because of their own interests on the sub-continent, had abstained in the voting. 'You have to be either on the side of justice or on the side of injustice, you have to be either on the side of the aggressor or the aggressed. There is no such thing as neutrality.'

As his impassioned words fill the chamber, I learn the lesson of acquiescence versus defiance. With the Superpowers dead set against Pakistan, the prudent course would be acquiescence. But giving in to the Superpowers would mean becoming a party to the act. 'Impose any decision, have a treaty worse than the Treaty of Versailles, legalise aggression, legalise occupation, legalise everything that has been illegal up to December 15, 1971. I will not be a party to it,' my father is thundering. '. . . You can take your Security Council. I am going.' And with that, he rises to his feet and strides out of the room. Hastily I collect my papers and through the stunned silence, follow him out with the rest of the Pakistani delegation.

*

The *Washington Post* termed my father's performance in the Security Council 'living theater'. But for us it was a real dilemma affecting the future of our country, if there was going to be a country called Pakistan at all. 'Even if we surrender militarily in Dacca, we must not be part of a political surrender,' he said to me later while we walked the streets of New York. 'By walking out, I wanted to make clear that though we can be physically crushed, our national will and pride cannot be.'

My father was very upset as we walked and walked, seeing the devastating repercussions ahead for Pakistan. 'Had there been a negotiated political settlement, perhaps a political referendum under the auspices of the UN, the people of East Pakistan could have voted whether to remain part of Pakistan or to become the separate country of Bangladesh. Now Pakistan will have to face the shame of surrender to India. There will be a terrible price to pay.'

The next morning, my father began his journey back to Pakistan. I returned to Cambridge. And Dacca fell.

The loss of Bangladesh was a terrible blow to Pakistan on many levels. Our common religion of Islam, which we always believed would transcend the 1,000 miles of India which separated East and West Pakistan, failed to keep us together. Our faith in our very survival as a country was shaken, the bonds between the four provinces of West Pakistan strained almost to breaking. Morale was never lower, compounded by Pakistan's actual surrender to India.

As television cameras focused in, General Niazi approached his Indian counterpart, General Aurora, on the race course at Dacca. I couldn't believe my eyes when I saw General Niazi exchange swords with the conqueror of Dacca (they had been at Sandhurst together), and embrace him. Embrace him! Even the Nazis did not surrender in such a humiliating manner. As commander of a defeated army, Niazi would have acted far more honourably if he had shot himself.

When my father landed in Islamabad, the city was in flames. Angry mobs were even putting a torch to the shops selling alcohol that had supposedly supplied Yahya Khan and the members of his regime. Watching Pakistan's surrender to India on television after weeks of the regime's claims that Pakistan was winning the war sent huge crowds in Karachi to storm the television station and try to burn it down. And bellicose editorials in the Indian press threatened further devastation to Pakistan, claiming our country was 'an artificial nation which should never have come into being'.

On December 20, 1971, four days after the fall of Dacca, the people's fury forced Yahya Khan to step down. And my father, as elected leader of the largest Parliamentary group in Pakistan, became the new President. Ironically, since there was no constitution, he had to be sworn in as the first civilian in history to ever head a Martial Law administration.

At Harvard I was no longer known as Pinkie from Pakistan, but Pinkie Bhutto, the daughter of the President of Pakistan. But my pride at Papa's accomplishments was compromised by the shame of our surrender and the price Pakistan had paid. In the two weeks of the war, one quarter of our air force had been shot down. Half our navy had been sunk. Our treasury was empty. Not only was East Pakistan gone, but the Indian army had captured 5,000 square miles of our land in the West and taken 93,000 of our men prisoners-of-war. Pakistan could not last, many were predicting. The united Pakistan Mohammed Ali Jinnah had founded after the partition of India in 1947 died with the emergence of Bangladesh.

Simla. June 28, 1972. A summit between my father, the President of Pakistan and Indira Gandhi, the Prime Minister of India. The future of the entire sub-continent depended on its outcome. And again, my father wanted me to be there. 'Whatever the result, this meeting will be a turning point in Pakistan's history,' he told me the week after I returned from my junior year at Harvard for the summer vacation. 'I want you to witness it first hand.'

If the atmosphere had been tense six months before at the United Nations, it was strained to breaking point at Simla. My father was coming to the negotiating table with Indira Gandhi empty-handed. India held all the bargaining cards, our prisoners of war, the threat of war trials and 5,000 square miles of our territory. On the presidential plane to Chandigarh in the Indian state of Punjab, my father and the senior members of the Pakistani delegation were sombre. Would tensions ease between our two countries at Simla? Could we make peace with India? Or was our country doomed?

'Everyone will be looking for signs of how the meetings are progressing, so be extra careful,' my father advised me on the plane. 'You must not smile and give the impression you are enjoying yourself while our soldiers are still in Indian prisoner-of-war camps. You must not look grim, either, which people can interpret as a sign of pessimism. They must have no reason to say: "Look at her face. The meetings are obviously a failure. The Pakistanis have lost their nerve. They have no chance of success and are going to make concessions."'

'So how should I look?' I asked him.

'I've already told you. Don't look sad and don't look happy,' my father said.

'That's very difficult.'

'It's not difficult at all.'

For once he was wrong. It was very difficult to maintain a neutral stance of the face as we transferred to the helicopter at Chandigarh that was to take us to the hill station of Simla, the former summer capital of the British Raj in the Himalayan foothills. It was even more difficult when we landed there on a football pitch and, under the scrutiny of televison cameras, were greeted by Mrs Gandhi herself. How tiny she was, much smaller than she seemed in the countless photographs I had seen of her. And how elegant, even in the raincoat she wore over her sari under the threatening skies. 'As-Salaam O alaikum,' I said to her, our Muslim greeting of peace. 'Namaste – Greetings,' she replied with a smile. I gave her what I hoped was a non-committal half-smile in return.

During the next five days, my father and the other members of the Pakistani delegation were on a roller coaster of emotions. 'The talks are going well,' a delegate told me halfway through the first session. 'It doesn't look good,' another told me that evening. The next day was an even wilder ride, optimism followed by pessimism. Acting from a position of strength, Mrs Gandhi was insisting on a package settlement, including India's claim to the disputed state of Kashmir. The Pakistani delegation wanted a step-by-step approach, settling separately the issues of the territory, the prisoners and our dispute over Kashmir. Any sell-out by Pakistan under pressure would be unacceptable to the people of Pakistan and heighten the chances of a new war.

But while the negotiating teams were deadlocked, a strange phenomenon was taking place on the streets. Every time I left the Himachal Bhavan, the former residence of the British governors of Punjab where we were staying, people lined the streets to stare at me. Cheering crowds began to follow me everywhere: past the old cottages and country gardens planted by nostalgic British inhabitants years before; on my arranged visits to a doll museum, a handicrafts centre, tinned fruit factories, and a dance programme at a convent where I ran into several of my old teachers from the convent in Murree. When I walked down the Mall where officials of the Imperial Government had once promenaded with their wives, the crowds grew so huge that the traffic had to be stopped. It made me feel quite uncomfortable. What had I done to draw such attention?

Letters and telegrams piled up welcoming me to India. One even suggested that my father appoint me Ambassador to India! Journalists and feature writers scrambled to interview me and I was invited to speak on All India Radio. To my chagrin, my clothes became a national fashion event, an embarrassment to me not only because they were all borrowed from Samiya's sister, my own wardrobe consisting mostly of informal khameezes and jeans and sweatshirts, but because I considered clothes irrelevant. I fancied myself more of a Harvard intellectual whose mind was occupied with the serious questions of war and peace, but the press persisted in asking me question after question about my clothes. 'Fashions are a bourgeois pastime,' I finally said in exasperation to one interviewer. But the story the next day had me blazing a new fashion path.

My father and the others among the Pakistani delegation couldn't understand either why I was receiving so much attention. 'You must be a diversion from the seriousness of the issues here,' my father decided one morning, looking at the front page picture of me waving at the crowd in the newspaper. 'Better be careful,' he teased me. 'You look like Mussolini.'

His diversion theory was probably right. The talks were being conducted in total secrecy, leaving the legions of international press gathered in Simla with little to focus on, except me. But I felt my overwhelming reception also represented something else.

I symbolised a new generation. I had never been an Indian. I had been born in independent Pakistan. I was free of the complexes and prejudices which had torn Indians and Pakistanis apart in the bloody trauma of partition. Perhaps the people were hoping that a new generation could avoid the hostility that had now led to three wars, burying the bitter past of our parents and grandparents to live together as friends. And I certainly felt it was possible as I walked the warm and welcoming streets of Simla. Did we have to be divided by walls of hatred or could we, like the once warring countries of Europe, come to terms with each other?

The answer to that question lay deep inside the panelled conference rooms of the British Raj buildings where the long and weary hours of negotiating were going nowhere. My father extended his stay, hoping for a breakthrough. But he wasn't optimistic. The Indians continued to refuse even to acknowledge Pakistan's position on Kashmir: a plebiscite to allow the Kashmiris themselves to decide which country they wished to join. And he was having difficulties with Mrs Gandhi. Though he had been a great admirer of her father, Prime Minister Jawaharlal Nehru, Mrs Gandhi, my father felt, did not have the vision and ideals of her father which had enabled him to build India into a country of international respect.

I was not at all sure myself about Mrs Gandhi. At the small working dinner she had given for our delegation on June 30, she kept staring at me, which made me quite nervous. I had followed her political career closely and admired her perseverance. After her selection as Prime Minister in 1966, the warring members of the Indian congress thought they had selected a malleable and token leader and had called her *goongi goriya*, dumb doll, behind her back. But this silk and steel woman had out-manoeuvred them all. To steady my nerves at the dinner, I tried to make conversation with her, but she was very reticent. There was a cold aloofness about her and a tenseness which only eased when she smiled.

My nerves were also unsettled by the fact that I was wearing a silk sari my mother had lent me. Even though she had given me a lesson in wrapping the yards of material securely around me, I was nervous that it would suddenly unravel. All I could remember was the story of my Auntie Mumtaz's sari in a supermarket in Germany. The hem had got caught in the escalator and her sari had unravelled until someone finally stopped the escalator. That memory didn't help. And Mrs Gandhi kept on staring.

Perhaps she was recalling the diplomatic missions on which she had accompanied her own father, I thought to myself. Was she seeing herself in me, a daughter of another statesman? Was she remembering the love of a daughter for her father, a father for his daughter? She was so small and frail. Where did her famed ruthlessness come from? She had defied her father to marry a Parsi politician of whom he had not approved. Their marriage had not worked and they ended up living separate lives. Now both her father and her husband were dead. Was she lonely?

I wondered also if perhaps the presence of the Pakistani delegation in Simla sparked more historical memories. It was in this very city that her father had met with Mohammed Ali Jinnah and Liaquat Ali Khan to carve out the boundaries of the new state of Muslim Pakistan from Hindu India. Now, as Prime Minister herself, she could ensure the survival of that separate Muslim state. Or she could try and destroy it. Which way would she go? The answer came four days later.

'Pack,' my father said to me on July 2. 'We're going home tomorrow.'

'Without an agreement?' I asked.

'Without an agreement,' he said. 'I'd rather go back to Pakistan with no agreement than with one imposed by India. The Indians think I can't afford to go home without a treaty and will therefore give in to their demands. But I'm calling their bluff. I'd rather face disillusionment in Pakistan than a treaty which sells out our country.'

A gloom fell over the exhausted delegation in Himachal Bhavan. Only the shuffling of papers being packed up broke the silence. All that was left was the courtesy call my father was going to pay on Mrs Gandhi at 4.30 and the dinner our delegation was giving for the Indians that night. Then we would be off to Islamabad.

I was sitting on the floor of my bedroom when my father suddenly appeared in the doorway. 'Don't tell anybody,' he said with a new gleam in his eyes, 'but I'm going to use this protocol visit to try one last time with Mrs Gandhi. I have an idea. But don't be disappointed if there are no results.' And he was gone.

I kept going to the window to watch for his return, looking out at the mist that blurred the pine trees on the hills, the curving mountain roads, the wooden lodges. Simla was so like Murree, yet the people who lived on either side of the border couldn't even visit the other. And suddenly my father was back.

'Hope has returned,' he said with a huge smile. 'We'll get the agreement, *Insha'allah.*'

'How did you do it, Papa?' I asked him as the sombre silence in the house lifted to be replaced by the humming sound of one delegate passing on the news to another.

'I saw that she was very tense during our visit,' my father told me. 'After all, failure was not only a setback for us, but for her, too. Both our political opponents would use it against us. She kept fiddling with her handbag and gave the impression that her tongue did not relish the taste of the hot tea in her cup. So I took a deep breath and talked non-stop for half an hour.'

We are both democratic leaders with a mandate from our people, my father had told her. We can take the region to a peace which has eluded it since Partition or we can fail, deepening the already existing wounds. Military conquests are part of history, but it is statesmanship which finds an enduring place in it. Statesmanship requires looking to the future and making concessions at the moment for the rewards they will reap. As the victor, it is India, not Pakistan, who must make those concessions for the reward of peace.

'Did she agree?' I asked my father with mounting excitement.

'She didn't disagree,' he said, lighting a cigar. 'She said she would consult her personal advisers and let us know at the dinner tonight.'

How we all got through the banquet toasts, the speeches, the pleasantries, I will never know. This time I was the one to keep glancing at Mrs Gandhi, but could read nothing from her face. After dinner, my father and Mrs Gandhi went into a small side sitting room while their negotiating teams went into the billiard room, the largest room available. They used the billiard table as a massive desk. Whenever they completed a point, or had a disagreement, one of the delegates would take the papers into the sitting room to elicit a 'yes' or 'no' from the two leaders.

The drafts and re-drafts, amendments and modifications, took hours. The house got more and more crowded with journalists, television cameramen and representatives from both countries. I kept coming and going between the press of people downstairs to my bedroom upstairs. 'Anything happened yet?' I periodically called from the staircase. Because no announcement could be made unless it was official, the Pakistani delegation devised a code to enable each other to know how things were going. 'If there is an agreement, we'll say a boy has been born. If there is no agreement, we'll say a girl has been born.' 'How chauvinistic,' I commented, but no one was listening.

'Make sure you're downstairs if and when an agreement is signed,' my father had said to me before going into the sitting room. 'It will be an historic moment.' As it turned out, I was upstairs in my bedroom when 'Larka hai! Larka hai! A boy has been born! A boy has been born!' rang out through the house at 12.40 am. I ran downstairs but in the crush of journalists and television cameramen I couldn't get into the room in time to see my father and Mrs Gandhi sign what would become known as the Simla Accord. But what did it matter? The longest lasting peace on the sub-continent had been ushered in.

The Simla Accord returned the 5,000 square miles taken from us by India. It laid the foundation for the restoration of communication and trade between our two countries and did not prejudice the stand of Pakistan or India on the Jammu and Kashmir disputes. The Accord also paved the way for the return of our prisoners-of-war without the humiliation of the war trials that Mujib was threatening in Bangladesh. But it didn't provide for their immediate return.

'Mrs Gandhi agreed to return either the prisoners-of-war or the territory,' my father said to me when he came upstairs later. 'Why do you think I chose the territory?'

'I really don't know, Papa,' I said, quite shocked. 'The people in Pakistan would have been much happier if the prisoners had been freed.'

'And they will be freed,' he assured me. 'Prisoners are a human problem. The magnitude is increased when there are 93,000 of them. It would be inhuman for India to keep them indefinitely. And it will also be a problem to keep on feeding and housing them. Territory, on the other hand, is not a human problem. Territory can be assimilated. Prisoners cannot. The Arabs have still not succeeded in regaining the territory lost in the 1967 war. But the capturing of land doesn't cry out for international attention the same way prisoners do.'

Returning without an agreement to free the prisoners was a hard decision for my father to make, and predictably, there were many protests from opposing Pakistani politicians and the prisoners' families. Perhaps the Indian side was banking on the inevitable turmoil to force him to capitulate. But he didn't. And all 93,000 prisoners were released after Pakistan's recognition of Bangladesh in 1974.

As we flew back to Rawalpindi on July 3, the mood was jubilant, a far cry from the sombreness that had accompanied us to India. Thousands of people were at the airport to welcome my father as we stepped out onto the red carpet. 'Today is a great day,' my father addressed the crowd. 'There has been a great victory. This is not my victory. Nor is it a victory of Mrs Gandhi's. It is a victory for the people of Pakistan and India who have won peace after three wars.'

On July 4, 1972, the Simla Accord won the unanimous approval of the National Assembly; even the opposition joined in the tributes. The Simla Accord still stands today.

Unfortunately, the Constitution of 1973, Pakistan's first democratic constitution framed by genuinely elected representatives of the people, does not. A year later, on August 14, 1973, while our whole family watched from the Prime Minister's box, the National Assembly unanimously adopted the Islamic charter which, unbelievably, had been supported by national consensus, by our regional and religious leaders, and by my father's opposition. As the leader of the majority in the National Assembly, my father became the Prime Minister of Pakistan.

Until Zia overthrew my father and suspended the Constitution four years later, the people of Pakistan enjoyed the first constitution in Pakistan's history to introduce fundamental human rights and ensure their protection. The Constitution of 1973 forbade discrimination on the basis of race, sex, or religion. It guaranteed the independence of the judiciary and its separation from the executive. The first representative government of Pakistan finally had the legal framework within which to govern: the sanctioned authority that Professor Womack had brought home to me so clearly in his seminar.

As I prepared to leave Harvard in the spring of 1973, the strength of the United States Constitution was being graphically demonstrated. In spite of the balmy weather and the Frisbee games in Harvard Yard, many of us were rooted to the televised Watergate hearings. My God, I thought. The American people are removing their president through democratic, constitutional means. Even a powerful president like Richard Nixon who had put an end to the Vietnam war and opened the pathway to China could not escape the law of his land. I had read Locke, Rousseau and John Stuart Mill on the nature of society and the state, the need to guarantee the rights of the people. But theory was one thing. Seeing it unfold in practice was quite another.

The Watergate process left me with a profound sense of the importance of nationally accepted laws, rather than whimsical or arbitrary laws imposed by individuals. When President Nixon resigned his office a year later in August 1974, the succession of power was smooth and peaceful. The leaders in a democracy like America's might come and go, but the United States Constitution remained. We would not be so fortunate in Pakistan.

As my Harvard graduation drew near, I grew increasingly sad at the thought of leaving Cambridge, of leaving America. I had been accepted at Oxford, as had several of my friends including Peter Galbraith, but I didn't want to go. I knew my way around Cambridge and Boston and had finally mastered the subway routes on the MTA. I knew and understood the people. I pleaded with my father to let me go on to the Fletcher School of Law and Diplomacy at Tufts before returning to Pakistan. But he was adamant that I go to Oxford. Four years in one place is more than enough, he wrote to me. If you stay longer in America you will begin to put down roots there. It is time for you to move on.

For the first time I felt my father was pushing me. But what could I do?

It was he, after all, who was paying for my tuition and expenses. I had no choice. And I was a practical person.

My mother came to graduation and she and my brother Mir who had just finished his first year at Harvard helped me pack. My roommate, Yolanda Kodrzycki and I gave away our furniture and took down our posters. Our rooms looked bare, as did Harvard Yard and the shelves at the Co-op bookshop. Maybe it was time to move on.

As the plane lifted off from Logan Airport, I strained to catch a last glimpse of the Boston skyline. Shopping at Filene's basement. Eating at the communal tables at Durgin Park. Going to the Casablanca to forget our hockey loss to Boston University. Man had reached the moon and I had seen the moon dust at MIT. With the lyrics to Peter, Paul and Mary's song – 'I'm leaving on a jet plane, don't know when I'll be back again' – running through my mind, I flew home to Pakistan.

4

REFLECTIONS FROM AL-MURTAZA:
THE DREAMING SPIRES OF OXFORD

January, 1980. In our third month of detention at Al-Murtaza, my ear starts to bother me again. Click. Click. The noises begin as they had during an earlier detention in 1978. Then the doctor called in by the Martial Law authorities in Karachi had diagnosed the problem as a sinus condition aggravated by the plane flights I'd taken every two weeks to visit my father in jail, and he'd cauterised the inside of my nose to open the Eustachian tube. Now, I start to feel the familiar buzzing in my ear and the build-up of pressure. The local doctor visits, but the noises continue. I ask the prison authorities to bring the doctor who had operated on me in Karachi. I'm surprised when they bring in someone I don't know instead. He is gentle and has a soothing voice. 'Relax. You have been under a lot of stress,' he consoles me as he examines my ear.

'Ouch!' I cry out. 'You're hurting me.'

'You're just imagining it,' he replies. 'I'm just taking a look inside your ear.'

When I wake up the next morning, there are three drops of blood on my pillow.

'You've perforated your ear-drum. You must have done it with a hairpin,' the doctor says when he returns. Hairpin? Why would I put a hairpin in my ear? He writes out a prescription for two drugs which he tells me to take three times a day. But all the pills do is make me sleep, and when I'm awake I'm depressed. My mother is shocked when by the third day I no longer get up at sunrise to go into the garden, care about eating, or even brush my teeth. She gets so upset she throws the medicine away.

For days afterward, the pain comes and goes while the noises increase. Click. Click. Click. Click. I can't sleep, can't get any peace at all. Has the regime's doctor deliberately punctured my ear-drum, or was it a mistake? Click. Click. Click. My ear feels full and I cannot hear properly.

I try to distract myself during the day by working harder in the garden. Sweat trickles through the hole in my ear-drum. Water from the showers I take seeps into my ear. I don't realise, and was not told by the doctor, that I should keep my ear dry, that water going into a perforated ear can make it septic. Click. Click.

Unable to sleep at night, I walk around inside Al-Murtaza. Like 70

Clifton, Al-Murtaza has been raided so many times that everything has either been moved or has vanished. My father's collection of antique guns passed down from my great-grandfather has been impounded by the regime and sealed in a storeroom in the garden. The Martial Law authorities come to Al-Murtaza every week to see whether the storeroom seal has been tampered with, as if they expect my mother and me to blast our way out with antique muskets.

I pass the now empty gunroom which we used as a family dining room and go on to the wood-panelled billiard room where my brothers used to challenge friends visiting me from Oxford. A small ceramic of a fat Chinese man surrounded by many children is sitting on a table in the billiard room, though it belongs in the drawing room. I pick it up to return it. My father loved the figurine, often joking that he wanted enough children to make up a cricket team, but educating eleven children in the modern world was too expensive, so he'd settled on the four of us.

Oxford, Oxford, Oxford, he'd drummed into all of us. Oxford was one of the best and most respected universities in the world. Oxford was steeped in English history. English literature, the church, the monarchy, parliament all had some connection with Oxford. American education was very good, he'd allowed, but was conducted in a more relaxed manner. Oxford would give us all a new horizon and a sense of discipline. He'd entered all four of us at birth. As the oldest, I was the only one who had the luxury of completing my Oxford education before the coup turned our lives upside-down. Mir left Oxford shortly after the beginning of his second year to fight for my father's life in England, while Sanam never got there at all. My years in my father's beloved Alma Mater meant a great deal to him.

'I feel a strange sensation in imagining you walking on the footprints I left behind at Oxford over twenty-two years ago,' my father wrote to me from the Prime Minister's House in Rawalpindi soon after I arrived at Oxford in the autumn of 1973. 'I was [made] happy by your presence at Radcliffe but, since I was not at Harvard, I could not picture you there through the same camera. Here I see your presence like mine in flesh and blood, over every cobble of the streets of Oxford, over every step you take on the frozen stone ladders, through every portal of learning you enter. Your being at Oxford is a dream come true. We pray and hope that this dream turned into reality will grow into a magnificent career in the service of your people.'

He had been far happier at Oxford than, at first, I was. Unlike Harvard, where my roommate and I had our own suite of rooms, my single room at Lady Margaret Hall was tiny with a communal bathroom down the passage. I missed having my own telephone, and had to rely instead on Oxford's antiquated message system which generally took two days. And I found the English reserved compared to my friends at Harvard who were instantly friendly. For weeks I sought out the company of my American classmates who had come on to Oxford. But my father kept after me, sending me a print of ancient Rome which had hung in his room at Christ Church in 1950. 'Before you went to Oxford this print could not have had any meaning for you,' he wrote from Al-Murtaza. 'Now I am sending it to you in case you want to keep it in your room.' I hung it on my wall, warming to the sense of continuity that now stretched from the dust of Pakistan to the clean-swept streets of Oxford.

My father had warned me that, compared to Harvard, Oxford would teach me to work under pressure. As I struggled to write the required two essays a week for my tutorials in Politics, Philosophy and Economics, I had to admit he was right. He was right, as well, in urging me to join the Oxford Union.

Of all the various societies at Oxford, and there were many – ranging from socialist, Conservative and Liberal political clubs to those focusing on rowing and beagling – the most well-known was the Oxford Union Debating Society. Established in 1823 and modelled on the House of Commons, the Union was seen as the training ground for future politicians. I had no intention of becoming a politician, having seen first-hand the pressures and strains of life in politics. I was aiming for a career in Pakistan's Foreign Service. Nevertheless, I joined the Oxford Union to please my father.

As well as fulfilling my father's wishes, I was drawn by the art of debate. The power of oratory had always been a great force on the Asian sub-continent where so many were illiterate. Millions had been swayed by the words of Mahatma Gandhi, Jawaharlal Nehru, Mohammed Ali Jinnah and, indeed, my father. Story-telling, poetry and oratory were part of our tradition. I didn't realise then that my experience gained in the polite and panelled walls of the Oxford Union would translate into speaking before millions in the fields of Pakistan.

For my three years reading PPE and the fourth year when I returned to take a post-graduate course in international law and diplomacy, the Oxford Union was one of the most important and pleasant focal points of my life. Its gardens and building in the centre of Oxford with a restaurant in the cellar, two libraries, and a billiard room became as familiar to me as the rooms at Al-Murtaza. In the debating hall we listened to speakers ranging from the feminist author Germaine Greer to the trade unionist Arthur Scargill. Two former British Prime Ministers came during my time at the Oxford Union, Lord Stockton and Edward Heath. Student speakers dressed in formal clothes with carnations in their lapels, forcing me out of my jeans and into the silks of Anna Belinda. After candle-lit dinners, we set to warring with words.

What tricks life plays on us. The first speech I was asked to give in the main debating chamber under the busts of such former British statesmen as Gladstone and Macmillan concerned the constitutional, not armed, removal of an elected head of state. 'That this house would impeach Nixon' was the motion which I was asked by the Union's president to propose.

'It is a paradox that a man who ran for the Presidency on the issue of law and order did his best to break the law and cause disorder in the length and breadth of his country,' I began my argument. 'But then American history is replete with paradoxes. Let me tell you the story of George Washington and his father. When young George's father found somebody had cut down his cherry tree, he was absolutely furious and wanted to know who did it. Bravely, young George stepped forward and said, "Father, I cannot tell a lie. I did it." Well, Americans began with a President who couldn't tell a lie and now they have one who can't tell the truth.'

With all the easy conviction of a twenty-year-old, I outlined the charges of impeachable offences against the American President, including his violation of the war-making powers of Congress in Vietnam and the secret bombings of Cambodia, his antedating the gift of his vice-presidential papers so as to claim a tax deduction, and his alleged involvement with the Watergate cover-up and the mysterious erasure of his secretary's tapes.

'Make no mistake, my friends,' I concluded. 'These charges are serious. Nixon has consistently considered himself above the law, able to do as he pleases. The last English sovereign to do so lost his head. We are proposing a less drastic but no less effective surgery. It is said that Nixon once went to see a psychiatrist who told him: "You're not paranoid, Mr President. You really are hated." Today Nixon is not only hated, but he has lost all credibility. By losing credibility with his people, Nixon has lost his moral authority to lead the American nation. This is the tragedy of Nixon and America.'

Codes of law. Credibility. Moral authority. All these democratic principles which I took for granted during my years in the West, would be lost in Pakistan. The motion to impeach President Nixon was carried by a vote of 345 to 2 in the Oxford Union. Guns, not votes, would overthrow my father in Pakistan.

But Pakistan seemed far away when I was at Oxford. Just as my father had predicted, the light, happy years I spent there became the best years of my life. Friends took me punting on the Cherwell River, and for picnics on the shaded greens of Blenheim Palace near Woodstock. Other weekends we drove in the yellow MGB convertible my father had given me as a graduation present from Radcliffe to watch Shakespeare at Stratford-on-

Avon, or to London where I satisfied my craving for American peppermint-stick ice cream at the newly opened branch of Baskin-Robbins. During 'eights week', when rowing crews from each college raced each other up the river, we all joined the garden parties held at the college boathouses, the men dressed in boaters and blazers, the women in hats and long flowered dresses. We took exams 'subfusc', wearing the traditional white shirts, black skirts and black sleeveless gowns which prompted even non-students in Oxford to call out 'Good Luck!' as we ran by.

Unlike Harvard where there were few foreign students – only four in my class at Radcliffe including an English girl whose definition as 'foreign' struck me as rather odd – there were many more up at Oxford. Imran Khan, the Pakistani cricketer was there as was Bahram Dehqani-Tafti, whose father was Iranian. Bahram, who was killed in May 1980, soon after the revolution in Iran, used to entertain us for hours at the piano, his repertoire ranging from Gilbert and Sullivan and Scott Joplin to Fauré's *Requiem*. But, though Asians were accepted at Oxford as rather exotic individuals who did not fit into any particular class or category, not all the British felt the same way.

In February 1974 I flew home to Pakistan to join my family at the Islamic Summit my father was convening in Lahore. Practically every Muslim monarch, president, prime minister and foreign minister was there, representing thirty-eight nations, states, emirates and kingdoms. After my father's call to the Summit members to extend diplomatic recognition to Bangladesh, Mujib ur-Rahman came too, flown in on President Houari Boumédiene's private plane. The Summit was a great success for my father – and for Pakistan. By extending the olive branch to Mujib, my father paved the way for the peaceful return of the Pakistani prisoners-of-war whom the Bengali leader was threatening with war trials.

I returned to England enthused with a sense of Asian identity – and promptly encountered my first case of racism.

'Where are you planning to stay in England?' the immigration officer asked me, studying my passport.

'Oxford,' I replied politely. 'I'm a student there.'

'Oxford?' he said sarcastically, raising his eyebrows. Fighting irritation, I produced my student identification.

'Bhutto. Miss Benazir Bhutto. Karachi, Pakistan,' he said in a contemptuous tone. 'Where is your police card?'

'Right here,' I replied, producing the up-to-date police card all foreigners were required to carry in England.

'And how do you plan to pay your bills at Oxford?' he said with condescension. I resisted quipping that I had brought pencils and a tin cup with me. 'My parents send funds to my bank account,' I said, showing him my bank book.

Still the nasty little official kept me standing there, going over my papers time and again, looking up my name which he obviously didn't recognise in a big, fat book.

'How can a Paki have enough money for an Oxford education?' he finally said, pushing my documents back to me.

I was furious as I turned on my heel and strode out of the airport. If that was how immigration officials were going to treat the daughter of the Prime Minister, how were they going to treat other Pakistanis who were not as fluent in English as I was or who were not as aggressive?

Long before I had gone to Oxford, my father had warned me about the prejudice I might find in the West. He had encountered it himself as a student when a hotel clerk in San Diego, California, denied him a room, not because he was a Pakistani, but because his dark skin made him look like a Mexican.

He warned me again of the perils of racism when my letters from Oxford and my references at home became as much Western as Eastern. He was worried, I suppose, that I might succumb to the Siren Song of the West and not return to Pakistan. 'They (the Westerners) know in their heart of hearts that as a student you are not going to remain permanently in their country,' he wrote to me. 'They accept you because they do not think of you as an immigrant, as a coloured liability. Their attitude changes completely once they come to know that you are one more Pakistani or one more Asian who has returned to their great country for refuge. They will begin to look down at you. They will think it unfair that you should compete with them for any avenue of success.'

His warnings really weren't necessary because I never really contemplated not returning to Pakistan. My heart was there. My heritage and culture were there. So was my future, I hoped, in the diplomatic corps. I was already getting diplomatic experience of sorts, just by being my father's daughter.

During a 1973 State Visit to the United States where my father set in motion the lifting of the arms embargo against Pakistan, I was seated next to Henry Kissinger at a formal White House dinner. All I could think of through the soup course was the irreverent *Harvard Lampoon* centrefold of the cigar-smoking Secretary of State lying on a panda-skin rug, a treasured issue I had immediately sent to my sister and Samiya in Pakistan. To distract myself during the fish course I chatted to him about elitism at Harvard and other non-controversial subjects. I was quite bewildered therefore the next night when Kissinger collared my father at another dinner to announce: 'Mr Prime Minister, your daughter is even more intimidating than you are.' My father had roared with laughter, taking the quip as a compliment. I'm still not sure . . .

Nuclear power was the subject in France where my father attended the funeral of Georges Pompidou in 1974. He had reached an informal nuclear assistance agreement with Pompidou the year before to provide Pakistan with a reprocessing plant. What he didn't know was whether Pompidou's successor would continue the negotiations. 'Who do you think the next President will be?' my father asked me over dinner with friends at Maxim's. 'Giscard d'Estaing,' I replied, basing my projection on the excellent course in French politics I was taking under my tutor Peter Pulsar at Christ Church. Luckily I was right, for President d'Estaing did indeed agree to honour the agreement, in spite of great pressure from Henry Kissinger and the United States.

My presidential projections had not been so astute three years before in China, where my father had sent my brothers, sister and me to observe a communist state. In a courtesy meeting with Chou En-lai, the Chinese Premier had asked me who I thought the next president of the United States would be. 'George McGovern,' I had replied firmly, repeating my choice again even after Chou said his American sources had pinpointed Richard Nixon. As a loyal anti-war activist at Harvard and resident of the liberal Northeast, I couldn't conceive of any other choice but McGovern. 'Write me your impressions when you return to America,' Chou En-lai asked me. I had. McGovern, I insisted again. So much for my political shrewdness as a student.

My own – and more successful – presidential elections were occupying me in the autumn of 1976 when I returned to Oxford for a one-year post-graduate course. Although I was anxious to leave the world of academia for that of diplomacy, my father felt strongly that his children, by virtue of being the Prime Minister's children, had to be doubly qualified for any job so that no one could accuse him – or us – of favouritism.

My brother Mir was beginning his first year at Oxford, and I looked forward to spending more time with him. But the real bonus to me of another year at Oxford was the chance to stand for the presidency of the Oxford Union. Over the years I had served on the Union's Standing Committee and as Treasurer, but I had been defeated in my first attempt at the presidency. This time I won. My victory in December of 1976 upset what was really an 'old boy's club', where only ten years before women had been restricted to the upstairs gallery and where the membership ratio still ran at seven men to one woman, and surprised everyone, even my father.

'In an election one side has to win and the other has to lose,' he had written to me shortly before the 1976 presidential election in America, bracing me for the same loss Gerald Ford was about to suffer at the hands of Jimmy Carter. 'You have to do your best but the result must be accepted in good grace.' A month later the message from my father was very different. 'OVERJOYED AT YOUR ELECTION AS PRESIDENT OF THE OXFORD UNION,' his cable read. 'YOU HAVE DONE SPLENDIDLY. OUR HEARTWARMING CON-GRATULATIONS ON YOUR GREAT SUCCESS, PAPA.'

My three-month term as President was to begin in January 1977. As Mir and I flew home to Pakistan for the Michaelmas break, there wasn't a cloud on my horizon.

'Come and meet Zia ul-Haq,' one of my father's aides said to me on the patio of Al-Murtaza during my father's annual birthday party a few days later. And for the first and only time I came face to face with the man who six months later would overthrow my father and subsequently send him to his death.

Having heard of the difficulty in filling the position, I was curious to meet my father's Army Chief-of-Staff designate. Six other Generals had been passed over for the top spot, all of them found by army intelligence sources to have some sort of character flaw: drinking, adultery, doubtful loyalty. General Zia was not without flaws either. He was rumoured to have links to the *Jamaat-e-Islami*, a fundamentalist religious organisation which opposed the PPP and wanted the country to be governed by religious, rather than secular leaders. He was also said to be a petty thief by one of my father's ambassadors.

But Zia also had a great deal in his favour. Unlike many of our army officers, Zia had been untarnished by the carnage in East Pakistan, because he had been out of the country during the civil war. And he was reported to be respected among the army. No other criterion was more important to my father in the lengthy selection process that he found increasingly exasperating. When the different army agencies all wrote favourable reports about Zia, my father chose him. 'The civilian government must not seem to be imposing their will on the military. Zia may not be among the most senior officers, but the men in the army seem to like him,' my father said with relief. And so at Al-Murtaza on January 5, 1977, I came face to face with the man who would so drastically change all our lives.

I remember being startled when I saw him. Unlike the childish image I carried of a soldier as tall and rugged with James Bond nerves of steel, the General standing in front of me was a short, nervous, ineffectual-looking man whose pomaded hair was parted in the middle and lacquered to his head. He looked more like an English cartoon villain than an inspiring military leader. And he seemed so obsequious, telling me over and over again how honoured he was to meet the daughter of such a great man as Zulfikar Ali Bhutto. Certainly my father could have found a more commanding Chief-of-Staff, I thought to myself. But I said nothing to my father.

'I'm going to call for additional land reforms,' my father confided in me as we walked in the garden of Al-Murtaza on the afternoon of his birthday. 'And I'm also going to call for elections in March. The Constitution doesn't require elections until August, but I see no need to wait. The democratic institutions we have installed under the Constitution are in place and the parliament and provincial governments are functioning. With a mandate now from the people, we can move on more easily to the second phase of implementation, expanding the industrial base of the country, modernising agriculture by sinking new tube wells, increasing seed distribution and fertiliser production. . . .' The ideas flowed out of him as we walked, his vision of a modern and competitive Pakistan coming nearer and nearer.

Many of his reforms had already begun. The PPP had delivered on its campaign promises to the poor, beginning the redistribution of the land held by the feudal few. My father had also begun his socialist economic policies, nationalising many of the industries monopolised by Pakistan's 'Twenty-Two Families' to channel the profits back into the country. His government had fixed minimum wages for those who had often worked for little or no compensation from the tribal chiefs and industry owners, and encouraged the workers to form unions, giving them a voice in management and a stake in their futures for the first time in Pakistan's history.

Electricity had been fed to many villages in the rural areas. Literacy programmes for men and women were established and new schools built for the poor. Parks and gardens were sprouting in the dust of the cities, and new, metal roads were being built to link the provinces where before there had only been dirt tracks. In a pact with the Chinese, a new highway was being carved out of the Hindu Kush which would run all the way to the border of China. My father was determined to bring modern prosperity to the people of Pakistan.

'My donkey keeps slipping on this new road,' one farmer complained to my father in Baluchistan. 'I will show you a better kind of donkey that will get your vegetables to market three times as fast,' my father assured him. The next week he sent the farmer a jeep.

There was opposition to my father, of course. He was certainly not a favourite of the industrialists whose private fiefdoms he had nationalised. Nor of the landowners whose holdings he had shared among the peasants who had been working the land for as many as eleven generations and who were only allowed to keep half the crop they had raised. The members of the *Jamaat-e-Islami*, many of whom were small shop-keepers, raised their voices against my father's social reforms, especially the government's outspoken support for women who worked outside the home and the new laws forbidding sexual discrimination. My father's policy of consolidation antagonised those with vested interests in separatism: the secessionists in Baluchistan and the Northwest Frontier who wanted independence; the tribal chiefs who wanted to continue imposing their own rule, not the central government's, on their hundreds of thousands of followers.

In fact, all the same factions which had existed at the birth of Pakistan in 1947 still existed in 1977: the regionalists against the central government, the capitalists against the socialists, the feudalists and *sardars* against the educated and enlightened, the inhabitants of the poorer provinces against the rich elite of the Punjab, the fundamentalists against those who favoured modernisation. And over all these lay the mighty shadow of the Army, the single most organised and smoothly functioning institution in fractious Pakistan.

Some Western political analysts and Pakistani military men argued that democracy was impossible for such a divergent and unsettled population where the literacy rate and annual income were so low. Many in Pakistan couldn't even talk to each other, as each region had its own language and customs. Such a population could only be kept in line by military rule, the argument went. But my father had disproved that theory by successfully establishing a democratic government where elections, not military might, determined who led the country. As 1977 began, there was no thought in anyone's mind that his government wouldn't be re-elected in March.

While my father prepared for the elections in Pakistan, I returned to Oxford to organise debates at the Union. 'That capitalism will triumph' was the subject of my first debate as President, which I invited Tariq Ali, an ex-President of the Union and a highly respected and articulate Pakistani leftist, to oppose. 'That the West can no longer live at the expense of the Third World' was another debate designed to focus attention on the North-South divide.

While the political opposition in Pakistan was banding together against the PPP in a nine-party coalition of regionalists, religious fundamentalists and industrialists called the Pakistan National Alliance, I was arranging the fifth debate, traditionally a funny one at the Oxford Union, whose motion was 'That this house would rather rock than roll'. Rock music resounded through the venerable debating hall for the first time ever, while two friends from Magdalen College sang a very loud duet about the Union to the tune of 'Jesus Christ Superstar', then carried me out of the hall on their shoulders.

While I was busy painting the President's office at the Oxford Union powder-blue and having the debate programmes printed in green and white (the colours of the Pakistani flag), in Pakistan Asghar Khan, a leader of the PNA and the former Commander-in-Chief of the Air Force, was announcing that the opposition coalition would not accept the March election results, claiming they would be rigged. I paid little attention to that charge, knowing that my father was following the electoral procedures found in all democratic countries and had set up an independent Election

Commission, Election Tribunals, and election laws under the jurisdiction of the superior courts to ensure that the elections would be fair and impartial. Still, it seemed a strange campaign tactic for Asghar Khan to be preparing the country not to accept the PPP's inevitable victory at the polls.

The election campaign became even more perplexing when on January 18, the deadline for registration of candidates, the PNA did not put up a single candidate for any of the constituencies where my father and his chief ministers were contesting. How odd, I thought, as I read the story in England. Why were they leaving the Prime Minister and the chief ministers of the four provinces unopposed? Perhaps the PNA candidates knew they could not defeat my father and wanted to save face. But that thought proved to be too rational. Their explanation was not only ludicrous, but made headlines.

'We were kidnapped and prevented from registering,' the opposition screamed, claiming that their proposers and seconders had also been snatched by the police until the deadline was passed. Their charges sounded ridiculous to me in England. I did not believe for a moment that the members of the PNA had been kidnapped, nor evidently did the Chief Election Commissioner who dismissed their charges for lack of substantiation. If they had been kidnapped, they must have arranged it themselves. But it was a clever move. Kidnappings for all sorts of reasons were common in Pakistan, and many people probably believed the PNA's claim of foul play.

I began to follow the campaign news more closely in the English newspapers as well as the Pakistani newspapers my parents sent me every week and other Asian publications. The PNA was getting more irresponsible and outrageous by the minute. Bhutto cannot be trusted, the opposition was trumpeting. He plans to nationalise everyone's private homes and to confiscate every woman's gold jewellery. Bhutto is a rich elitist, not a man of the people, they scoffed. He wears Savile Row suits, Italian shoes and drinks Scotch whisky.

Ayub Khan's ministers had made the same charge. My father's retort then had delighted me, for he was an open person and never hid in public what he did in private. 'I don't deny that after an eighteen-hour working day I take an occasional drink,' he had shot back during a public meeting in Lahore. 'But, unlike other politicians, I do not drink the blood of the people.'

I never doubted the outcome of the election. The PNA leaders were not great men or even fine men. Most were much older than my father and had had their time. They hadn't had the benefit of my father's education, nor his extensive experience in government and international diplomacy. In Pakistan, my father was, in fact, unique. Under the rule of the

Generals, politics had not on the whole drawn the cream of the crop; real power was seen to lie in the Civil Service, the Army, or in industry. Many of those opposing my father were small, provincial men whose myopic views had failed Pakistan in the past and would do so again in the future.

And their lies were growing preposterous. Bhutto is such a bad Muslim, Asghar Khan was claiming, that he is only now learning how to perform the five daily prayers. I could hardly believe my eyes when I read that charge in the *Far Eastern Economic Review* in February; I had prayed often with my parents at home. But I loved my father's retort to that one, too. When a reporter asked him why Yasir Arafat, leader of the PLO, was coming to see him, my father quipped: 'He is coming to teach me prayers.'

Under the campaign slogan of *Nizame-e-Mustafa*, the 'Regime of the Prophet', other coalition leaders were shamelessly using religion for political ends. A vote against the party, the head of the *Jamaat-e-Islami* party told one rally in a rural area, was a vote against God. A vote for the PNA was equal to 100,000 years of prayer.

Saner opposition leaders, however, knew the religious issue was explosive and avoided expanding on it. For all the spiritual muckraking going on, they knew the PPP's adherence to Islam was unquestionable. It was my father who had given the country its first Islamic Constitution in 1973, and he who had created Pakistan's first Ministry of Religious Affairs. It was his administration which had printed the first error-free Holy Quran in Pakistan, lifted the quotas past governments had set to limit the number of Pakistanis permitted to travel to Mecca on pilgrimage, and made *Islamiyat* – religious education – compulsory in primary and secondary schools. My father's government had instituted Arabic language programmes on televison to teach Pakistanis the language of the Holy Quran, and a *Ruet-e-Hillal*, or moon-sighting committee, to end confusion over the beginning and end of the Ramazan fast. Under my father, the government had even insisted that Pakistan change the name and symbol of the Red Cross to the Red Crescent to commemorate its connection to Islam instead of Christianity.

I was therefore not too disturbed when I read about the fundamentalist elements of the opposition campaign. The vast majority of the people, I thought, knew that implementing the fundamentalist interpretation of *Shariah* would turn back the gains Pakistanis had made in human rights and economic development one thousand years. Banking would have to be abolished altogether, for example, for strict interpretation of Islam sees the charging of interest as usury. And women would lose every step forward my father had encouraged them to take.

He had opened the Foreign Service, the Civil Service, and the police force to women. To promote female education, he had appointed a woman to the position of Vice-Chancellor of Islamabad University and, in the government, had named a woman as Governor of Sindh and as the Deputy Speaker in the National Assembly. Communications, too, were opened to women, female newscasters appearing on television for the first time.

He had encouraged my mother, as well, to take a more active role. In 1975 she had headed Pakistan's delegation to the United Nations' international conference on women held in Mexico City. I had been very proud when she was elected Vice President of the conference. Now she was standing for election to the National Assembly, a symbol of my father's positive attitude toward women in politics.

But, as election day drew near, the PNA's attacks against the PPP only grew wilder. Asghar Khan was promising to send his least favourite PPP leaders to concentration camps when he took over the government on March 8. And he was boasting of killing my father.

'Shall I hang Bhutto from the Attock Bridge? Or shall I hang Bhutto from a Lahore lamp post?' the opposition leader was saying. That truly jolted me. Asghar Khan had been rumoured to have relatives among the junior army officers who had staged an unsuccessful coup attempt in 1974. Was he working up factions in the army again?

I felt so far away in Oxford. My father had worked to bring democracy to Pakistan. But not all the people, it was turning out, had learned the self-discipline that democracy requires. In one Karachi neighbourhood, a PNA candidate sprayed a poster of my father with machine-gun fire, killing a young child standing by.

'The opposition has behaved quite badly, so much so that even a politically apathetic cabbage like myself has been jolted into taking notice,' a school friend wrote to me from Karachi in February. '. . . Now, more than ever, all of Pakistan realises how desperately we need your father. God forbid, if anyone else were to even come close to taking over the reins, I think it would destroy us as a nation.'

On election night I joined Mir in his rooms opposite Christ's College to wait by the phone. The Pakistani Ambassador in London and one of my father's ministers had both promised to ring as soon as they had any news of the results. Mir was predicting that the PPP would win between 150 and 156 seats in the National Assembly. When the phone rang, it was my father, his voice hoarse from campaigning, calling with the news that the PPP had won 154 of 200 seats. 'Congratulations, Papa. I am so happy for you,' I yelled into the phone. I was as excited by the PPP victory as I was relieved that the election tension was over. But it wasn't.

True to the coalition's threat, the PNA claimed the national election results were rigged and announced it would boycott the Provincial Assembly elections scheduled three days later. And the agitation increased.

Swarms of young men on motor scooters were suddenly reported to be racing through Karachi, leaving cinemas, banks, shops that sold alcohol, and any houses flying the PPP flag burning in their wake. Thirteen members of one family were put to the torch in one home and, when in his final agony one of the victims asked for water, the hooligans responded by urinating in his mouth. A PPP member was lynched, his body left to hang from a public lamp-post until the police cut it down. Death threats were issued to innumerable other PPP ministers and parliamentarians, as were threats to kidnap their children from school.

A nightmare was unfolding in Karachi. Every morning I rushed to the common room in St Catherine's College to snatch up the English papers before collecting the Pakistani papers from my mailbox. Mir and I pored over them in disbelief. We had seen democracy in America and England where political opponents did not often resort to such terrorist attacks and goondaism, and both of us found the PNA's tactics apalling. We also grew increasingly suspicious about their implications. It was obvious that the PNA had no interest in elections. Perhaps their continued agitations were paving the way for some intervention in the government, like an army take-over.

The Army was the key. But there was no reason to doubt the loyalty of the armed forces. My father was very popular among the army and his selection of Zia as Army Chief-of-Staff over six more senior officers seemed to ensure Zia's support as well. In our culture, one does not betray one's benefactor. Still, Asghar Khan was trying to win over the army, circulating a letter he had written to the armed forces implicitly calling on them to take over the government. But it fell on deaf ears. Instead the Chiefs-of-Staff − Navy, Air Force, and Army − released a statement supporting my father's elected civilian government. The PNA was getting nowhere.

After almost three weeks of unrest in Karachi and Hyderabad, the PNA tried to carry the rioting and looting to Lahore. Again, packs of twenty to thirty men on scooters were dispatched, this time to the bazaars where they pelted shoppers with stones, forcing merchants to pull down their shutters in fear. At times the hooligans doused banks and buses with petrol and set them on fire before riding off.

Reading the papers at Oxford, Mir and I were becoming increasingly disgusted at the PNA's attempts to stir up agitation. Instead of accepting a democratic defeat, these old-style politicians were resorting to violence and rumour. 'Begum Bhutto has fled with her suitcases,' one such PNA rumour went. 'Bhutto will follow soon.'

My father was so sure of the PPP's strength that he offered to hold new provincial elections and, if the PNA won a majority, to re-run the general elections, but the leaders of the PNA refused even to sit down and talk with him. Nothing would satisfy them but his resignation. Having just been returned overwhelmingly to office in a fair and democratic election, my father naturally refused.

The PNA's terrorist tactics even reached me at Oxford. I was startled one afternoon in late March to find a member of Scotland Yard waiting for me when I returned from the Bodleian Library. 'I don't wish to alarm you, Miss Bhutto, but there have been reports that you may be in some danger,' the British officer told me.

I didn't think Scotland Yard would bother to send anyone all the way to Oxford to tell me something if it were not in my best interest. So from that day until I left Oxford in June I followed his instructions carefully, looking under my car to check for any explosives before opening the door, and inspecting the lock to see if it had been tampered with. I also followed Scotland Yard's instructions to vary my schedule and not to follow a routine. If I had a ten o'clock class, I would leave for it as early as 9.30 or as late as 9.55. I still use some of the security measures Scotland Yard taught me today.

In Pakistan, the PNA's agitations were fizzling by early April. The trouble seemed to be over when the news from home took a new and ominous turn.

People had fistfuls of American dollars and were leaving their jobs, my friend Samiya wrote, including my cousin Fakhri's servants and those of their friends. 'We get better pay by demonstrating for the PNA,' the servants claimed. Since March, she wrote, the flood of American currency had driven the value of the dollar in the black market down by 30 per cent. Without apparent financial loss, private truck and bus drivers had gone on strike in Karachi, forcing a factory slowdown because the employees couldn't get to work. Those same trucks and buses, however, were available to transport the people to PNA demonstrations.

Asians have always been prone to conspiracy theories. But in this case my father and other members of the PPP were convinced that the unrest was due to American involvement. I could see for myself when the truck drivers went on strike that the pattern of economic dislocation was similar to the one in Chile during the CIA-sponsored military overthrow of President Allende and his democratically elected government. Our intelligence had also noted frequent meetings between American diplomats and members of the PNA.

The effectiveness of the PNA-sponsored strikes was suspicious as well. When my father came to power, he learned that in 1958 the US had held top secret manoeuvres with the Pakistani army to teach them the art of immobilising a government through strikes. These secret manoeuvres had been called 'Operation Wheel Jam'. Now the PNA was calling for a nationwide strike. Its name? 'Operation Wheel Jam'.

I didn't want to believe the United States was actively destabilising the democractically elected government of Pakistan. But I kept coming back to a remark Henry Kissinger had made to my father during a visit to Pakistan in the summer of 1976. The issue then had been my father's determination to move ahead with negotiations with France on a nuclear reprocessing plant; a plant which would give Pakistan energy at a time when skyrocketing oil prices had adversely affected the economies of even the prosperous West. Dr Kissinger had been equally determined to dissuade my father from continuing these negotiations. The US government ment evidently saw the plant only in terms of its potential to produce a nuclear device, and the 'Islamic bomb', as it came to be known, was decidedly not in the best interests of the Free World.

The meeting had not gone well and my father had been flushed with anger when he returned home. Henry Kissinger, he told me, had spoken to him crudely and arrogantly. The US Secretary of State had made it clear that the Reprocessing Plant Agreement was not acceptable to the United States. The agreement either had to be cancelled or delayed for several years until new technology excluded the possibility of the nuclear device option. During the meeting Kissinger had claimed that he considered my father a brilliant statesman. It was only as a 'well-wisher' that he was warning him: Reconsider the agreement with France or risk being made into 'a horrible example'.

Now I couldn't wipe that conversation from my mind, even though Jimmy Carter had taken office as President of the United States three months before and Cyrus Vance, not Henry Kissinger was now Secretary of State. But changes in the US administration did not necessarily mean changes in all the US centres of power. From my seven years of government studies I knew that the CIA often acted autonomously and that their policies were not established overnight. Had it been their policy option to get rid of my father if they could not get him to cancel the Reprocessing Plant Agreement? Had my father inadvertently played into their hands by calling elections a full year ahead of schedule?

I could just picture the CIA dossier on my father. Here was a man who had spoken out against American policy during the Vietnam War, who had promoted normalised relations with Communist China, who had supported the Arabs during the 1973 war and advocated independence from the superpowers at Third World conferences. Was he getting too big for his boots?

Another intelligence report came in, this one a taped conversation between two American diplomats in Islamabad. 'The party's over! He's gone!' one had said, referring to my father's government. 'Gentlemen, the party is *not* over,' my father had responded in an address to the National Assembly, 'and it will not be over till my mission is completed for this great nation.' Meanwhile the subsidised fundamentalists in the streets were sinking to a new low. 'Bhutto is a Hindu, Bhutto is a Jew,' they chanted, as if the two religions, neither of which my Muslim father practised, were mutually compatible.

'I do not know what to write about the situation here,' my mother wrote. 'I know what we read in the newspapers and you get the papers there, too. The *Morning News* is the most correct paper and does not believe in sensationalism, so actually you know as much as I know.

'I have written to Sanam [my sister had entered Radcliffe in 1975] and Mir not to invite any friends this summer. I do not know if they have got my letters as many have gone astray. If you get this letter, let the others know just in case.'

The leaders of the PNA continued to refuse my father's offer to negotiate a peaceful solution. In the face of looting, arson and murder of PPP supporters, my father was forced to detain several of the PNA leaders. Perhaps the temporary silencing of their calls to violence would calm the country. But on April 20, the long-planned-for 'Operation Wheel Jam' paralysed Karachi's streets. The truck drivers were on strike, and shops, banks, markets and textile mills remained closed. On April 21, in accordance with the constitution, my father called out the army to help the civil powers restore order in the major cities of Karachi, Lahore and Hyderabad. The protests subsided. A massive demonstration and nationwide strike called for April 22 never materialised. Nor a week later did the 'Long March', the PNA's call for two million people to march to Rawalpindi and surround the Prime Minister's House. The failure of the Long March punctured the balloon of the PNA agitation once and for all. My father drove through the streets of Rawalpindi greeted by cheering crowds.

But the PNA agitation had taken its toll. Thousands of new cars and buses had been burned. Factories in Karachi were closed or behind schedule. Millions of rupees worth of property had been destroyed. Lives had been lost. I breathed a sigh of relief when the papers reported on June 3 that the PNA had finally agreed to talk with my father, while my father seemed amenable to the idea of dissolving his government in preparation for fresh elections.

Reason seemed to be returning at last to Pakistan. Four days into the negotiations my father withdrew the army, and a week later the PNA leaders and others detained during the troubles were freed. Following my father's announcement that he would hold new elections in October, even the most stubborn PNA leaders seemed optimistic about the future. 'I now see a light at the end of the tunnel. Let us pray it is not a mirage,' one of the opposition was quoted as saying in the June 13 issue of *Newsweek* after a meeting with my father.

Relations with the United States, too, seemed to be improving. The Pakistani Foreign Secretary Mr Aziz Ahmed flew to Paris for a meeting with the US Secretary of State Cyrus Vance. He took with him a fifty-page Foreign Office report containing the grounds of our suspicion about American involvement in the destabilisation of the government. My father told me that Secretary Vance put it to one side. 'No, Mr Aziz Ahmed, we want to start a new chapter with Pakistan,' the Secretary of State reportedly said. 'We value greatly the long and close friendship we have with your country.'

Did the Americans play a role in disrupting my father's government? We will never have proof. I have since tried through friends in America to find out more information through the Freedom of Information Act, but was unsuccessful. The CIA sent back six documents, including an analysis of China's support for Pakistan during the 1965 war with India when my father was Foreign Minister, and a cable reporting the movement of civilian convoys through Rawalpindi during the same period. Only one document dealt with my father and the PPP, and that only with the resistance to his proposed Constitution of 1973.

'We can neither confirm nor deny the existence or nonexistence of any CIA records responsive to your request for records pertaining to Zulfikar Ali Bhutto,' the covering letter read. 'Such information, unless, of course, it has been officially acknowledged, would be classified for reasons of national security. By this action, we are neither confirming nor denying the existence or nonexistence of such records. Accordingly, this portion of your request for documents pertaining to Zulfikar Ali Bhutto is denied. . . .'

Whatever happened in Pakistan in 1977 happened because there were people who allowed it to happen. If the leaders of the PNA had acted in Pakistan's national interest rather than their own, if my father's Chief-of-Staff had acted in Pakistan's national interest rather than his own, the government could not have been overthrown. It was – and is – an important lesson for all of us to learn. The United States was acting in its national self-interest, but we were not acting in our own. Some people take the easy way out by putting the whole blame for the events of 1977 on the USA. Had there not been those among us who collaborated, who looked to their own chance of power rather than that of serving their country, no harm could ever have come to the elected government of Pakistan. But as a student at Oxford, I did not yet understand that.

The sun was shining brightly when I woke up on my 24th birthday. June 21 promised to be a hot summer day and I looked forward to the big birthday and farewell party I was giving myself in the gardens of Queen

Elizabeth House before returning to Pakistan. I must have invited the entire contents of my Oxford address book and, judging from the crowd of people, everybody came. Over bowls of strawberries and cream, we reminisced and exchanged home addresses.

I was sad at leaving Oxford and so many friends. I was sorry, also, to leave my little yellow car which Mir was planning to sell for me in the autumn. For four years my MGB had served as a bulletin board for messages from my friends as well as parking tickets from the zealous traffic wardens. But I was also very excited about the prospects awaiting me in Pakistan. My father had discussed some of his tentative plans for me, which included working for the Prime Minister's office during the summer as well as for the Inter-Provincial Council of Common Interests so that I could familiarise myself with common provincial concerns. In September, he told me, he was going to send me to the United Nations as part of the Pakistani delegation which would give me good exposure. I would return to Pakistan in November to study for my foreign ministry exams in December. There was my future, all neat, clean and laid out for me.

My father was evidently looking forward to my return as much as I was looking forward to going home. 'I promise you that I will do everything within my capacity to make your readjustment to Pakistan short and pleasant,' he had written. 'After that you will swing on your own. Of course you will have to tolerate my nasty sense of humour. Unfortunately I cannot change my temperament at this age although I shall try very hard while dealing with my first-born. The trouble is that you also have a temper and tears trickle from your eyes as readily as they come down from my own. This is because we are of the same blood and flesh.

'Let us make a pact to understand each other. You are a motivated person. How can a motivated person want the desert to be without heat or the mountains to be bereft of snow? You will find your sunshine and your rainbow in your values and in your inner morality. It will turn out to be perfect. Both of us will work together for a laudable achievement. You bet we will make it.'

On June 25, 1977, Mir and I flew to Rawalpindi to join our parents and the rest of the family, Shah Nawaz returning home from school in Switzerland and Sanam from Harvard. It was the last time our family would ever be together again.

5

RELECTIONS FROM AL-MURTAZA:
THE HIGH TREASON OF ZIA UL-HAQ

Through the windows of Al-Murtaza I see the February sun glinting on the guns held by our captors. As our detention drags on into the fourth month, I feel the house itself is being held prisoner. Heads of State and international politicians used to come here to visit my father: the Shah of Iran from neighbouring Persia, the ruler of Abu Dhabi and President of the United Arab Emirates Sheikh Zayyed, the Aga Khan Prince Karim, Senator George McGovern from the United States, British Cabinet minister Duncan Sandys. My father often organised shooting parties for his guests, though he didn't really care for hunting. My brothers, however, were crack shots and occasionally bolstered the guests' egos by discreetly downing the birds or deer for them.

Even on ordinary days Al-Murtaza was filled with laughter and fun. Often my father burst spontaneously into song, giving off-key but enthusiastic renderings of Sindhi folk songs or his favourite tunes from the West: 'Some Enchanted Evening' from the musical *South Pacific* which he'd seen in New York, 'Strangers in the Night', the Frank Sinatra hit which had been all the rage in Karachi during his courtship of my mother, and his speciality, 'Que Será, Será'. I could still hear him singing it – 'whatever will be, will be, the future's not ours to see. . . .'

Who could have foreseen the dark future which overtook him so suddenly in the early morning hours of July 5, 1977, the military coup d'état which began our own personal tragedy and the agony of Pakistan?

July 5, 1977, 1.45 am. The Prime Minister's residence, Rawalpindi.

'Wake up! Get dressed! Hurry!' my mother called out sharply, rushing through my room to wake my sister. 'The Army's taken over! The Army's taken over!'

Minutes later I nervously joined my parents in their bedroom, not knowing what was going on. A coup? How could there be a coup? The Pakistan People's Party and the opposition leaders had reached a final settlement over the contested elections the day before. And if the Army had taken over, what military factions were staging it? General Zia and the Corp Commanders had come personally to see my father two days before to pledge the Army's loyalty to him.

My father is on the telephone, placing calls to his Army Chief-of-Staff General Zia and the Federal Ministers. The first call to come through is from the home of the Education Minister. The Army has been there already. 'The soldiers beat my father and took him away,' sobs the daughter of Hafiz Pirzada who had left my father just a few hours ago after celebrating the agreement with him. I had seen the glow of their cigars and heard their laughter on the lawn while I gossiped inside with my sister. 'Stay calm,' Papa is telling Pirzada's daughter in a steady voice. 'Retain the dignity of your family.' In the midst of his next call to the Governor of the Frontier, the telephone goes dead.

My mother's face is deathly pale. Papa found out about the coup, she whispers to me, from a policeman who saw the military forces beginning to surround the Prime Minister's residence. Risking his life, he had stolen through the ranks and inched his way to the front door on his stomach. 'Tell Mr Bhutto the army is coming to kill him!' he had urgently told Urs, my father's valet. 'He must hide quickly! Hide!' My father had evidently taken the message calmly. 'My life is in God's hands,' he had told Urs. 'If the army is going to kill me, they'll kill me. There is no point in hiding. Nor in any of you resisting. Let them come.' The policeman's warning, however, probably saved all our lives.

'The Prime Minister wishes to speak to the Chief-of-Army-Staff,' my father is saying on Sanam's phone, the private line on which she speaks endlessly to her friends. Miraculously, the line is still intact.

Zia takes the call immediately, astonished that my father has found out about the coup.

'I'm sorry, Sir, I had to do it,' Zia blurts out, making no reference to the peaceful agreement just concluded. 'We have to hold you in protective custody for a while. But in ninety days I'll hold new elections. You'll be elected Prime Minister again, of course, Sir, and I'll be saluting you.'

Now my father knows who is heading the coup. His eyes narrow as Zia tells him he can be taken anywhere he wants, to the Prime Minister's rest house in nearby Murree, to our own home in Larkana, anywhere. Zia would like the family to stay at the Prime Minister's residence in Rawalpindi for a month. The army will come for him at 2.30.

'I will go to Larkana, and my family will return to Karachi,' my father says. 'This is the residence of the Prime Minister. As it appears that I am no longer the Prime Minister, my family will be gone by nightfall.'

My father's face is grim when he hangs up. When he lifts the receiver to place another call, Sanam's line, too, is dead.

My brothers, Mir and Shah Nawaz, rush into the room. They had obviously dressed very hurriedly.

'We must resist,' Mir says.

'Never resist a military coup,' my father says quietly. 'The Generals want us dead. We must give them no pretext to justify our murders.'

I shudder, remembering the coup and assassination two years before of President Mujib and almost his entire family gathered at his home in Bangladesh. The Bangladesh Army was the breakaway Pakistani Army of yesterday. Why should that army act any differently from ours?

'Zia has instigated the coup,' my mother tells my brothers, filling them in on the little we know. 'Asghar Khan and the other PNA leaders have been arrested. So have Ministers Pirzada, Mumtaz, Niazi and Khar. Zia says he's going to try Asghar Khan for treason and won't spare Niazi and Khar. He says he'll hold elections in ninety days.'

'He'll do all that and hold elections in ninety days?' says Shah, who as the youngest has spent more time at home than the rest of us in recent years and is more politically astute. More unanswerable questions hang in the air. Why has Zia singled out these political leaders for arrest? Is it a cover-up? Are they in fact in cahoots with him? We try to absorb the bits of information, to make sense of a world where suddenly there seems to be no sense.

Why had Zia waited so long to launch the coup? The agitation had petered out in April. The talks with the PNA had been successfully completed just a few hours ago.

'Zia miscalculated,' my father says. 'He thought the talks with the PNA would break down and he would have a pretext to take over. He struck before the formal agreement could be signed.'

'God knows what will happen to us,' my mother says quietly. She goes into her dressing room, opens her safe and returns with some money. 'You're already scheduled to leave for Karachi early in the morning,' she says to my brothers, giving them the money. 'Benazir, Sanam and I will join you there. If we don't arrive by evening, leave the country.'

It is almost 2.00 am. We wait for the Army to come and take Papa away. None of us wants to leave the bedroom to get ready for our own departures. We are still unsure of what lies ahead. Was General Zia waiting for all of us to return home to Pakistan so the whole family could be wiped out together? Such macabre thoughts. I try to push them away, but I can't. Two of President Mujib's daughters had survived the massacre, as they were out of the country at the time. One had gone on to become the leader of the Opposition. Did the Pakistani Army want not to make the same mistake with us?

My brothers, sister and I had all flown home separately: Shah from school in Switzerland, Sanam from Harvard, Mir and I from Oxford. Our parents did not permit us to travel together for fear of an accident. 'Thank God you've completed your education and are home,' my father had greeted me just ten days ago. 'Now you can help me.'

I had moved into an office near his at the Prime Minister's Secretariat, taken the Official Secrets Act oath, and begun summarising the contents of some of his files, making my own observations in the summaries. How much could change in a week. In hours.

My mother turns on the radio, looking for any news, though it is rare to have any broadcasts at such an early hour. There are none. As we continue to wait for the Army, my father seems almost relieved. 'The burden of responsibility is off my shoulders,' he says. 'Government is a trust and I upheld it faithfully. Now the burden is no longer on me.'

We sit numbly on the sofa in my parents' bedroom while my father calmly follows his customary routine of reading the files piled high on the table behind his armchair. One black file he doesn't read at all, but just signs all the contents. 'My first act as Prime Minister was to commute the death sentences of the condemned,' he says. 'My last act will be the same. I always hated reading appeals for life.' I reach to hug him, but he gently pushes me away. 'There is no time for sentimentality,' he tells me. 'This is a time to be tough.'

2.30 comes and goes. 3.30. No one comes for my father. I feel increasingly uncomfortable. What is the Army planning? Around 4.00 am my father's Military Secretary arrives. His eyes are red and he looks shocked. He has just come from General Headquarters where he had been summoned by General Zia, he explains. General Zia regrets that it is not possible for my father to go to Larkana. If it is not too much of an inconvenience, my father will be taken to the Prime Minister's rest house in Murree instead where he will be held in accordance with the dignity of his office. Arrangements have been made for a 6.00 am departure.

'I wonder why they keep changing the plans?' Sanam asks. 'My phone call must have thrown Zia off balance,' my father says. 'He's probably wondering if I had time to alert loyalist officers to mount a counter-attack before I spoke to him.'

And so we begin the uncomfortable wait again. An hour later, one of our bearers tells us that the Household Manager has been awakened and asked to proceed to Murree to prepare the Prime Minister's rest house.

'General Zia said they were going to come for me at 2.30. Now it's 6.00. They hadn't even prepared the rest house. They'd made plans for the arrests of the rest of them, but not for me,' Papa says quietly.

The significance of the words sits in the silence of the room.

'The bastard was planning to murder us all in our beds,' Shah whispers to me.

'Go and pack,' my mother tells my brothers. 'Your flight leaves at 7.00.' We tune in to the BBC early morning Urdu report to hear the bare news that the Army has taken over the government of Pakistan.

'You are a student of world government,' my father says to me. 'Do you think Zia will hold elections?'

'Yes, I do, Papa,' I tell him, still full of student idealism and academic logic. 'By supervising the elections himself, Zia will be able to deprive the opposition of any claim they were rigged and the pretext to start new agitations.'

'Don't be an idiot, Pinkie,' my father says in a quiet voice. 'Armies do not take over power to relinquish it. Nor do Generals commit high treason in order to hold elections and restore democratic constitutions.'

Reluctantly I leave my parents' room to pack. My father had prepared us for the moment of leaving the Prime Minister's residence for years, though I had never thought it would be at the point of a gun. We were not to think of the residence as home, he had insisted, but as an official government building. When he was voted out of office, he wanted us to be able to leave the official residence quickly, unlike his military predecessor Yahya Khan who had stayed on for months after he left office. 'Don't keep any more here than you can pack in a day,' my father had always told us. But I had broken this cardinal rule. I had come straight to Rawalpindi from Oxford two weeks before with my accumulation of books and clothes. I had planned to ship them on to our home in Karachi, but I hadn't got round to it. I had been too busy working for my father.

I feel totally distracted while I pack, rushing back and forth between my bedroom and my parents' bedroom to make sure my father isn't taken away without my knowing. I keep tripping over my Persian cat, Sugar, who senses the tension and persists in meowing and rubbing herself against my legs. The room is almost bare when Mummy comes in.

'It's 8.00,' she says, 'and the Army still hasn't come. The aide-de-camp tells us that they're still preparing the Murree rest house. But who knows? Thank God the boys were allowed to leave.'

Somehow daylight has brought an element of calm. My own tension has been eased somewhat by the mundane task of packing. My mother and I go through the interconnecting door to Sanam's room to find her throwing all her clothes, pictures and record albums into her trunk, even her back copies of *Harper's Bazaar* and *Vogue*. 'I don't want them touching any of my things,' she says angrily, dressed in jeans and a sweatshirt, her long hair still uncombed.

'Pinkie! Sunny! Come quickly. Papa is leaving,' I hear my mother shout just before 9.00.

'*Jaldi.* Hurry! Sahib is leaving!' a turbaned member of staff says at my door, wearing the red and white uniform of the Prime Minister's house. He has tears in his eyes.

I feel a rush of tears spring to my own eyes. Sanam's eyes are also red. 'How can we say good-bye to Papa looking like this?' I say. 'Quickly. I have some eye drops,' Sanam says. We rush to her dressing room and, with shaking hands, put eye-drops in each other's eyes. Blinking hard, we run down the white and gold panelled corridor to the front entrance. I can hear the sound of wailing from the lawn where the staff has gathered.

Papa is already seated in the Prime Minister's black Mercedes. As the car begins to move, Sunny and I rush past the weeping staff to the front porch. 'Good-bye, Papa!' I cry out, frantically waving my arms. He turns and gives a half-smile as the car sweeps through the gates of the Prime Minister's residence, the early morning sun glinting off the Prime Minister-ial gold seal of entwined leaves on the licence plate.

My father is taken to Murree in a convoy of army vehicles where he is placed under 'protective custody', a term coined by Zia to justify the arrest of his political opponents. He will be held there for three weeks, in the white colonial rest house built by the British in the hills leading to Kashmir. We had spent summer holidays there as a family, passing idle hours playing Scrabble on the colonnaded front porch. Now my father is returning to Murree in the custody of the Army. My father's civilian government has ceased to exist. Once again the Generals are ruling Pakistan.

I should have realised that the coup was final, that my father's first arrest marked the end of democracy in Pakistan. The Constitution of 1973 was suspended, Martial Law imposed. But I clung stubbornly to my academic reasoning and personal naïvety that Zia would hold the elections he promised the country over and over again in the next few weeks. 'I want to make it absolutely clear that I have no political ambitions nor does the Army want to be taken away from its profession of soldiering,' Zia had announced to the country the morning of the coup. '. . . My sole aim is to organise free and fair elections which will be held in October this year. Soon after the polls, power will be transferred to the elected repre-sentatives of the people. I give solemn assurances that I will not deviate from this schedule.' He was lying.

> Martial Law Order No. 5: Anyone organising or attending a meeting of a trade union, student union, or political party without permission from the Martial Law Administrator will receive up to ten lashes and five years im-prisonment.
> Martial Law Order No. 13: Criticising the army in speech or writing punish-able by ten lashes and five years imprisonment.
> Martial Law Order No. 16: 'Seducing' a member of the army from his duty to the Chief Martial Law Administrator, General Zia ul-Haq, is punishable by death.
> 'No person shall loot,' read Martial Law Order No. 6 issued on the day of the coup. 'Maximum punishment: amputation of hand.'

To further intimidate the people, Zia unleashed the forces of the religious fundamentalists. Whether or not to fast during the holy month of Ramazan had always been the personal choice of Muslims in Pakistan. Under Zia, public restaurants and food concessions were ordered to close from sunrise to sundown. At the universities, water was shut off in the campus water fountains and even the bathrooms to prevent anyone from taking a drink during the fast. Fundamentalist gangs roamed the streets freely, banging on doors in the middle of the night to make sure people were preparing *sehri*, the pre-dawn meal. Smoking cigarettes, drinking water or eating in public was punishable by arrest. There was to be no room for personal choice in Pakistan any more, only the strong arm of the supposedly religious regime.

Anxious about my father's detention and the darkness overtaking Pakistan, PPP supporters crowded into our garden at 70 Clifton when we returned from Rawalpindi. While Mir talked to the men, my mother who was suffering from her recurring struggle with low blood pressure, sent me to meet the women. 'Just say *"howsla rakho* – keep your spirits up",' my mother told me. '*Howsla rakho, howsla rakho,*' I repeated to one visitor after another, stumbling in the Urdu which had dwindled during my eight years abroad.

Zia took his campaign to discredit my father to the newspapers. 'Bhutto tried to kill me.' 'Bhutto kidnapped me,' ran the headlines from my father's political opponents, all of whom were obviously alive and free. 'You have to brace yourself for a smear campaign. It's part of "Operation Fairplay",' my father said drily in one of his daily phone calls from Murree, referring to the term which Zia had used to describe the coup. Zia was also cutting the staff at Murree one by one – 'as though that bothers me,' my father said.

My father's spirit remained high, as did his sense of humour. 'A journalist phoned today and asked me how I was passing the time,' he reported one day. 'I told him I was reading a lot of Napoleon to learn how he had kept his Generals in line when I couldn't control mine.'

My father's high spirits helped all of us to keep a sense of balance at home. Rather than feeling depressed, we felt strong, confident and on top. First, my father was alive. Second, the people were supporting him. Also, the PPP was as popular as ever. While Papa sent Mir off to Larkana to look after his constituency, Shah and I had meetings with the scores of people who continued to come daily to 70 Clifton to reiterate their support. A reporter and photographer from our family-owned newspaper, *Musawaat*, recorded each session. The next day, *Musawaat*, the only paper carrying the PPP point of view, would report what was going on in PPP circles and debunk the anti-PPP propaganda in the regime-backed papers. After my father's detention, the circulation of *Musawaat* swelled dramatically, from a few thousand to 100,000 in Lahore alone. When the presses couldn't keep up with the demand, clever entrepreneurs began to sell copies of *Musawaat* at ever higher prices under the counter in the bazaars. '*Musawaat* is selling for rupees ten on the black market,' I reported to my father in delight, rupees ten being more than the average Pakistani earned in a day. These circulation figures were even more phenomenal in a society with a high rate of illiteracy and where the lack of official patronage in terms of advertisments and distribution restricted sales.

'Zia is coming to see me today,' my father said on the telephone on July 15. In the photograph in the paper the next day, my father looked grim, his face reflecting the political situation confronting the country. Zia, in turn, looked guilty, his hand half-held across his chest, an obsequious smile on his face. 'Zia reiterated his intention to hold elections and to act as an honest referee between the political parties,' my father rang to tell us after their meeting. Why did Zia feel it necessary to tell us he was going to be honest? My father didn't believe Zia was going to be even-minded and fair. Nor did we. Given the climate of hysteria being created against my father and the PPP in the media controlled by the regime, this was a little hard for us to believe.

There were just too many unknowns. For the first time in the history of Pakistan and its two earlier periods of Martial Law, public servants had been arrested, including Afzal Saeed, Secretary to the Prime Minister, Rao Rasheed, Adviser to the Prime Minister, Khalid Ahmed, Deputy Commissioner of our home district of Larkana, Masood Mahmood, head of the 500 strong Federal Security Force, and many others. What did public servants have to do with politics? What was the regime up to?

Zia had gone on to state in interviews that the Army had 'contingency plans' for a coup, thus admitting that the coup had been planned well in advance. This indicated that the arrest of the public servants was not a spur of the moment action, but part of a well-conceived military plan. Who was behind it? The military plan to concoct slanderous stories about us in the press was also puzzling. If Zia was planning to hold fair and impartial elections, it didn't make sense.

Meanwhile, journalists were ringing up 70 Clifton asking for information about my father, about the PPP, about the elections Zia was still promising to hold. 'Invite them all to tea,' Papa suggested. I did. And to my amazement, the dining room at 70 Clifton was packed, so packed that the air conditioning barely dented the heat. My cousins Fakhri and Laleh came to help, as did Samiya and her sister. I was very nervous as I tried to answer the journalists' questions. But one shocked me completely.

'Is it true that Mr Bhutto and General Zia planned this coup together to bolster Mr Bhutto's popularity?' a journalist asked over tea and samosas.

'Of course not,' was all I could think of to say, recalling the fear and uncertainty of the night of my father's arrest. But when I repeated the story to PPP visitors the next day, I was even more surprised to learn that this was a widespread rumour, apparently spread by the Army to confuse our supporters and defuse hostility to the military takeover. That rumour, and many others, persisted.

In a country like Pakistan where literacy rates are low, rumour and bazaar gossip often substitute for the truth. No matter how illogical, rumours gain a force of their own, even among the educated upper classes. 'Is it really true that you carry a miniature video-tape camera in your handbag to film meetings with political leaders?' an old school friend asked me one day. I couldn't believe it. 'How on earth could a camera film through a handbag?' I asked her. 'Oh, I didn't think of that,' she conceded. 'I read it in the newspaper.'

Even the particularly heavy summer rains which began two weeks after the coup, were blamed on my father. 'The fundamentalists are spreading the story that Bhutto Sahib caused the rains as revenge for his overthrow,' a PPP visitor told me. Some people probably believed the rumour, looking for some explanation for the flooding that washed away homes and destroyed crops. But not in the underprivileged section of Lahore, a bastion of PPP support, which was particularly hard hit by the floods.

'Go to Lahore as a gesture of solidarity with the people who have suffered during the rains,' my father said. 'The flooding there has been devastating.'

Go to Lahore on my own? I had never been on a party assignment before. My stomach churned with nervousness. 'Announce your programme in *Musawaat* and take Shah with you,' my father told me. Within twenty-four hours Shah and I arrived in Lahore.

Hundreds of PPP supporters greeted us at the airport shouting PPP slogans in spite of Martial Law Order No. 5 which threatened those attending or organising a political meeting with five years imprisonment. The crowd was so enthusiastic that Shah and I had difficulty making our way through the supporters to reach our car. My eighteen-year-old brother and I were both a bit overwhelmed by the unexpected demonstration. We were just the Prime Minister's children, not political figures.

The crowds were even bigger at the bungalow of Begum Khakwani, the President of the Women's Wing in Punjab, where the people spilled out of her huge gardens into the street. Shah and I were soon sweating profusely from the crush in the reception room and blinded by camera lights as people took endless photographs of us. In the middle of the reception, I was called to the telephone. 'It's Prime Minister Bhutto,' the message rippled around the hushed crowd. 'Chairman Bhutto is calling.'

Scores of people crowded into the living room with me. 'How are you?' my father asked, unaware of the reception Shah and I were receiving. When I told him about the hundreds of people at the airport and now here in Lahore, he was very pleased. 'Give them a message from me,' he told me. When I hung up the phone, I turned to the expectant crowd. 'My father sends his condolences to all those who have suffered the loss of home and crops,' I stumbled along in Urdu. 'The PPP calls for relief assistance to the affected families.'

In the face of the obvious support for my father and the PPP, Zia moved to show the popularity of the PNA. The detained leaders of all parties, he announced in the middle of July, could now receive visitors. But his gamble didn't work. Bigger and bigger crowds gathered every day outside the Prime Minister's rest house in Murree to see my father, while the detention houses of the opposition leaders were ignored. Quickly Zia fabricated a reason to cut short his losses. 'Due to misuse, the right of the people to visit political leaders in detention is revoked,' the Chief Martial Law Administrator proclaimed on July 19.

The coup was not going according to Zia's plan. Traditionally, the people of Pakistan had always deserted any leader who had fallen from power and transferred their support to the perceived winner and new leader. But in this instance, Zia's overthrow of my father was backfiring. Instead of deserting my father, the people's loyalty was returning one hundred fold. When Zia released my father and the other political leaders three weeks after the coup, millions, literally millions of people violated Martial Law to greet my father as he visited the major cities of Pakistan. No crowds in the West ever come close to the size of Asian crowds. But even by our standards, the crowds who came to hear my father were overwhelming.

He had returned first to Karachi, where his progress through the massive crowds was measured not in city blocks, but in inches. What was normally a half-hour trip from the train station to our home took my father ten hours. His car was dented and scratched by the time it arrived at 70 Clifton. My brothers, sister and I didn't dare go outside the gates to greet him for fear of being crushed. Instead, we went up on the roof to watch his arrival. And, though we had seen impassioned crowds before, we'd never seen a crowd like this one. So many people were straining to see him, to touch him, to get close to him, that the twelve foot cement wall surrounding our house collapsed under their weight.

'Oh, Papa, I'm so glad you're free,' I told him when we all gathered in my mother and father's bedroom that night.

'Free for the moment, anyway,' my father said.

'Zia wouldn't dare arrest you again,' I said. 'He's seen the size of the crowds.'

'Don't,' my father cautioned me, moving his finger in a circle to show me that the room was probably bugged.

I pressed on stubbornly. 'Zia is a coward and a traitor. He has committed high treason!' I said loudly, hoping my words were being picked up, foolishly believing that my father's massive support would protect him.

'You are being careless,' my father said to me sharply. 'You are not in the democracy of the West now. You are home under Martial Law.'

The shadow of Martial Law became darker when all of us accompanied my father on a visit to our hometown of Larkana. Once again the crowds turned out to welcome my father home, giving me a sense of false security and adding to my joy at having my father back with the family. As we gathered in my parents' bedroom at Al-Murtaza, everything seemed familiar and normal. But it wasn't. One of my father's relatives came in with a message from a senior bureaucrat in Islamabad. The regime, the bureaucrat said, was preparing to implicate my father in a case of murder.

Murder? A chill ran around the room. My mother and father looked at each other for a second in silence. 'You should start making arrangements now for the children to return to school abroad,' he told her. 'All their papers and bank books should be in order. God knows what will happen.' She nodded in agreement as Papa turned to me. 'Pinkie, you too, should think seriously about leaving Pakistan for a while. Take graduate courses abroad if you want until the situation here is resolved.' I looked at him numbly. Leave Pakistan? I had just arrived home.

'The servants too, may face hardship,' my father continued. 'No one is safe under Martial Law.' In the morning, he summoned the staff. 'There may be suffering ahead for all of you,' he said. 'If you would like to leave our employ now and return to your villages until the trouble passes, I will understand. I may not be able to offer you my protection under General Zia.' Not one of the staff chose to leave. Nor did I. And my father moved on to Lahore.

Jiye, Bhutto! *Jiye*, Bhutto! The crowd in Lahore, the capital of Punjab and the stronghold of the army, was estimated at three million, the largest turnout ever in Pakistan. There was no way that Zia could diminish my father's support politically. And a second message came in. 'Sir,' an intelligence officer said, slipping into the former Chief Minister's house where my father was staying. 'General Zia and the Army are determined to kill you. They are torturing the public servants under detention in order to prepare a false case of murder against you.' The officer was trembling. 'In God's name, leave the country, Sir,' he begged my father. 'Your life is at stake.' But my father was not one to give in to threats or terrorist tactics. 'I may not be free for long,' was the only hint he gave of this latest message when he phoned home from Lahore that night.

When he returned to 70 Clifton, the political meetings went on non-stop. Zia had scheduled the elections for October 18, and was allowing one month of campaigning, due to start on September 18. While my father had meetings with party leaders downstairs, I was in the upstairs dining room being tutored in Urdu. 'You need to brush up on your Urdu,' my father had told me. 'I may need you to speak for me.' Every day for two hours in August, I poured over Urdu language newspapers and learned political vocabulary from a tutor. 'How's she doing?' my father would say, coming to the door of the dining room during breaks from the political meetings downstairs.

In late August, I flew with my father to Rawalpindi. Hoping to prevent huge turnouts like the ones my father had drawn at the railway stations in Karachi and Larkana, Zia had issued a military order forbidding politicians to travel by train. In Rawalpindi, he had taken the extra precaution of ordering military patrols to block all approaches to the airport. But many people managed to evade the barricades, lining the route to the airport and thronging around the car.

While our car was being mobbed in Rawalpindi, Bashir Riaz, a journalist and PPP supporter was in Karachi alerting my mother to yet another threat to my father. 'I beg of you, tell Bhutto Sahib to leave the country,' Bashir Riaz said to my mother. 'One of Zia's confidants who is a friend of mine told me to forget Bhutto Sahib, that he will never come back to power. "Zia has decided to execute him on a murder charge," he told me. 'He offered to buy my loyalty with a blank cheque, but I refused.'

And Zia tightened his noose, for the first time extending it to me. The next day in Rawalpindi I attended a tea at the Khokhars, a large family of PPP supporters, which around one hundred women went to. 'Say a few words,' the three Khokhar sisters urged me: two of them were PPP officials and the other, Abida, one of my mother's former secretaries at the Prime Minister's residence. '*Howsla rakho,*' I told the assembled women in the two-minute speech in Urdu I had learnt by heart. 'Keep your spirits up.' When I left, I was surprised to see a large contingent of police, including policewomen, waiting outside the gates. 'They are here because of you,' one of the sisters told me.

I was even more surprised later that night to be served with a notice from General Zia, the Chief Martial Law Administrator, signed if I re- member correctly by General Arif, warning me not to indulge in political activities. Just a month and a half after the imposition of Martial Law, I had received my first official warning from Zia. But I didn't take it at all seriously. 'Imagine,' I laughed to my father, slipping into his bedroom. 'They consider me a threat to Martial Law for attending a tea.' 'It's not a laughing matter,' my father said quietly. 'Martial Law is a deadly and dangerous business.'

And the deadly business escalated. It was obvious to everyone by then that there was no way the opposition was going to defeat my father's Pakistan People's Party fairly at the polls. Two weeks before the campaigning was to begin, Zia sent his agents to arrest my father again.

September 3, 4.00 am. 70 Clifton, Karachi.

I am asleep in my bedroom when I hear the loose step on the stairway creak. As it is the fast of Ramazan, I think it is one of the staff bringing me the pre-dawn meal. Instead five men suddenly burst through my door, dressed all in white. I recognise them immediately as commandos of the Pakistan Army with their crew cuts and strong physiques. How often I had seen them on duty at the Prime Minister's House. But why are they in plainclothes?

They point their machine guns at me while a sixth jumps around the room, sweeping everything off my dressing-table, yanking my clothes off their hooks, throwing my books off the bookshelves, smashing my table lamp and ripping the wires out of the telephone on my bedside table.

'What do you want?' I ask, terrified. Men never come into the room of a Muslim woman like this. 'If you want to live, keep quiet,' says their leader. He and his team move to the door, leaving my room in a shambles. 'Are you going to kill my father?' I ask the man who had jumped around my room. For a second he seems to take pity on me. 'No,' he says, after a moment's hesitation. Then his face hardens. 'If you know what's good for you, don't move,' he says, waving his pistol at me. And he slams my door and is gone with the others.

Quickly I throw on some clothes over my T-shirt, snatching anything from the pile on the floor. My sister rushes in in a panic. 'Don't! Don't! Where are you going? They're going to kill all of us,' Sanam cries.

'Keep quiet,' I snap at her. 'I have to get to Papa.'

I rush out of the room followed by Sanam to find the hall swarming with army commandos all dressed in white clothes and waving their guns round. Immediately they herd us downstairs into the reception hall where there are even more of them. I bolt for the front door, intending to cross the compound to the small annexe where my brothers live, but the commandos surround me and force me at gunpoint to sit on the sofa with my sister. The men are ordered to stand in pairs in front of all the doors leading into the room, their guns raised.

I have to get to my father. He is in danger. I must reach him. The commandos had chosen to break into our house in the middle of the night, without wearing their uniforms. It was all so unnecessary. My father could have been taken away quietly any time with an arrest warrant or a Martial Law order. Instead they were trying to intimidate and insult us. What were they up to? Perhaps they didn't want the people to know what they were doing to my father. But I was determined they weren't going to keep it from his daughter.

'*Kya aap fauji hain?*' I ask the men at the kitchen door in Urdu. 'Are you soldiers?' They look at each other but, in keeping with military discipline, do not answer. I take a deep breath. 'Look at these soldiers,' I say loudly to my sister in Urdu. 'How can they be so *besharam*, so shameless? It was their Prime Minister, Zulfikar Ali Bhutto, who brought them back from the camps of India where their Generals had left them to rot. And this is how they repay him, by entering his home and violating its sanctity?'

Out of the corner of my eye, I see the men glance at each other nervously. '*Yeh kis ka ghar hai* — Whose house is this?' one of them asks. I suddenly realise that some of them don't even know where they are — or why. 'Don't you know you have forced your way into the home of the Prime Minister of Pakistan?' I ask them scornfully. Sheepishly they lower their rifles. There is my chance. Quickly I dart up the stairs and into my parents' room. Nobody stops me.

Papa is sitting on the edge of the bed. My mother is still against the pillows, the covers pulled up to her chin, the ear plugs she wore so that her sleep wouldn't be disturbed by Papa coming to bed late in her hands. Commandos with drawn weapons surround them. The man who had jumped around my room destroying things is now jumping around my parents' room, trying to wrestle my father's crossed ceremonial swords off the bedroom door. 'What are you doing?' my father is saying to him quietly when I come into the room. My father's voice never loses its ring of authority and the man immediately stops.

My father motions me to sit down next to him. In an image that seems particularly grotesque, a fat thug of a man is lolling on one of Mummy's delicate blue and white brocade Louis XV chairs. 'Who is he?' I whisper to my father. 'Saghir Anwar, Director of the Federal Investigative Agency,' he tells me. 'Do you have an arrest warrant?' my father asks the FIA Director. 'No,' he replies awkwardly, looking down at the carpet. 'Then under what charge are you taking me from my home?' my father asks. 'I am following orders to take you to military headquarters,' Anwar says. 'Whose orders?' my father asks. 'General Zia's,' the man replies.

'Since I was not expecting you at this hour, I will need half an hour to get ready,' my father says calmly. 'Send for my valet to pack my clothes.' Saghir Anwar refuses, saying that no one is permitted to see the Prime Minister. 'Send for Urs,' my father quietly repeats. And Anwar motions to one of the commandos.

Urs, I find out later, was being held at gunpoint with the rest of the staff in the courtyard. 'Be quiet! Hands behind your backs!' the commandos had yelled at them in English. Those who hesitated, not understanding

English, were pistol-whipped. Their money was stolen, along with their watches.

'Who is Urs?' asked the commando who had been sent from the house. 'I am,' Urs replied, and was smashed on the head with a pistol butt for speaking. Farcically, the commando then went down the whole row, asking each if he was Urs. After several people had shaken their heads, he came to my father's valet, who had learned by then just to nod. Urs was grabbed by the throat and feet and carried bodily up the stairs where, at gunpoint, he packed my father's clothes. When he took the bags to the waiting unmarked car, six commandos kept their automatic weapons levelled at his head and chest.

Upstairs my father takes a shower and dresses. I can't get over his composure. What a far greater weapon that is than the cowardly arsenal of guns being held all over our house. 'Stay behind!' one of the commandos yells at me when I start to walk downstairs with my father. I ignore them. They let me pass.

Downstairs Sanam and Papa exchange glances. 'You shameless cowards,' my normally shy sister shouts at his captors as he is taken towards a car. 'You shameless cowards.'

Once again I watch my father being driven away, not knowing where he is being taken, not knowing if I will ever see him again. I waver for a moment, half my heart breaking, the other half turning to ice. 'Pinkie,' I hear a voice call. I turn to see my brother Shah Nawaz lined up with the staff in the courtyard. '*Usko choro!* Leave him!' I shout at the soldiers holding him. I am frightened myself at the new tone of my voice. But the soldiers step away.

Back inside the house, my mother's face is as white as chalk. Her blood pressure has dropped even further and Shah Nawaz, Sanam and I take turns massaging her feet to stimulate the circulation. I try to phone for a doctor, but the lines have been cut. I plead with the guards at the gate to let me fetch her doctor, but that, too, is to no avail. Only when our major-domo arrives at 70 Clifton in the morning and, eliciting the sympathy of a Sindhi guard, manages to find out what has happened, does the word get out about my father's arrest at all. Dost Mohammed races around Karachi for hours on his motor scooter, alerting the party leaders and my brother Mir at Al-Murtaza, our relatives, the media – and my mother's doctor. But when Dr Ashraf Abbasi comes to the gate, she is refused entry. A regime-approved doctor finally arrives at noon to give my mother the injection she so desperately needs.

An Army Colonel arrives in the afternoon with a blank paper. 'General Zia, the Chief Martial Law Administrator, has ordered that you and your mother sign this,' says the Colonel who is dressed in battle fatigues with the name Farooq written on his green and brown shirt. I refuse. 'I'll make you sign it,' he threatens me, his beady eyes becoming even beadier and his little mouth more cruel. 'You can kill me, but you can't make me sign it,' I say in my new tone of voice. 'Even your General Zia can't make me sign it.' 'You don't know what's good for you,' he says in a clear and deadly voice. And he turns and walks away.

At 5.00 pm the army is finally withdrawn from the house. Immediately Shah Nawaz and I rush to the PPP office where fear is already setting in among some of the Party officials. While some members call for a nation-wide protest strike and other demonstrations, the people at the top of the party call for restraint until contact is made with my father. Contact with my father? Who knows how long that will take?

My mother's news the next day is even worse. She has talked to my father's lawyer. The secret warnings my father had received were true. The charge against my father, now, is conspiracy to murder.

Murder? I didn't even know who my father was being accused of conspiring to murder.

A minor politician named Ahmed Raza Kasuri who was still very much alive, my mother explained to me. Someone had ambushed the car he and several members of his family were travelling in three years before near Lahore. Kasuri's father, a retired magistrate, had been killed. But Kasuri, a member of the National Assembly elected on the PPP ticket, claimed he had been the real target. The politician, who had since joined the op-position, was known to have many enemies, and was said, unbelievably, to have survived fifteen prior attempts on his life. In this latest attempt, he had said he suspected my father's involvement and filed a report with the police. Such was the freedom then in a democratic Pakistan, that the police had filed the report against the Prime Minister. The resulting en-quiry by the High Court had cleared my father of any connection to the crime and the whole sorry incident had been forgotten.

Until 1977. Kasuri had rejoined the PPP and had even applied for a PPP ticket to Parliament in the March elections. After the PPP had decided to offer the ticket to someone else, Kasuir had evidently decided to refile charges against my father. Now, two weeks before the new election cam-paign was due to begin, Zia had used the old charge against my father as an excuse to arrest him. But once again, Zia's ploy backfired.

The Justice who heard the charges found the material on record 'con-tradictory and incomplete', and saw no reason to believe my father guilty of the offence. He set my father free on bail ten days after his arrest. Again, I was optimistic about the future. 'If the civil courts have released the Prime Minister then I see no reason to detain him under a Martial Law order,' Zia commented to the press.

My father came straight home to Karachi on September 13, planning to leave early the next morning with Shah Nawaz to join my brother Mir in Larkana to celebrate *Eid* at the end of Ramazan. The pressure was really on now. There were only five days left before campaigning began and my father had scheduled ninety meetings during the thirty days. As usual, the family gathered in my parents' bedroom that night, where the conversation took an unexpected turn.

'You know, Nusrat, it's time for Pinkie to get married,' my father said suddenly as he lay on the bed, smoking a cigar. 'I'm going to find her a husband.'

I sat up bolt-upright on the couch, almost scattering my mother's game of Patience onto the floor.

'I don't want to get married,' I protested. 'I've just returned home.'

Sanam and Shah seized the opportunity to revert to childhood teasing. 'You've got to get married. You've got to get married,' they chanted.

'In fact,' my father continued, 'I've already seen a boy I like.'

My mother smiled, probably already planning the wedding.

'I don't want to marry yet, and you can't get me to say yes,' I said mutinously.

'You can't say no to your father,' Papa said, which Shah and Sanam then echoed in chorus.

'No. No. No.' I said, saved by the arrival of my father's late night dinner trolley. Mercifully, the conversation changed. But the new subject was even more threatening.

'I am told Zia won't spare me and I should escape,' Papa said while he ate. 'One of the PPP leaders asked me for money today so he could flee. Go if you like, I told him, but I'm not a rat who runs. I'm going to stay here and face Zia.'

'And you're going to win the elections and try General Zia for high treason,' I said loudly.

'Be careful, Pinkie,' my father cautioned, motioning again to the bugged walls. But I had forgotten all restraint in my relief at seeing my father out of prison and at home again. On I railed about Zia's treachery until my father got angry.

'Be quiet,' he admonished me sharply. 'You don't know what you are saying.'

We stared at each other across the room. In fury and hurt, I stormed out of the room.

I realise now that he knew just how bad things were going to get, that from the beginning he had seen the realities that I was trying to deny. He knew just how ruthless General Zia was and was trying to keep me from making provocative statements. But I was too headstrong then to see that. How many times since have I thanked God that he woke me before he left for Larkana.

'Don't take to heart what I said to you last night,' he said, sitting on the edge of my bed. 'I just don't want any harm to come to you.'

He held me in his arms.

'I understand Papa, and I apologise, too,' I said to him, kissing him good-bye. I remember distinctly the sight of his grey *shalwar khameez* and the scent of Shalimar. It was the last time I ever saw him free.

September 17, 1977, 3.30 am. Al-Murtaza.

Bahawal, one of the Larkana staff, recounts what happened, for I wasn't there.

70 army commandos and policemen scaled the walls of Al-Murtaza around 2.00 am, clubbing the *chowkidars* and swarming towards the house.

'Open the door,' they yelled, pounding on the front door while I and the other servants inside held the door closed.

'What do you want?' we called out.

'Bhutto.'

'Wait. We must wake him up.'

'Open the door,' they yelled, leaning all their weight against it until it bulged.

Mir heard the commotion and went to wake Bhutto Sahib. 'Tell them it's not necessary to break the door down,' his father said to him. 'Allow two officers to enter. I will need time to collect my things.' But he knew they would come. His suitcase was all packed. So was his briefcase.

Bhutto Sahib was taken away ten minutes later. All of us were forced into the house at gunpoint and locked in. There were security forces posted inside and outside the house. We wept.

Mir *baba* was very angry. He tried to call Karachi but the phone lines were cut. The next morning I slipped through the guards and ran to another house to call Begum Sahiba. The word had spread by then through the village and hundreds of people were gathered outside the gates of Al-Murtaza. *Jiye,* Bhutto! they were chanting. Long live Bhutto!

The police arrested them.

My father was taken to Sukkur jail, then to jail in Karachi and then on to Lahore. Zia didn't dare risk letting the people know where he was. This time Zia was determined to finish off my father once and for all. Again my father was charged with the same old murder. But this time, Zia had arranged to make it stick.

6

REFLECTIONS FROM AL-MURTAZA:
THE JUDICIAL MURDER OF MY FATHER

March, 1980. Time, dripping grain by grain through a bottomless hour-glass at Al-Murtaza. I feel as if I am in a living grave, cut off from all human experience. My mother passes many of the endless hours of detention playing Patience. But after five months of being locked up at Al-Murtaza, I am more restless than ever. I have no idea when and if we'll be released. It all depends on Zia.

The United States government has made its choice. As winter heads towards spring, it becomes clear that the Americans are opting for Zia's military dictatorship and not the return of democracy. Prompted by the increasing Soviet presence in Afghanistan, President Carter offers Pakistan 400 million dollars in aid in March, 1980, but Zia dismisses the package as 'peanuts'. A growing number of refugees from Afghanistan are entering Pakistan, indicators of the flood which will pour in as the civil war in Afghanistan intensifies. The refugees and the Soviet troops on our doorstep will result in a cornucopia of foreign aid for Zia, eventually making Pakistan the third largest recipient of US aid after Israel and Egypt. The Soviet invasion of Afghanistan becomes known in Pakistan as 'Brezhnev's Christmas present to Zia'. And my mother and I remain incarcerated at Al-Murtaza.

Sanam arrives for a rare and much anticipated visit, surrounded by the usual retinue of prison and army officials. Even a daughter is not allowed to visit her mother and sister without the constant presence of the military authorities. My mother is feeling ill from her continuing low blood pressure and is lying down in her bedroom. I ask if the meeting can take place there in the presence of the female officials. As Sanam and I move towards the family quarters, I hear footsteps behind us. It is not a police matron. It is Captain Iftikhar, one of the army officers. I stare at him in disbelief. No man, unless he's a relative, is permitted to enter the family quarters. Some people in our culture prefer to die than to have strangers violate its sanctity.

'Even jail rules state that only women police officials can enter a woman prisoner's room,' I remind him.

'I will be present,' he says.

'Then we won't have the meeting at all. I'll call my sister.'

Sanam had already gone ahead to my mother's room, so I keep walking down the corridor to the family quarters to tell her and my mother that the meeting has been postponed. I hear a noise behind me. Captain Iftikhar is still following me.

'Where do you think you are going? You can't come in here,' I tell him, momentarily stunned.

But he is oblivious. 'Do you know who I am?' he says loudly. 'I am a Captain of the Pakistani Army and I can go where I want.'

'Do you know who I am?' I reply just as loudly. 'I am the daughter of the man who brought you back after your disgraceful surrender at Dacca.'

Captain Iftikhar lifts his hand to hit me. And the rage I have suppressed, the anger I have tried to control, erupts.

'You raise your hand in this house, you shameful man! You dare to raise your hand in this house, near the shadow of the grave of the man who saved you. You and your army fell at the feet of the Indian Generals. It was my father who gave you back your honour. And you are raising your hand to his daughter?'

He lowers his hand abruptly. 'We'll see what happens,' he spits out, turning on his heel and stalking off. Sanam's visit is cancelled.

I write a letter to the court where my mother and I had challenged our arrests as soon as we had been locked up at Al-Murtaza. Under Martial Law in 1979, civil courts were still authorised to review arrests made under military regulations. I describe what happened in our family quarters. General Zia had often spoken of the sanctity of *Chador* and *Char Divari*, the Veil and the Four Walls, meaning the sanctity of family life. Yet neither he nor Captain Iftikhar seemed to have much regard for it. I give the letter to the jailer who promises to forward the letter to the court and gives me a receipt for it. I have no idea at the time just how valuable that receipt will be.

Cogito, ergo sum – I think, therefore I am. I always had difficulty with this philosophical premise at Oxford and I am having much more difficulty with it now. I think even when I don't want to but, as the days slowly pass, I am not sure whether I exist at all. To truly exist, a person must effect something, act and cause a reaction. I feel that I have nothing on which to leave my imprint.

My father's imprint on me, however, keeps me going. Endurance. Honour. Principle. In the stories my father used to tell us as children, the Bhuttos always won a moral fight. 'Rupert fell upon me in the forests of Woodstock,' my father would begin the tale of his encounter near Oxford with Rupert of Hentzau, the evil character in the novels of Anthony Hope. Rising to his feet, my father would brandish an imaginary sword. 'He slashes me in the shoulder, slices my leg. But I fight back because an honourable man fights to the death.' While we watched spellbound, Papa would parry. He'd thrust. He'd ignore the blood now seeping from a wound to the stomach. Lunging suddenly, he would finish Rupert off, then sink exhausted into his chair. 'A noble scar,' he'd say, lifting his shirt to show us his appendix scar.

Fortified by this and other Bhutto legends, I saw no reason after the coup to believe that my father would not also triumph over Zia. I had not yet made the distinction between the inspirational challenges my father had made up for us in his stories and the real evil that awaited him.

September, 1977. Massive brick walls jagged with barbed wire. Tiny, high-set windows covered with rusted iron grilles. Huge iron gates. Kot Lakhpat Jail. The door in the gate rattled and creaked as I stepped through. I had never been inside a jail before.

I faced another steel wall, this one guarded by police carrying guns. All around me men, women and children carrying tiffin boxes of food were pushing towards the one small door in the blanket of steel. There are no amenities in Pakistani jails — clothing, bedding, dishes, even food must be brought by the inmates' families. Those whose families are too poor to supply these 'luxuries' or who have been sentenced to rigorous imprisonment are put in Class C confinement — group cells where fifty sleep on lice-filled mats on the floor with a single hole in the corner for their lavatory, and subsist on a daily ration of two bowls of watery lentils and a piece of bread. There are no fans to stir the over 100 degree heat, no showers to cool the prisoners or allow them to wash. The police took me to meet my father in the jail superintendent's office.

'With this recycled murder charge Zia is coming out more openly against us now. The other children must leave the country quickly, before Zia makes it impossible,' my father tells me. 'Especially the boys. I want them out of the country in twenty-four hours.'

'Yes, Papa,' I say, knowing that Mir and Shah would hate leaving now. How could they concentrate on their studies with their father in prison? They were both working so hard in Larkana and Karachi preparing for the elections Zia was still promising to hold . . .

'You have completed your education. But, if you want to return to England and live a safer life, I will understand. You can go,' my father continues. 'If you choose to stay here, know that we are in for heavy weather.'

'I will stay here, Papa, and help with your case,' I tell him.

'You will have to be very strong,' he says.

Mir left reluctantly for England a few days later. He was never to see his father again. Nor was Shah Nawaz who made the long trip to Kot Lakhpat Jail a few days before returning to school in Switzerland.

'I have permission to see my father,' Shah told the guards inside the first gate. 'I have come to say good-bye to him.'

'We don't have permission to admit you,' the guards said. 'We can't let you in.'

My father, who happened to be passing by the inner steel wall on the way to a meeting with his lawyers, overheard Shah arguing with the jailers.

'You are my son. Don't ask them for any favours,' he called out loudly to my brother. 'Go for your studies and work hard. Make me proud of you.'

Shah Nawaz left two days later for the American College in Leysin. Sanam left shortly thereafter to return to Harvard. Ten days after that, September 29, 1977, I was arrested for the first time.

People. Swarms of people. Young men in *shalwar khameez* clinging to tree branches and lamp-posts, balancing on the tops of buses and trucks. Families craning to see from their windows, roofs and balconies. People wedged so tightly that anyone fainting will be held upright, women in *burqas* hovering on the edges of the crowd, daring for this cause to be seen in public. The daughter of their imprisoned Prime Minister had come to talk to them.

A woman standing on a political podium was not as strange to the crowd as it felt to me. Other women on the sub-continent had picked up the political banners of their husbands, brothers and fathers before me. The legacies of political families passing down through the women had become a South Asian tradition. Indira Gandhi in India. Sirimavo Bandaranaike in Sri Lanka. Fatima Jinnah and my own mother in Pakistan. I just never thought it would happen to me.

Standing on the makeshift stage in the industrial city of Faisalabad, I was terrified. At twenty-four years old, I did not think of myself yet as a political leader or a public speaker. But I had no choice. 'Darling, you have to campaign. We have to divide up your father's schedule,' my mother had said to me the week before in Karachi. 'The other PPP leaders are either in detention or already committed to their schedules. We are the only ones left.'

'But I won't know what to say,' I had told her.

'Don't worry,' she had said. 'We'll give you a speech.'

'Bhutto *ko reha karo* — Free Bhutto!' the masses are chanting, the same cry a million had raised the day before in Rawalpindi for my mother. I had stood behind her on the stage, watching, learning. 'Do not worry if the father is in jail. You have the mother who is still free,' she had called out to the crowds. 'I do not have either tanks or guns, but I certainly have the unconquerable power of the downtrodden to face any power in the world.'

Her voice was firm but her hands shook slightly as she rallied the people and my heart went out to her. My mother hadn't wanted this public life, hadn't wanted to assume the leadership of the PPP while my father was in prison. She was still ill from her low blood pressure and feeling very weak. When the party leaders squabbling over the chairmanship had proposed her as a compromise candidate, she had refused. But after my father had written from prison to ask her to accept the party decision she had had to accept. The first promised elections were only two weeks away. And the people were more than ready to welcome back the PPP.

Zia's 'Operation Fairplay' was turning out to be anything but fair for the vast majority of the population. Less than two months after the coup, Zia's regime returned the flour and rice mills my father had nationalised to their original owners, and promised further denationalisation. Industrialists throughout the country were celebrating by firing union organisers. Fifty thousand workers in Lahore alone were laid off. 'Where's your Father Bhutto now?' the industrialists taunted the workers who had lost the only job security they had ever had.

Other workers were threatened with massive dismissals and wage cuts. Peasants expecting to sell their crops for guaranteed prices were offered 'take it or leave it' prices instead. Once again the feudal landowners and the factory owners were pocketing the profits, onions now selling for five times the 1975 price, potatoes for twice as much, eggs and flour up by 30 per cent. The outrage at the reversal of my father's policies was being shouted at PPP rallies all over Pakistan. Bhutto *ko reha karo!* Bhutto *ko reha karo!* Free Bhutto!

In Faisalabad, I clutched the speech which I had practised over and over again in my room in Islamabad. Look up. Don't look down. Speak to the back of the room. What a tidy technique that had been at the Oxford Union. Stretching in front of me now in a sports field was a seemingly infinite mass of humanity. 'Don't antagonise the junta and give Zia any pretext for cancelling the elections,' my mother had cautioned me. But the crowds were irrepressible. 'I can't believe it,' a local party worker said, mopping her brow. 'I've never seen such a big public meeting in my life.'

Somebody handed me the microphones which were connected to the loudspeakers with unearthed wires. Sparks were crackling and flying off the wires. While I spoke, the people on stage tried to wrap cloth around the wires or hold the microphones for me. No. This was not the Oxford Union.

'When I was in India with my father during the negotiations with Indira Gandhi, my father refused to sleep in his bed but slept on the floor,' I called out in my own contribution to my prepared speech. '"Why are you sleeping on the floor?" I asked him. "I cannot sleep in a bed in India," he answered, "when our prisoners-of-war have nothing to sleep on in the camps but the ground."' And the roar rose.

Kasur one day. Okara the next. Past the rolling green fields where farmers bent to weed and water. The PPP was cutting a swathe through the agricultural heartland of the Punjab, our progress on the roads slowed by cheering crowds. The Punjab was the home of the army *jawans*, the rank and file who were devoted constituents of my father's. He had treated the *jawans* with simple decency: issuing warm clothing for the soldiers lying in the winter trenches of West Pakistan, raising their pay, and offering them greater opportunities for promotion to officer rank. Now the families of the soldiers were turning out in force to support us. We were getting too close to Zia's quick.

'The magistrate is here to see you,' said my hostess nervously when I arrived in Sahiwal on September 29, the third stop on my tour.

'This house has been declared a sub-jail. You are detained for fifteen days,' the magistrate told me.

I couldn't believe it. The house was surrounded by the police. The telephone was cut off as periodically were the water and electricity. The roads to the whole neighbourhood were cordoned off, keeping the residents from their homes. My host and hostess, who subsequently left the party, were detained with me. I spent three days pacing up and down my bedroom in a fury, a policewoman posted in the hallway outside.

What were the charges? I hadn't broken any law, even a Martial Law. I was merely standing in for my father during the month of campaigning sanctioned by Zia himself. How little I understood then about the high-stakes game I had been drawn into. 'My daughter is used to wearing jewellery. Now she will be proud to wear the chains of imprisonment,' my mother said at a campaign rally in Karachi where the size of her crowds swamped previous records. The tremendous turnouts we were receiving dashed Zia's hopes of politically defeating the PPP. Bhutto in jail was even more powerful than Bhutto on the campaign trail.

The next day, Zia announced on television that the elections were cancelled.

From that moment, I knew there were no more laws.

October 24, 1977. The day my father's trial for conspiracy to murder began. Unlike ordinary murder cases which started in the lower courts, this one started in the Lahore High Court, depriving my father of one level of appeal. The Justice who had released my father on bail six weeks earlier had been removed from active duty in the High Court, and a bench of five specially selected judges had been set up. One of the first acts of this new bench was to cancel my father's bail. Now he was being held under criminal charges and under orders of the Chief Martial Law Administrator, Zia ul-Haq.

At least I was free to continue working with my mother on my father's behalf: I had been released from my detention shortly after the elections were cancelled. A party supporter lent us an unfurnished house in Lahore, the capital of the Punjab, to use as an office and meeting place for the PPP during my father's trial. Every day one of us attended the court hearings in the handsome building built by the British in 1866. The trappings of justice were everywhere in the carved wooden-ceilinged courtroom with its rich, red carpet. Everyone stood as the judges entered, preceded by a bearer wearing a long green coat and a white turban and carrying a wooden sceptre topped with a silver knob. The judges, wearing black robes and white wigs, took their places in five high-backed chairs under a red satin tasselled canopy. My father's lawyers were already in court, dressed in black silk gowns over their black jackets, starched white shirts with winged collars, morning suit trousers. Sitting with the other onlookers filling the rows of wooden benches in the court-room, I should have felt comforted. It looked like a trial being held in the finest traditions of British law. It wasn't.

The case against my father rested primarily on the confession of Masood Mahmood, the Director General of the Federal Security Force. Masood Mahmood was one of the public servants who was arrested soon after the coup and who we had been told was tortured to give false evidence against my father. After almost two months of detention by the military, Masood Mahmood had decided to become an 'approver', a witness who claims to be an accomplice in a crime and is pardoned on the promise that he will tell the 'truth' about the other participants. Now Masood Mahmood was claiming that my father ordered him to murder the politician Kasuri.

Masood Mahmood's statement was the only testimony directly linking my father to the alleged conspiracy. The other four 'co-accused' were also members of the Federal Security Force who allegedly took part in the attack and who took their orders from the Director General. Like Masood Mahmood, they had all been under arrest since shortly after the coup. There were no eyewitnesses to the attack.

While the four accused members of the FSF sat next to their lawyers, my father was surrounded by intelligence agents and kept within a wooden dock constructed just for this trial. 'I know you are used to a very comfortable life, so I am providing you with a chair instead of a bench,' Acting Chief Justice Maulvi Mushtaq Hussein said sarcastically to my father on the first day of what was to be a five-month trial. One of Zia's top judicial appointees, Maulvi Mushtaq was from Zia's home area of Jullandar in India, and was an old enemy of my father's. He was the judge who had tried my father during his challenge to Ayub Khan. Under the PPP government he had been passed over for the post of Chief Justice and denied promotion to the Supreme Court after the Law Minister, the Attorney General and my father had all deemed him unfit. And shortly after the coup he had accepted Zia's appointment as Chief Election Commissioner, making a mockery of the separation between the executive and judicial branches of government. He could hardly be impartial.

The court's bias was clear. On the first day of the trial, Mian Abbas, one of the FSF accused and a good and brave man, stood up and denied his own testimony. 'My confession was extracted from me under torture,' he announced. The next day he did not appear in court. He was ill, the prosecution explained.

The defence requested copies of the witnesses' statements against my father. The request was deferred by the Chief Justice 'until some appropriate time'. As the trial progressed Mr D. M. Awan, the chief defence counsel, was called into the Chief Justice's chambers where he was advised to 'think about his future'. When Mr Awan persisted in mounting a proper legal defence of my father, the Chief Justice retaliated by giving unfavourable rulings in Mr Awan's other cases being heard by the court. Finally, Mr Awan advised his clients to find another lawyer.

I was present when Maulvi Mushtaq misrepresented the testimony of Masood Mahmood's driver, trying to establish a link between my father and the Director General of the FSF. 'Is it true that you took Masood Mahmood to see the Prime Minister?' the Chief Justice asked.

'No,' the frightened driver replied.

'Write: "I drove Masood Mahmood to see the Prime Minister",' Maulvi Mushtaq directed the court stenographer.

'Objection, my Lord!' the defence lawyer said, rising.

'Overruled!' Maulvi Mushtaq snapped, his heavy white brows gathering in anger. Then he turned to the witness. 'What you meant to say is that you don't remember, but you may have driven Mahmood to see the Prime Minister,' he said.

'No, sir. I didn't drive him,' the driver responded.

'Write: "Masood Mahmood drove himself to see the Prime Minister",' the Chief Justice instructed the stenographer.

'Objection!' the defence lawyer said again, rising.

'Sit down!' roared Maulvi Mushtaq. He turned back to the driver. 'Masood Mahmood could have driven himself to see the Prime Minister, couldn't he?' he asked.

'No, sir,' the driver said, shaking.

'Why not?' shouted Mushtaq.

'Because I had the keys, sir,' quivered the driver.

John Matthews, QC, a lawyer from England who came to attend the trial in November, was shocked by the proceedings. 'Particularly I was concerned at the way a witness's favourable answer would be the subject of immediate interruptions from the Bench, who would take over the case and cause him to whittle down or change his answer,' he told an English journalist later. The defence lawyers were even more concerned. At the end of the trial, not one of the objections they raised or the contradictions in the evidence they pointed out appeared in the record 706 pages of testimony.

There wasn't even a pretence of impartiality. When I arrived at court one morning, I overheard the deputy director of the Federal Investigative Agency, Abdul Khaliq, briefing a group of witnesses on what they were to say during their testimony. 'What sort of justice is this?' I protested loudly. People began to gather. 'Take her away,' Khaliq ordered the police. 'I will not go,' I shouted, quite willing to create a scene to embarrass the prosecution. 'Take her!' Khaliq yelled again. As the police moved towards me, the murmur began to run down the corridor that my father was arriving from prison. I didn't want my father to be upset at the sight of his daughter being bullied and pulled from the court, so I withdrew from the confrontation. Later I heard that the prosecution had rented a house near the court, complete with good food and drink, to polish the testimony of the witnesses.

Ramsey Clark, the former Attorney General of the United States, came to observe my father's court proceedings. Later he wrote an article about it in *The Nation*. 'The prosecution case was based entirely on several witnesses who were detained until they confessed, who changed and expanded their confessions and testimony with each reiteration, who contradicted themselves and each other, who, except for Masood Mahmood (the Director General of the FSF) were relating what others said, whose testimony led to four different theories of what happened, who were absolutely uncorroborated by an eyewitness, direct evidence, or physical evidence,' he wrote.

I believed in justice. I believed in laws and codes of ethics, sworn testimonies and the judicial process. But there was not to be any during the farce of my father's trial. The defence got hold of an army log-book showing that the jeep allegedly used during the attack on Kasuri was not even in Lahore on the day in question. 'The travel log has not been proved correct,' the prosecution objected, though they themselves had submitted the log to the court in their papers relating to the case.

The defence produced FSF travel vouchers showing that Ghulam Hussein, the officer who had supposedly organised and supervised the murder attempt, was in Karachi on another assignment on the day it took place. In fact, the vouchers revealed, he'd been in Karachi for the ten days prior to and the ten days following the attack as well. 'Those documents were intentionally falsified,' the prosecution back-pedalled, though no mention of this had been made before by them or by any of the 'confessing accused'.

Irrefutable evidence that the whole murder case had been fabricated came when my father's lawyers obtained a copy of the ballistics report on the actual shooting. The positions the 'assailants' claimed to have fired from did not match the bullet holes in the car. There had been four assassins, not two as the prosecution had claimed. Moreover, the FSF guns which the 'confessing accused' claimed to have used in the murder attempt did not match the empty cartridges found at the scene. 'We have won the case!' Rehana Sarwar, the sister of one of my father's lawyers and a lawyer herself, said to me jubilantly in the court-room.

I rushed to tell my father during the tea break, wasting no time. While the 'confessing accused' were allowed to chat with their families in the court-room for as long as they liked, my father was often hustled off to a little room in the back under heavy police guard. 'Papa, we've won! We've won!' I said to him, telling him about the ballistics report. I'll never forget the look of kindness on his face while he listened to my excitement. 'You don't understand, do you, Pinkie,' he said gently. 'They are going to kill me. It doesn't matter what evidence you or anyone comes up with. They are going to murder me for a murder I didn't commit.'

I looked at him dumbstruck, not believing him, not wanting to believe him. None of us in the room, including his lawyers, wanted to believe him. But he knew. He had known since Zia's soldiers came for him in the middle of the night in Karachi. 'Flee,' his sister had begged him when she had first heard rumours of the impending murder charge. Others, too, had urged him to leave. His answer had always been the same as it was now. 'My life is in God's hands, not anyone else's,' he said to me in the tea room. 'I'm prepared to meet God whenever He calls me. My conscience is clear. What is most important to me is my name, my honour, and my place in history. And I am going to fight for that.'

My father knew that you can imprison a man, but not an idea. You can exile a man, but not an idea. You can kill a man, but not an idea. But Zia was blind to that, and was trying to send another message to the people. Look at your Prime Minister. He is made of flesh and blood like any ordinary man. What good are his principles to him now? He can be killed just as you can be killed. See what we are doing to your Prime Minister. Imagine what we can do to you.

My father tried to tell me what lay ahead. But I heard his words as if from a great distance. And I kept them there. Otherwise, I could not have gone on to fight the one new charge after another that was being brought against him. The fight to save his honour became my own.

On the day after my father was arrested in Karachi, Zia had issued Martial Law Order No. 21. All members of the National Assembly, Senators and members of the Provincial governments from 1970 to 1977 (the years of the Pakistan People's Party) were required to submit financial statements to the military regime detailing all properties and purchases, from land-holdings, machinery and jewellery to insurance policies and office supplies. The penalty for a failure to comply was seven years rigorous imprisonment and confiscation of the property.

If the military regime deemed that the properties and assets were acquired through political influence or that government property had been misused, the guilty party would be disqualified from any elected or appointed political post.

Arbitrarily choosing whom to disqualify, the Martial Law authorities used the new law to threaten members of parliament into acquiescence to the military regime. The only avenue of appeal open to victims of disqualification was a Tribunal set up by the same regime which had disqualified them in the first place. Of course those who co-operated with the regime were miraculously requalified.

Heading the first list of disqualified politicians was my mother, although she had been a member of parliament for only three months. She had to make repeated appearances before the Tribunal, where the regime found it difficult to frame any charges against her. Her hearings had to be postponed time and again. But the biggest target in the autumn and winter of 1977 was my father whose reputation Zia wanted desperately to discredit.

Bhutto used government funds to buy motorcycles and bicycles for People's Party Workers. Mr Bhutto had his houses at Larkana and Karachi air-conditioned at government expense. Mr Bhutto used our Embassies abroad to purchase dishes and clothing for his personal use with official funds. The regime heaped charge after charge of corruption, misappropriation of funds, even criminal charges against my father, knowing that he would find it hard to refute them from his prison cell. They had taken the extra precaution of jailing his personal secretary. But my father's filing system proved to be a formidable opponent in the sixty-plus cases now facing us.

I found everything we needed to refute the charges against my father in his papers in Karachi. Day after day I waded through the family accounts, rushing copies of what was needed to the lawyers, receiving new instructions on what was required next in return. My father had kept a record of every single expense, right down to the receipt for 24 dollars worth of cloth bought on a trip to Thailand in 1973, or 218 dollars worth of Italian wall-paper paste from 1975. I was astonished to discover that he had even paid for his own reading glasses, although health care was provided free to the Prime Minister. But our refutations of the charges never appeared in the newspapers, only the charges themselves. We mimeographed the refutations on our own machines and distributed them among the people.

We also put together a pamphlet, later bound as a book, called *Bhutto: Rumour and Reality*, in which the rumours against my father were outlined and then contrasted with the reality. Producing the pamphlet was a risky business, since any literature that was positive about my father was regarded as 'seditious' by the regime, and those printing or distributing it were likely to be jailed and the material confiscated. The refutations were useful for both Pakistani and foreign journalists who were flooded with the regime's propaganda against my father and the PPP. But there was always something more to do.

'We've got to send out a call to the people for a strike, for demonstrations, for something,' I said in frustration to the Party leaders who came to our rented house for secret meetings at night. But timidly they demurred. 'Don't do anything until we have a party line,' they kept repeating. I was impatient with their apathy, as were the other young members. 'Let's go to the *mazaars* to pray,' I suggested, believing that the regime which was pounding Islam — Islam — Islam — into everyone's heads wouldn't dare arrest us while we prayed at the tombs of our saints. The idea took hold. PPP workers began to gather in mosques and *mazaars* all over the country to read the Holy Quran and pray for my father's release. But I was wrong. The regime came down with a heavy hand even at the *mazaars*.

And the arrests and floggings continued, totalling 700 by December, 1977. The case of Khalid Ahmed, the Deputy Commissioner of Larkana, indicates what the regime must have done to Masood Mahmood and the other civil servants arrested after the coup to make them give false evidence against my father. Two army men came to Khalid Ahmed's house in Lahore with a written order from Zia, his wife Azra told me. 'If I don't call you tomorrow, you'll know something is wrong,' he told her as he was taken away. There was no call. When she finally located him in a prison in Islamabad a month later, she almost wished she hadn't. 'I cannot forget that day,' she told me. 'His face was ashen, his lips dry and cracked. There was white spittle caked around his mouth. He had been given electrical shocks in his delicate parts. They wanted him to give evidence to use against Mr Bhutto in court.'

Khalid was held for five months in solitary confinement. Every evening Azra went to a public garden with a view of the prison terrace. 'He was allowed to exercise for half an hour a day,' she said. 'I sat on a bench for hours just to catch a glimpse of him, to make sure he was still alive.'

Khalid Ahmed's life, and probably many others, was saved by a petition my mother filed in the Supreme Court shortly after my father's first arrest, challenging the legal authority of Martial Law to detain him. In November 1977, the Supreme Court upheld the legality of Martial Law, declaring it to be a 'law of necessity' in keeping with a Quranic law which permitted a Muslim to eat pork in order to survive if no other food was available. But the Court also made it clear that Martial Law was only valid for a limited period, the nine months quoted by the regime as the time needed to organise free and fair elections.

The justices also ruled that superior civil courts would continue to have the power of judicial review over the actions taken by the military courts. Without this provision of civil review, thousands of people, including political activists and public servants arrested after the coup, would not have been able to appeal for review of their detention. Though the appeals – including my own appeals when I was in detention – took many months to reach the bench, at least there was some hope of relief through the civil courts at that time.

The High Court released Khalid Ahmed in December 1977 because there wasn't a shred of evidence against him, not even an arrest order. 'We had orders from higher up,' the army officers said. But just as the regime had gone around every court decision to rearrest my father, now they did the same to Khalid. A week after his release, the former commissioner was warned by a friend that he was about to be rearrested under Martial Law Order No. 21 for the misuse of a government car and an air-conditioner. An air-conditioner! 'I begged him to leave,' Azra said, her eyes filling with tears. Her husband left that night for London. The cases are still pending against him, forcing him to remain abroad. Azra has brought up their two children alone. The persecution of this family, and many others, was just beginning in December of 1977. Two weeks later, it escalated sharply.

Tear gas. Screaming. People running. A wrenching pain in my shoulder. 'Mummy, where are you? Are you all right? Mummy!'

December 16, 1977. The anniversary of the Army's surrender to India. Qaddafi Stadium, Lahore. My mother and I decide to go to a cricket match to take our minds off the trial. We have tickets to the women's enclosure, but when we arrive we find one gate after another locked. We enter the only one that is open. As we are spotted the applause and cheers of the spectators begins. But the cricket players suddenly run off the field. There are policemen kneeling three deep where the cricket teams had been.

Whoosh. Something heavy hurtles past my face.

'Tear gas! Tear gas!' I hear the screams beginning.

The people panic, rushing towards the locked exits. I can't breathe, can't see. I begin to suffocate in the poisonous clouds billowing towards us. Can lungs catch fire? My shoulder! I almost fall from the blow. All around me in the murk are police clubbing people to the ground.

'Mummy!' I call out. 'Mummy!'

I find her bent over the iron railing of the stands. She lifts up her head at my voice. Blood is streaming from a gash in her scalp.

'The hospital. We've got to get my mother to the hospital,' I scream.

'No,' my mother says quietly. 'First we are going to see the Martial Law Administrator.'

The blood is streaking down her face, dropping in red rivulets to her dress. We move through the crowd and find a car. 'Take us to the Martial Law Administrator's house,' she says. The security at the gate is shocked to see us and lets us in. As my mother gets out of the car, the General's jeep pulls in behind us.

'Do you remember this day, General?' she says, confronting Iqbal, Zia's appointed Martial Law Administrator of the Punjab. 'On this day you surrendered to the Indian army at Dacca and today you have shamed yourself again by shedding my blood. You do not know the word honour, General, only dishonour.'

He looks at her, stunned. With great dignity my mother then turns and gets back into the car. We drive straight to the hospital, where it takes twelve stitches to close her wound.

That afternoon I am arrested at home. My mother is arrested in the hospital.

The next day Zia appears on television to congratulate the Punjab administration for its handling of the incident. And my father is removed from the court for saying 'damn it' when he tries to find out what happened to us. 'Take him away until he regains his senses,' the Chief Justice says. The next day my father files a petition for a mistrial. The petition is denied.

Locked up in our unfurnished house in Lahore and with my mother in hospital, I saw clearly for the first time the lengths to which Zia would go to crush our spirits. There was no doubt in my mind that the attack on us at the cricket match had been premeditated. The police had locked the gates themselves to force us to walk into their barrage of tear gas and bamboo rods. The implications were enormous. Women had never been singled out for punishment or harassment. We were entering a period the likes of which had never been experienced in Pakistan before. Those days locked up alone in Lahore among mimeograph machines and typewriters were dark ones indeed.

Within a week my mother joined me in detention, her scalp held together by stitches. What is happening, we kept asking each other in disbelief. Are we really witnessing what we are witnessing? Our minds just weren't prepared to absorb it. But that, I'm sure, is what sustained us throughout. Every new atrocity brought another shock – and a new burst of determination. From anger I moved on into a state of defiance and resolve. They think they can humiliate me? Try it, I remember thinking.

I spent my first New Year back in Pakistan in detention. Just a year before I'd been home from Oxford at Al-Murtaza and had actually met Zia on my father's birthday. Now my father was spending his birthday in prison. My mother and I checked off each day of our fifteen-day detention order. Mummy passed the time playing Patience and occasionally watching the television set we left on just to hear voices.

My scheduled visit to my father came and went, making me very sad. It always cheered me to see him, and to take away the instructions he wrote out for me on the yellow legal pads he had stacked in his cell. I thought his cell was bad then, with its dirt floor and poor running water. Little did I know that there were far worse cells awaiting him.

The authorities had lodged him next to a group of mentally disturbed prisoners who hooted and howled all night. They also made sure he heard the other political prisoners being lashed in the courtyard, sometimes inserting microphones into their mouths. But the regime couldn't break him. 'My morale is high,' my father assured me during one of my visits to his prison. 'I am not made of the wood which burns easily.'

The fires of outrage were burning outside the prison, however, when in early January, 1978 the regime committed its first mass murder. Before my mother and I were arrested, the PPP had called for a Day of Democracy on January 5, my father's birthday. At the Colony Textile Mill in Multan, the workers, who were striking for the bonuses they had received in the past but which had been cut back by their industrialist owners, were planning to use the date to demonstrate. They never got the chance.

Three days before the Day of Democracy, the Army locked the gates to the mill, got up on the roof, and fired into the workers trapped below. It was among the worst massacres the sub-continent had ever seen. We were told hundreds died. Nobody knew how many. Some said two hundred, others three hundred. Bodies kept popping up for days, in fields, in gutters. Zia had put the members of the working class who formed the backbone of PPP support on warning: cower down or be massacred.

The Day of Democracy turned out to be one of the worst days of oppression. Thousands of PPP supporters were arrested all over the country. And the brutalisation of the country deepened.

Lashes were administered to anyone saying 'Long live Bhutto', or 'Long live democracy'. Lashes were administered to anyone displaying a PPP flag. They were administered quickly, often within an hour of the sentence, because appeals were still being heard then by the civil courts. In Kot Lakhpat Jail, the prisoners were spreadeagled and tied with thongs to the whipping rack. Doctors were called in to check the pulses of the victims so that the whippings would stop short of death. Often the victims were revived by smelling salts so that the prescribed number of lashes, usually numbering ten to fifteen, could be completed.

Outside prison, public lashings were also becoming more frequent. Instant judgments and punishments from mobile military courts were meted out by a single Martial Law officer who toured the bazaars deciding whether the merchants were cheating on weights, over-charging or selling inferior goods. In Sukkur, one officer demanded that a man, any man, be handed over. 'We need someone to lash,' he said. The stall keepers didn't know what to do and finally led the officer to a man suspected of selling sugar on the black market. Though the 'crime' was being committed by almost everyone in the bazaar, the man was promptly – and very publicly – lashed.

Nothing in my life had prepared me for such barbarity. The whole framework of society as I had known it in America and England, and as experienced by those living in Pakistan under the Constitution of 1973, was vanishing.

On the day our detention ended, the gates opened to let the magistrate in – but not to let us out. Instead he handed us a new detention order for another fifteen days. Another legal precedent shattered. Under my father's civilian government, orders for preventive detention had been extremely restricted. No one could be detained for a cumulative, not consecutive, period of three months within a year, and the courts heard petitions within twenty-four hours. Now a new and terrible history of Pakistan was being written.

Released. Detained. Externed. Detained. Throughout my father's trial the regime used its arbitrary powers to keep my mother and me off-balance, releasing and rearresting us so constantly that any kind of planning was impossible. During those first few months of 1978, I was detained and restricted repeatedly. Even the regime didn't seem to know if I was coming or going.

In the middle of January my mother and I were released from our detention in Lahore. I flew immediately to Karachi, where I had been ordered to appear by the Income Tax Authorities. The charge? To list the assets and liabilities of my grandfather who had died when I was four years old. I wasn't even an heir and not liable to answer questions relating to my grandfather's estate under any civil or military law. But that didn't matter to the authorities. Failure to comply, the notice had insisted, would result in an automatic *ex-parte* decision against me. I arrived at 70 Clifton at midnight.

Bang! Bang! I shot out of bed at 2.00 am. 'What is it?' I called out in the panic that had never really left me since the commandos had burst into my room four months before. 'The police have surrounded the house,' Dost Mohammed called to me. I dressed and went downstairs.

'We have booked you on the 7.00 am flight to Lahore,' the officer said. 'You are externed from the province of Sindh.'

'Why?' I asked. 'I've just arrived to answer the charges your regime brought against us.'

'General Zia is planning to take Prime Minister Callaghan of Great Britain to a cricket match,' the officer told me.

For once, I was speechless. 'What does that have to do with me?' I asked. 'I didn't even know there was a cricket match.'

'The Chief Martial Law Administrator doesn't want any trouble. You may decide to go to the match, so he has ordered your externment,' the officer said. At 6.00 am I was driven to the airport under police guard and put on a plane to Lahore. Why couldn't I just be restricted in Karachi for the day?

Two days later I was having lunch with friends in Lahore when the police surrounded that house. 'You are being detained for five days,' the arresting officer told me. 'Why?' I asked again.

'It is the anniversary of Data Sahib's death,' the officer said — a fact I well knew, Data Sahib being one of our most revered saints. 'You may decide to go to his tomb.'

Back I went into detention with my mother. She played Patience while I paced the floors. Our mail was stopped. Our telephone was cut off. When I got out in early February I went immediately to see my father. Because of all our detentions, I had missed three precious meetings with him. But I wasn't missing any court sessions.

Though the Chief Justice had assured the world press that the trial would take place 'in the full light of day', the court-room was closed to all observers on January 25, the day after my father had begun his testimony. The world had been invited to hear the prosecution. But no one was to hear the defence. Disgusted with the court's bias, my father had already withdrawn his lawyers. Now he declined to testify at all, sitting silently

114

through most of the rest of the proceedings. The Chief Justice from the Punjab took advantage of the *in camera* proceedings to reveal his racial prejudice against Sindhis, the race from the southernmost province of Pakistan to which my father belonged. Both my father and the PPP high command called for retrial on the basis of his bias – to no avail.

While I helped with the case, my mother had been visiting different cities in the Punjab, including Kasur where she had prayed at the shrine of the Muslim Saint Buba Bullah Shah. 'I want you go to Sindh,' my father told me in Kot Lakhpat Jail. 'You and Mummy have both been spending all your time in the Punjab. Get the PPP activists to arrange a tour.'

I was apprehensive as I prepared to go from Karachi to Larkana on the pretence that I was going to pray at the graves of my ancestors. Mummy sent me a cautioning note in Karachi. 'DON'T abuse or criticise Zia, but concentrate on issues like high prices. You must be there to hold the flag and run the party,' she wrote from Lahore, after returning herself from a secret trip to Multan to comfort the families of the workers massacred at the textile factory. She sent me the names of families to visit, who had had members arrested, and the amounts of money to give them, depending on the number of children they had. 'If the worker is the only earning member, take his address so that we can send money to the family every month until the release,' she wrote, then concluded: 'You should go in the Mercedes. It is strong and reliable with good acceleration. All my love, Your Mummy.'

Musawaat announced my departure and the cities en route. And on February 14, off I went on my first Sindh tour, taking with me a speech-writer, a reporter, and a photographer from *Musawaat*. Begum Soomro, the head of the Women's Wing of PPP Sindh, came as my chaperone.

Thatta, where Alexander the Great rested his troops. Hyderabad, where ancient roof windcatchers funnelled cooling breezes into the houses below. Huge crowds thronged our car along the way. Public political gatherings had been banned by Zia, so we held ours within the four walls of the biggest family compounds we could find. Standing on the roofs of one compound after another, I looked down at people packed into the court-yards like sardines. 'My Brothers and respected Elders,' I yelled down to them at the top of my lungs, since microphones and loudspeakers had been forbidden by the regime. 'I bring you *salaams* – greetings – from Chairman Zulfikar Ali Bhutto. The crime against him is a crime against the people.' Therparkar. Sanghar. Whenever possible I also addressed Bar Associations and Press clubs, always speaking of the illegality of the regime and the injustice meted out to my father and the PPP.

Leaving Sanghar, army trucks suddenly cut off the car from the front and the rear. We were escorted to the house we were to stay in for the night at bayonet point.

'You are not to continue your trip,' the District Magistrate told us.
'Where are your orders?' I asked him. 'I want to see it in writing.'
He had none.

'The regime has just sent him to frighten us,' said Makhdoom Khaliq, a
PPP leader travelling with us. 'Let's go on.' The next day we set out for
Nawabshah where the meeting was to be the biggest of all. But as the car
reached the Khairpur-Nawabshah border we found the road blocked by
security forces. This time they came with papers.

I was externed from Nawabshah to Karachi on February 18 and forbidden to leave the city. Once again I missed my fortnightly meeting with
my father.

March, 1978. 'I have learned from a Zia source that the Lahore High
Court will sentence Bhutto Sahib to death,' a journalist in Karachi told me.
Mechanically I passed the news on to my mother in Lahore and the PPP
chiefs of Sindh and Karachi, though I myself didn't want to believe it. But
the signs were everywhere.

Three criminals, not political prisoners, were sentenced in early March
to be hanged in public in Lahore. Hanged in public! The newspapers gave
the news wide coverage, as did the television. The hangings were to take
place on public ground and they were being advertised like the opening
of a play. 200,000 people showed up to watch the gruesome spectacle,
the men dangling from the gallows wearing black hoods. I realise now
that the regime was psychologically preparing the country for a death
sentence for my father. But then I just took it as an extremely ominous
sign. All I could remember was the campaign promise of Asghar Khan
during the election campaign just a year before: 'Shall I hang Bhutto from
the Attock bridge or from a lamp-post?'

The momentum was building towards the court decision. Soldiers in
plain clothes were deployed at all government buildings and banks. Ar-
moured cars full of soldiers began to patrol Rawalpindi. In Sindh, trucks
with machine guns mounted on them rolled through the streets. And a
massive round-up began of PPP members, guilty of nothing but the
government's anticipation that they might make trouble when my father's
sentence was announced. The charge read: 'Since you, _____ (fill in
the name), are likely to incite trouble on the announcement of verdict in
Bhutto's trial you are hereby detained. . . .' How did the regime know
what the verdict would be if the courts were independent and the trial fair
as Zia claimed?

80,000 arrested from the Punjab, 30,000 from the Frontier Province,
60,000 from Sindh. Incomprehensible numbers. So many people arrested
that the regime opened detention camps all over Pakistan. Race courses

Generations of politicians: My grandfather, Sir Shah Nawaz Khan Bhutto, founded the first political party in Sindh before Pakistan came into being in 1947.

My father, Zulfikar Ali Bhutto, studied politics at Berkeley and read law at Christ Church, Oxford, before becoming a lawyer and government minister in Karachi.

My Iranian-born mother, Nusrat, was later elected to the National Assembly herself. I learned at the knees of them all.

Dressed in our clothes from Saks Fifth Avenue, Mir, I, Sanam and Shah Nawaz, meet Chinese dignitaries Chen-Yi (*left*) and Chou En-lai.

'You are human beings and have rights,' my father exhorted the masses after he resigned as Foreign Minister and founded the Pakistan People's Party in 1967.

While I was experiencing democracy at Radcliffe College, my father was waging a successful campaign in Pakistan to become the first leader directly elected by the people.

Eight months after I was elected President of the Oxford Union Debating Society, my father was overthrown.

(*Opposite*) High treason: General Zia visited my father in detention at Murree ten days after the military coup. No wonder Zia looks so guilty. He was soon to cancel the elections he had promised, and to order public lashings to bludgeon the people into submission.

Many PPP supporters felt the lash of Martial Law. It took twelve stitches to close the wound on my mother's head after we were tear-gassed and beaten by Zia's police for attending a cricket match in Lahore. I was arrested at home that afternoon and my mother was arrested in her hospital bed.

While my father attended his farcical trial in Lahore, I toured Pakistan to keep the people's spirits up. In England, my brothers Shah and Mir (*bottom, centre*) led the international campaign to save my father's life. Zia sent him to his death on April 4, 1979.

(*Opposite*) 'Revenge! Revenge!' cried the crowd mobbing the train bearing me to Larkana to visit my father's grave after I was released from my sixth detention. 'We must turn grief to strength and beat Zia at the polls,' I told the

I felt a part of me had died as I laid rose petals on my father's grave before returning to Karachi to continue receiving the mourners crowding into our garden. Five months later, Zia cancelled the second scheduled elections and rearrested my mother and me.

were converted into open-air prisons, open fields with no facilities surrounded by barbed wire and patrolled by armed personnel, sports stadiums
turned into temporary jails. Even women were being arrested, some with
their infants.

March 15, 1978. Kishwar Qayyum Nazami, wife of a former member
of the Provincial Assembly:

My husband and I were arrested at 1.00 am. The police cordoned off
the whole house. Our baby was only a few months old, so I had to take
him with me to jail in an open military truck. At Kot Lakhpat Jail the
administrators said there were no facilities for women political prisoners.
They finally locked me in a tiny storage room with six other ladies, including Rehana Sarwar, the sister of one of Mr Bhutto's lawyers and Begum
Khakwani, the president of Punjab Women's Wing. 'Why have we been
arrested?' Begum Khakwani asked the police. 'Because the decision is about
to be reached on Bhutto,' the policeman said. 'How do you know the
decision is going to go against Mr Bhutto?' she'd asked. The policeman
had said nothing.

We were searched roughly by the matrons who took my wedding ring
and my watch. When I was released they said they'd lost them. There was
no toilet in the room, just a pile of bricks in the corner, and no bedding.
We couldn't have slept anyway. The police started lashing the political
prisoners in the next courtyard at midnight. Lines were painted on the
men's backs to show the number of lashes to be administered. The man
who whipped them, a wrestler who wore a loin cloth and greased his
body, ran towards the men from a distance to gather strength while an
army officer sat on the side and counted the strokes. Twenty to thirty men
were whipped in each session. We could hear their screams all night long.
'Jiye Bhutto!' they shouted every time the lash landed. Long live Bhutto! I
covered my ears and prayed my husband wasn't among them. He had
already been lashed in September 1977.

The second morning of our imprisonment, the police suddenly released
us. As we hurried out of the gate, we were re-arrested, this time on charges
of maintaining law and order. The regime must have realised that it didn't
look good to have arrested us on charges pre-empting the court decision.
And we were returned to the storage room.

Mr Bhutto, whose cell we could see from our own, found out we were
there, and had his lawyer bring us a basket of fruit. 'See how Zia treats
women from respectable families,' his note read. I was returned to house
arrest two weeks later because my baby got very ill in prison and I had no
medicine. The other women didn't get out for a month.

My own detention orders came in three days after theirs, in the early hours of March 18. 'The police are here to see you,' came the all too familiar message at 4.30 am. I knew why, but I didn't want to know. I wanted to run to my mother, but she was already in detention in Lahore. I wanted to run to my father. I wanted to run anywhere, to Samiya, to the lawyers, to Mir or Shah Nawaz or Sunny. I couldn't take this alone. I couldn't. My God, help us all, I said over and over to myself, pacing through the empty house.

The wailing began in the late afternoon. I could hear it coming from the kitchen, from the garden, from the gate to 70 Clifton. My heart speeded up until I thought it would explode. Suddenly the front door burst open and my cousin Fakhri threw herself on the entrance hall floor. 'Murderers!' she screamed, banging her head on the floor in her grief. 'Murderers!'

Zia's judges had found my father guilty and sentenced him to death. Fakhri, who had rushed past the startled army guards at the gate, was served with her own detention order within the hour. She would be detained with me for a week. I would be detained for three months.

Iron gates, one after another. Long dirty passageways in between. Police matrons searching me, going through my hair, running their hands over my arms, my chest, my shoulders. Another iron gate. Then three small cells with iron bars in the doors.

'Pinkie? Is that you?'

I peer into the cell, but I am blinded by its darkness. The jail officials open the door and I step inside my father's death cell. It is damp and fetid. No sunlight has ever penetrated its thick cement walls. The bed covers more than half of the tiny cell, and is bolted to the ground with thick iron chains. For the first twenty-four hours my father was in the cell, he was chained to the bed. His ankles still bear the scars. Beside the bed is an open hole, the only lavatory facility provided for condemned prisoners. The stench is nauseating.

'Papa!'

I embrace him, my arms easily circling his body. He has lost a tremendous amount of weight. When my eyes adjust to the light, I see that he is covered with insect bites. Mosquitoes breed in the heat and dampness of his cell. No part of his body is without angry red swellings.

I feel tears welling in the back of my throat. I swallow them down. I will not let myself cry in his presence. But he is smiling. Smiling!

'How did you get here?' he is saying.

'I filed a petition with the provincial administration saying that as a family member I was being prevented from my rightful weekly visits to you under the Jail manual,' I tell him. 'The Home Secretary gave me permission to see you.'

I tell him how I was brought to Kot Lakhpat Jail in a convoy of army trucks, cars and jeeps. 'The regime is very nervous,' I tell him, bringing him up to date on the riots that had brought curfews to villages throughout Sindh since the announcement of his death sentence less than a week before. 120 had been arrested in a 146 mud hut village near Larkana. The police had also detained a shopkeeper who had kept my father's picture on the wall next to that of a film star.

'The numbers of countries that have appealed to Zia for clemency is incredible,' I tell him. 'I hear it all on the BBC. Brezhnev has written a letter, as has Hua Kuo Feng citing the close co-operation you forged with China. Assad has appealed from Syria, Anwar Sadat in Cairo, the President of Iraq, the Saudi government. Indira Gandhi. Senator McGovern. Practically everyone, with the exception of President Carter. An unanimous resolution was adopted in the Canadian House of Commons appealing to the regime to commute your death sentence and 150 members of the British Parliament are urging their government to take steps. Greece. Poland. Amnesty International. The Secretary-General of the United Nations. Australia. France. Papa, there is no way Zia can go through with this.'

'That's heartening news,' he says. 'But there will be no appeal from us.'

'But Papa, you must appeal,' I say, shocked.

'Through Zia's courts? This whole process is a farce. Why prolong it?'

As we talk, he motions with his head for me to come closer. The jailers are just outside the cell door, listening, looking. I feel a piece of paper being pressed into my hand.

'Papa, you can't just give up,' I say loudly to distract the jailors.

'My God knows that I am innocent,' my father replies. 'I will file my appeal in His court on the Day of Judgement. Now go. The hour is almost up. Go when you decide, not when they do.'

I hug him. 'The paper must not fall into the hands of the authorities, or your visits will be cancelled,' he whispers rapidly into my ear.

'Till we meet again, Papa.'

I was searched on the way out of the prison. Nothing was found. I was searched for the second time when I was taken to see Mummy in detention in nearby Lahore, and again after I left her. Nothing was found. Sometimes the searchers were sympathetic, merely going through the motions. But I never knew until the moment came. At the airport to be flown back to my own detention in Karachi, I was made to sit under guard for three hours in a car, surrounded by the convoy of other military vehicles.

Finally, the plane was ready. I could see through the car windows that the passengers were all aboard. The engines were turned on. The headlights shone down the runway. The police got me out of the car and started walking me rapidly, always rapidly, towards the steps, one in front of me, one behind, guns drawn. A two-way radio crackled. And suddenly they reversed themselves and headed me back towards the car.

I can still see her fat body as she waddled towards me on the tarmac that night, her arms akimbo. I knew her all too well, an airport security woman who always seemed to be on duty when I flew in and out of Lahore and who was so unsympathetic I suspected the regime had deliberately planted her to search me. She looked mean, like the sort who took rings and watches during the searches and never returned them. Nothing was too small for her to search. She emptied lipsticks out of their cases and studied every page of my appointment diary. She enjoyed her work.

'I will not be searched by her. I will not be searched!' I yelled, backing away from the car into the circle of guns surrounding me. 'I was searched going into jail to see my father. I was searched coming out. I was searched going to see my own mother in detention and searched coming out. I have been searched enough!'

The convoy of military vehicles pulled into position around me. More guns. More police. 'You have to be searched again,' the police officer insisted. 'Otherwise, you won't be allowed to leave in time for the plane.'

'That's fine with me,' I screamed. 'What do I have left? You've sentenced my father to death. You've broken my mother's head. You've sent me to live alone in Karachi, my mother to live alone in Lahore, put my father in a death cell. We can't even speak to each other, comfort each other. I don't care whether I live or die. So do what you will!'

I was almost hysterical. What other option did I have? I was up against the wall. The security woman hovered in the background, frightened by my outburst. But if she searched me she would surely find my father's message.

'Come, come, let her be,' the men began to murmur.

'You can go,' the officer said.

On the flight to Karachi, I was near collapse. My ear ached for the first time. Click. Click. The noise was so irritating that I found it hard to sleep when I returned to 70 Clifton. The regime finally called in a doctor, who began to conduct tests.

I read the piece of paper from my father. It was advice to me on points to make in contesting my illegal detention. I tried to write out a draft for the court, but I felt too ill.

The animals. It was strange what was happening to our family's animals. On the day my father's death sentence was handed down, one of his poodles died. One minute he was perfectly all right. The next he was dead. The following day the female poodle died, again for no apparent reason. I had a Siamese cat with me at 70 Clifton. She died too, on the third day.

When there is danger to the master of a house, some Muslims believe, the animals sometimes deflect it and they die instead. All I could think of as I lay ill was that the danger to my father was so great that it had killed not one, but three of our pets. The thought was not comforting. Every morning when I turned on the BBC news at 6.00 am, I prayed I'd hear that Zia was dead. But he was still alive.

I challenged my detention at 70 Clifton, using the pointers from my father. The court postponed hearing my case in April and again in May. Each time I had to re-submit the petition for a hearing. On June 14, my lawyer brought me the best pre-birthday present I could have. There were no grounds for my detention, Justice Fakhr ud-Din had ruled in the first ruling in a preventive detention case. I was free. At last I could attend to my health.

I had my first operation for my ear and sinuses at MidEast Hospital in Karachi at the end of June. As I came round from the anaesthetic all my suppressed fears surfaced. 'They're killing my father! They're killing my father!' I heard myself screaming. My nose was stuffed with packing and I couldn't breathe, though I felt calmer after my mother, who was still in detention in Lahore, was finally given permission to visit me under police escort.

What a sorry world I found when I recovered. The Karachi branch of our newspaper, *Musawaat*, had been closed down by the regime in April and its presses seized. Both the editor and the printer had been arrested for printing 'objectionable material', the term the regime used for our side of the story in my father's case. Journalists at other newspapers had gone on strike in protest. Ninety were arrested and four sentenced to lashing, including a senior editor of the *Pakistan Times* who was physically handicapped.

The international community was finally taking notice. By the summer of 1978, both the editor of *Musawaat* and the printer were among fifty political prisoners 'adopted' by Amnesty International, the world-wide human rights organisation which monitors the status of political prisoners. Amnesty was investigating the cases of thirty-two others – with no help from the regime. Though Zia had promised his co-operation to two of Amnesty's delegates during a fact-finding mission to Pakistan earlier in the year, the regime never responded to Amnesty's report which was issued in March.

I myself had met the delegates during their visit in January. I told them of our concern about the loss of fundamental human rights under Zia's Martial Law regulations, the trying of civilians and political prisoners by military courts, and the 'cruel punishments' being meted out, including the amputation of the left hand of a right-handed person or the right hand of a left-handed person convicted of theft. I was also anxious to get them to understand the unfairness of my father's trial and told them of the inhuman conditions he was being held in in solitary confinement. Naturally, they wanted to verify it. The delegates requested permission to visit my father in jail. The request was denied.

April 28, 1978. Kot Lakhpat Jail. Dr Zafar Niazi, my father's dentist:

When I visited Mr Bhutto in Kot Lakhpat Jail in April, I found his gums were rapidly deteriorating. The conditions in the prison were unsanitary and his diet inadequate. The sub-tissue in his gums was inflamed and painful, but there were no facilities for me to give him any treatment. I'm not sure any treatment would have been effective, however, in these sub-human surroundings. I issued a report to the regime after my visit, stating that I could not be effective as Mr Bhutto's dentist, unless his conditions were improved. I knew the regime would not take kindly to such a report. Many of my patients were foreign diplomats, and the regime was concerned, I am sure, that I would share my findings with them. As a precaution, I gave a copy of my report to my wife. 'If the army arrests me,' I told her, 'give it to the foreign press.' The police came for me two days later.

The persecution of Dr Niazi and his family was just beginning. He was arrested twice, once while he was treating a patient under anaesthesia in his clinic. 'Just give me an hour to finish my patient,' he asked the police. But they refused and he had to leave the patient in the chair. During this first arrest, the police raided his house at 2.00 am, turning over mattresses, pulling clothes out of the cupboards, looking for anything to pin on him. All they found was a half-bottle of wine left behind by an American associate of Dr Niazi's, an orthodontist who practised at his clinic every three months. Dr Niazi was charged with having alcohol in his house.

Dr Niazi, who was not a member of the PPP, nor in any way political, was held for six months in prison on the alcohol charge. By the time he was released, my father had been transferred from Kot Lakhpat Jail to another death cell in Rawalpindi Central Jail. Dr Niazi immediately applied for permission to see my father again. His application was denied.

June 21, 1978. Rawalpindi Central Jail. My 25th birthday.
I sit in a small room at Flashman's Hotel in Rawalpindi, waiting to visit my father. I keep looking at my watch. Where is Mummy? My father's lawyers had managed to get a court order allowing us to visit my father together on my birthday. But it's noon, and I have been waiting since 9.00 am for the police to fly her in from her detention in Lahore. Once again, they are stalling.

I am worried about my mother. She has been having terrible headaches and is almost always exhausted. The strain is taking a terrible toll on her and her blood pressure keeps dropping. Twice when flying from Lahore to see my father in 'Pindi she has fainted. The lawyers have petitioned the regime to detain her in Islamabad within driving distance of the prison, but she is still being held in Lahore. Once more she is alone, her only company a little kitten I smuggled in for her in my pocket. Chou-Chou is giving her comfort, Mummy says. The kitten puts her paw on Mummy's hand when she lays out her card games of Patience.

I smooth out my *shalwar khameez*. I want to look smart for my parents on my birthday to show them my morale is high. 1.00 pm. 2.00 pm. This is one of the regime's favourite tricks. I cannot count the number of times in my own periods of detention when I have been ready at the appointed hour to be taken to visit my father, only to wait hour after hour with no word. My visits to him every two weeks help keep me going. The regime knows that. So they either delay taking me, so that I only have half an hour with him, or they don't come for me at all. Why haven't they come? How can the regime violate a court order?

3.00 pm. 3.30 pm. The jail rules stipulate that all visitors must leave by sunset. I remember my last birthday. My party on the lawns of Oxford seems more like ten years ago. I wonder now whether it ever happened at all.

4.00. The message that my mother has finally arrived comes from the airport. 'Pinkie, happy birthday!' she says, giving me a hug when we meet at the entrance to the jail. Together we begin the walk to my father's cell.

'It was your great good fortune to be born on the longest day of the year, Pinkie,' my father says when we reach him. 'Even the regime couldn't make the sun set early on your birthday.'

He is being held now in another dim cell in an interior courtyard of the prison. Army tents are set up all around the inner courtyard. Military guards are posted at the locked and barred entrance. What a farce of a civil trial. It's a military operation. We are in a military outpost.

His dim, damp cell is only six feet by nine feet. There is no gauze netting over the bars in his cell door as there is over the guards' doors in the cells next to his. The air is thick with flies and mosquitoes. A sleeping bat clings to the ceiling while pale, colourless lizards scuttle up and down the walls.

We look at his bare metal cot. 'Didn't they give you the mattress I sent you two weeks ago?' my mother asks him. 'No,' he says. My father's back has sores and bruises from the thin jail bedding. He's had two bad cases of influenza, and severe stomach problems from unboiled water. On three different occasions he has vomited blood and bled from the nose as well.

Unbelievably he is quite cheerful, though very thin. But then he always seemed fine to me. Perhaps I just didn't want to see otherwise.

'I want you to go to Larkana for *Eid* and pray at the graves of our ancestors,' he is saying.

'But Papa, then I'll miss my next meeting with you,' I protest.

'Your mother is still in detention. There is nobody else to go but you,' he says.

I swallow hard. I had never been to our family graveyard on *Eid*, or to receive the traditional visits from the villagers and family at the nearby house in Naudero. The men in the family had always officiated, my brothers accompanying my father if the end of Ramazan fell during their school holidays. I felt a shiver of loneliness. I hoped my father would soon be free.

'Go to pray at Lal Shahbaz Qalander,' my father also urges me. 'I never got there last *Eid*.' Lal Shahbaz Qalander. One of our most renowned saints. My grandmother had gone to pray at his shrine when my father became very ill as a baby and nearly died. Would God be able to hear a daughter's prayer for the same person?

We sit in the courtyard for a precious hour, our heads close together so that the three jailers under orders to listen to us cannot. But they are sympathetic this time and do not press in on us.

'You are twenty-five now,' my father jokes, 'and eligible to stand for office. Now Zia will never hold elections.'

'Oh, Papa,' I say.

We laugh. How do we manage it? Somewhere in the jail stand the hangman's gallows which shadow our lives. The army, my father tells us, is trying to bait him into an outburst. Every night they climb up on the roof of his cell and clomp around in heavy boots, the same ruse they had used during the imprisonment of Mujib ur-Rahman during the civil war in Bangladesh. The hope is that the prisoner will lose his temper and use strong language with the guards, giving the army the excuse that some trigger-happy soldier had been provoked into shooting him. But my father knows their tricks and instead includes the harassment in his legal defence.

I returned to Flashman's followed by the now familiar convoy of two or three military vehicles which, in time, would swell to seven, eight, sometimes ten different military trucks. The people in the streets stared at the convoy as I passed. Some looked on in sympathy. Others lowered their eyes as if they didn't want to believe what was happening.

An eerie silence had fallen over the city, over the whole country. The entire nation was in suspended animation. It was said over 100,000 had been arrested. 'Zia won't carry out the sentence against the Prime Minister. It's not possible,' people whispered among themselves. The only topic of conversation was my father's trial, his death sentence, his Supreme Court appeal.

124

In spite of my father's reluctance, we had brought an appeal before the Supreme Court of Pakistan in Rawalpindi. 'I am obliged to respect the views of my wife and daughter, not only because of the relationship, but for a loftier reason,' my father had written to Mr Yahya Bakhtiar, the former Attorney General of Pakistan and the leader of my father's legal team at the Supreme Court. 'Both have played a heroic and gallant part in these dangerous times. They have a self-evident word and political claim on my decision.'

The court had begun hearing the case in May. Though in other cases, the accused was given a month to bring an appeal before the Supreme Court, my father had only been given a week. My father's lawyers were staying at Flashman's where we had set up an office to follow the appeal as closely as possible. Yasmin Niazi, Dr Niazi's teenage daughter, had joined in the work, keeping my appointments straight, as had Amina Piracha who was working as a liaison to the foreign press for the team of lawyers. In addition, my old friend from Oxford, Victoria Schofield, who had succeeded me as President of the Oxford Union, had come to Pakistan to help.

On some days I had to force myself to get up in the morning. Quickly. Get up. Get dressed. Face the day. More charges to refute. Meet with the few party workers not in jail. Give interviews to the press gathering in Rawalpindi. The regime-controlled press was only reporting the charges against my father. *Musawaat* in Lahore, which remained open despite the closure of the Karachi branch, and the world press were our only hope of getting the true story out. *Guardian* correspondent Peter Niesewand and Bruce Loudon of the *Daily Telegraph* became familiar faces.

The regime issued the first of a series of 'White Papers' at the end of July, this one criticising the conduct of the March 1977 elections. At Flashman's we worked constantly on my father's rejoinder to the false charges, which he wished to file in the Supreme Court in his defence. Every day Victoria and I transcribed the handwritten pages which the lawyers brought us from Rawalpindi Central Jail. My father's handwriting on both sides of the paper was cramped and difficult to read. It must have been far more difficult for him to write – fasting in his death cell in the August heat of Ramazan. The lawyers took the typed pages back to my father who edited them and sent them back to us for retyping. We sent his finished rejoinder – our code name for it was 'Reggie' – to a secret press in Lahore.

But before the document was submitted to the Supreme Court the printed copies were seized. In order to reproduce the document for the Supreme Court and distribute it to the foreign press, PPP workers had to stay up all night making photocopies of the three hundred page document. The location of the photocopier we used and the identities of the people who helped had to be kept entirely secret.

The net was tightening around Flashman's. One night the police formed an intimidating flank in front of the hotel, arrested one of our assistants, and sentenced him quickly in a military court. We worked under constant threat of not knowing what would happen next.

When the rejoinder was finally submitted to the Supreme Court, the Chief Justice banned its publication. By this time, however, several copies had already found their ways overseas. The rejoinder was later published in India as a book, *If I am Assassinated*, and became a best-seller.

There were constant rumours that the decision from the Supreme Court was coming any minute. At the beginning of the hearing the Chief Justice, Anwar ul-Haq, had announced that the appeal would be completed as soon as possible, and my father's lawyers had been optimistic. Of the nine judges on the bench, five were asking questions and reviewing the testimony in a way that seemed dismissive of the Lahore judgment. But, suddenly in June, Anwar ul-Haq had adjourned the court and gone to Jakarta for a conference. We all felt the appeal was prolonged and postponed until the judge most obviously in favour of acquittal and the only one on the bench with extensive murder trial experience, had been required to retire at the end of July. Despite our request, Chief Justice Anwar ul-Haq refused to allow him to complete the hearing. Another independent-minded judge was forced to drop out in September when a haemorrhage behind his eye left him temporarily dizzy and weak. His request that the court adjourn briefly until he recovered was also denied. That left the balance against us, four to three.

The Chief Justice of the Supreme Court was as biased as his counterpart on the Lahore High Court had been. Like the Chief Justice of the High Court, with whom he was very friendly, Anwar ul-Haq was also from Zia's home area of Jullandar in India. And again there was no pretence of separation between the executive and judiciary. When Zia went to Mecca on pilgrimage in September, 1978, Anwar ul-Haq was sworn in as acting President. There was even a hotline from the Chief Justice's chambers to the office of the Chief Martial Law Administrator.

I learned just how prejudiced Anwar ul-Haq was years later in exile from one of the other Supreme Court Justices, Safdar Shah. Anwar ul-Haq had taken Justice Shah aside during the appeal. 'We know Bhutto is innocent. But he must be eliminated if Pakistan is to be saved,' he had told him. Safdar Shah had gone on to vote for my father's honourable acquittal, and was himself persecuted by Anwar ul-Haq and the regime and forced into exile. Yet during the Supreme Court hearing, both Zia and Anwar ul-Haq continued to claim my father's appeal was being held in front of an independent judiciary. 'We are going through the evidence with an open mind,' insisted Anwar ul-Haq.

What could we do? The regime had control of the courts, the army, the newspapers, the radio and television. Other conveniently timed White Papers filled with false allegations designed to smear my father's reputation were being released by the regime in four languages and distributed among the foreign embassies. At the same time, my father's accuser Ahmed Raza Kasuri launched on a tour of Europe and America, staying at expensive hotels and holding press conferences about the 'just trial' my father was receiving in Pakistan. Kasuri claimed he was paying for everything himself, but the financial disclosures he and every other member of the PPP had been required to file under Zia's Martial Law regulations didn't support his claim. Where was the money coming from if not from the regime?

'I want you to go on a tour of the Frontier,' my father told me in September. 'We have to keep the people's morale up. Take my Mao cap with you. It's in my dressing room at 70 Clifton. Wear it while you're speaking, then take it off and put it on the ground. Tell them "My father said his cap should always be placed before the feet of the people."'

I listened to him carefully, but I was worried about his health. Every time I saw my father in jail he looked thinner. His gums had turned deep red and at places become infected. He often had a fever. Mummy and I used to take chicken sandwiches with us and try to tempt him into eating. We would wrap the sandwiches in a moist cloth to keep them fresh and soft.

But my father paid little attention to food during the September visit, concentrating instead on coaching me on the themes for the speeches I would be making. 'The whole issue of autonomy will be re-opened as a consequence of Martial Law,' he said. 'Remind the people that I, through democracy, gave them faith in a unified Pakistan. And only the return to democracy will hold the country together.'

His face seemed concerned as I left. 'Pinkie, I hate to put you in any danger. You may be arrested again if they get even more desperate. I've wrestled with this problem from the beginning. But then I think of the thousands of others who are being whipped and tortured for our cause . . .'

'Papa, please,' I said quickly. 'I know you are concerned as a father for a daughter. But you are more than a father to me. You are also my political leader, just as you are the political leader of the others who are suffering.'

'Be careful, Pinkie,' he called after me. 'You are going into the tribal areas. Don't forget how conservative they are. Sometimes your *dupatta* falls off your head while you're speaking. Remember to put it back up.'

'I'll be careful, Papa,' I assured him.

'Good luck, Pinkie,' I heard him call after me.

*

Victoria came with me to the Northwest Frontier province and the tribal areas which are bordered by Afghanistan to the west and China to the north. Yasmin accompanied me too, a brave act for a young girl who'd grown up in the traditional protectiveness of a Pakistani family. She'd never spent a night away from her home until I'd asked her late one night to stay with me at Flashman's. Her grandmother had agreed reluctantly, not because of the danger from the regime, but because tradition did not permit an unmarried girl to spend a night away from home.

But the Niazis, like many families, were radicalised by the brutality of the regime. At great cost to themselves, the Niazis insisted that I stay with them and have some semblance of a family atmosphere rather than staying at the hotel. In retaliation, the family was constantly harassed. Tax liens were filed against them. The lane in front of their house was filled with intelligence trucks which followed Mrs Niazi to the market and her children to school. Intelligence agents trailed Dr Niazi's dental patients as well until his practice fell off to practically nothing.

Together with local PPP leaders we travelled to Mardan, once a centre of the Gandharan Buddhist civilisation; Abbotabad, a former British hill station; Peshawar, the capital city of the Northwest Frontier whose walls of ochre brick had guarded against invaders from Central Asia for centuries. The words poured effortlessly from my heart at every stop in the Frontier province and the autonomous tribal areas ruled by the Pathans' strict code: revenge for any insult, and hospitality for any guest. 'The Pathans are famous for their belief in honour. My father is fighting not only for his honour, but for the honour of our country,' I called to the crowds whose features were as rugged as the nearby mountains of the Khyber Pass. We went on to Swat, with its lush, terraced rice fields, and Kohat, where salt blew in the air from the jagged salt-range in the distance. I spoke in Urdu, not knowing the regional language of Pashtu, but the Pathans listened all the same. There was no resistance to me, either, as a woman, even in these areas where the tribal women were fiercely guarded. The suffering in the country, the suffering of my family, of all of us, had risen above the barrier of gender. 'Rasha, rasha, Benazir rasha!' the people yelled back in Pashtu. Welcome, welcome, Benazir welcome!

'Bravo,' my father greeted me, standing in the door of his cell and clapping his hands when I returned briefly to Rawalpindi before setting out to tour the Punjab.

Hundreds of PPP activists gathered to hear me at the home of a party official in Lahore. In spite of the regime's harsh punishments, the dedication of the party workers was undiminished. 'The trial is unfair. We'll protest by courting arrest,' the PPP loyalists told me. 'Zia will have to arrest all of us before he can go ahead with the death sentence.' At Sargodha, where feudal landlords still held sway, more crowds turned out. There was a tempo building up, and the regime quickly moved to crush it. Scores of PPP supporters were arrested shortly after my departure from Sargodha, including my host whose only crime was allowing me to use his house. For this he was sentenced to a year's rigorous imprisonment and a fine of rupees 100,000, or 10,000 dollars.

'The regime is edgy. Let's not go on to Multan right away,' some in the party argued back in Lahore. 'We have a momentum going,' countered others. 'We might as well be arrested while sentiment is high.' 'If we back off a little now, we'll be able to gain more time to visit more places and reach more people,' the discussion continued. The second strategy won, and I returned briefly to Karachi to answer another charge from the regime.

Meanwhile, the people's commitment to democracy was reaching new heights. One after another, men in different cities began to set themselves on fire, immolating themselves in the ultimate protest against the perceived fate of their leader. Looking at their photographs in *Musawaat*, I realised with a start that I had met at least two of them. One, Aziz, had come to me at Flashman's with a simple request a few months before: to pose for a photograph with him. Though I was exhausted, I had agreed, a small effort on my part for which I was very thankful when I read that he had burned himself alive.

Another, a Christian named Pervez Yaqub who was the first to immolate himself, had come to me with a desperate proposal shortly after my father's arrest in September, 1977. He was going to hijack an airliner and hold the passengers hostage, he told me, until the regime was forced to release my father. 'You mustn't,' I'd told him. 'Innocent people might die. And that would make you no different from the lawless thugs in the regime. We must fight by our rules, and not descend to theirs.' Now he had made the ultimate sacrifice, burning himself to death in Lahore.

Pervez's life could have been saved by the crowd which had rushed to put out the flames, but the Martial Law authorities prevented anyone from reaching him. They wanted the people to watch his agony, in order to scare any other Bhutto loyalists who might want to do the same thing. But the depth of passion only intensified. Over the next weeks, five more men would burn themselves to death to try and save the life of their elected Prime Minister.

'The regime claims that those who burned themselves to death were paid to do it by the party,' I wrote in my notes for my forthcoming speech at Multan. 'Can there be such a price on a human life? No. These brave men were idealists whose dedication to democracy and decency transcended their own pain. We salute them.' I never got the chance to deliver the speech.

*

October 4, 1978. Multan Airport.

The flight from Karachi to Multan to continue our tour of the Punjab is delayed and delayed. Yasmin and I arrive at the airport at 7.00 am. The flight doesn't take off until noon. When we arrive at Multan, we understand why. Instead of taxiing to the terminal, the plane is shunted off to the far end of the tarmac and is immediately surrounded by army trucks and jeeps.

'Where is Miss Benazir Bhutto sitting?' say two men in plain clothes, boarding the plane.

The steward points to me.

'Come with us,' they say.

'On what grounds?'

'Don't ask questions.'

A small plane is standing nearby when Yasmin and I come down the steps.

'You get in the Cessna,' the officers say to me. 'She stays here.'

I look at Yasmin. Her eyes are huge in her face. Here she is, a young girl in a strange city, alone. God knows what could happen to her. 'Dogs!' the fundamentalists and the Martial Law authorities have begun yelling at the women all over Pakistan who have left the sanctuaries of their homes for the first time – to demonstrate against my father's arrest, my mother's arrest, the arrests of their own husbands and sons and, increasingly, their daughters. Yasmin is also concerned about what will happen to me. There is safety in numbers.

'I won't go without her,' I say to the police.

'Get in the plane,' they say, their eyes narrowing.

'I won't,' I say, taking a firm grip on Yasmin's hand.

Unbelievably, they move towards me, grab me, and start dragging me across the tarmac. 'Don't let go, Yasmin!' I yell to her, as she struggles to hang on to me.

While the passengers in the plane we've just been taken from look on horrified, Yasmin and I are pulled along the cement. My *shalwar* tears. The skin on my legs scrapes and bleeds. Yasmin is screaming. But we don't let go of each other.

The police's two-way radios crackle at the steps of the Cessna. As usual, they aren't sure what to do and are requesting instructions. While the policemen are preoccupied, Yasmin and I dash up the steps into the little three-passenger plane. The pilot informs the police that if he doesn't take off immediately it will be too dark for him to land. Land where? We don't know. The Corps Commander of Multan is furious when the pilot's message is radioed to him. He instructs the police to let us proceed. But the plane still sits on the runway.

'I haven't had food or water since 7.00 this morning,' the pilot says quietly to the police. They quickly bring him a lunch box. When we are airborne, he turns – he had heard my request for water turned down by the Corps Commander – and hands it to us. 'I've eaten. I got this for you,' he says.

Five hours later, we land back in Rawalpindi. I only know it is 'Pindi because I recognise one of the policemen who comes to take me from the plane. At least Yasmin is home. As I struggle towards the door of the plane, the pilot turns to me. I can still see the concern on his kind face, the tears that spilled out of his eyes. 'I'm a Sindhi,' he said. That was all. That was enough.

My mother was delighted to see me when I arrived at the house where she was in her tenth month of detention. 'What a pleasant surprise,' she said, thinking that I'd come for a visit. Her eyes widened when she saw my torn clothes, my bloody legs. 'Oh, I see,' she said, her voice tapering off. Both of us detained again.

I wrote a letter to Mir in America where he had gone to appeal to the United Nations to exert more pressure on the regime. 'Papa has asked me to give you some guidelines. He is *advising*, not criticising. Hence, here we go:

'1. Caesar's wife must be above suspicion. The press here has said you are living lavishly in London which Papa knows you are not, but he wants me to remind you that your personal life must be most circumspect. No films, no extravagance, or people will say you are enjoying yourself while your father languishes in a death cell.

'2. No interviews to, and keep completely away from, India and Israel. Your interview with an Indian paper has been misconstrued here.' And on and on. I hated writing Mir such a seemingly bossy letter: I knew how hard he was working. He had sold my little MGB and used the money to pay for the printing in London of my father's rejoinder to the charges against him. He was having meetings with every foreign member of government who would see him and leading demonstrations of the Pakistani population in England to protest against my father's death sentence. I wished so much we could be fighting together, but there was no way he or Shah, both of whom had abandoned their studies to lead the fight abroad, could return to Pakistan without being arrested. We all had to fight on, alone.

December 18, 1978. Supreme Court, Rawalpindi.

The court-room was swamped with people desperate to catch a glimpse of their Prime Minister. After a lengthy court battle, my father's lawyers had won the right for him to appear before the Supreme Court in his own defence. The court-room seated only 100. 300 to 400 packed themselves in for the four days of his address, sitting on the radiators, squashed into the aisles, perched on stacks of law books in the well in front of the bench. The thousands who were turned away waited outside behind barricades to watch my father's arrival in a police van at 9.00 am and his return to prison at noon.

I wanted badly to be there, but I was in detention and my request for permission to attend was denied. My mother, however, had been released by the court in November after almost a year of detention, and so was able to go. My father's valet, Urs, also managed to get a court pass. So did Mrs Niazi and Yasmin, as well as Victoria and Amina. Later, Victoria would write a book about my father's ordeal entitled *Bhutto: Trial and Execution*. It should have been called *Judicial Murder*.

My father's address, my mother told me, was brilliant. Over the four days allowed him by the court, he refuted the charges against him of complicity in the murder case, citing the irregularities and contradictions of the 'witnesses' in the Lahore trial; of the charges that he was a Muslim in name only; of the charges that he had personally rigged the elections. 'I am not responsible for each and every thought and idea born in the minds of officials or non-officials of our fertile Indus Valley,' he said. Speaking extempore and without notes, my father once more cast the spell of his intellect and oratory over the spellbound crowd.

'Everyone who is made of flesh has to leave this world one day. I do not want life as life, but I want justice,' he said. '. . . The question is not that I have to establish my innocence; the question is that the prosecution has to prove its case beyond reasonable doubt. I want my innocence to be established not for the person of Zulfikar Ali Bhutto. I want it established for the higher consideration that this has been a grotesque injustice. It puts the Dreyfus case in the shade.'

My father's performance was even more remarkable considering the conditions he'd been kept in. He had been kept awake by the army for nights on end. He had not seen the sun for more than six months, and had been without fresh water for twenty-five days in his death cell. He was pale and weak, Mummy told me, but he seemed to gain strength as his address went on. 'I feel a little dizzy,' he admitted in the courtroom. 'I can't adjust myself to the momentum and the people.' He looked around the packed crowd. 'Yes, it's nice to see people,' he said with a smile.

People in the court-room rose in respect every time he entered or left. And he insisted on appearing before the public as he always had, the impeccably dressed and stylish Prime Minister of Pakistan. Urs had brought him the clothes he requested from 70 Clifton and he appeared on the first day in court in a tailored suit, a silk shirt and tie, with a colourful handkerchief in his pocket. Only the loose fit of his trousers indicated the amount of weight he had lost.

At first the authorities allowed him to enter the court-room freely down the centre aisle. But when they saw how the people reached out to shake his hand, and how he responded to the first affection he'd received in over a year by smiling and touching them back, the security guards formed a human barrier around him. For the last three days of his appearance, he was kept inside a tight circle of six security men, their arms linked around him.

The appeal was completed on December 23. My mother and I applied for permission to visit him on December 25, the birthday of Pakistan's founder Mohammed Ali Jinnah. This was denied. We were not permitted to see him either on New Year's Day or five days later on his 51st birthday.

On February 6, 1979, the decision came down from the Supreme Court. By a vote of four to three, the death sentence was upheld.

My mother and I heard about the decision at 11.00 am, soon after it was announced. We had hoped for a miracle from Zia's packed bench. But the four Punjabi judges from the military heart of the country — two of them had been appointed *ad hoc*, and their tenure was confirmed by the military regime after the verdict — had voted to uphold the lower court, while the three senior judges from the minority provinces had voted to overrule. The reality of my father's death sentence made me feel physically ill.

My mother was about to leave for her regular Tuesday visit to my father when the Martial Law authorities arrived at our rented house with a detention order for her. But she thwarted them. Before they realised what was going on, my mother rushed out the door and got into her car, a fast-moving Jaguar. 'Open the gate,' she commanded the police guards stationed around the house where I had been in detention since my arrest at Multan airport. Not realising that detention orders had been issued for my mother as well, they obeyed. At high speed she drove herself to Rawalpindi Central Jail, outdistancing the pursuing army jeeps. Because they were expecting her, the jail authorities let her in.

She got through one steel gate. Then another. She was just ahead of her detention order being relayed to the prison, thereby cancelling her permission to visit. She rushed on. The interior courtyard was right in front of her. Steadily she moved through the army tents and the arsenal of weapons surrounding my father's compound. The last gate finally opened.

My father was in his death cell. 'The appeal has been rejected,' she managed to tell him before the jail authorities and police caught up with her. Her face was remarkably serene when she was returned to the house. 'I made it,' she told me. 'I was not going to give them the perverse satisfaction of telling your father the verdict.' Once more we were both locked up. And there was only a week to appeal against my father's sentence.

At Flashman's, the lawyers worked non-stop on the review petition. They had requested four copies of the Supreme Court's 1,500 page decision, over 800 of the pages written by Anwar ul-Haq. They received only one copy. A secretary was dispatched to photocopy it. In the midst of the copying process, he was arrested as was the owner of the photocopying machine.

Somehow the defence team managed to procure its own photocopying machine and move it into Flashman's. This was very risky. Since the beginning of the year, the regime had restricted the sale of typewriters and photocopying machines to commercial businesses so that the equipment could not be used by the PPP or any other political organisation to produce underground literature. Just using a typewriter or a photocopying machine was now deemed 'anti-state', while anyone selling us any new equipment risked arrest. The lawyers worked on.

Locked up with my mother in Islamabad, I felt trapped in a never-ending nightmare. Another sweep of arrests followed the Supreme Court decision. Schools and universities were closed. Zia was bent on suppressing any disturbance before it could occur. He quickly mopped up outbreaks of protest before they could spread.

The repression unleashed by military regimes has a numbing effect on people. When the danger or tension becomes too high, people turn to their own survival. They detach themselves. In silence lies safety. They seek refuge in apathy. They don't want to reach out for fear that they, too, will become victims.

But I was not so fortunate. I could not detach myself from the relentless momentum towards my father's death. When I looked in the mirror, I didn't recognise myself. My face was red and blotchy from acne caused by stress. I'd lost so much weight that my chin, jaw and eyebrows jutted out. My cheeks were sunken, my skin tightly stretched.

I tried to keep up a regimen of exercise, jogging in place for fifteen minutes every morning. But I kept losing my concentration and stopping. If only I could sleep. But I couldn't. Mummy gave me Valium. I took two milligrams, but I kept waking up, my mind in a turmoil. 'Try Ativan,' my mother suggested. It made me cry. I tried Mogadon instead. Nothing.

February 12, 1979. Sihala Police Camp.
The authorities came in the morning to tell Mummy and me that we were being moved to a police training camp in Sihala a few miles from my father's prison in Rawalpindi. We were taken to a remote building

surrounded by barbed wire on the top of a barren hill. Nothing was provided for us, no blankets, no food. Nothing. Ibrahim and Basheer, two of our household staff from Al-Murtaza, had to make the long trip back and forth every day with provisions.

February 13, 1979. The lawyers finished writing their petition at 5.00 am, the morning it had to be submitted. The court granted my father a stay of execution while the petition was reviewed. On February 24, the court hearing began. Meanwhile appeals for clemency flooded into Pakistan once more from heads of state around the world. 'All the politicians are asking to save a fellow politician but not many non-politicians have asked me for clemency,' Zia scoffed, describing the pleas from the heads of state as nothing more than 'trade union activity'.

I visited my father from Sihala at the beginning of March. I don't know how he kept going. He had refused all medical treatment since the death sentence had been upheld, and had stopped taking any medication. He had also stopped eating, not only because of the pain in his gums and teeth, but as a protest against his treatment. He was being kept locked in his cell now, unable to use the commode the prison officials had set up for him in another cell.

As usual, I was looking forward very much to seeing him, even more so that day because I had a surprise for him. Before my mother's latest arrest, she had gone to Karachi and brought back my father's dog, Happy, to keep me company in detention. I loved Happy. We all loved Happy, a fluffy white mongrel my sister had given to my father. 'Now you be quiet,' I whispered to Happy when I arrived at Rawalpindi Central Jail with him under my coat.

At the search area at the first barrier, I found to my great luck that the jail superintendent wasn't there. Nor was Colonel Rafi, the head of the army contingent posted inside the jail who always stood around watching our every move. Happy and I moved on to the second barrier. Luckily the policewomen searching me didn't object. 'We don't have orders to search for a dog,' one of them said sympathetically. I stepped inside the final prison enclosure. 'Go and find him,' I said to Happy, letting him loose.

Happy put his nose to the ground and dashed from cell to cell. I heard him yapping with excitement when he found my very surprised father. 'How much more loyal dogs are than men,' my father said when I caught up with the two of them.

The authorities were furious when they found out about the dog. Happy was never allowed to visit my father again. But at least I had been able to give my father that one moment, a reminder of life when we were a normal family: a mother, father and four children living under one roof, with dogs and cats in the garden.

*

During the first weeks of March, our lawyers flooded the court with more grounds for review. They were exhausted by the enormity of their burden. When Mummy and I tuned in to the BBC evening news at Sihala at the beginning of March, we heard that Ghulam Ali Memon, a member of my father's defence team and one of Pakistan's most highly respected lawyers, had died at his desk at Flashman's of a heart attack. 'Allah, Ya Allah,' he had reportedly said in the midst of dictating what was to be his final legal attack against the majority decision of the Supreme Court. Another victim of Martial Law was claimed. We turned off the radio. What could we say?

On March 23, the anniversary of the day Pakistan's founder Mohammed Ali Jinnah called for the establishment of an independent Muslim state, Zia announced that he would hold elections in the autumn. The next day, the Supreme Court announced its decision. Though my father's petition was dismissed, the Court unanimously recommended that the sentence be commuted to life. Once again, hope surged. The decision now rested solely with Zia.

Seven days. There were seven days for somebody, anybody, to persuade Zia not to send my father to his death. And Zia had every reason to spare him. A split decision, especially such a close one of four to three like my father's, had never resulted in the death sentence in Pakistan. No executive government in judicial history had refused to accept the unanimous recommendation of the highest court in the country to commute the death sentence. And no one in the history of the sub-continent had ever been put to death for conspiracy to murder.

There was pressure on Zia, too, from abroad. Messages were pouring in again from foreign heads of state. Prime Minister Callaghan of Great Britain appealed to Zia for mercy for the third time. Saudi Arabia, the seat of fundamentalist Islam, appealed again. Even President Carter joined in and appealed this time. But there was no reply from Zia. The minutes ticked by towards my father's fate.

No date of execution was announced, giving the people false hope. No one wanted to accept what my father had always known, preferring to cling to the unanimous recommendation of the court and Zia's promises to Muslim governments to commute the sentence to life. A plea from my father or his immediate family, Zia had also let it be known, would give him a way to save face and commute the sentence. But my father, who had accepted the inevitability of his death long before, continued to refuse. 'An innocent man does not appeal for mercy for a crime he did not commit,' my father insisted, forbidding us to appeal as well. His oldest sister, one of my aunts in Hyderabad, went ahead and appealed anyway, delivering her petition at the gate to Zia's house an hour before the deadline was to expire. But there was still no reply from Zia.

The signs were increasingly ominous. In Rawalpindi Central Jail, what pitiful pieces of furniture there were in my father's cell were taken away, including his bed. He was left to sleep on the floor on his roll of bedding. They even took away his razor, leaving my usually cleanly-shaven father with a stubble of grey beard on his face. He was ill and very weak.

In Sihala, I was served with another detention order, restricting me for another fifteen days on the grounds that I would 'resort to further agitational politics as a final bid to secure the release of [my] father, posing a serious threat to peace and tranquillity and to the efficient conduct of Martial Law.'

Nobody knew what was going to happen. Would Zia actually go ahead and hang my father in spite of world condemnation and the recommendation of the court? If so, when? The answer seemed tragically clear on April 3, when my mother and I were taken to our last meeting.

Yasmin! Yasmin! They are going to kill him tonight!

Amina! You here, too. It's tonight! Tonight!

The lawyers drew up another review petition. Amina flew to Karachi where she and one of my father's lawyers, Mr Hafiz Lakho, tried to submit it to the court. The registrar refused to accept it. Give the petition to the judges, the registrar told them, but the judges wouldn't accept it either. One judge even slipped out of the back door of the court house to avoid them. Amina and Mr Lakho went to the senior judge's private house and pleaded at the gate. The judge refused to see them. Broken-hearted, Amina flew back to Islamabad.

April 3, 1979.

Tick. Tick. The Martial Law forces are cordoning off our family graveyard, cutting off all the roads to Garhi Khuda Bakhsh. Tick. Tick. Amina goes directly to the Niazi's house from the airport, not wanting to be alone. Tick. Tick. 'It's tonight,' Dr Niazi is saying quietly into the phone over and over again, as Yasmin and Amina lie silent and wide awake in the darkened house. Tick. Tick.

An army truck pulls away quickly from Rawalpindi Central Jail in the early morning. A short time later, Yasmin hears a small plane fly across Islamabad. She convinces herself that it belongs to one of the Arab leaders who has got into the prison and is spiriting my father away to safety. But the plane she hears is taking my father's body home to Larkana.

7

RELEASE FROM AL-MURTAZA:
DEMOCRACY'S CHALLENGE TO MARTIAL LAW

As the first anniversary of my father's execution nears on April 4, 1980, people are pressing past Al-Murtaza towards my father's grave in Garhi Khuda Bakhsh. Now in our sixth month of detention, my mother and I apply to the regime for permission to visit his grave but I know this won't be granted. The regime is so apprehensive about any public demonstration of support for my father's memory and the PPP that the roads leading to our ancestral village have been blocked for a hundred miles radius.

No matter how many guns the regime levels at the people, Zia continues to be haunted by my father's ghost. In his lifetime, my father was admired as a statesman and social visionary. By his murder, he has been elevated in the minds of his followers to the rank of martyr, and to some, a saint. No two forces are more powerful in a Muslim country.

Miracles are being reported from my father's burial ground ten miles away from Al-Murtaza. A crippled boy walks. A barren woman delivers a son. In the year since my father's execution, thousands have made the pilgrimage to our family graveyard to hold a rose petal or a piece of mud from my father's grave on their tongues while they pray. The local administrators have torn down the sign pointing to the graveyard isolated in the desert. But still the people come.

Police and army patrols harass them, demanding their names, writing down their number plates if they've come by car or truck, their addresses if they've made the journey on foot. Often their food is confiscated and the jugs of water put out for them by local villagers smashed. But still the people come, heaping framed photos of my father and strings of roses and marigolds on his grave in the desert.

Eight days after the anniversary of my father's death, the court hearing challenging our detention finally comes up in Karachi. When our lawyer mentions the letter I'd written protesting against the disrespect of Captain Iftikhar during Sanam's attempted visit the month before, the Advocate General claims to have no knowledge of any such letter. But I have the signed receipt from the jailer, and our lawyer asks for a day's adjournment so we can produce it. To prevent a letter from reaching the court is contempt, punishable by six months imprisonment. They know I have the proof. The authorities have to do something to pre-empt the contempt charge.

That night my mother and I are abruptly freed. I never see the jailer again. Later I hear he was denied promotion and given a 'punishment post'.

Freedom. But who knew for how long. My mother stayed in Karachi after our release from Al-Murtaza while I flew to Rawalpindi to catch up on the developments during our six months of detention. The pressure in my ear was almost unbearable during the flight, especially during the descent into 'Pindi. When I woke up the next morning at Yasmin's house, the pillow case was splattered with stinking pus and blood. My friends rushed me to the hospital. 'You're very lucky,' the doctor told me at the emergency room after cleaning my ear. 'The air pressure in the plane forced the infection to burst outwards. It could have burst inwards and caused serious damage.'

I didn't know what to think. First the regime's doctor at Al-Murtaza had insinuated that I was imagining the discomfort in my ear, then had accused me of perforating it. Now this doctor, after telling me how lucky I'd been, simply gave me a note advising me to have my ear checked every two weeks by my doctor in Karachi. Were the doctors inept or were they deliberately ignoring my condition? No one told me that I had a serious mastoid infection which was slowly melting the delicate bones of the middle ear. That's what was causing my partial deafness. Without surgery, I learned later, the chronic inflammation could lead to permanent deafness and facial paralysis. But I was told nothing.

My mother was very concerned when I returned to Karachi. 'Write to the regime and request permission to travel abroad for a check-up,' she urged me. 'Your health has nothing to do with politics.' I wrote to the regime. We received no reply. The regime wanted to keep us where they could see us.

Military intelligence vans were parked twenty-four hours a day outside 70 Clifton. Whenever my mother or I left the house, they followed us. Whoever came to the house was photographed and their licence plates noted. Our telephone lines were tapped. Sometimes there was a clicking noise. Other times the line just went dead.

'Why don't you go back to Larkana and try to straighten out the farm finances?' my mother suggested when I felt stronger. 'No one in the family has been able to check through our accounts for two years.'

Intelligence agents never left my trail as I headed back to Al-Murtaza to see our farm managers and go over the planting and harvest reports. I had no idea what to expect or even to look for. My father or brothers had always tended the lands.

While I went over the books, I often felt as if I was back in the kitchen as an eight-year-old struggling with the household accounts with Babu. But it was a relief to have something concrete to deal with and to stop even momentarily the endless whirling in my mind. Every morning before the summer heat became unbearable I drove across the guava orchards and the fields of rice and sugar-cane in a jeep to familiarise myself with my new responsibilities. I roamed the fields in trainers with a scarf or straw hat on my head as protection from the scorching sun, learning about our system of irrigation canals bolstered with tube wells, helping with the summer planting of rice and cotton, and reading up on sugar-cane cultivation and the problems of water-logging and salinisation. The physical exertion became a balm.

The tenant farmers, the *kamdars* or managers, and the *munshis* or accountants, were greatly relieved to have a member of the Bhutto family back among them. 'There is gold in the step of the owner. Now that you are here we will prosper,' one said to me. 'We are no longer orphans.'

I loved being on the lands. Still, it felt odd to be working side by side with men in Larkana. Women in the rural areas were very conservative, rarely leaving their homes without wearing *burqas* and certainly not driving cars. But I had no choice. There were no male members of my family left in Pakistan. My father was dead and my brothers, who would have been arrested immediately if they returned to Pakistan, were living in Afghanistan. So back and forth I went to the fields every morning. There was little room left in my life, in any of our lives, for tradition.

In a way I had transcended gender. There was not a person who did not know the circumstances that had forced me out of the pattern of landowning families, where young women were guarded zealously and rarely, if ever, allowed to leave their homes without a male relative. Our tradition holds that women are the honour of families. To safeguard their honour, and themselves, a family keeps their women in *purdah*, behind the four walls and under the veil.

My four aunts, my grandfather's daughters from his first marriage, formed part of this tradition. With no suitable first or second Bhutto cousins available for marriage, they had been consigned to a life of *purdah* behind their compound walls in Hyderabad. They had great status within the family because everyone understood why they had never married. And they always seemed very cheerful, never having known any other sort of life. 'They have no worry lines in their faces,' my mother would often say in wonder when she came back from visiting them.

To me it seemed a life of boredom, but my aunts seemed happy enough. They learned enough Arabic to read the Holy Quran, supervised the cooking, made delicious carrot pickle and sweetmeats, sewed and knitted. For exercise they took walks around the courtyard. Occasionally the cloth man would discreetly leave bolts of new fabric outside the walls for them to pick and choose from. They were the old generation. I was the new.

In the evenings at Al-Murtaza, I had meetings with student delegations and other visitors who brought news of those still in jail and reports about resistance to military rule. We drew up lists of people to visit in prison and of families to console. In the afternoons I finally had the time and freedom to arrange for a *shamiana* to be built to shade my father's grave and to fulfil a request from my mother to replace the old wooden windows at Al-Murtaza with glass. 'I'd rather see than be cool,' she had said during the almost daily power failures we'd experienced in our long months of detention at Al-Murtaza. 'Who knows when we'll be detained here again? We might as well be ready.'

I also found myself thrust into an unfamiliar Eastern tradition. As the only Bhutto around, I was suddenly considered the 'elder' by the local villagers who began to come to the courtyard of a mud hut on the lands to get me to settle their feuds and problems. A hangover from feudal times when the heads of clans held sway over every decision affecting their people, an abbreviated system of tribal justice still remained in the rural areas as did the tribes themselves. Though I was certainly not the head of the Bhutto tribe, the people insisted on coming to me anyway. Justice in Pakistan was too slow, too far away, too expensive and considered too corrupt to bother with. The police had the reputation of arresting people for 'pocket money', releasing them only upon payment of a bribe. The people felt better served by the *faislas*, or judgments, from a family they knew. But, after eight years in the West, I was discovering I was not well versed in dealing with the intricacies of rural life.

'His cousin murdered my son forty years ago,' a toothless old man argued in front of me one morning while I sat on a rope bed holding court. 'The *faisla* from your great-uncle then was my marriage to the first daughter born to his family, if there was one. And there is. Look at her! But he won't give her to me.'

I looked at the eight-year-old girl cowering behind her father. 'He never said a word when my daughter was born,' the father retorted. 'I thought he had forgiven us for the crime committed so many years before. If I'd known he was going to claim her, I would have brought up my daughter knowing that she was not ours and that one day I would have to give her up. Now we are thinking of arranging a marriage for her with another family and they want her. We have given our word to the others. How can we break it?'

I shuddered at the thought of this poor little girl being haggled over. The fate of women in the rural areas was not always a happy one. Few of them had any choice in their lives, or were ever asked what they wanted, 'You will not get the girl, but a cow and rupees 20,000 in compensation,' I said to the old man. 'That is my judgment. You should have made your claim before she was betrothed to another.' A cow for a girl – not an equation that had ever come up in discussions about the women's movement at Radcliffe. But this was Pakistan. And the old man was furious, grumbling loudly when he left.

My *faisla* the next day turned out to be a disaster. 'My wife has been kidnapped,' a man cried in front of me. His father-in-law added to the din. 'The sky has fallen on our heads. Our lives are finished. All day my daughter's children are crying for their mother. You must help us get her back.'

'Who do you suspect?' I asked, alarmed for the woman. When they told me I sent someone to the village to negotiate with the village elders. The young woman was successfully returned. And she was furious.

'I don't want to live with my husband. I am in love with someone else,' was the message she sent me. 'This is the third time I've run away and been returned. I thought you as a woman would understand and sympathise with me.'

I was flabbergasted. Did everyone but me know that the only way a woman could leave her husband in the harsh codes of tribal traditions was by being 'kidnapped'? An unhappy wife cannot go voluntarily. The poor young woman, I discovered later, never managed to escape again. Not for the first time I realised the conflict between tribal traditions and the human values of equality and free choice.

The gap between a democratic Pakistan and Pakistan under military dictatorship was also widening. While I was passing *faislas* in the fields of Larkana, the special military courts Zia had set up in every province, presided over by one magistrate and two officers with no legal training were dispensing more and more sentences of death and life imprisonment. Injustice was also being speeded up in the hundreds of summary military courts where a single untrained officer heard testimony and awarded up to a year's rigorous imprisonment and fifteen lashes on the spot. While the *faislas* I issued were not binding and the disputes could be taken to court, the accused in the military courts were allowed no lawyers and no right of appeal. Only by bribing the presiding officer at the rate of rupees 10,000 per lash, then about 100 dollars, could the victims escape on-the-spot punishment. The noose of Martial Law was tightening.

Martial Law Order No. 77, May 27, 1980: The jurisdiction of the civil courts is replaced with the military courts in such crimes as treason and subversion of members of the armed forces. The punishments run from death by hanging to whipping and imprisonment for life.

Martial Law Order No. 78: The twelve-month period of detention without trial for political prisoners is reiterated, but with a new twist. There no longer needs to be any explanation at all to the people arrested in their homes or on the streets. 'Reasons or grounds for detention . . . shall not be communicated to any person,' the order states. The detention order can now be extended for as long as the Martial Law authorities feel 'the circumstances so warrant'.

Now anyone, anywhere, can be arrested without any right of appeal, on a charge he or she is unaware of, and be held indefinitely. On June 19, a procession of lawyers calling for the withdrawal of these new orders and for elections to return the government to civilian rule set out in Lahore. Eighty-six lawyers were beaten up and arrested. So were twelve others among a group arrested in Karachi in August for calling for the restoration of the Constitution of 1973. Students and trade union leaders were also being swept up by the regime in a reign of terror seemingly without end.

When I returned to Karachi during the summer, my mother cautioned me to be very careful. But the regime was not taking any risks. When we went to Lahore for the wedding of a family friend in August, our hotel was surrounded by the police and we were externed from the province of Punjab. The police drove us under armed escort to the airport and put us on a plane bound for Karachi.

It was clear that three years after the coup and the imposition of Martial Law Zia had still not been able to bludgeon the people into acquiescence nor win their support. Instead he was losing ground. Zia had almost no political support, just the control of the military. Even the members of the PNA, the coalition of politicians who had opposed my father and the PPP in the 1977 elections, some of whom had subsequently become Zia's ministers, were defecting. When, six months after my father's death, Zia had dispensed with their ministries and banned all political parties, the PNA found themselves in the political wilderness.

As a result, shortly after my mother and I were detained at Al-Murtaza in October 1979, some components of the PNA had started offering to co-operate with the PPP against Zia. We had taken their advances then as political manoeuvring aimed at gaining leverage with the military regime. 'If you don't want us as Ministers,' they were effectively telling Zia, 'we'll go to the PPP.' Now, in the autumn of 1980, the overtures from our old adversary, the PNA, began again. This time we had to take them seriously.

Desperate to create a political base, Zia and his few remaining supporters were resorting to bribes. Every day brought new reports of Zia's seduction campaign. Dhoki, the son of a poor PPP leader, who worked in a bicycle shop and earned rupees two a day, was offered rupees 1,000 to forsake the party for the Muslim League, a PNA faction still supporting Zia. A PPP member as powerful as Ghulam Mustafa Jatoi, the President of Sindh and a former Chief Minister, was offered – and considered accepting – the Prime Ministership of the regime by Zia himself. There was great danger of a political re-alignment orchestrated by Zia, fooling the people into thinking that a civilian solution to Zia's hated military regime had been reached.

'We have to outmanoeuvre Zia before he outmanoeuvres us,' my mother said to me in September after Jatoi was offered the Prime Minister-ship. 'Much as I hate the idea, perhaps we should take up the feelers put out by the PNA. There is no point in splintering the opposition to Zia.'

At first I was appalled. 'It will cause a storm among the party leaders,' I protested. 'How can we forget that it was the PNA who brought the charges of election rigging against the PPP in the first place; the PNA who paved the way for the Army takeover? They were Zia's ministers when he sent Papa to his death.'

'But what other choice do we have?' Mummy said. 'Now it is Jatoi. Tomorrow it will be others. When ideal conditions do not present them-selves, you have to deal with ugly realities.'

She called for a secret meeting of the thirty-odd members of the PPP Central Executive Committee. We knew we were taking a great risk – political gatherings had been banned – but if we just sat silently by we were in fact acquiescing to the regime. This meeting, like all the others, was called at 70 Clifton. The leaders came from as far away as the Northwest Frontier province and Baluchistan. And predictably, the debate was bitter.

'The PNA are murderers, murderers,' said one member from Sindh. 'If we do a deal with them today, then what is there to stop us from dealing directly with General Zia tomorrow?'

'But Mao Tse-Tung co-operated with Chiang Kai-Shek when the Japan-ese invaded China,' countered the aged Sheikh Rashid, the Marxist in the party. 'If they could co-operate in the national interest, I say we should co-operate with the PNA.'

Back and forth the argument raged. 'We agree that they are opportunists and self-seekers,' I offered. 'But what can we do? We can either wait for the initiative to slip out of our hands or swallow the bitter pill of the PNA and seize the initiative ourselves. I suggest we compromise and form an alliance without giving up our separate party identities.'

After seven hours pragmatism finally prevailed and each one of us reluctantly agreed to respond to the PNA overture. The framework for the MRD, the Movement to Restore Democracy, was formed.

'There is no use in both of us landing up in jail again at the same time, so you keep a low political profile,' my mother told me. 'That way one of us, anyway, can stay on the outside to lead the party.'

Reluctantly, I agreed. But at the same time I was somewhat relieved. Though it made good political sense to form the MRD, I still found it difficult to accept an alliance with my father's former enemies. The leaders of the former opposition parties evidently found it just as difficult to negotiate with the PPP – and with each other. Deeply suspicious, the leaders of the fiercely opposed parties wouldn't talk to each other directly during the preliminary meetings, but only through emissaries.

The process was further complicated by the bitterness of many of the exchanges leading to the shaky new coalition, especially over the wording of the proposed MRD charter: whether the elections of 1977 were or were not rigged, whether 'execution' or 'assassination' should be used in describing my father's death. It took four months, from October 1980 to February 1981, to break the deadlock and work out a draft agreement among all ten parties, and an uneasy one at that.

The Muslim League party of Mohammed Khan Junejo, who went on to become Zia's hand-picked Prime Minister, backed out at the eleventh hour. The other leaders and party deputies finally met together face to face for the first time on the night of February 5, 1981, at 70 Clifton.

I looked at my father's former opponents now sitting in his house to strike a political deal with his widow, the Chairperson of the PPP, and his daughter. What a strange business politics is. Nasrullah Khan, the fez-wearing leader of the Pakistan Democratic Party sat on my mother's right. Opposite me sat Kasuri, the fleshy faced representative of Asghar Khan's more moderate Tehrik-e-Istiqlal. Bearded leaders from the religious party Jamaat-ul-Ulema-e-Islam were on one side of the room; on the other, Fatehyab, head of the small leftist Mazdoor party, wearing starched white *churidaar-kurta*, loose shirt with tight pyjamas. There were around twenty people in all, most of them from the former PNA coalition. I had to keep reminding myself that the point was to unseat Zia, that the point, despite our divergent views, was to cement a political coalition to force Zia to hold elections. But it was hard.

Cigarette smoke and tempers rose among the velvet-panelled walls and chandeliers in the drawing room, and the meeting went on so long it had to be reconvened in the morning. At one stage a former PNA leader tried to justify his party's role in the agitation of 1977. I was surprised by the implied criticism of the PPP here in our own house.

'We are here to discuss a coalition for democracy, not to discuss what you think of us or we of you,' I said in an icy tone.

'Yes, we must look to the future, not to the past,' Nasrullah Khan said, trying to calm us both.

Still, I found it difficult to watch the politicians drinking coffee out of my father's china, sitting on his sofa, using his telephone to make excited

145

calls to friends around the country to explain: 'I'm at 70 Clifton! Yes, really. Mr Bhutto's house!'

Yasmin, Amina and Samiya prevailed upon me to calm down. 'They have come to you. It's a vindication of the strength of the PPP,' Samiya said.

'You wanted to form this coalition,' Amina added. 'It makes political sense, so take the difficulties in your stride.'

I swallowed my objections, as did the other leaders who finally, one by one, signed the charter uniting all the parties. And on February 6, 1981, the Movement to Restore Democracy was born.

The news of the signing of the MRD charter, which many heard on the BBC, electrified the length and breadth of Pakistan. The psychological boost it gave to the people led many to interpret it as a signal to launch a protest against the injustices of the Martial Law regime. The students in the Frontier province were the first to take to the streets. Immediately Zia served my mother and me with externment orders to keep us from visiting the wounded.

The discontent soon spilled over into Sindh and Punjab where university professors, lawyers and doctors joined the swelling protest movement. More student protests broke out in Multan, Bahwalpur, Sheikupura, Quetta. 'Thank God for the MRD,' taxi drivers, shopkeepers and small traders began to whisper. 'Zia's time is finally over.' Our cook came back from Karachi's Empress Market to report that 'even the butchers are ready to strike at the call of the MRD.'

Zia knew he was in a corner. He closed down universities all over Pakistan and banned meetings of more than five people. But the demonstrations continued, described by *Time* magazine as 'the most serious wave of opposition that has faced General Zia'.

A secret meeting of the MRD was called for February 27 in Lahore. Zia reacted quickly, arresting many of the MRD leaders on February 21. Other members of the MRD and PPP were issued restriction orders externing them from the Punjab. '. . . Your entry in the Punjab is deemed as prejudicial to public safety and maintenance of public order as well as public interest,' my own order from the Governor of the Punjab read.

My mother tightened the agreement we had made about limiting my political activity. 'Do nothing political for the time being. If I am arrested you must be there to provide leadership,' she told me firmly. The situation was becoming explosive, close to toppling Zia, and I chafed under the restrictions. It fell to my mother to try and attend the secret meeting of the MRD in Lahore. All the roads to the city were sealed off by the police and every car was being searched. The members of the MRD still at large had to travel to the meeting by circuitous routes. My mother went by train disguised as a grandmother in a *burqa*, accompanied by her 'grandson', the thirteen-year-old son of one of our staff.

146

The police raided the meeting and arrested the members, including my mother who was externed back to Karachi. But not before the MRD delivered its ultimatum, a call for the end of Martial Law and for elections within three months. 'We demand that Zia quit immediately, failing which the Martial Law regime will be removed by the irresistible will of the people,' the MRD announced in Lahore.

The MRD set March 23 as the target date for massive strikes and demonstrations across Pakistan. Some of the PPP councillors elected in the 1979 local elections agreed to resign and call for Zia's resignation at the time of the strike. The countdown had begun for Zia's downfall and the return of civilian government to Pakistan. The clock was finally ticking for Zia.

March 2, 1981.

I am sitting in the living room of 70 Clifton with a group of party workers when the telephone rings. It is Ibrahim Khan, the Reuters representative in Karachi.

'What is your reaction to the news?' he asks me.

'What news?'

'A Pakistan International Airlines plane has been hijacked.'

'By whom?' I ask, startled. A PIA plane had never been hijacked before.

'Nobody knows yet,' he says. 'Nobody knows anything, who the hijackers are, where they're taking the plane, or what they want. I'll try and keep you posted. But may I have a reaction?'

'All hijacking is bad, whether it is a plane or a nation,' I respond automatically. When I hang up the phone, the PPP members are looking at me expectantly.

'One of our planes has been hijacked,' I say. 'That's all I know.'

8

SOLITARY CONFINEMENT
IN SUKKUR JAIL

Sukkur Central Jail, March 13, 1981.

Why am I here? I don't understand. Jail, now. A remote jail in the desert of Sindh. It is cold. I hear the prison clock strike 1.00, then 2.00. I can't sleep. The chill desert wind sweeps through the open bars of my cell, four walls of open bars. The cell is more like a huge cage, an enormous space with only a rope cot in it.

I twist and turn on the cot, my teeth chattering. I have no sweater, no blanket, nothing. Only the *shalwar khameez* I had been wearing when I was arrested in Karachi five days ago. One of the jailers had felt sorry for me and quietly passed me a pair of socks. But she was so frightened of being caught for her charity that this morning she had asked for them back. My bones ache. If only I could see, I could at least walk around. But the electricity is turned off in my cell at night. From 7.00 onwards, there is nothing but the cold darkness.

The police had come for me on March 7 at 70 Clifton. But I wasn't there. I had spent the night with Samiya, keeping away from the policy meeting my mother was holding at 70 Clifton with the leaders of the MRD. The police had evidently gone quite berserk in their efforts to locate me, raiding my cousin Fakhri's house and 70 Clifton where they first arrested my mother, then tore the place apart searching for me. 'What do you think she is, a beetle?' my sister Sunny had asked the police when they emptied matchboxes searching for me.

Fanning out across Karachi, the police had gone on to raid the houses of my old school friends, including that of the Punthakeys, a Zoroastrian family. Their 25-year-old daughter Paree was taken to the police station where the police interrogated her for seven hours. Paree and her family were members of a religious minority, and under Zia's policy of Islamisation, anyone who was not a Muslim was now particularly liable to punishment. 'We know how to deal with religious minorities in this country,' the police had warned Paree's relatives when they contacted the authorities to protest against her detention. 'You have no place in politics in this country. You shouldn't get involved.'

148

After searching the houses of two other friends, Putchie and Humo, the police finally caught up with me the next day at the home of Dr Ashraf Abbasi, the former Deputy Speaker of the National Assembly and one of my mother's doctors in Karachi. 'The police are here and want to search the house,' Dr Abbasi's son Safdar told us as I was preparing to take advantage of her direct-dial phone to ring up some friends in Islamabad. We looked at him in amazement. As I knew nothing about the raids and had steadfastly avoided any MRD political activity, I thought the police had come for Dr Abbasi, or possibly her son Munawwar. 'Tell them there's no need to raid the house,' I told Safdar. 'Ask them who they want.' He came back a moment later. 'They have come for you,' he said.

There was something new and terrible about this arrest. I sensed it when I was told to get into the back of an open jeep crammed with constables rather than one of the cars they had used to take me into detention before. I refused, and finally they let me get in front. The size of the military convoy following me through the empty streets was also bigger, and the destination ominous: a police station. I had never been taken to a police station before. What was going on? No one would tell me as I sat for 5 hours in the bare room, watching the policemen smoke cigarette after cigarette and spit betel-nut juice at the already stained walls. A look of fear was frozen on all their faces. This time, I was to find out shortly, Zia had gone beyond his previous bounds of repression and brutality.

What the authorities knew, but I didn't, was that thousands of people were being rounded up all over Pakistan in the biggest sweep ever. Amnesty International, whose figures were always conservative, estimated that over six thousand people were arrested in March 1981 alone. In the five days since the hijacking of the PIA airliner on March 2, Zia had decided to use the hijacking as a pretext to stop the groundswell of support for the MRD movement. Everybody with the slightest connection with the MRD or the PPP was being imprisoned.

The Niazis were arrested in Islamabad. The police came for Amina, too, though when they saw she was nine months pregnant they took her husband Salim instead. She went into labour out of shock. Yahya Bakhtiar, the head of my father's legal defence team and former Attorney General of Pakistan, was arrested in Baluchistan. Faisal Hayat, a former member of the National Assembly and the nephew of Khalid Ahmed, the Deputy Commissioner of Larkana who had been forced into exile, was arrested in Lahore, as again, were many of the women members of the PPP. Qazi Sultan Mahmood, the assistant manager of Flashman's Hotel, was arrested for the third time in Rawalpindi. So were Irshad Rao, the editor of *Musawaat* in Karachi, and Pervez Ali Shah, a leading member of the Sindh PPP. The list went on and on. And our treatment was reaching a new level of barbarity.

'Where is my mother?' I asked a group of policemen at the station.

'In Karachi Central Jail,' they said.

'In the Rest House?' I asked. The Rest House was the relatively comfortable accommodation for visiting jail officials where my father had been held at the beginning.

'In a cell,' they told me.

I gasped. My mother, the widow of the former Prime Minister, in a Class C cell with no running water, no bedding, no air?

'Where are you taking me?' I asked the police.

'To join your mother,' they said.

They were lying.

I was held incommunicado for five days in the Karachi Central Jail Rest House, now stripped of its furniture to the barest minimum. The officials there claimed they didn't know my mother's whereabouts, and denied that she was even being held in Karachi. I was also refused permission to see my lawyer. I had no clothes with me, only what I had on when I was arrested. I had no hairbrush or comb, no tooth brush or toothpaste, no supplies at all. I was also under medication for female problems brought on by the cumulative stress. I needed more medicine, but there was no doctor or woman I could talk to to say what I needed.

'You will be leaving here at 2.30 am,' the superintendent said, coming to my cell on the night of the 12th. He looked frightened. 'Be ready.'

'Where are you taking me?' I asked. There was no reply.

'Where is my mother?' I asked. Again there was no reply.

For the first time, I felt afraid. I had heard rumours that the jail authorities sometimes took controversial prisoners into the desert at night and simply killed them. Their bodies were buried before their families were notified that their relatives had either been killed while trying to escape or had suffered mysterious and sudden heart attacks. When I first arrived at the Rest House I'd written a letter to the Sindh High Court challenging my arrest and asking either to be allowed to conduct my own defence in court or to have a lawyer sent to me. Now I was desperate that the letter should reach its destination.

'You must send this letter to the court,' I urged one of the jailers while I waited for the regime's officers to arrive in the early hours of the morning. He quietly took my letter and stuffed it into his pocket. Thank God for that. If he delivered it, at least there would be some record of where I was and where I had been taken from.

A van load of policewomen came for me at 2.30. So did trucks full of police and army personnel. We raced through the empty streets at breakneck speed in a car with darkened windows, as if we were expecting an ambush. Suddenly the car lurched to a stop and there was much whispering and talking back and forth on two-way radios.

'Isolate her on the tarmac,' I heard the instructions come through. I was relieved. At least I was at the airport. But where were they taking me? I knew the plane schedule by heart by now, and there were no flights to anywhere in Pakistan at this hour. Perhaps to Larkana, I consoled myself. Perhaps in their concern for secrecy they had arranged for a special plane. I kept waiting for one to land, but none came. Instead I sat and I sat and I sat for four hours until I saw the dawn break.

At 6.30, an ordinary passenger plane appeared on the tarmac. I was loaded onto the flight, a policewoman in the seat beside me, two behind me, and two across the aisle. 'Where are we going?' I asked the air hostess. The policewoman cut off her answer. 'You are under arrest and can speak to no one,' she said.

What was going on? I hadn't seen a paper during my five days in Karachi Jail and had no idea why my mother and I were being treated so harshly. It was the formation of the Movement to Restore Democracy and our challenge to Zia, I was sure, that had brought on these last waves of arrests. The newspapers had been filled with little else for the week before I was arrested. But what was allowing the regime to treat us so severely? And why was there such fear on the faces of the other passengers, even on the faces of the policemen?

The air hostess passed me a newspaper. It was dominated not by news of the MRD, but by news of the hijacking. Calling for the release of fifty-five Pakistani political prisoners, the hijackers had ordered the plane to Kabul, Afghanistan, where they had shot one of the passengers, an army officer named Major Tariq Rahim who had once been an aide-de-camp to my father. The pilot had then been forced to fly to Damascus in Syria.

I caught my breath as I read on, half of me refusing to believe the newspaper report, half of me dreading it was true. The hijackers were claiming to be members of a resistance group called Al-Zulfikar. Al-Zulfikar was said to be based in Kabul, where my brothers were living. The group's leader, the article claimed, was my brother Mir.

Thirty-one, thirty-two, thirty-three. Seven strokes to go with the hairbrush. Ninety-seven, ninety-eight. Count to one hundred while brushing the teeth. Walk now for fifteen minutes in the open courtyard. Discipline. Routine. I must not deviate. Up and down the open sewer running through the dusty prison yard, along the empty, barred cells facing my own cell in the locked enclosure. The prison compound, the jailers tell me, has been entirely emptied because of me. The regime has placed me in utter isolation.

Besides the jailers who unlock my cavernous open cage in the morning to bring me a cup of weak tea and bread for breakfast, weak lentil soup, boiled pumpkin and a twice-weekly tiny serving of fish for lunch or supper before locking me in again, I see no one. On the rare occasions I hear a human voice in the five months I am in solitary confinement in Sukkur, it is to give me depressing news. 'Today fifty more were arrested,' the jail authorities would say on their weekly rounds. 'Today a political prisoner is to be whipped.'

Like the Soviet move into Afghanistan, the hijacking had come at a critical time for Zia. On the threshold of being forced out of office by popular uprising, Zia was using the event to falsely link the PPP with terrorism. The timing was so incredible that it led many to conjecture that Zia had orchestrated the hijacking himself. If so, it was very effective. Thirteen days after the hijacking began and only minutes before the hijackers' deadline to blow up the plane, the regime agreed to meet their demands to release the fifty-five political prisoners. What did fifty-five prisoners matter now that the regime had imprisoned thousands of its political opposition, and charged many of them with terrorism? The MRD challenge was no longer even mentioned in the papers. The hijacking and Al-Zulfikar had all the coverage.

Locked up in my cell in Sukkur, I didn't yet know about Zia's efforts to link the PPP, and particularly my mother and me, to Al-Zulfikar. Instead, I concentrated on getting released. I felt relieved when my lawyer, Mr Lakho, visited me at Sukkur to draw up an appeal against my detention. Once again I'd been helped by an honest jailer. The letter I'd written to the Sindh High Court had been delivered after all. But both the jailer's efforts and those of Mr Lakho would prove to be fruitless.

On March 23, three or four days after Mr Lakho's visit, the military regime issued a 'Provisional Constitutional Order'. 'General Zia shall have, and shall be deemed to always have had, powers to amend the constitution,' it read. Using the new Order, Zia immediately struck down the authority of the civil courts to hear challenges to Martial Law sentences. The appeal I'd filed through Mr Lakho, and that of every other political prisoner, was now irrelevant. We could be arrested, tried, sentenced and executed by a military court without any legal recourse at all.

Zia also used the new Provisional Court Order to purge the courts of any judicial opposition. All judges were now required to swear an oath upholding the supremacy of Martial Law and Zia as Chief Martial Law Administrator. The judges who refused to take the oath were dismissed. Others were dismissed before they had the chance to take the oath. One quarter of Pakistan's judiciary was eliminated by the regime's new order, including all the judges who had been overruling the verdicts of death and rigorous imprisonment for political prisoners. 'If it is a question of sharing power with the judiciary, I will not have it,' Zia was quoted as saying in the *Guardian*. 'They are there to interpret the law.' International law associations and again Amnesty International lodged strong protests with the regime, but they did no good. Civil law in Pakistan had effectively ceased to exist. And Mr Lahko was not allowed to contact me again.

Time, relentless, monotonous. To keep my brain stimulated, I recorded everything that was happening to me in a thin little notebook a sympathetic jailer smuggled into my cell. That passed some of the time. I was allowed one newspaper a day, a new edition of *Dawn* for interior Sindh. Read it slowly, I kept reminding myself, word for word. Fishing stories. Puzzles for children on Friday, the Muslim sabbath. Recipes. But I would be finished with the paper in an hour.

'Can you bring me *Time* or *Newsweek*?' I asked the jail superintendent on his weekly visit.

'They are communist publications and are not allowed,' he told me.

'They are hardly communist, but from the centre of capitalism,' I argued.

'They are communist.'

'What books do you have in your library?' I tried.

'We have no library here.'

As March turned into April, I began to dread the arrival of the newspaper. The hijacking continued to be front page news. So did the involvement of my brother Mir. In one interview I read, Mir took responsibility for the hijacking of the PIA plane. In another, he denied it. All the government papers insinuated, however, that Al-Zulfikar was the armed wing of the PPP.

What a fraudulent charge. The whole premise on which the PPP was based was to effect change peacefully by political means, to work within a legal framework. Why else had we pressed so hard for elections, entered the elections in spite of every trick Zia had thrown at us, continued to press for elections in the face of his Martial Law guns? The hearts and loyalty of the people could never be captured by force. Even Zia must have known that. Still the regime was continuing to twist whatever truth there was about Al-Zulfikar to destroy the MRD, the PPP, and the Bhuttos.

Alone in my cell at Sukkur, I was becoming convinced that the authorities were preparing to kill me. One jail official told me nervously that I was going to be tried secretly by a military court right here in the prison and sentenced to death. Another said that the death cells in another courtyard were being emptied in preparation for my transfer. Security at Sukkur was being stepped up, he reported, following rumours that my brothers were going to try to rescue me following my death sentence. There were other rumours, too, that I was about to be moved to a torture centre in Baluchistan to extract a 'confession' of my involvement in the hijacking of the PIA plane. 'There are terrible days ahead for you,' one whispered sympathetically to me. 'You should pray for your survival.'

The Inspector General of Jails came to Sukkur on his inspection rounds and confirmed the rumours. 'They are torturing people to get them to involve you in Al-Zulfikar,' the kind-looking grey-haired man whispered to me, trying to caution me of the dangers that lay ahead.

'But I am innocent. They cannot implicate me,' I said naïvely.

The Inspector General shook his head. 'I have seen a boy from your own home town of Larkana with his toe-nails pulled out,' he said, tears filling his eyes. 'I don't know how many can put up with that without breaking.'

I didn't want to believe him or the jail staff. In order to survive, it was important not to accept reality. To accept reality was to accept the threat. Subconsciously, however, my body registered the tension. My internal problems worsened. As there was no privacy in my cell, the jail matron had learned of my gynaecological condition soon after my arrival at Sukkur and a doctor had been summoned. But I had been told nothing about her diagnosis.

I began to push away the food the jailers brought to me, finding it difficult to swallow. I ate almost nothing, yet I became convinced that I was getting fat. My stomach seemed to extend. My rib cage felt larger. I realise now that I had become anorexic.

As I lost more and more weight, the jail authorities who had been telling me that the regime wanted to sentence me to death now became nervous that I might die on my own. 'Pack up all your things. You are being shifted to Karachi,' the jail matron told me early on the morning of April 16, five weeks after my arrival at Sukkur.

'Why?' I asked.

'Your health is poor. We are taking you to Karachi.' At Karachi airport, the police told me they were taking me home.

I was ecstatic. 70 Clifton. Pure, cool water instead of the yellow jail water. My own bed instead of the rope cot. Four solid walls instead of bars. I thought my ordeal was over. It wasn't.

'This isn't my home,' I protested when, exhausted after the journey, I was taken inside a house I'd never seen.

'We want you to see another doctor first,' my police escort explained. 'Then we will take you to your house.'

I looked at the unfamiliar woman coming towards me. 'Why don't you take me home where my own doctor will see me?' I said. The policemen said nothing.

The doctor had a kind face, at least. 'The doctors in Sukkur think you have uterine cancer,' she told me quietly, after examining me. 'I'm not sure. We'll have to do an exploratory operation.'

Cancer? At twenty-eight? I looked at her disbelievingly. Was the threat of cancer real? Or were they just trying to disorient me again? She, like all the doctors I had seen, was chosen by the regime.

As we talked, she was scribbling on a pad. 'Don't worry. I am a friend and sympathiser,' read the note she passed me. 'You can trust me.' But could I? I didn't have one reason to trust anyone.

'You said you were taking me to 70 Clifton,' I told the police when we continued on through Karachi in the jeep. 'This is not the way.'

'You'll go home later,' they told me. 'First we are taking you to visit your mother in Karachi Central Jail.'

I got very excited. I hadn't seen my mother or heard from her since our arrests over a month ago. I needed to talk to her badly about my condition, about the state of the MRD, about the charges of high treason I was sure the regime was going to lodge against us.

'Mummy! Mummy!' I called out as I rushed into the Rest House. 'Mummy, it's Pinkie. I'm here!'

There was no answer. Another lie. My mother was being held in another ward, one jailer told me in secret. I applied to see her immediately. I never received a reply. The next day, instead of taking me to 70 Clifton, the police took me to a large public hospital. Its corridors were deserted, without the crowds of family who usually accompanied their relatives right up to the door of the operation room. I felt so alone without my own family. When I woke up after the operation, I was relieved to see my sister Sanam there. At least the regime had given her permission to come. But she was very upset by her visit:

Sanam:

The hospital was huge. I didn't know where to go or who even to ask about my sister. As soon as I mentioned her name, everyone froze and stared at me. I was so frightened. I hadn't been out of the house for months. Pakistan was a terrifying place at that time, especially for anyone named Bhutto, but I had nowhere else to go.

'Please, can you help me?' I asked one person after another in the endless halls. Go here. Go there, they told me. Suddenly I heard a woman screaming. 'My God, it's my sister,' I said to the woman next to me. 'That's not your sister. She's just here for a little operation,' replied the woman, who must have been an intelligence agent. 'The woman who is screaming is in labour.'

I knew it was Pinkie. I just knew it. I rushed after the sounds of the screaming to find her being pushed rapidly down the hall from the operating room on a hospital trolley, surrounded by policemen. There were tubes coming out of her arms and her nose. 'They're going to kill me! They're going to kill Papa!' she was shouting, still half under the anaesthetic. 'Stop them! Somebody, stop them!'

I saw one white hair on her head. To me that was the limit, the last straw. She'd been locked up for so many birthdays, locked up without a single human soul. And what had she got for it? One white hair.

I sat by her bed in the ward until she woke up. I thought they'd let me spend the afternoon with her. They only let me stay half an hour. On the way out, I saw her doctor. 'Tell your sister she's all right,' the doctor said. But I never got the chance. That afternoon they took her back to Karachi Central Jail.

Roaring in my ears. Blackness advancing then receding. I open my eyes in Karachi Central Jail to find a policewoman going through my handbag, taking out the tiny notebook with my notes in it from Sukkur. 'What are you doing?' I say groggily to her. She looks at me, startled. 'All right,' she says, putting the notebook back in my bag. When she leaves, a sixth sense forces me out of bed. Feverish and delirious, I drag myself into the bathroom and burn the notebook. Within an hour, a policeman and policewoman are back. 'Your sister passed you something. Where is it?' they demand. So that's what they think the notebook was. 'I don't know what you're talking about,' I say. 'You're lying,' they yell at me, going through my handbag and my few items of clothing. Their anger increases when they find nothing.

'Get up. Hurry,' two policewomen shout at me the next morning. I feel too weak to stand. 'The doctor said I shouldn't be moved for forty-eight hours,' I try to protest. The police pay no attention, throwing my few things in a bag. As they hurry me into a car and then onto a plane, I feel myself sinking. Their voices seem to come from far away. Waves of darkness roll towards me. Please don't let me sink into them. I don't want to faint. But I fall into blackness. When I start to regain consciousness several hours later in my cell at Sukkur, I hear voices. 'She's alive,' I hear someone say. Another voice breaks in. 'She shouldn't have been moved so soon,' it says. I sink back into the darkness, but this time it is more peaceful. I have survived.

I didn't know then how lucky I was. Jam Sadiq Ali, a former minister in the PPP government living in political exile in London told me years later that he'd received a desperate call from Pakistan during my brief hospitalisation. 'Do something,' he was told. 'They're planning to kill her on the operating table.' He had held a press conference and disclosed the threat on my life, thereby pre-empting whatever plans the regime might have had to kill me.

For weeks after the operation, I remained tired and anaemic at Sukkur, too depleted to walk. The junior jail staff became much more open in their sympathy. At great risk to themselves, they smuggled me a pen and a new notebook, as well as a few copies of *Newsweek*. One even brought me some fresh fruit. I spent as much time as possible recording events taking place outside the Sukkur walls, writing in my notebook, on the margins of newspapers, on every scrap of paper I could find. The jailers took the papers away with them every night in case there was a surprise inspection. If anything was found, they would lose their jobs. I waited impatiently for the papers to be returned in the morning.

Notes from jail diaries:

April 20, 1981: 'The regime-backed Urdu newspaper *Jang* headlined a BBC interview with Mir Murtaza Bhutto who said that he was in Kabul at the time of the hijacking but he did not know about it until after it had occurred. Mir Murtaza said his mother and sister who are in Pakistan, had not given their agreement to Al-Zulfikar. He was not working with the Pakistan People's Party and had had no contact at all with his mother and sister.'

April 21: Dawn. 'Radio Australia last night quoted Mir as having said in Bombay recently that his Al-Zulfikar organisation, also known as the Pakistan Liberation Army, could "turn Pakistan up and down" and was now pledged to violence to oust the administration. Al-Zulfikar, Mir said, had conducted at least fifty-four other operations inside Pakistan, including the bomb explosion in the stadium at Karachi before the Pope arrived there. Asked about reports that his organisation's headquarters were in Kabul, he replied: "We do have a presence there, but our headquarters are inside Pakistan."'

My heart sank as I recorded the news items. If only I could talk to Mir, see him. It had been five years. I only knew what he and Shah Nawaz looked like now from pictures in the press. As much as I understood Mir's frustration and anger, his statements, whether real or misconstrued by the regime, were making it far more dangerous for me and other members of the PPP. Zia could use them as a pretext to finish the PPP off. He couldn't get to my brothers, but he could get to us.

On April 28, Mir was put on Pakistan's 'most wanted' list. And the Deputy Martial Law Administrator unexpectedly came to see me during an inspection tour of the prison. He walked into my cell accompanied by the jail superintendent and some other official. We sat on the only two chairs.

'Why have I been detained?' I asked him.

'Because of Al-Zulfikar,' he replied.

'I had nothing to do with Al-Zulfikar.'

'We found the blueprint of Al-Zulfikar in your room which gave away their plans in detail,' he said. I didn't know what he was talking about.

'I never even heard of Al-Zulfikar until the hijacking,' I insisted.

'It is for the court to decide about your association with Al-Zulfikar, the stadium bombing, and Lala Assad.'

Lala Assad? The vice-president of the student's wing in Sindh? I knew Lala Assad. He was an engineering student in Khairpur. I couldn't believe he was involved in Al-Zulfikar, if indeed such a group existed at all. But the regime was obviously using Al-Zulfikar as an excuse to rid themselves of as many PPP loyalists as possible. Another man had been arrested as an accomplice of the hijackers, the Deputy Martial Law Administrator told me — Nasser Baloach. I knew him too. Nasser Baloach was the labour representative of the PPP in the gigantic Karachi Steel Mills.

'What I can conclude from the talks this morning,' I wrote in my diary after he left, 'is that the regime thinks I conspired with Lala Assad and the others in the Stadium blast as part of Al-Zulfikar. I can hardly believe it. It sounds so surrealistic and eerie. The innocent are persecuted. The criminals rule. What a world.'

The world grew infinitely more ominous two days later.

'PAPERS PROVE THAT BHUTTO LADIES HAD KNOWLEDGE ABOUT THE PROCEEDINGS' read the headlines of *Jang*. My heart stopped beating for a second and a chill crept up my spine. They must have been referring to the 'blueprint' the Deputy Martial Law Administrator claimed to have found in my room. The regime was obviously preparing the country for another trial of the Bhuttos.

'We seem to be caught in a nightmare,' I wrote in my diary on April 30. 'First the shock of learning about Al-Zulfikar and Mir. Now the regime's determination to make us part of what we were not. It seems so fantastic. But then, why should it? They did the same thing with Papa. Now they want to repeat a fraud which the world knew was a fraud. Or perhaps they think the world won't know it's a fraud. What matters is the truth. But what opportunity does a military court provide for showing that? Unable to defeat us politically, Zia is seeking physical elimination and destruction.' What I didn't know was the depth of brutality the regime had sunk to in its efforts to destroy us.

Baldia Centre and Division 555 in Karachi. Lahore Fort and Birdwood Barracks in Lahore. Attock Fort in the north of Punjab. Chaklala Air Force Base outside Rawalpindi. Mach Jail and Khalli Camp, Baluchistan. The

names of these torture centres were creeping into the lives of PPP supporters, as well as into the increasingly concerned reports of Amnesty
International and other human rights organisations. And all to implicate
the PPP, my mother and me in Al-Zulfikar.

It would be years before I learned the details of what happened in
these torture centres. Chains. Blocks of ice. Chilis inserted into the prisoners' rectums. It sickened me to hear the stories of my friends and colleagues, to have to recognise the cruelty that human beings are capable of.
But there has to be a record of the suffering people endured under the
brutality of Zia's Martial Law regime.

Faisal Hayat, lawyer, landowner, former member of the National Assembly from Punjab:

Four hundred police headed by the superintendent of the police and a
colonel of the army intelligence surrounded my house in Lahore on April
12, 1981, at 3.30 in the morning. They beat the servants and broke into
the house. My sister, who was recovering from liver surgery, was dragged
from her bedroom. They dragged my mother out of her room and broke
down my bedroom door. 'This is the headquarters of Al-Zulfikar,' they
told me, grabbing me by the neck. 'We are here to confiscate the rocket
launchers, bazookas, submachine guns and ammunition you have stored in
your basement.' I looked at them dumbstruck. 'Search all you want,' I said.
'This is a family home, not a headquarters. We don't even have a basement.'
They arrested me anyway.

I spent the first twenty-four hours in jail with no food or water. Then I
was blindfolded and taken to Lahore Fort, the 450-year-old brick-walled fort
from the time of the Moguls. Shah Jehan, the creator of the Taj Mahal, built
the beautiful Palace of Mirrors in Lahore Fort. My family and I used to stroll
in the shade of the Summer Pavilion where the Mogul emperors created
pools of water lilies. But after the hijacking, the Lahore Fort was known only
for its tortures. It became Pakistan's answer to the Bastille in France.

There were about twenty-five to thirty of us arrested at the same time:
Jehangir Badar, additional Secretary-General of the PPP Punjab, Shaukat
Mahmood, the General Secretary, Nazim Shah, our Finance Secretary, Mukh-
tar Awan, a former Minister, all high government officials. It was a miserable, very miserable state of affairs.

Every two days I was taken to be interrogated. I never knew exactly
when. They came for me at 6.00 in the morning, in the evening, in the
dead of night. I never knew. Though we were already in prison, we were
taken in handcuffs to be grilled by Brigadier Rahib Qureshi, Chief-of-Staff
to the Martial Law Administrator of Punjab, and Abdul Qayyum, the
Chief of Provincial Intelligence. The names and faces of these two men
will be with me for the rest of my life.

'We are giving you the chance of your life,' they said to me while I was forced to stand in front of them hour after hour after hour. 'You are a young man. You come from a good family. You have a future. All you have to do is agree to testify against Begum Nusrat Bhutto and Miss Benazir Bhutto in the hijacking case.'

I refused. And their temptations escalated. 'You are in politics,' they said. 'We will make you a minister.'

'You are in textiles,' they said. 'Your permission to put up a new mill was cancelled because of your political activities. We will reinstate that permission now. You will be rich.'

When I continued to resist them, they changed their tactics. 'We can put you behind bars for twenty-five years,' they threatened. 'We are a Martial Law government. We don't need evidence. We can convict you here and now.'

I spent three months locked into a cell five feet by four feet. Being six feet tall, I could never stretch out day or night. There were four identical cells in my block with the open bars facing west. From noon on, the sun blazed in on us with no relief, the temperature often reaching 115 degrees. There was no way to get away from the heat. Fans were installed on pedestals outside our cells, positioned to blow through the corridor of heat until the air reaching us seemed to be on fire.

My lips swelled and were so painful I couldn't swallow any water. My skin blistered and round, dark circles spread all over my body from my face to my toes. I had sores all over. In desperation, I tied my shirt to the bars one afternoon to block the sun, and the guards snatched it away from me altogether. I didn't get my shirt back for three days.

One by one the others in my cellblock began to succumb to heatstroke. I could hear them fainting and calling out in their delirium. I was the youngest, twenty-seven then, and held out the longest. But after two months I collapsed. When I woke up two days later I was in an underground cellar the jail authorities had turned into a makeshift hospital. When the doctors were sure I had regained my senses, I was returned to my cell.

The nights soon became a bigger torment than the days. Neither I, nor any of the others, had any bedding, not even a sheet. We had to curl up on the broken cement floor of the cell next to the open stinking hole which served as a toilet. Ants crawled over us, cockroaches, lizards, rats, every insect and rodent which lives in the earth. And there was no respite from the heat. The prison authorities installed 500 watt bulbs into the seven foot ceilings and left the lights on all night. They were careful to sink the sockets deep into the ceiling so none of us could commit suicide by plunging our hands into the wiring. I think I might have, had it been possible.

My health deteriorated rapidly. The conditions were so unsanitary it's remarkable that anyone lived. The miserable food they brought us, which we had ten seconds to grab from a tray outside the bars, consisted of bread with pebbles and sand in it, and thin curry encrusted with flies. I suffered from repeated bouts of dysentery, malaria, cholera. At one point my temperature went up to 105. My head was splitting with pain, the light at night slicing into my eyes so that I could not keep myself from screaming in agony. My body alternated between burning and freezing and I couldn't stop being sick. For days I lay in my own vomit.

'Look who is here to see you,' Brigadier Qureshi and Major General Qayyum said to me one day. I blinked at the familiar figure standing in front of me in the interrogation room. They had brought my mother.

'Twenty-five years he will be in prison,' the Martial Law Administrators said to my mother. 'Twenty-five years unless he consents to testify against the Bhuttos.'

My mother's face was streaming with tears. She was a broken woman, with her brother-in-law tortured and driven into exile, her son almost destroyed, and our ancestral agricultural lands brown and withered because the regime had cut off our water supply. But in spite of the fact that she was a lady of soft heart and very kind soul, she showed an inner strength that day I had never seen before.

'Don't let them intimidate you, Faisal,' she said to me right in front of them. 'Don't let them force you into going against your will. You must do what your conscience tells you to.'

'I have put my faith in God,' I told her. 'These men are merely human beings. If it is God's destiny for me to spend twenty-five years in prison, I can't help it. But I will not betray the trust of the Bhutto family.'

I couldn't betray them. None of the political prisoners in Lahore Fort could. We all came from good families with long histories of religious and government service. We were educated. We had names in society. We couldn't have lied and then lived with the dishonour, in spite of all the regime's temptations and threats.

Not one of the former government officials agreed to give false evidence against the Bhuttos. After three months the authorities finally gave up and transferred us to local district jails. I was sent to Gujranwala Jail forty miles north of Lahore for another two months. The regime didn't dare release us directly back into society from Lahore Fort. Even they would have been embarrassed by our condition.

Qazi Sultan Mahmood, former employee of Flashman's Hotel, Rawalpindi, General Secretary of the PPP in Rawalpindi City:

I had already spent one year's rigorous imprisonment in Central Jail Mianwali for leading processions in protest against Chairman Bhutto's death sentence. I had also been fired without compensation from my position at the hotel because of my work with the PPP. After the hijacking I was arrested again and taken first to Rawalpindi Jail, then Gujranwala Jail, and then to the Lahore Fort. It was a terrible place.

'Tell us the connection between Miss Bhutto and Al-Zulfikar,' the jail authorities asked me over and over again. When I said she had never talked to me about it, that I knew nothing about the hijacking, they whipped me with leather straps and beat me on the head with bamboo rods. That was just the beginning.

I am a very small man, three feet high and weighing forty-eight pounds. So it was easy for them to make great sport of me. When I refused to support their lies, they put heavy handcuffs on me and told me to raise my arms over my head. My arms are quite short and when I fell down with the effort, they stepped on me, laughing uproariously. Often, they picked me up by the flesh on my stomach and either hurled me to the ground, or tossed me back and forth between them like a ball.

They blindfolded me and led me around, I don't know where. 'You are going to die now unless you confirm the Bhutto ladies' involvement with Al-Zulfikar,' they told me during these sessions. When I refused, they held me by one foot and hung me over the high walls of the prison. 'Why do you want to die?' they said. 'Just sign this confession.' 'Go ahead and kill me,' I told them. 'But I can't tell you what I don't know.'

For thirty-five days they tortured me like this constantly. One of their favourite cruelties was to make me stand naked in front of them, then to weave a pole between my legs and tell me to hang on to it. It was not possible for me to stay in this position for even two or three minutes and I would pitch forward on my face. Blood would spurt from my nose and my teeth, making them laugh.

'Oh, you are a very important leader,' they taunted me. 'What was it about you that Mr Bhutto liked? Is there something special? You are the sort of man people should hate. You are not a beautiful chap. The something special must be that you are doing something secret with Al-Zulfikar.' Then they would kick and beat me. The wounds on my back, on my legs, on my hands became infected, but they wouldn't let me see a doctor.

I spent another thirty-five days in solitary confinement, locked in total darkness. I was just left in the dirt, in a living grave. I was given very little food, one rusk of bread and perhaps a chapatti with thin lentil sauce. They dropped the food through the small hole in the cell door. I was not tall enough to reach the opening so I had to scrape the food out of the dirt. They dropped my one cup of tea a day as well. I tried to catch the cup, but it almost always spilled. If I was lucky, I got one or two sips. My head and feet were often scalded.

When I was released after two months, I addressed a reception for other political prisoners in Rawalpindi. My speech dwelt on the horrible conditions and treatment of political prisoners under General Zia. The *Guardian* carried the story in England as did the Associated Press all over the world. I was arrested again and kept in solitary confinement in Kot Lakhpat Jail for two years and four months. A military summary court then sentenced me to three years hard labour in Multan Central Jail, then Attock Jail. I was finally released on June 15, 1985.

My nephews have been supporting me ever since because I am still blacklisted by the government. But I continue to work for the PPP. I will never give in. I will not leave Benazir Bhutto while I am alive.

Pervez Ali Shah, now Senior Vice President Sindh PPP; then a leading member of the Sindh PPP and former publisher and chief editor of *Javed*, a weekly magazine:

I was playing a game of cricket with my sons on March 24, 1981, when an unmarked car drove up and men in plain clothes told me to get in. They said they were police but had no warrant. They took me away without telling my family where I was going.

I had been arrested three times before, the first time with my 62-year-old father on October 1, 1977, the day Zia first cancelled the elections. Then cars and jeeps full of police had come to our home in Khairpur in interior Sindh, where I was running for the Provincial Assembly on a PPP ticket. 'Get moving,' the police ordered us, handcuffing my father's arm to mine and parading us through the streets while the cars and jeeps followed behind. People gathered on the footpaths in amazement to watch us walk by. Common criminals weren't treated this way, much less members of respectable families. At first I felt so ashamed that I took my handkerchief and tried to cover up the cuffs. But when I saw that there were tears in the people's eyes I took the kerchief off. After sleeping on the floor of the police station for twenty-five days, a major released me but sentenced my father to a year in Sukkur jail.

A year later, when thousands in Khairpur began courting arrest by calling for Mr Bhutto's release, they came again. This time I wasn't at home, though the police looking for me even entered the women's quarters which for generations no outsider had ever entered. They pulled the clothes out of the cupboards, and emptied drawers on the floor. They finally arrested me at a friend's wedding I was attending, and put me in a cell measuring ten feet by seven feet with twenty-one others. I was charged with arson. When they could find no witnesses, they sentenced me to a year in jail for inciting crowds.

But the arrest in 1981 was the worst. I was blindfolded and driven the six hours from Karachi to Khairpur Central Jail, where I was held for three days without food. Then I was moved again, first to Hyderabad, and then in the middle of the night back to Frere police station in Karachi. 'At least give me a cup of tea,' I begged the police. 'You'll get everything you need at 555,' they told me. 555 was notorious, the headquarters of the Central Intelligence Agency in Karachi.

163

Once again I was loaded into a police van. This time I was released into a pitch-black cell whose ceiling just touched my head. 'Watch out,' voices cried out as my foot trod on other prisoners. I don't know how long we all huddled there in the darkness.

I was taken to Colonel Salim, the head of Interservices intelligence. He handed me a piece of paper and a pencil. 'Write down that Miss Benazir is the leader of the bomb blast and that Begum Bhutto is involved in the hijacking,' he told me. 'How can I write something I don't know,' I answered. He asked again. I refused. He called in Lala Khan, the famous torturer of 555, who strapped my legs to a wooden rack, and began to rap my kneecaps with a long wooden stick. The pain built up and built up until tears ran down my cheeks. 'I don't know anything about the bomb blast or the hijacking,' I begged. Lala kept hitting. When he finished I could not move either leg. 'Stand up, or you will never be able to walk again,' he told me coldly.

I was moved to another cell. Often members of the four different branches of intelligence came to ask me to implicate Benazir and Begum Sahiba. When I refused, they called Lala.

Sometimes he made me watch while he hung others upside-down and beat them until they screamed. Sometimes I was tied to the ceiling so that just my toes touched the floor and left to hang there for hours. Often at night guards stationed around my cell kept me from sleeping, asking me silly questions like my name and jabbing me with sticks if I didn't respond. When I was completely exhausted and starving from the two glasses of water and watery lentils I was given every day, I would be called in to have lunch with an interrogator. 'Look at yourself. You're an educated man from a good family,' they would say as I sat in my filthy jail clothes over a sumptuous lunch and glasses of hot tea. 'Why make things hard? Just say that Benazir and Begum Bhutto were involved in the hijacking and all this will be over.' When I refused, I was taken away and tortured.

After three months I was moved to Karachi Central Jail, and later to Khairpur where my family was allowed a monthly visit. In the seven times I was hauled before a military court, the regime produced no witnesses and framed no charges. In February of 1985, the regime finally sentenced me to a year's imprisonment for 'propagating political opinions prejudicial to the ideology, integrity and security of Pakistan'. No allowance was made for the then almost four years I had already spent in prison. My wife had a nervous breakdown under the strain of trying to manage our small business in Karachi and bring up our three children.

Pervez Ali Shah was adopted as a 'prisoner of conscience' by Amnesty International. In the dreadful period following the formation of the MRD and the hijacking, so were many others. Throughout 1981, Amnesty reported, the number of political prisoners being tortured in Pakistan in-

creased dramatically. Most of the victims were students, political party workers, trade unionists and lawyers belonging to political parties. But the
hijacking brought a new category of prisoner as well. 'In 1981, for the first
time, Amnesty International received press reports that four women political
prisoners had been tortured,' stated Amnesty's report covering this period.
'Nasira Rana and Begum Arif Bhatti, the wives of PPP officials; Farkhanda
Bukhari, a PPP member; and Mrs Safooran, mother of six.' I knew them all.

Nasira Rana, April 13, Lahore:

My husband, who was a member of the MRD, was in Karachi in early
April when the police suddenly burst into my living room. 'Who are you?'
I said in a fright to the man holding a rifle to my head. He was not
wearing a uniform, but an open shirt and black trousers. I can still see the
gold chain he had around his neck.

'I will tell you who I am,' he said menacingly. 'I am a Major in the
Pakistan army.' He was pressing the gun into my forehead, hurting me.
I pushed it away. He took the rifle butt and hit me with it, breaking
the bones in my hand and finger while my twelve-year-old daughter
screamed.

'Where is your husband?' he demanded, while other army men ransacked
the house. 'He is not here,' I told him. He raised his rifle butt again. 'Where
is the door to the secret passage?' he said. 'There is no secret passage,' I
replied. He locked my daughter and me in a room and finally they went
away. They came back fifteen days later.

'Come with us. You are under arrest,' said the Additional Superintendent
of Police and the local magistrate.

'Where are your warrants?' I asked them.

'We are the warrants,' they replied.

They took me to jail where I was forced to stand the whole night.
Every hour a new interrogator was brought in.

'Your husband is a member of Al-Zulfikar as are Benazir Bhutto and
Begum Bhutto. We know this to be a fact. Confirm. Confirm.'

Hours passed. But I was adamant. Whatever they said, I would have
will. I felt my knees begin to buckle. I reached for the chair right beside
me. 'Get away!' they shouted.

Two days later, I was taken to Lahore Fort where I was locked in a tiny
cell with another political prisoner, Begum Bhatti, whose husband had
been a Provincial Minister as well as the Revenue Minister for the Punjab.

Begum Bhatti:

Eleven different government agencies interrogated us. 'Where are your
husbands?' they kept yelling. 'They are terrorists, working with the Bhutto

ladies.'

The jail officials kept us awake all night, our third without rest. 'No sleep, Mrs Rana,' they yelled into our cell, banging the bars with clubs. 'Wake up, Begum Bhatti.'

The next day they took us to Major-General Qayyum, the Chief of Intelligence. The same questions. The same answers. At one point Major-General Qayyum grabbed me by the hair and smashed my head against the wall.

'Where is your husband?' he yelled at me.

'I don't know.'

He held cigarettes to our arms until we could smell the burning of our own flesh.

'Where are your husbands?'

I began to faint. From a distance I heard Nasira scream.

'We'll break you!' Major-General Qayyum yelled, the last words I heard before blacking out.

Nasira:

We were in the Lahore Fort for five weeks, the hottest part of the year. The heat of the sun was merciless. 'Now you'll tell us what we want,' they said, leaving us under guard in the central courtyard at noon. We stood there for hours, black spots dancing before our eyes, heads aching, tongues swelling. The guards drank water in front of us, laughing. One hour passed. Another. Who knows how long we stood there? The guard changed every three hours.

Three times they took us to a special room. Wet sponges were tied around our wrists, and wires were run through them. Every few seconds, they sent electric shocks through the wires, one after another after another. Our bodies twitched, went rigid. My broken hand was in a cast and was particularly sensitive. I finally screamed. I couldn't help it. 'We'll bring your father to be tortured,' they threatened. 'We'll bring your daughter.' The shocks went on for two hours.

Begum Bhatti:

'We had no bed in our cell and no bedding. They gave us a gunny-sack. When I went to lay it on the floor, a three-foot snake wiggled out. 'Don't scream,' I hissed at Nasira as much as to myself. Somehow, the snake made me the angriest. I grabbed it up in the sack, mashed it against the wall then twisted its neck. The policewoman screamed when she saw it.

The authorities tried to make us sign a statement that they were not responsible for the snake, that the snake had got into the cell on its own. We refused to sign it.

Implicate Benazir. Implicate Begum Sahiba. Implicate your husbands, our interrogation continued. 'If your wife were in my position, would she tell?' I asked the interrogator. 'Yes,' he said. 'Then she is a very shameful woman,' I said.

Nasira:

I got word from one of the guards that my husband had been captured and brought to the Fort. I don't know what they did to him. I don't want to know. He had a heart attack after he was tortured. He turned blue and gasped for breath. They took him to the hospital because they didn't want it said he died under torture. It was a miracle he survived.

I didn't know about any of these tortures in my isolation at Sukkur. I didn't know that Dr Niazi, at the urging of his wife and family after the hijacking, had fled Pakistan minutes before the police came to arrest him for the third time. He suffered a near fatal heart attack in Kabul from the strain and barely survived by-pass surgery in London where he would remain until 1988.

Yasmin, too, barely escaped arrest. 'Is Yasmin Niazi at home?' the police had asked at the family's gate. 'No,' Yasmin had the presence to say. When the police decided to take her mother instead, Yasmin and Mrs Niazi had a brief and whispered fight. 'I'm going to tell them who I am,' Yasmin said to her mother out of hearing of the police. 'Yasmin, if you do this I will die. So either you have me in prison or you have my dead body. You can choose which you want,' she replied. Yasmin stayed quiet as the police took Mrs Niazi to Rawalpindi Central Jail where she was held with three other women in the cell directly across from my father's former death cell. For the five days of Mrs Niazi's imprisonment, the cell was so crowded that the women had to take turns sleeping.

Yasmin went into hiding for three months while the police continued to search for her. She was in great danger. In very poor health and worried about his daughter, Dr Niazi bought a PIA airline ticket for Yasmin to join him in London. But how was she to be got out of the country? After her release from prison, Mrs Niazi telephoned the British Embassy. Luckily, Yasmin had been born in England and the embassy said they could get her a British passport within forty-eight hours if Mrs Niazi could find the passport Yasmin had travelled on with her as an infant. Mrs Niazi found the eighteen-year-old passport in the bottom of a box in their basement.

'I couldn't go to the airport with Yasmin because I was afraid I'd be recognised. I put a *burqa* over her and sent her with her sister,' Mrs Niazi told me years later in a voice that still trembled. 'Yasmin was wanted on

Zia's personal orders. There were arrest orders on her in Islamabad. She was wanted in every province. There wasn't a list that didn't have her name on it. She got out by an act of God.'

'There's no entry visa on your passport,' the immigration officer said to Yasmin at the airport. 'That's very odd,' Yasmin bluffed. 'There must be a mistake.' As he turned to look up her name on a list, the lights suddenly went out in the airport. For over a minute the airport was plunged into darkness, creating chaos among the passengers trying to reach their flights. When the lights came back on, the immigration officer was in such a hurry that he just stamped her passport quickly and sent her through.

Yasmin arrived safely in London where she later married my cousin Tariq, himself a political refugee. They are still living there with their two small children.

The heat reached Sukkur in May: a dry, searing heat which turned my cell into an oven. The winds blew constantly through the open sides of my cell, winds heated to 110 degrees, 120 degrees, by the surrounding desert of Interior Sindh. A constant dust storm swirled in my cell. Sticky with sweat, I was often coated with grit.

My skin split and peeled, coming off my hands in sheets. More boils erupted on my face. The sweat dripped into them, burning like acid. My hair, which had always been thick, began to come out by the handful. I had no mirror, but I could feel my scalp with my fingertips: damp, gritty, and naked. Every morning I would find new clumps of hair on my pillow.

Insects crept into the cell like invading armies. Grasshoppers. Mosquitoes. Stinging flies. Bees. They were forever buzzing in my face or crawling up my legs. I flailed my arms to keep them away, but there were so many it was often useless. Insects came up through the cracks in the floor and through the open bars from the courtyard. Big black ants. Cockroaches. Seething clumps of little red ants. Spiders. I tried pulling the sheet over my head at night to hide from their bites, pushing it back when it got too hot to breathe.

Water. I dreamed of cool, clear water. The jail water I was given to drink was pale brown or yellow. It smelled like stale eggs, did not taste like water or quench my thirst. But the jail authorities cut off the fresh water Mujib, a lawyer who lived nearby, had tried to send to me. 'It is for your own good,' the jail superintendent told me. 'These people are your enemies. Your own party leaders want you out of the way.' On another day, he told me that instead of delivering the fresh oranges Mujib had sent me, he had eaten them himself. 'It was to save your life,' he added. 'He could have injected them with poison.' It was theatre of the absurd.

'Can you please provide me with insect spray?' I asked the prison authorities.

'Oh, no,' they said. 'It is poisonous. We wouldn't want anything to happen to you.'

What was all the talk about poison? I suddenly realised they were implanting the idea of suicide in my head. What tidier solution could there be for the regime than to announce that Benazir Bhutto had killed herself? Problem solved. The proof came in the shape of a bottle of Phenyle, a strong cleaning detergent left all the time in my cell. The label was covered with a picture of a skull and crossbones. 'Be sure not to leave it in her cell,' the jail superintendent said loudly to the woman who cleaned the cell each time he came on his weekly visit. 'Don't let the Phenyle out of your sight. She might want to end her misery.' But the bottle of poison remained where it was.

Were they playing with my mind? My ear began to trouble me again, my chronic condition being aggravated by the dust and sweat trickling constantly down my face. But the jail doctor kept telling me nothing was wrong. 'You are in solitary confinement and under a great deal of stress,' he said to calm me. 'Many people in your situation imagine aches and pains where there are none.' I began to half-believe him. Maybe I was just imagining the clicks which disturbed me night and day. If only it weren't so hot.

'My dearest Pinkie,' my mother wrote to me from Karachi Central Jail on May 23, telling me about her recipe for the heat. 'I pour water three to four times a day over myself to beat the heat. You should try it. I first bend my head and pour mugs of water on the back of my neck and on top of my head, then all over with my clothes on. Then I sit on my bed under the fan and it is so cooling until the clothes dry. As a matter of fact, even after the clothes dry, one is kept cool for quite sometime thereafter. With this method you don't get prickly heat [rash]. It's just marvellous. I strongly recommend it . . . With love, your Mummy.'

I followed her suggestion, dumping the entire bucket of water over my head every morning. It was much hotter in Sukkur than it was in Karachi, and I had no fan. But for the hour it took my clothes to dry in the hot wind, I was comfortable, little realising that as more water seeped into my ear, the infection was growing. 'You're just imagining it,' the jail doctor continued to say soothingly. He wasn't a specialist. I'll never know whether he did it deliberately or out of ignorance.

250 times running-on-the-spot. Forty bending exercises. Swing the arms. Twenty deep breaths. Read the papers. Ignore the continuing stories attempting to implicate my mother and me in the hijacking. Concentrate instead on the embroidery kit Mujib and his wife Almas had sent in to me: cloth, thread and a pattern book.

169

'I have finished a trolley cloth and four napkins,' I noted in my diary in mid-May. 'When I'm free I can bore everyone with "and this is what I did in jail". On a less frivolous note, the concentration that needlework requires does not permit wandering thoughts. Moreover, in the vacuum of solitary confinement, it provides a point of focus, something to do, something to build the day about and so it has a salutary effect.'

I forced myself to write at least an hour a day in my journal. 'François Mitterand has been elected by France to become the first socialist President of post-war France,' I noted in my diary on May 11. 'The Anglo-American media had run quite a ferocious anti-Giscard campaign. This election will have far-reaching effects on the politics of Europe. France may become embroiled in internal controversies while adjusting to socialist policies. This will take the thrust out of aggressive French foreign policy. Who will step in to fill the French influence among the Arab and African nations? How will France's relationship with the Federal Republic of Germany shape up now that the partnership of 'technocrats' and 'friends', Giscard and Schmidt, is broken. What of the spillover effect in Italy?'

On the same day I noted the death of Bobby Sands, an Irish political dissident. 'After sixty-six days of hunger strike, Bobby Sands finally fell victim to death in a British jail. To the British, Bobby Sands was a terrorist. But to his country, Bobby Sands fought for political liberty and rights. It is the story of the world.' Too often, though, I would let days go by without writing at all. 'I have not written properly for some time,' I chided myself in my diary on June 8. 'It is no use asking myself what there is to write about because the news from the papers can always be summarised. Without writing one loses the flow of expression and familiarity with words and sentences as well as the ability to express ideas.'

Slowly but surely, I settled into a pattern. 'Each hour has passed more slowly than a day or a week and yet I have come so far,' I noted on June 11. '"Adjusted"is not the right word. I cannot adjust to a situation which is abhorrent. To adjust is to give in. I have coped. Each moment has dragged, but it has also passed. God alone has helped me in this ordeal. Without Him, I would have perished.'

My detention at Sukkur was to end at noon on June 12. I had no idea whether I'd be set free or detained longer, possibly to face trial and execution. 'Death comes in the end and I do not fear it,' I wrote in my notes. 'The animals in the regime can only eliminate people. They cannot eliminate concepts. The concept of democracy will survive. And in the inevitable victory of democracy, we will live again. At least I will be free from the monotony of solitary confinement where one lives, but does not live.'

At 11.00 am on the day my detention ended, the order from the Deputy Martial Law Administrator arrived. He was 'pleased', he wrote, to give me a new detention order. My incarceration at Sukkur was extended until September 12.

June 21, 1981. My 28th birthday. Sukkur Central Jail.
  My sister, Sanam:

I was given permission to visit my sister on her birthday, her third in detention. My flight from Karachi was delayed, leaving me only an hour to see her. I was crying when I finally reached her cell, I was so frustrated. I had been searched and searched and searched. The prison matrons had gone through my hair which was very short at the time, emptied my bag, turned every page of the *Cosmopolitan* magazine I was bringing her. They even made me taste the food I had brought my sister to make sure it wasn't poisoned. 'I won't have any time with her at all,' I protested as the jailors slowly unlocked and relocked the four gates between her and the jail walls. They just wanted to hurt her, even on her birthday.

She received me as if she were a gracious hostess and I an honoured guest. On that day she had been sent some oranges by a friend in Sukkur and she offered me one, apologising that she had no plate to put it on, or a knife to peel it with. 'They're afraid I'll slit my wrists,' she smiled. I felt so guilty. There I was, crying and complaining about my frustrating journey. And there she was in the furnace of Sukkur, not complaining at all. She looked so ill, so skinny. I saw to my horror that her hair had got thin. I could see her scalp.

'Tell me the gossip,' she said, as if we were back in our bedrooms at home. I did have something very important to tell her, but there was a big burly policeman sitting right outside the open bars and a policewoman in the cell with us, listening to every word we said. There was no place to sit but her bed. I leaned close to her.

'Nasser wants to marry me,' I whispered.

'Don't let them whisper!' the policeman said, gripping the bars of the cell.

The policewoman moved towards us. 'Oh, Sunny, that's wonderful news. I'm so happy for you,' my sister said. The policewoman moved closer, putting her face practically between my sister and me.

'I don't want to get married with both you and Mummy in jail,' I told my sister quietly. 'I told Nasser we should wait until I have my family around me again.'

'But that's just why you shouldn't wait,' Pinkie told me. 'Who knows when we'll get out? We've both been worried about you living alone. You'll be much happier with the protection of a husband. And we'll feel more secure about you.'

'Oh Pinkie, why does it have to be this way?' I said, putting my arms around her.

'No! No!' the policeman shouted. The policewoman pulled us apart, putting her foot up on the bed to separate us.

'For goodness sake,' Pinkie said. 'We are not talking politics, but personal family news. I haven't seen my sister for months. It's my birthday. Can't you give us some privacy?'

The policeman ignored her, busy scribbling notes about our conversation in his notebook. For the rest of the hour, the policewoman stood between us. I could barely keep from crying again when I had to leave her alone in that barren, empty cell with those horrible people. 'I wish you and Nasser much happiness,' she called after me. 'Happy birthday, Pinkie,' I managed to call back while the policeman hurried me away.

To Miss Benazir Bhutto   From Begum Nusrat Bhutto
Sukkur Central Jail   Karachi Central Jail
                                         June 9, 1981

My darling Baby,

By the time this second letter of mine reaches you, it will be near your Birthday. My memory has taken me back to the day when I was happily informed by the doctor in England where your father was studying that I was pregnant. Oh! How excited and happy we were. You were our first born, our love. How we celebrated at the good news. Then at Pinto's hospital in Karachi I couldn't sleep the night after you were born because I just wanted you to be in my arms and to stare at your beautiful golden curls, your rosy face, your beautiful long-fingered hands. My heart fluttered at the sight of you.

When Papa arrived from England, you were three months old. He was shy in front of his parents but when we were alone, he stared and stared at you, then touched your face and hands, looking with wonder at the miracle of having such a lovely baby. He wanted to know how to hold you and I lifted you and gave you to him, telling him 'one hand under her head and another around her body'. He said you looked just like him. How thrilled he was. He went round and round in a circle in the room with you in his arms – I can't go on into more details because my eyes are filled with tears for the beautiful days gone by.

I remember the day you took your first step when you were only ten months old. I remember the day you talked intelligently a week before your first birthday in Quetta; the day I took you to nursery school at the age of only three and a half; the pretty little dresses I used to sew and embroider with love and affection, praying after each of my five daily prayers for your future happiness, health and long life.

Now June 21 is here and I wish you a very happy birthday, with many, many, many more to come. I cannot give you a little gift, not even a little kiss being locked up so far away from each other for another ninety days. . . . I hope, my love, you eat a proper diet and drink lots of water. Don't forget to eat fruit and vegetables also. I end with my wishes for a good future for you.

> Your ever loving
> MUMMY

Fruit and vegetables. Water. What nice thoughts from a mother. I felt terribly for her. A new detention order. How long were they going to make her suffer?

My own new detention order had elevated me to 'A' class, entitling me to a radio, television set, a refrigerator which I imagined filled with chilled, pure water, and an air conditioner. I was briefly thrilled, though I couldn't figure out how a totally open cell could be air conditioned. I needn't have bothered. The only privilege my much touted elevation to 'A' class brought me was the freedom to wander around the compound courtyard at night. No longer, the jail superintendent told me as if it were a great gift, would I be locked in my cell at night. 'I decline your "A" class status,' I wrote to the jail superintendent. 'I will not be party to your lies.'

I dreamed of being free. I dreamed of eating steak and mushrooms at the Sorbonne restaurant in Oxford. I dreamed of fresh apple cider in New England and peppermint stick ice cream from Brigham's. My father had passed the time in his death cell by conjuring up someone he knew, then remembering every single detail about him. I thought of Yolanda Kodrzycki, my roommate at Radcliffe, who, the last time I'd heard, was working as an economist in Massachusetts. I thought of Peter Galbraith who was now working for the Senate Foreign Relations Committee in Washington and had married his long time girlfriend and another of my contemporaries Anne O'Leary. I had introduced them to each other at Harvard. The time droned on. 'These days will pass,' my father had told me in prison. 'What is important is that we pass them with honour.'

I didn't have his patience. I had to get out of there. I just had to. General Abbassi, the Martial Law Administrator of Sindh, Sunny told me, had said that the regime was out to crush us physically, morally, and financially. They had moved on the latter, filing a civil suit in May to sell 70 Clifton, Al-Murtaza, our agricultural lands and other properties at public auction. I had no idea what had happened. If I lived, would I still have a home to return to, would I ever sleep in my own bed again? As the summer heat baked on, I became obsessed with getting myself transferred to 70 Clifton or Al-Murtaza. Somehow I felt that my physical presence in either of our homes would prevent the regime from seizing them. My repeated requests, not surprisingly, were turned down. 'We can't spare that many guards,' they told me, as if it required an entire regiment to detain one young woman in her home.

The jail superintendent started a new tactic to demoralise me. 'Your party officials are deserting you,' he told me, telling me stories about members of the PPP having meetings with members of the opposition parties, or even with the regime itself. 'They are all leaving you. Why are you wasting your life here? If you give up politics, your troubles will be over.'

I prayed to God to give me strength. 'If I am the only person left resisting the tyranny of the regime, then so be it,' I told them. 'I don't believe your lies. Even if everybody else capitulates, I will not.' I didn't believe the PPP leaders, some of whom had been released by July, would desert the party. I did not allow myself to believe it.

I started to pray a special prayer for my release that one of the jail matrons told me about. '*Qul Huwwa Allahu Ahad*, Say He is One God,' I started the 112th *surah* of the Quran, reciting the verse forty-one times, then breathing over a mug of water and sprinkling a little of the water in each of the four corners of the cell. I prayed for every prisoner. I prayed for my mother. I prayed for myself. By the fourth Wednesday, the jail matron told me, the prison door was supposed to open. And it did.

On the fourth Wednesday of the fourth month of my detention in Sukkur, my cell door opened and the jail authorities took me to see my mother in Karachi briefly. Four Wednesdays of rituals after that it was my mother's cell door which opened. She was released from detention in July after vomiting blood. The jail doctors diagnosed her as having an ulcer. She had a bad cough as well, which they thought might be TB.

I knew nothing about my mother's health, and only found out about her release from a jail matron. I was thrilled that my prayer had worked and redoubled my efforts at Sukkur, adding additional prayers and sprinkling more and more water for other prisoners, including me. '*Allahu Samad*', the Eternal God. On the fourth Wednesday in August, the cell door opened again. 'You're leaving,' the matron told me.

I threw my things together. Please God, I prayed, let them take me home to 70 Clifton.

The convoy of army and police didn't go near 70 Clifton. Instead they took me to Karachi Central Jail, and locked me up in my mother's old cell.

9

LOCKED IN MY MOTHER'S OLD CELL
AT KARACHI CENTRAL JAIL

Karachi Central Jail, August 15, 1981.

Flaking cement. Iron bars. And silence. Utter silence. I am back in total isolation, the cells around me in the locked ward all emptied. I strain for the sound of a human voice. There is only silence.

The cell is hot in the damp, humid weather of Karachi, and the ceiling fan provides no relief. The electricity is off again. Every day the power fails, sometimes for three hours, sometimes for longer. The jail authorities tell me it is because of a problem at the main power station. But I know that's not true. At night I can see the sky lit up by lights in other parts of the jail. Only my cell-block is in darkness.

The authorities have put me in an A-class cell reserved for high-ranking political prisoners, but once again I am not allowed A-class privileges. The cells to the right and left of mine, ordinarily used as a sitting room and kitchen, are now empty and locked. The cell in which I am held is small and dirty. The 'toilet' has no flush, and swarms with roaches and flies. Its stench mingles with that of the open sewer which runs through the jail yard outside. The only water bucket is coated with dead insects.

In the mornings I hear the jangling of keys and clicking of locks which signals the arrival of my food. Without saying a word, the grey-uniformed prison matron who sleeps in the courtyard at the far end of the cells brings me the tiffin boxes of food which the authorities allow to be sent from 70 Clifton. My throat tightens the first few times I open them to find carefully prepared creamed chicken with mushrooms, kebabs and chicken *sheeks*. Though I have little appetite, and can only take a few mouthfuls, I keep thinking of the care my mother has taken to have the food made in our kitchen at home.

I am worried about Mummy. She was allowed to visit me my second week in Karachi Central Jail and, though I was relieved to see her alive, I was shocked by her appearance. The pale, haggard woman with her nervous movements and grey hair parted in the middle and tied in a plait looked so different from the elegant and self-confident woman I knew as my mother.

Her eyes had filled with tears when she saw me, still a captive in her old cell. But we both tried to smile bravely, ignoring the jailers who crowded around us to listen to the news she hesitantly delivered. She'd caught a cough in jail, she told me quietly. She thought it was the dust, but then she started coughing blood. After several visits, the jail doctor and the authorities told her they suspected tuberculosis, a diagnosis which came as no surprise. Many people in Pakistan have tuberculosis, their lungs irritated from the constant dust, their systems depleted from malnutrition. The insanitary conditions in jail make the inmates especially susceptible to TB as well as to every other sort of disease. The prisoners often spit on the ground, releasing the viruses into the air.

Her own doctor's suspicions were even worse, my mother told me. Though she was still too weak for the bronchoscopy necessary for a diagnosis, he was not ruling out lung cancer. Lung cancer. I embraced her, trying not to register my shock, trying to be strong both for my mother and for the intelligence agents among the jailers who I knew would report back to General Zia.

'Perhaps it is not lung cancer. Wait for the bronchoscopy,' I consoled her in the firmest voice I could muster.

'He thinks it can be cured if treated in time,' she continued. 'If necessary, I can get treatment abroad.'

'You must go as soon as you can,' I heard myself saying, though inside my heart was breaking at the thought of her leaving Pakistan.

'But what about you, my darling? How can I leave you here alone?'

I assured her that I was fine. But I wasn't. For three days after her visit I lay on my bed staring up at the ceiling, immobilised by a sense of overwhelming, irrational depression. I had no will to exercise, wash myself, or change my clothes. I couldn't eat or drink. My God, I thought, I've lost my father: now I'm losing my mother. I knew I was being self-pitying, but I couldn't shake off my sense of abandonment. Even my mother's good news, that Sanam and Shah would be marrying their fiancés in September, deepened my despair. During my father's imprisonment he had cautioned us never to give the appearance that we were enjoying ourselves. 'If you go to the cinema, wear a *burqa*,' he had instructed me. Now my family seemed to have reconciled themselves to my being permanently in jail. They were carrying on with their lives and having wedding celebrations as if I didn't exist.

After three days without water I felt weak and disoriented. Don't play into Zia's hands and fall apart, a voice in my head warned me. I felt better after I forced myself to take a mugful of water from the water bucket, and to begin a puzzle in one of the Pakistani newspapers which my mother sent to the cell every day and which for days I'd ignored. But the newsprint looked fuzzy. I felt the beginnings of one of the migraine headaches I had developed since moving to Karachi Central Jail. My teeth and gums ached, as did my ear. And my hair continued to fall out.

My health problems, I learned later from a doctor, were due partly to a breakdown in the harmony of the body's systems. Normally, he told me, the cardiovascular, muscular, digestive, respiratory and nervous systems each take their due share of energy and food intake. In times of stress, however, the nervous system goes on full alert, diverting more than its share from the other systems and weakening them. The heart was particularly vulnerable, which explained why so many political prisoners suffered heart attacks. Our wills may have remained strong, but our bodies were paying the price. There was so much uncertainty.

September 13, the day my detention order was due to end, was not far away. Several times the jail matron had whispered to me that she had heard of political prisoners being released. If the regime had begun freeing the people arrested after the hijacking, why shouldn't I be freed too?

There was no longer any mention in the press of my mother's and my alleged connection with Al-Zulfikar. Despite all its tortures and planted 'evidence', the regime had not been able to concoct a case against us that would hold up in the court of world opinion. And Zia could not risk losing the potential largesse of the West, especially the United States.

Pakistan had not received aid from the United States since 1979 when, suspicious that Pakistan was developing or already possessed nuclear capability, the Carter administration enforced its nuclear non-proliferation policies and cut Pakistan off. But that was before the Soviet invasion of Afghanistan. Now Zia was successfully banking on the presence of the Russians right on Pakistan's border to overshadow America's concern about Pakistan's nuclear programme.

The Reagan administration had offered Pakistan a six-year, 3.2 billion dollar economic and military aid package — more than twice as much as the offer that Zia had summarily dismissed from the Carter administration. The US had also added what Zia wanted most of all: 40 F—16 planes. The package, due to come before Congress in the autumn of 1981, was more than acceptable to Zia, though a great disappointment to those of us who believed that America's eagerness to bolster Pakistan against the Communist threat should have been balanced by a concern for human rights and the restoration of democracy.

Zia's position was being further strengthened by the hundreds of millions in refugee relief Pakistan was receiving from the US, Saudi Arabia, and China, as well as from the United Nations High Commissioner for Refugees, the World Food Programme, and other international relief organisations. The numbers of Afghan refugees trekking through the ancient traders' and smugglers' passes of the Hindu Kush to wait out the war in Pakistan or to join the rebel forces of the *mujahideen* had swelled into millions. Refugee camps, hospitals, schools and service centres had been set up all along the border, giving members of the regime the opportunity to skim the international aid flooding into Pakistan. One UN official estimated that only one third of the aid actually reached the refugees, I would read later in Richard Reeves' book *Passage to Peshawar*. Weapons sent to the *mujahideen* also went through Pakistan, giving Zia and his men a chance to siphon them off into the arsenals of the Pakistani army and take fat commissions on arms sales. Another American journalist later told me that Washington officials only expected about a third of them, too, to reach their intended destination.

I suspected that the CIA was deeply involved in Pakistan's role in the war in Afghanistan. But I didn't realise the extent of the CIA's stake in maintaining Zia and his regime until years later when I read *Veil: The Secret Wars of the CIA* by the American journalist Bob Woodward. 'No leader ruled a country in a more precarious situation,' Mr Woodward wrote. 'Most crucial was President Zia's willingness to allow the CIA to funnel growing amounts of paramilitary support to the Afghanistan rebels through Pakistan. [CIA Director] Casey, the CIA and the Reagan Administration all wanted Zia to stay in power and needed to know what was going on inside his government. The CIA station in Islamabad was the biggest in the world.'

I hadn't realised the depth of CIA Director Casey's interactions with Zia, either. 'Congress had made it illegal for American business to make payments or bribes abroad to obtain business,' Woodward wrote. 'The payments and favors to foreign leaders or intelligence sources were the exception – legal bribes, Casey realised. For example, he made certain to visit Pakistan's Zia once or twice a year. Soon he had the closest relationship with Zia of any member of the Reagan Administration.'

All this was helping Zia transform his image from that of a hangman and a brutal dictator to a 'world statesman'. His famous quotes like the one to a *Daily Mail* correspondent over tea in 1978 – 'We'll hang people. A few.' – were now replaced by his references to Pakistan as a 'front line state' helping to fight a *jihad*, or holy war, against the godless Communists. The Americans were especially willing, if not eager, to swallow Zia's new rhetoric. For the first time I saw, in a reprint of an *International Herald Tribune* article in the local press, Zia being described as a 'benevolent dictator'.

I distracted myself from the discouraging press reports by resuming my exercise regime, pacing up and down the narrow corridor that ran in front of the cell-block for an hour every day. Even when I had no appetite I forced down the food sent from 70 Clifton. As August turned into September, I allowed myself a slight feeling of optimism. Sanam's marriage had been set for the 8th, and I had applied for permission to attend. Perhaps I might even be released.

I began to fantasise that the footsteps approaching my cell were bringing news of my release. I fantasised as my cell-block was unlocked for the delivery of my tiffin box, and then again with the arrival of the night matron. I fantasised at hearing the footsteps that came regularly on Monday mornings, the light footsteps of a small, nervous man. They belonged to the jail superintendent. Sometimes he came with his deputy, sometimes alone. His message was always the same.

'Why do you want to ruin your life behind prison walls while other members of the party are free and enjoying themselves?' he asked me each week. 'If you agree to give up politics for a while, you will be freed.'

What was the regime up to? I knew the superintendent would never dare say such things without official support. Yet, if Zia wanted to set me free, he would. If he didn't, he wouldn't. But what was the point of trying to blackmail me, to compromise me? Did they really think I would consent? Or were they just trying to break me as Ayub Khan had attempted to do to my father?

'You can be free tomorrow,' the superintendent would tell me. 'Only you are keeping yourself in jail. Wouldn't you like to travel to London, to Paris? You're a young woman, wasting her youth in prison. And for what? You can wait for your time to come, and it will, it will.'

I always felt unsettled after he left. Though I never had the slightest inclination to accept the temptations he offered me, I wasn't sure of his motives. Did he wish me well – or ill? I hated my new and necessary tendency to be suspicious about everyone. But how else had I survived? The regime was just trying to unbalance me, I suspected. They were trying to destabilise me further, I decided, by making mysterious noises round my cell at night.

Whispers. Two men and woman speaking in hushed voices. Sometimes I woke to the sound before dawn. No one was allowed in my ward or even near by ward except for the police. I complained to the prison authorities that they were disturbing my sleep deliberately. 'There is no one in your ward,' the deputy superintendent assured me. 'You are imagining it.'

Footsteps. A man's heavy footsteps coming closer and closer to my cell. 'Who is it?' I called out, peering at the door from under my sheet. Silence. 'Did you hear the footsteps?' I asked the matron. 'I didn't hear anything,' she said. I made another complaint. 'You're just imagining it,' they said.

Tinkle. Tinkle. A new sound, like the jingle of bells on a woman's anklet. Then the whispers. I woke earlier and earlier, and finally couldn't go to sleep at all. When the old matron was replaced by a new one, I tried again. 'Don't you hear any noises at night?' I asked the toothless, wizened old Pathan woman who now slept in the courtyard.

'Hush! Pretend you have heard nothing!' she replied, her eyes darting from side to side, her hands nervously smoothing down her thin grey uniform.

'But who is it?' I asked, thrilled to have some confirmation at last.

'It is the *chur-ayle*,' she whispered.

A *chur-ayle*, the spirit of a woman whose feet point backwards instead of forward? 'There is no such thing as a *chur-ayle*,' I told the matron, clinging to rationality. 'Yes there is,' she insisted. 'Everyone in the women's wing has heard her. Pretend you do not hear her and she will not harm you.'

Tinkle. Tinkle. That night and for many others, my reasoning vanished altogether. Why doesn't she stay in the women's wing instead of coming into my ward, I shivered in bed. And the noises continued.

Clank. Clank. Someone, something, was rattling what seemed to be rubbish bins outside by ward, searching through the refuse inside. Footsteps approached my cell again, though there was no sound of the ward door being unlocked. *Ya Allah*, what is that! *Ya Allah*, help me! I heard my empty tiffin box being picked up right outside my door, the lid opened, the box knocked against the wall. *Allah!* I gathered my nerve and rushed to the cell door. The tiffin box was upside-down in the dirt. There was no one there.

'You're under a lot of stress,' the jail superintendent told me the next time he visited. Finally he told me that my cell-block had been built over a *phansi ghat*, a former hanging ground used by the British. 'Maybe it is some soul who has not found rest,' the jailer suggested. The thought was not comforting. Neither was the explanation offered by the Pathan matron. 'My husband was a night watchman and he was murdered by thieves,' she told me, her eyes blazing. 'His murderer was never found. It must be his soul which has not found rest.'

I am not superstitious, and suspected that the regime was trying to strain my nerves as they had my father's in Rawalpindi Jail. But, as a precaution, I began to pray for the lost souls of the *phansi ghat*. After some months the voices stopped. I still don't know what caused them.

I resumed the prayer ritual I had learned from the matron at Sukkur, breathing the *surah* of the Quran over the bucket of water and sprinkling a little in the corners of my cell. The cell was an odd shape and didn't have four square corners and I was afraid the ritual wouldn't work. Would I at least be able to attend Sanam's wedding? I had heard nothing about my application. '*Qul Huwwa Allahu Ahad* – Say He is One God,' I prayed. After the second Wednesday and before the third, the Pathan matron came to my cell early in the morning. 'I heard the voices near my cot,' she told me. 'They said "she's going today".' This old woman is mad, I thought to myself. Two hours later the jail authorities came. 'You are leaving immediately,' they told me. 'You have permission to go to your sister's wedding.'

70 Clifton. The brass plaques were still gleaming next to the gate. Sir Shah Nawaz Khan Butto. Zulfikar Ali Bhutto, Bar-at-Law. The tensions of the last six months eased a little as the police convoy delivering me drew up in front of the gate. I had been convinced that I would never see this house again, that 70 Clifton would either be confiscated by the regime, or that I would be quietly put to death at Sukkur without ever going home again. But here I was, alive. And here was my home, the compound walls draped with strings of lights to celebrate my sister's wedding. We had both survived.

I felt a new surge of life when the familiar gates swung open. As the *chowkidar* saluted me and the convoy moved into the courtyard, I felt that God had sent me a second life. With His help, I had not been defeated by the enemy. A new sense of strength and resolve swept through me. In that instant, I was reborn.

Drums. Dancing. Garlands of jasmine and roses. The entire household staff was gathered on the front porch, beating on the *dholak* and dancing folk dances with their arms undulating in time with the beat. *Chowkidars*. Bearers. Secretaries. I saw Dost Mohammed, our major-domo, who had run faster than the prison guards to reach my father in jail; Urs, my father's valet who had been pistol-whipped and beaten by the army during the raid to arrest my father; Basheer and Ibrahim who had been with my mother and me at Sihala when my father was hanged; Nazar Mohammed from Larkana who had received my father's body, and buried him.

Their faces were wreathed now in smiles as they danced and sang. What a wonderful wedding atmosphere I thought as I got out of the car. They rushed towards me to drape the garlands around my neck. 'Save them for the wedding guests,' I said as the garlands mounted to cover my ears. 'No, no, we got the flowers for you,' they said. 'We are so happy to have you home.'

Home. I couldn't believe it. Ululations vibrated in the air as my relatives streamed out of the carved wooden front door. My mother's sisters were there, Auntie Bejhat, who'd come from London, Cousin Zeenat from Los Angeles, my cousin Fakhri, who had been detained with me after my father's death sentence. My father's sister Auntie Manna greeted me as did his three half-sisters from Hyderabad who had petitioned Zia to spare my father's life unsuccessfully. Other relatives had travelled from India, from America, from England, from Iran, from France, filling every bed in our house as well as the separate apartments belonging to my brothers, which had been empty for the last four years. Laila! Nashilli! We hugged each other and laughed and cried. I had never expected to see them again, nor they me. Left unspoken was the fear that I'd never come out of prison alive.

The luxury of a hot bath. Carpeting under my feet. Pure, cool water to drink. The feast of my family. I didn't sleep for two days and two nights, not wanting to squander a single moment of freedom. My mother went to bed early and I stayed up until dawn talking to Sanam. Soon after Sanam went to bed, Mummy got up. I couldn't get enough of them or of my other close relatives.

In the time I had to myself, I devoured the back issues of *Asia Week*, *Far Eastern Economic Review*, *Time* and *Newsweek*. I also scrubbed the walls of my bedroom. In the last raid, I soon discovered, the regime had stolen many of the letters my father had written to me while I was studying abroad; also irreplaceable photographs of my brothers, sister and me, and my jewellery including a favourite ring given to me by my mother and a gold *kohl* holder from my grandmother. But it was the feeling of the violation of my bedroom which bothered me most. I scrubbed and scrubbed, trying to erase their psychological fingerprints from my walls. Be thankful that God left you this room and this house, I kept reminding myself. Just a few months back you didn't know whether you would have that. 'They won't take you back to prison, will they?' said my cousin Abdul Hussein, forgetting that he was in Pakistan and not in San Francisco. I did not allow myself to share his hope, though it was hard not to.

Everything at 70 Clifton seemed so normal, so comfortingly traditional. The staff were rushing in and out, setting up buffet tables in the patterned tent in the garden, arranging upholstered armchairs to seat the guests. Sunny was having her hand hennaed by the *mehndi* artist who had come to the house to trace delicate and intricate patterns on the hands of the women in the wedding household. The *mehndi* artist made beautiful scrolls and arabesques on my sister's palm with a toothpick, then sealed the henna with lemon juice and sugar.

Sanam's wedding was small by Pakistani standards, only five hundred guests. And not every tradition could be followed. I hadn't been able to have new silk *shalwar khameez* made for the *mehndi* ceremony or for the *nikah* or wedding ceremony, as had most of the other women thronging through the house. But it didn't matter. I hadn't seen the clothes in my cupboard nor worn anything dressy for so long that my old pink silk *shalwar khameez* seemed like new to me.

'Mom is forcing me to wear make-up,' Sunny said, rushing into my bedroom. 'And I have to wear a sari. I wish I could just get married in a pair of blue jeans. Do something.'

'You only get married once,' I said. 'And Mummy's suffered a lot. Make her happy by listening to her.'

This bride is fairer than the moon. Yes she is, yes she is. The sound of singing, not silence, filled the house the first night I was home. *This bride is fairer than the moon.* Our female relatives clapped along with Sanam's girl-friends, practising the traditional songs and dances for the *mehndi* ceremony. Not wanting to waste a moment of my freedom and not knowing how long it would last, I went to talk to relatives and friends instead. Our worlds had become so different. But which world was real? Twice I caught myself referring to my jail cell as 'home'.

Sunny looked beautiful as she joined her husband-to-be Nasser Hussein on a green cushion inlaid with mirrors for the *mehndi* ceremony. As theirs was not an arranged marriage, there was little tension between them. But there were traditions to be gone through. Sunny kept her *dupatta* carefully over her face so that her groom wouldn't catch a glimpse of her before the wedding, though she raised it and talked to me while I sat beside her.

'Nasser *ji*, Nasser *ji*, about-to-be brother-in-law. Seven conditions you have to accept before Sanam can become your bride,' Sunny's friends and relatives sang in front of us. 'The first condition is that Sanam will not make food.'

'I will get a cook,' Nasser sang back.

'Sanam will not wash clothes,' the bride's side sang.

'I will take them to the laundry,' Nasser sang back, responding to each condition until his side had a chance to return the teasing.

Relatives from both sides brought in platters heaped with henna and decorated with burning candles and silver foil. One by one Nasser's relatives pressed a pinch of henna into a betel nut leaf laid on Sanam's palm, placed a fingerful of sweet in her mouth, and waved money over her head to protect her from evil. Led by my mother, we on the bride's side did the same to Nasser.

The festive air came to an abrupt end when one of the staff suddenly came up to us. 'The police are at the gate,' he said, casting a terrible silence over the entire room. I assumed the police had come for me, but our major-domo returned to say that they wanted my mother. The guests sucked in their breath. Mummy would never survive another detention.

'Call them in, Dost Mohammed. I don't want the police breaking down gates while our guests are here,' my mother said calmly. The police came in looking quite uncomfortable. 'What do you want with me?' my mother asked them, her voice firm in spite of her illness. They sheepishly handed her a Martial Law Order. It wasn't for her arrest, thank God, but instead notified her that she was externed from the Punjab. She didn't have any plans to visit the Punjab, and Zia knew it. He just wanted to harass us and dampen and spoil any happiness the Bhuttos might be having.

And the harassment continued. The next morning, the wedding musicians my mother had engaged suddenly sent word that they weren't coming. They couldn't get a permit for a microphone from the authorities, they told us: the use of loudspeakers had been banned under Martial Law. We didn't know whether the regime had interfered or if the musicians had just got cold feet.

The harassment extended to our wedding guests whose number plates were noted by the regime's intelligence agents stationed in vans across the street from 70 Clifton. The regime had already tried to obtain the guest list. My mother's secretary had confessed to her in tears that the regime had threatened him with dire consequences if he didn't hand it over to them.

The country, however, was to be kept in the dark about the wedding. The Bhutto name was not allowed to appear in the newspapers unless the stories were negative, though journalists in Pakistan had become used to getting around restrictions. To announce Sunny's engagement they had noted that Nasser's grandfather, like our own, had once been Prime Minister of Junagadh state. 'GRANDCHILDREN OF TWO FORMER PRIME MINISTERS OF JUNAGADH STATE TO MARRY' the headlines had read. To announce Sanam's wedding and my temporary release from Karachi Jail, the headline read: 'SISTER ATTENDS SISTER'S WEDDING'.

Inside the gates of 70 Clifton, we remained determined to carry off Sanam's wedding as a personal, family affair. My sister had suffered enough, dragged into the world of politics in which she had no interest just because her name was Bhutto. She had graduated from Harvard alone, two months after our father had been assassinated. She had been admitted to Oxford, but unable to concentrate on her studies, had returned to Pakistan. But to what? To become a prisoner of sorts herself, living alone at 70 Clifton, her mother and sister in and out of prison, her brothers in exile. She had always chosen to keep her circle of friends small, disliking the attenton she got as a Bhutto and the constant questions about her father. She mixed now with only a handful of people she had known for years, including Nasser who had gone to school with Shah Nawaz and Mir.

'Don't marry Sanam. The regime will ruin you,' his uncles had warned him when he had asked them to propose for her. 'That is my decision, not yours,' he told them. 'I love this girl. Whatever the price is, I will pay it.' And he has. The regime has all sorts of ways of punishing those out of favour: opening tax investigations, withholding permits, cutting off water to farmlands. Nasser's vulnerability lay in his successful telecommunications business in Pakistan which sold state-of-the-art equipment primarily to the government. His bids for contracts were soon ignored, causing his business to drop by over 75 per cent. He and Sanam now live in London where Nasser had to start virtually all over again. Their wedding, however, was beautiful.

Holding a Holy Quran over her head, my mother and I escorted Sanam down the staircase to the *nikah* stage in the front hall. The sari Sanam wore for the ceremony was green, the colour of happiness. 'Do you accept Nasser Hussein, son of Nasim Abdul Qadir, as your husband?' asked our cousin Ashik Ali Bhutto. Sanam smiled at my mother and me and remained silent, knowing Ashik Ali had to ask her the question three times in the presence of two other witnesses to be sure of her consent. Again he asked her. Again Sanam remained silent. Islam wants to make sure that the woman understands and agrees freely to the marriage. After the third repetition, Sanam finally consented and signed the marriage contract. Ashik Ali went to bring the good news to the men gathered in another room. The *maulvi* read Nasser the marriage prayers. And my sister became the first Bhutto woman to marry a man of her own choosing.

Two of Nasser's close friends brought him onto the dais to join his bride. The female cousins and Nasser's friends held a silk shawl over the couple's heads like a canopy while a mirror was placed between them. I fought back tears as Sanam and Nasser looked at each other in the mirror, the traditional moment when the bride and groom see each other as partners for the first time.

The dais was wreathed in roses, marigolds and jasmine, sending their sweet perfume into the night. Sanam and Nasser sat on a blue velvet footstool surrounded by dishes of candied almonds, eggs painted in gold, walnuts and pistachios dipped in silver. Candles burned in silver candelabra beside the couple so that their lives would be filled with light. Sanam's happily married cousins ground sugar cones over the couple's heads so that their lives would be sweet. The sound of ululating filled the air. The celebration had begun.

My mother and I sat with Sunny and Nasser while the guests lined up to offer their congratulations. Many of them had spent time in jail and some showed it, looking thin and drawn. 'How well you look,' they said to me. I hoped they meant it, wanting to appear as unbroken by the regime as my father had in his appearance before the Supreme Court. 'How nice to see you,' I murmured automatically again and again. For all that my head was high, I felt shaky underneath.

Would I have to go back to prison? I had heard nothing from the authorities. In the crowd I saw my lawyer Mujib, who told me he had an appointment with the Home Secretary of Sindh early the next morning. Since my detention was due to expire in less than a week anyway, he told me he would ask the authorities to let me stay at 70 Clifton for the remaining period.

After the guests departed, I collected magazines and newspapers to try and smuggle back into jail if the police came for me, along with kleenex and insect killer. I stayed up all night, talking with my cousins, with Samiya, and writing a last minute letter to Peter Galbraith, my old friend from Harvard and Oxford. Peter was handling the South Asia portfolio for the US Senate Foreign Relations Committee, my mother told me, and had recently come to Pakistan to review American security interests. He had tried to visit me in Karachi Central Jail, she said, but he had received no response from the regime to his request. Later he told me what happened.

Peter Galbraith, August, 1981:

I carried a letter with me to Pakistan from Senator Claiborne Pell, the minority leader of the Senate Foreign Relations Committee, requesting the regime to permit me to visit Benazir. I made a big pitch to the Pakistani Foreign Ministry as well as to the US Embassy, which at that time was quite hostile to the Bhuttos.

The regime didn't even respond to Senator Pell's request, nor to mine. Although the US Embassy tried to discourage contact with the Bhuttos, I went around to 70 Clifton to see Begum Bhutto anyway. She was pale and looked very tired. She was very concerned about Benazir's confinements in Sukkur and Karachi jails over the previous five months.

Begum Bhutto invited me to join her, Sanam and Fakhri at the Karachi Boat Club. As we left 70 Clifton she told me to smile for the security men who were taking pictures with a telephoto lens from a car across the street. I gave them my best politician's wave.

Through lunch, I could not keep my mind off Pinkie's imprisonment. The last time I had seen her was at Oxford in January 1977. Pinkie had just been elected President of the Oxford Union and was holding court before fawning undergraduates in the President's office.

Since then, her life had taken such an unexpected, almost incomprehensible direction. I kept thinking of her returning home only to see her father overthrown, put on trial for his life and then executed. And then for Pinkie to spend so much time in prison, and under such terrible conditions. As I often handled human rights cases I knew these things happened, but it was still hard to comprehend that it was happening to a friend. As I left the Boat Club, I gave Begum Bhutto a long, newsy letter for Benazir which I had written the night before on a legal pad.

Back in the United States I prepared a report for the Foreign Relations Committee on the prospective resumption of assistance to Pakistan. The report argued that the assistance risked identifying the United States with an unpopular military dictatorship and could lead to a repetition of the American experience in Iran. I urged a forceful human rights policy as a signal that our assistance was intended to benefit the country as well as the rulers. Privately, I briefed Senator Pell and Committee head Senator

Charles Percy on the treatment of the Bhutto women. Both were eager to help. I wished Benazir knew she wasn't forgotten.

The sun was barely up in Karachi when I read and re-read Peter's chatty letter, cherishing the news of his wife Anne and the birth of their son. Old memories of a simpler time were rekindled. I wrote back to him:

September 10, 1981

Dear Peter,

Last night was Sunny's wedding. The whole house is sound asleep. It is now 6.00 am, and a few hours of freedom remain to me. I wanted to quickly write to tell you how happy your letter made me, to hear from you, to receive news of our friends and to know how well you are doing in life. My prayers for your success and for your brother Jamie's success will always be there.

So unsettling in a way to hear from Harvard, a voice from the past, harkening back to an age of innocence. Did they teach us that life could be full of such terrible dangers and tragedies? Were they words we read or did not read, meanings I, at least, can now say I failed to grasp. Freedom and liberty, the essays we wrote on them, papers for our tutors, for *grades*, but did we know the value of those words which we bandied about, of how precious they are, as precious as the air we breathe, the water we drink. But then, the harsh realities seemed so remote in the snows of Vermont and the yards of Harvard . . .'

Later in the morning I went up to Mummy's bedroom with tea. 'Stay with me,' she said. 'Maybe we'll hear the good news from Mujib together.' Shortly afterwards, my lawyer arrived. The Home Secretary had turned down his request, he told me. Until I signed a promise not to violate the ban on politics, he'd been told, I would stay in jail.

The police came at 10.00 am. My relatives and the staff crowded into the courtyard to see me off, running after the car as it moved down Clifton past the Iranian Embassy, past Clifton Gardens where children gathered to fly kites, past the Soviet Embassy, the Libyan Embassy, the Italian Embassy. As always, I was whizzed at full speed through half-empty back streets to the jail.

The familiar sound of the jailer's keys opening padlock after padlock greeted me at Karachi Central. I walked briskly through the small iron door cut in the high brick wall, kept my back straight as I moved down the windowless muddy corridor toward my ward. I didn't want anyone to think my two days of freedom had softened me. I also hoped they wouldn't search me. Before leaving 70 Clifton, I had stuffed the magazines and newspapers into my bag.

The electricity was off as usual when I made it safely to my cell. Automatically, I registered a complaint. For the next two days I was sick, throwing up bile and brown gastric juices. Whether it was psychological or something I had eaten, I don't know, but I was very ill.

On the third day, September 13, I luckily felt stronger. A jailer came with a depressing, but not unexpected, order from the District Martial Law Administrator. My detention at Karachi Central Jail was extended for another three months.

I started reading my Wednesday prayer every day instead of once a week. The prayer had always worked for me before. Perhaps, by reading it daily, the doors of my cell would open permanently after the second Wednesday and before the third. My target date for the prayer to work now was September 30, the third Wednesday. Failing that, the next target date was Margaret Thatcher's visit to Pakistan at the beginning of October.

Zia had to free me some day and I was always looking for dates on which to pin my hopes for release. I knew Margaret Thatcher, having met her first with my father in Rawalpindi at the Prime Minister's House when she was opposition leader. I had met her again in London over tea at her offices in the House of Commons when I was the President of the Oxford Union. If the Thatcher visit passed without my being freed, perhaps I'd be let out on *Eid* which this year fell on October 9. The regime always released some prisoners at the end of Ramazan as a mark of respect to the religious occasion.

I was not to be released on any of those dates. On September 25, 1981, Chaudhry Zahur Elahi, one of the ministers in Zia's military cabinet who had accepted Zia's pen as a gift after Zia signed my father's death warrant and who had passed out sweets after my father was hanged, was ambushed in Lahore and shot dead. Riding in the same car and wounded in the attack was Maulvi Mushtaq Hussein, the former Chief Justice of the Lahore High Court who had sentenced my father to death. Also in the car was M. A. Rehman, the special public prosecutor in my father's murder case, who escaped injury.

I felt there was divine retribution when I read the headlines about Elahi's assassination in the paper. 'Now his wife, his daughter, his family will know what it is like to feel grief,' I noted in my diary. 'I do not rejoice, for a Muslim does not rejoice over death. Life and death are in God's hands. But there is consolation in knowing that the bad guys don't get away scot free.'

My gratification was short lived. The regime claimed that Al-Zulfikar once again was responsible for this latest violence, and the arrests began.

Mir didn't help when, the day after the assassination, he took credit for it in the name of Al-Zulfikar in a BBC interview. A debate about the attack might have exposed the immoral role Elahi had played in the death of my father; instead, all the attention was focused on routing out the supposed members of Al-Zulfikar.

Terrorists! Murderers! Political assassins! the headlines screamed. Once again the regime used Al-Zulfikar to suppress political opposition. One young leader of the PPP after another was arrested, and warrants issued for hundreds of others. Four young men were taken to Haripur Jail where they were badly tortured. The father of one of them, I learned later, Ahmed Ali Soomro, came to see a member of the PPP in a terrible state. He paid an enormous amount of money to the police just to glimpse his son from a distance, so he'd know whether he was alive or dead. According to press reports, there were 103 young men in Haripur Jail alone, 200 in another town nearby.

Women were being rounded up again, including Nasira Rana Shaukat who was taken back to the Lahore Fort. Once more the wife of the PPP's General Secretary was given electric shocks and interrogated for twenty-three days without sleep. 'Implicate your husband in the assassination,' she was ordered. 'Implicate Benazir. Implicate Begum Bhutto.' What that brave woman endured is beyond comprehension. She was held for the next seven months in a cell with no toilet facilities, just a tray which was changed twice a week. She spent the winter lying on the cement floor with no sweater, no bedding, no blankets, and nearly died of pneumonia. When she was finally transferred to house arrest, she could neither walk nor speak.

In the midst of this new wave of brutality, Margaret Thatcher arrived for her visit. Two years before, a BBC report carried in the press pointed out, it would have been unthinkable for a Western head of government to visit Pakistan — after Zia had dismissed pleas from all over the world to spare my father's life. But the Soviet invasion of Afghanistan had overridden all these reservations of the West. Instead, the BBC reported, Britain was now making every effort to build up Zia's image. It was heartening to hear that the world press, at least, realised that Zia was still the deplorable murderer that he had always been, and continued in office only with the patronage of outside powers. Still, it was a shock to read in the newspaper that after a tour of the Afghan refugee camps Margaret Thatcher presented Zia with a certificate declaring him 'the last bastion of the free world'.

I was increasingly frustrated as well to read about the twisting of the political situation in Pakistan by the Reagan administration in its congressional campaign to restore US aid. 'Bhutto's PPP might be opposed to it [the aid], but not the great mass of the common people who realized that Pakistan was having to face a great threat to its security with antiquated weapons,' Ambassador-designate to Pakistan Ronald Spiers had reportedly testified before the Senate Foreign Relations Committee in September. He was completely wrong. First, the PPP was the only voice of the 'great mass of the common people'. And second, we were not then – nor are we now – opposed to foreign aid *per se*, but only aid designed to perpetuate the military occupation of Pakistan. Yet the arguments remained reversed. Undersecretary of State James Buckley, who was responsible for organising the aid package, even testified that elections were not 'in the security interest of Pakistan', as if we, the democratic party were the enemy, rather than the dictator!

I didn't know then that behind the headlines certain American politicians were quietly challenging Mr Buckley's conclusions. Peter Galbraith had returned to Washington determined to raise the issue of human rights abuses in Pakistan and to win my release. Working with Senator Pell, Peter developed a very straightforward strategy. Each time Pakistan was raised in the US Senate, the issue of human rights and my detention would also be raised. Neither the American administration nor the Zia dictatorship would be allowed to forget about the political prisoners in Pakistan. Eventually, they hoped enough pressure could be brought to bear to make the regime decide it was easier to release me than to continually confront the issue of my and others' unfair detentions.

I would read later how Senator Pell, an opponent of resumed assistance to Pakistan, had implemented the strategy. 'The F–16 is the most visible symbol of American support for the Zia regime,' *India Today* quoted Senator Pell as saying to Undersecretary of State Buckley. 'Amnesty International believes that human rights violations in Pakistan amount to a consistent pattern ... do you feel they are correct?' When Mr Buckley tried to answer in vague terms Senator Pell apparently got very specific. 'It appears as if President Zia is conducting a vendetta against the widow and daughter of executed – murdered – former Prime Minister Bhutto,' the Senator charged. 'I am wondering if the Administration has made any representation to the Government of Pakistan about the confinement and maltreatment of the Bhutto family.' In reply, Undersecretary Buckley promised efforts through 'private diplomacy', a codeword for doing nothing at all. But at least Senator Pell had made his point.

The American Congress's traditional deference to the request of a new administration as well as concerns about Afghanistan outweighed objections from Senator Pell and others about Zia's human rights record and about Pakistan's nuclear programme. While Congress approved the proposed aid package, Senator Pell was able to persuade his colleagues to go along with an amendment stating 'in authorising assistance to Pakistan, it is the intent of Congress to promote the expeditious restoration of full civil liberties and representative government in Pakistan.' While the Pell amendment had little practical effect, it was a useful shot over the bow of the Zia dictatorship.

At Karachi Central Jail, *Eid* came and went without my release. The Pathan matron told me that political prisoners were among those freed for the holiday, which made me very happy for them and their families. Many among the jail staff showed me their own warmth and respect for *Eid*. The wife of one jailer requested one of my *khameez* so she could have *Eid* clothes made for me, while another jailer sent me a message that he would remain at the front desk and put pressure on the authorities until the electricity was restored to my cell block. 'I hope we remember such people in the good times,' I noted in my diary.

For every political prisoner freed for *Eid*, however, ten were being arrested. The student leader Lala Assad, I read in the paper, was now the subject of an intensive manhunt. Lala Assad was a loyal supporter of the party, and I prayed that he would elude the police. Towards the end of my period of freedom in 1981, when I had travelled to Khairpur to give certificates to students who had been jailed for protesting against Martial Law, I had used the birthday celebration of Lala Assad's son Zulfikar, who was named after my father, as a cover. Lala Assad himself had spent two years in prison for his support of my father. His own father, a former minister of West Pakistan, who had fought with Mohammed Ali Jinnah, for Pakistan's independence, had asked to see me during my visit. Ill and bedridden, the old man had begged me to urge his son to give up politics.

'I don't have long to live,' Lala Assad's father said to me. 'I never interfered with my son's political activities while Mr Bhutto was in jail. But now that the Prime Minister is dead, I need my son to look after me, to look after his wife and child. When I am gone, he will be free to work for you and your party. But in my dying days, I need my son.' I promised him that I would speak to Lala Assad, which I did. I had no idea what happened after I left, for I was arrested a month later and taken to Sukkur. Now a year later Lala Assad was being sought as a leader of Al-Zulfikar. I had no idea whether the charge was true.

Terrorism. Violence. Was there to be no end to the cycle? Three presidents had been assassinated in the last few months alone, President Zia ur-Rehman in Bangladesh, President Rajai in Iran, and most recently Anwar el-Sadat in Egypt on October 6. I felt sad for President Sadat, for his family, for his violent end. As a child, I had been an avid supporter of his predecessor, Gamal Abdel Nasser, greatly admiring his fight against British colonialism and American imperialism during the Suez War. Nasser had seemed a colossus to me, promising a new world of equality to be built from the ashes and rubble of yesterday's obsolete kings and monarchs. I had spent hours in my father's library at 70 Clifton, reading every book about Nasser I could, including his own, *The Philosophy of the Revolution*.

I had not been fond of Sadat, who had turned against his mentor and reversed his policies when he assumed the presidency of Egypt in 1970. But, reading of Sadat's death in my cell, I found myself unexpectedly moved. Though Papa had been sharply critical of the separate peace Sadat had made with Israel, Sadat had appealed for my father's life. The Egyptian President had also given refuge to the Shah of Iran and his family, despite incurring unpopularity for it. And when the Shah died of cancer, Sadat had ordered a full-scale funeral for him, showing a generosity of spirit rare in the world of *realpolitik*. He had not let political differences and disputes stand in the way of what he thought was right. Now he too was dead.

A depression settled over me. Night after night, as I sat over my embroidery, I got splitting headaches. On the night of November 21 — my brother Shah's birthday — I suddenly felt my throat constrict and tears rush to my eyes. I went to lie down but could not control the tears which flowed freely. Where were my brothers? How were they? Both Mir and Shah had got married just after *Eid*. They had married two Afghan sisters in Kabul called Fauzia and Rehana, the daughters of a former government servant. That was all we knew about them. I was very glad that my brothers had found a source of love, warmth and emotional comfort in these difficult times. Why then was I so depressed?

I sank into a troubled sleep. Mir was secretly back in Pakistan, I dreamed in a recurrent dream. He had walked over the mountain passes from Afghanistan, forded the Indus and was hiding in a cupboard in 70 Clifton. The Army raided the house. Just as they opened the cupboard and saw him, I woke up.

I had the wrong victim. The next morning, I read that Lala Assad had been shot dead by the police. The pain in my head intensified. Lala Assad had been killed in a gun battle with the police in Karachi's Federal B area, the newspaper reported, after he shot and killed a policeman. I didn't learn the truth for months. Lala Assad in fact, had been unarmed at the time of the shooting. The policeman had been shot by another policeman in the crossfire. When Lala Assad tried to escape the ambush, he had been gunned down in cold blood.

Lala Assad dead. Now his blood, too, was on General Zia's uniform. What must Lala Assad's father be feeling? Instead of having his son to care for him in his last days, he was receiving his son's body. When would it end?

'A country-wide hunt for Al-Zulfikar terrorists has continued and police have arrested several hundred people,' the paper reported on November 26. The police were staking out houses, youth hostels, the airports all over the country. Check-points were set up on all routes leading out of Karachi – land, sea, and air. Special binoculars, the papers reported, were being used by the police to peer through the tinted glass of car windows. Make-up artists had been contacted by the police to prevent the 'absconders' from adopting disguises.

My anxiety deepened. I was racked by remorse over Lala Assad's death. I prayed for him to forgive me for the times I had spoken sharply to him. I tortured myself for keeping pictures of him and other student leaders at 70 Clifton, pictures the police had taken in the last raid. Had they used the photographs to identify him?

I looked at the weblike lines on the back of my hands, the lines around my eyes, across my cheeks, on my forehead. I thought they were a reaction to the hot dry weather and winds at Sukkur. But they appeared to be permanent. I was ageing much too fast.

On December 11, the day my detention order ended, I prepared myself to receive a new one. I knew I wouldn't be released after the crackdown. My food arrived an hour early – with the expected detention order. But Senator Pell's message had apparently found its way into Pakistan. Two weeks later, the Deputy Superintendent came to see me unexpectedly in the late afternoon. 'Pack your belongings,' he told me abruptly. 'You are being taken to Larkana tomorrow morning at 5.45 under police escort.'

The day matron wept at our parting. The Pathan matron wept too, and asked my forgiveness if her stupidity had aggravated me. I wept and wept myself. Though I had dreamed and fantasised of being transferred to sub-jail at home, I suddenly dreaded leaving the secret network that had been established at Karachi Central Jail. I had cherished the occasional copies of the *International Herald Tribune*, *Time*, or *Newsweek* the sympathetic jailers allowed to be sent to me. In Karachi I was also near my mother and my sister. Now I would be cut off from them in the rural isolation of Al-Murtaza.

The police came for me soon after dawn on December 27, 1981. I took one last look at my horrible, dank cell. How could I possibly be sad at leaving? But I was, just as I had been when I'd left the familiarity of Sukkur. The years of detention were having their effect. I had come to dread the unknown.

10

TWO MORE YEARS ALONE IN SUB-JAIL

Familiarity. Comfort. Home. Leaving aside the fact that the paramilitary Frontier Forces were once more posted inside the compound walls and a prison staff came daily to Al-Murtaza to supervise my detention, I revelled in my apparent good fortune. Some members of the household staff would be permitted to enter Al-Murtaza during the day, the Martial Law authorities told me. I could use the telephone and, best of all, receive three visitors a fortnight. After almost ten months of solitary confinement, these privileges sounded tantamount to a stay in a five-star hotel. I celebrated my first night home by taking a long, hot bath and manicuring my nails.

But I had celebrated too soon. My telephone calls were restricted to conversations with my relatives and I was not allowed to talk about political matters. The telephone rarely worked. Often my calls were disconnected or the line simply went dead. Later I found out why. All the phone lines were run through a military communications outpost set up outside the walls.

In the year that the regime kept me locked up at Al-Murtaza, the promise of three visitors a fortnight soon became a myth as well. Only my mother, Sanam, and my Auntie Manna were on my allowed list. Each lived in Karachi, over an hour away by air, a journey made more difficult by the infrequent and inconveniently timed flights to interior Sindh. Sanam, who now had a house and a husband to look after, came only once or twice. My mother, who was in poor health, was only able to visit infrequently. I had political acquaintances in Larkana who could have visited me easily, but the jail authorities did not allow substitutions. Essentially, I was back in solitary confinement. When I did have a visitor, more often than not a jail official, my jaws ached afterwards from the unaccustomed exercise. I probably should have talked to myself in the endless silence if for no other reason than to hear a human voice, but I didn't think of it.

New detention orders, however, came regularly every three months. I knew the words now, by heart. 'Whereas the Deputy Martial Law Administrator is of the opinion that for the purpose of preventing Miss Benazir Bhutto from acting in a manner prejudicial to the purpose for which Martial Law has been proclaimed, or to the security of Pakistan, the public safety or interest, or the efficient conduct of Martial Law, it is necessary to detain the said Miss Benazir Bhutto. . . .'

Time weighed more heavily than ever. There were no afternoon papers to read, no *International Herald Tribune*. There was little on television apart from Arabic language study programmes, Zia's news in Sindhi, Urdu and English, brainwashing documentaries about the regime's political activities, and a few half-hour plays. I succumbed to periods of self-pity followed by attacks of remorse. You shouldn't be ungrateful to God, I chided myself. You have your home. You have food and clothing. Think of all those less fortunate. My emotions swung back and forth like a pendulum.

I taught myself cooking to pass the time, practising recipes from my mother's old cookbooks left in the kitchen. The ovens didn't work and the kitchen utensils were limited: there wasn't even an egg-beater. Every dish I produced then – curries, rice, *dahl* – became a mini-triumph of sorts. Like the ladyfingers and chillies my mother had managed to grow at Al-Murtaza during our detention three years before, the food I was making now took on special significance. I could look at a bowl of rice I'd made and see in it proof that I existed. I had caused it to become edible. *Coquo ergo sum*. I cook, therefore I am.

I worried constantly about my mother. It had been four months since her visit to me in Karachi Central Jail when she told me that her doctor suspected she had lung cancer. If indeed she did have cancer, she was in a race against time. Early detection and treatment of lung cancer can arrest it. Left untreated, lung cancer can kill quickly. To build up her strength for further diagnostic tests, she had been put on a special diet by her doctor. The last series of tests had been more conclusive. The shadow on her left lung, the doctors decided, was very likely malignant. They reported to the regime that she was in need of a CATSCAN and treatment which was unavailable in Pakistan. Yet my mother's request for the restoration of her passport so she could travel abroad for medical attention was being ignored. It was rumoured that the Interior Ministry could do nothing because Zia had taken my mother's file with him on a trip to Beijing.

One month passed without the regime granting permission for my mother to leave Pakistan. Then another. Losing hope, my mother's doctor in Karachi began chemotherapy. My frustration when Mummy first told me the news over the phone deepened to bitterness after her subsequent calls. Her hair was thinning and she was losing weight, she confessed, regretting that she could not come and visit me. As a daughter, I felt inadequate that I could not be with her or help her.

In spite of press censorship, the news of her ordeal was spreading through the country. 'The people haven't forgotten Mummy,' Sanam tried to reassure me over the phone. 'We're getting constant calls inquiring about her, and so is Fakhri. Apparently her health is a major topic of conversation at diplomatic receptions and coffee parties, at bus stops and cinemas.'

'Zia will have to let her go,' I said hopefully, trying to convince myself. But, even when the pressure on Zia began to tell, he didn't let her go. Instead, three months after the doctors' report of probable cancer, Zia convened a Federal Medical Board to determine whether or not she was sick enough to warrant medical treatment abroad.

A Federal Medical Board. Another petty discrimination. Not since the time of Ayub Khan when foreign travel was restricted had citizens of Pakistan needed the authorisation of a medical board to obtain a passport. Under my father, the right to a passport had become a fundamental right for every Pakistani, and with it the right to travel freely. It was quite common for members of Zia's regime to travel abroad at government cost for minor ailments easily treatable in Pakistan. But for his political opponents Zia had reinstituted the medical board. Now he was using it to delay my mother's departure for treatment.

When the board finally met, it was stacked with Zia's men. Just as the Supreme Court's decision upholding my father's death sentence had been effected by diminishing the size of the judicial bench, seven doctors, instead of the usual three, were now appointed to the medical board to make sure Zia got the decision he wanted. All seven were employees of the regime. The head of the board was a serving Major-General.

'Begum Sahiba seems well enough to me,' this General said irresponsibly shortly after the board's first meeting. Others on the stacked board demanded that my mother undergo another fourteen lung X-rays and a blood test, a process so exhausting that she developed a fever, began coughing blood and fainted immediately after its conclusion. Although the tests showed that the shadow in her lung had grown larger and that her haemoglobin count had dropped, the head of the board suggested that she have another bronchoscopy, which was not only unnecessary but could aggravate any malignancy. My mother's physician in Karachi, Dr Saeed, who was himself a member of the board, was outraged and refused to endorse the board's decision. The anaesthetist at the hospital backed him up, insisting that my mother could not withstand the general anaesthetic necessary to insert the diagnostic tube into her lung.

I prayed for my mother at Al-Murtaza. There was nothing else I could do. But, in the rest of the country, the fear that Zia might actually let my mother die began to move people to action. 'We could not save Mr Bhutto,' people began to whisper among themselves. 'We must not stand by while Begum Bhutto wastes away.' Indignation at my mother's callous treatment at the hands of the regime cut across traditional lines of PPP support to include military families and those high in Zia's bureaucracy.

'Guess what! The wife and sisters of the Martial Law Administrator of

Sindh took part in a ladies' demonstration to save Auntie's life,' Fakhri said excitedly on the telephone.

'Did the police arrest them?' I almost shrieked, not believing what I was hearing. After General Zia, the four provincial Martial Law Administrators were the most powerful men in the country.

'They didn't dare. When they came, all the demonstrators ran into the Martial Law Administrator's house and closed the gates,' Fakhri said.

My mother's ordeal, I would find out later, was also sparking protest abroad. In England, a group of my old friends from Oxford joined with Dr Niazi, Amina Piracha and some human rights activists to mount a campaign called 'Save the Bhutto Ladies'. The group concentrated first on freeing my mother, lobbying Parliament with the assistance of Lord Avebury, a member of the House of Lords. Two MPs, Joan Lestor and Jonathan Aitken, quickly responded by sponsoring an Early Day Motion in the House of Commons – 'Medical Treatment for Begum Bhutto: That this House urges the Government of Pakistan to allow Begum Bhutto to travel abroad for medical treatment for the cancer from which she suffers.' On November 4, Lord Avebury held a press conference in the House of Lords, at which a British doctor outlined the gravity of my mother's condition.

Members of the United States government were also making pleas on my mother's behalf. 'Dear Mr Ambassador,' Senator John Glenn, a member of the Senate Committee on Foreign Relations, wrote to Ejaz Azim, the Pakistan Ambassador to Washington on November 8. 'More than two months ago Mrs Nusrat Bhutto, widow of the late Prime Minister, requested permission to go abroad to seek treatment for a probable malignancy on the lung. . . . On humanitarian grounds I would urge your government to act expeditiously in approving Mrs Bhutto's request. Prompt approval would be seen here as a compassionate act and would help strengthen the relationship between our two countries.'

Zia, however, had grown used to ignoring pleas for compassion from Western governments. Away on a visit to Southeast Asia, he was so confident that the board was going to go his way that he beat them to their decision. 'There is nothing wrong with Begum Bhutto,' the press quoted him as saying in Kuala Lumpur on November 11, the day the board had scheduled its final meeting. 'If she wants to go abroad on a holiday to do some sightseeing, then she can apply for that and I'll think about it.'

But General Zia had not counted on my mother's physician, Doctor Saeed. 'I will not sign your report,' Dr Saeed told the Major-General heading the medical board when it convened later that day. 'My conscience as a doctor will simply not allow me to put my patient's life in jeopardy.'

'Neither will mine,' another of the doctors on the board suddenly announced, breaking the unspoken rule that all members of a Federal board follow the lead of their commander.

'Nor mine,' added a second, then a third. The Major-General watched in shock as the defiance of the doctors snowballed: one after another, they all signed a statement produced by Dr Saeed calling for my mother's immediate release from Pakistan. 'You must sign, too,' Dr Saeed told him with delight. 'When all the officers agree, how can the General refuse?' The Major-General's shock no doubt deepened when, shortly after he did indeed place his signature on the document, Zia summarily removed him from both his civil and military posts.

The regime gave my mother permission to go abroad the day after the board's surprise announcement. I was overjoyed when I read the news in the morning paper and immediately applied to the authorities for permission to see her before she left. After almost a year's incarceration at Al-Murtaza, I was suddenly told to pack my things. A convoy of twelve police cars, trucks and jeeps took me to Moenjodaro airport. There, the police confiscated the cameras of the photographers recording the first sight the public had had of me for eleven months. Policemen armed with Sten guns followed me to the plane. When I arrived in Karachi, a helicopter flew over the car as I was driven in another convoy to 70 Clifton. All this for a daughter to say good-bye to her mother.

Mummy, lying pale and weak on her bed. Mummy, who had aged well beyond her years. Once again, I was torn with personal conflict. More than anything I wanted her to get the medical treatment abroad she so urgently needed. Yet I dreaded being left alone in the emptiness of detention. I fought not to think about the feelings of loneliness that lay ahead in sub-jail as Fakhri rushed in and out of the bedroom with last-minute messages from the Secretary General of the MRD and other party people. 'What will happen if Begum Bhutto leaves?' the messages ran. But Mummy had no choice.

'It is with a heavy heart, and under medical duress, that I take leave of our Land and our People for a temporary period,' Mummy wrote in her farewell statement. 'My thoughts will constantly be with you, with the struggling masses, with the hungry and the oppressed, with the exploited and the discriminated [against], with all those who have a vision for a progressive and prosperous Pakistan. . . .'

The regime kept announcing false dates in the newspapers for my mother's departure, hoping to discourage the people from gathering. Wise to the deviousness of the regime, a steady stream of PPP supporters constantly drove by 70 Clifton, searching for signs of her impending departure. We could hear their shouts from inside the walls. 'Jiye, Bhutto,' they called out. 'Begum Bhutto, zindabad! Long live Begum Bhutto!'

On the night of November 20, 1982, I kissed Mummy good-bye and gave her lockets filled with soil from my father's grave to give to my brothers and for my newly born nieces pendants engraved with the Quranic verse for safety. We both wept, not knowing what lay ahead for either one of us. 'Take care of yourself,' Mummy said to me. Together we walked out of the carved wooden front door of 70 Clifton where, thirteen years before, she had passed the Holy Quran over my head as I left for Harvard. And she was gone into the masses of people waiting outside the gates.

Samiya Waheed:

Dost Mohammed drove Begum Bhutto to the airport with Sanam and Fakhri in the back seat. The crowds were enormous as we pulled away from 70 Clifton. Defying the regime which had tried to keep her departure secret, Begum Bhutto turned the light on in the car so the people could see her. Mrs Niazi, Amina, my sister Salma and I followed in the car behind. At every intersection more cars joined us, until we formed a giant cavalcade of well-wishers. When we reached the top of the airport bridge, I looked back. The cars escorting Begum Bhutto to the airport had taken over seven lanes of the highway. Cars going in the opposite direction were forced into one lane.

The crowds waiting for her at the airport were even bigger. As we pulled up to the terminal, they overran our cars. I saw one man's bare feet through the windscreen as he climbed onto our roof. 'God go with you,' he called to Begum Bhutto as party members struggled to get her into a wheelchair and inside the terminal. They finally had to pass her wheelchair over the heads of the crowd. The airline crew for the Air France flight was finding it equally difficult to get through. They had to throw their flight bags to each other. At the end of their 100-yard struggle, their uniforms were rumpled, their hats knocked off, and the flight attendants' hair unpinned. It was the most tumultuous farewell Pakistan had ever witnessed. The people didn't know if they were going to see their Prime Minister's widow and beloved leader of the PPP again.

Mummy underwent a CATSCAN and further treatment in West Germany. She responded well and, luckily, the cancer was arrested. Meanwhile I remained under guard at 70 Clifton. Eleven jail personnel were posted inside the house. Outside, members of the Frontier Force were stationed every two feet around the house. Intelligence agents kept an eye on everything from their positions across from the front and back gates. I was to remain behind this hostile barricade at 70 Clifton for fourteen more months.

With great interest I read Jacobo Timerman's *Prisoner without a name, Cell without a number*, the newspaper publisher's chronicle of his two and a half years as a political prisoner in Argentina. 'It was the mirror of our souls, pain-filled eyes reflected in pain-filled eyes,' I noted in my diary. 'When he spoke of the torture in the electric chair, the words on the page leapt out at me. The body was torn apart, Timerman wrote, and yet, miraculously, there was no mark or scar on the flesh. The political prisoners were dumped after the chair treatment to recuperate, then returned to be tortured again. Was he speaking of Argentina or was he speaking of the military regime's interrogation cells in Pakistan?'

Presidential Order No. 4, issued March 24, 1982. Trials by special military court could now be held secretly, *in camera*. No one needed to be informed when a trial was taking place, who the accused were, what the charges were against them, or the resulting sentence. To make sure there were no leaks, it became a crime for the lawyers or anyone in any way connected with the case to disclose any information about it to the public.

Martial Law No. 54, issued September 23, 1982, and retroactive to the day of the coup against my father, July 5, 1977. The death penalty was now authorised for anyone committing an offence 'liable to cause insecurity, fear or despondency among the public.' The death penalty was also prescribed for anyone who had knowledge of such an offence and failed to inform the Martial Law authorities. Further, the accused was now assumed to be guilty until proven innocent. 'The military court . . . may, unless the contrary is proved, presume the accused has committed the offence charged,' the ordinance stated.

In October, two thousand lawyers met in Karachi to demand the restoration of civil liberties. The organisers of the conference were arrested and sentenced to one year's rigorous imprisonment. Two weeks later, Mr Hafiz Lakho, who had been one of my father's lawyers, was arrested, along with the Karachi Bar Association's Secretary.

In December I read in the papers that Zia was in Washington to have meetings with President Reagan and the members of Congress. In the month of December alone, there were more than twenty executions of prisoners in Pakistan. Did the members of Congress know about the human rights abuses in Pakistan? Did they care?

I would not find out the answer for another three years. Zia had expected his visit to Washington to be a great celebration of his new found respectability in the West, but he had run instead into a barrage of criticism during a meeting with the Senate Foreign Relations Committee. 'Those who were present recall that the General was cool and confident – until [Senator] Pell handed him a letter expressing the committee's concern about a number of Pakistan political prisoners,' Jack Anderson wrote in the *Washington Post*. 'Heading the list was Benazir Bhutto.'

Zia reportedly blew up when Senator Pell pressed him about my detentions. 'I can tell you this, Senator,' he snapped, claiming that I had broken the 'law'. 'She lives in a better house than any senator.' Zia then went on to claim that I was allowed visits from relatives and friends and 'even had use of a telephone'.

Upon hearing Zia's claims, Peter Galbraith put them to the test and telephoned 70 Clifton. A male voice answered and he asked to speak to me.

'You cannot speak to her. She is in jail,' the man replied.

'I am calling from the US Senate,' Peter ventured. 'Your president was just here and told us that Miss Bhutto could use the telephone.'

'You cannot speak to her. It is forbidden,' the man said firmly and slammed down the phone.

I spent December 25, the birthday of the founder of Pakistan, in detention at 70 Clifton. I was alone on New Year's Day and on my father's birthday. As 1983 began, I realised there had only been one New Year's Day that I had been free since 1977. I began to grind my teeth at night. In the morning I often woke up to find my knuckles swollen and my fingers so tightly clenched that I couldn't open them.

'I am truly grateful to God for all that He has blessed me with,' I wrote in my journal. 'My name, my honour, my reputation, my life, my father, mother, brothers, sister, education, ability to talk, having both my hands and legs, eyesight, hearing, no disfiguring scars. . . .' On and on my list of blessings went to eradicate my feelings of self-pity. Other political prisoners were far worse off than I was in the cold of their winter cells.

A member of the household staff came to the house one day with a new woollen scarf. There were many being sold cheaply on the black market by the Afghan refugees, he told me. I smuggled out a message to a party worker to have scarves made with the red, green and black colours of the PPP at the ends. We sent thousands to the prisoners in jail all over Sindh, along with socks and sweaters.

My ear began to hurt again, as did my teeth, my gums, and my joints. 'There's nothing the matter with your ear,' the regime's ear doctor at the

Naval hospital told me. Their dentist was equally inept, asking me which tooth I wanted him to X-ray. 'I don't know specifically which tooth,' I told him. 'You're the dentist, not me. It's in this general area.' 'We can't waste X-rays,' he said.

Stories about my health began to appear in the British press to which the Minister of Information at the Pakistani Embassy responded. 'Whenever she complained of any ailment she was taken to the best hospital in Karachi,' Qutubuddin Aziz wrote to the *Guardian*. 'Due to heavy smoking, she developed gum troubles for which she was treated by an eminent dentist of her choice.' How the regime lied. None of the doctors were of my choice. And I didn't smoke.

I was starved of conversation, of communication, of any exchange of ideas. I was lucky to have my cats with me at 70 Clifton, but they didn't make up for human company. The regime wanted me to remain completely incommunicado. I was surprised, therefore, when I received a request to appear in court in March, 1983, to give evidence at the trial of one Jam Saqi, a Communist who was being tried on various charges, among them working against the ideology of Pakistan and spreading dissatisfaction against the Armed Forces.

I had never met Jam Saqi. He had in fact opposed my father. But Jam Saqi, it turned out, had called upon a number of prominent politicians to define the issues to determine whether the charges against him were valid or not. I was more than willing to discuss the illegality of Martial Law, although I wasn't sure of the regime's motives for permitting me to appear in person. Perhaps they wanted to paint me as a 'communist sympathiser'. But the more important issue to me was the right of every defendant to an open and free trial. Besides, the court would provide me with a platform to air my own political views for the first time in almost two years.

When my first summons to appear arrived from the special military court on March 25, I wrote back through the jail authorities that I was a prisoner and couldn't simply go to the court at the appointed time. If the court wanted me to give evidence, the court would have to make the arrangements.

Word came back immediately from the Home Office to be ready at 7.00 am the following morning. I was. At 11.00, a new message arrived. My appearance had been rescheduled for the same time for the following day. I was ready again at 7.00 am on March 27. Again I waited for four hours. And again, they delayed my appearance for twenty-four hours. I consoled myself by thinking that the regime wanted to confuse the supporters who would gather to see me. When they did come for me on the third day, every precaution had been taken to isolate me from the public.

The streets we travelled by were totally deserted, as the entire route had been blockaded by the police. Heavy contingents of police were posted at all the entry points to Kashmir Road and pedestrian crossings were criss-crossed with barbed wire. When I arrived at the makeshift military court set up in a sports complex, I discovered the court, too, had been cleared. Jam Saqi's relatives and the relatives of the others were permitted to sit in the waiting room only, on condition that they did not speak to me. I didn't care. I was so happy to see the few lawyers who were there, as well as Samiya, Salma and my cousin Fakhri who had somehow managed to get special permission to pass through the blockades. Most of all, I welcomed the opportunity to talk.

The court-room was small, with a Colonel sitting behind a desk flanked by a Major and a magistrate. We sat in the three rows of chairs in front of them – Jam Saqi remained shackled throughout the proceedings. I thought it sad that even in this small room the army considered it necessary to keep the iron bars on. Jam Saqi was also asking the questions, as military courts didn't permit lawyers to defend the accused.

I was scheduled to testify for one day, but I gave such long answers to the questions Jam Saqi asked me that my testimony spread over two days. His questions did not have easy or short answers: 'We have been accused of working against the ideology of Pakistan – is there an ideology of Pakistan? What do you think of the Iranian Revolution? Is there any question of Martial Law in Islam?'

I knew that a culture of underground literature had grown up, with photostatted leaflets and poorly printed booklets circulating amongst the intelligentsia in the major cities, passed surreptitiously from hand to hand. Some printers, at a price, kept their presses open at night, secretly printing by torch-light, then destroying the plates. This was my one chance to give the party line and to discredit Martial Law. I was going to take it.

'In determining with clarity whether Martial Law has a place in Islam or not, we need to understand the concept of Martial Law and the concept of Islam,' I responded to the third question. 'Islam is the submission before the will of Allah whereas Martial Law is submission before the army commander. A Muslim submits only before the will of Allah.

'The term Martial Law, if I remember clearly, is a term derived from the days of Bismarck and the Prussian Empire. To integrate the territories he conquered, Bismarck superseded the law prevailing in those territories with his own law based on his whim and enforced at the point of a gun. Martial Law, before the second world war, also referred to the rule of an occupying army. The word of the commander of the occupying army superseded the existing law.

'Under colonialism, the indigenous people were treated as second-class citizens, denied a government of their choice, denied the right to shape their own destiny according to their hopes and desires and according to what would be economically beneficial for them. In the wake of World War II and the withdrawal of colonial powers from most of the colonies, the people of the newly independent countries enjoyed freedom and liberty for a little while. This was the period when nationalist leaders such as Nasser, Nkrumah, Nehru and Soekarno insisted on bringing social equality and justice to their people. But the former colonial powers, now restructured in shape, intended to keep their own people happy and, whether they consciously decided this or not, they ended up supporting a military-mullah complex. This mullah-military complex denied the people charge of their own destiny and the fruits that would avail from guiding this destiny. The situation was further complicated by the rivalry between the Soviet Union and the United States of America.

'Many of the newly independent states are now ruled by some form of military administration. However, an administration which is based on force and not consensus can not be congruent with the central principles of Islam which lays emphasis on consensus. Second, military regimes always come into power at the point of a gun or the threat of the use of force, whereas in Islam there is no concept of the usurpation of power. Therefore, we can see that there is no question of Martial Law in Islam.' My photostatted words would later find their way into press rooms, Bar Associations and even the prison cells of political activists.

The court-room was closed to the press, but one British correspondent evidently managed to gain admittance. No one knew he was there until suddenly a man entered and whispered into the Colonel's ear.

'Where?' the Colonel asked. The man inclined his head toward the back of the room.

'I believe you are a journalist,' the Colonel's voice boomed. 'Journalists are not permitted. You are to leave immediately.'

I caught a quick glimpse of a man dressed in *shalwar khameez* whom everyone had taken for a fair-skinned Pathan being escorted out of the court-room. But at least he had got a piece of the story. 'Miss Bhutto appeared composed and in good health and proceeded to demonstrate that she has lost none of her eloquence or wit,' the correspondent for the *Guardian* wrote subsequently.

My health, however, was not as good as it appeared. My generally depleted condition was aggravated by the disloyalty of some PPP leaders in April, 1983. Once more Zia was on the move, trying to establish the political base which had eluded him since the coup. Planning to announce the latest step to 'Islamise' the country in August, Zia was seizing the occasion to tour Sindh for the first time since he overthrew my father and buried the Constitution of 1973. Not surprisingly, the people reacted to his visit with fury and anger.

Under my father's government, Sindhis had made great strides, winning government jobs in Customs, the Police, in PIA. Quotas were set aside for them in universities, they were given plots of land and earned high wages in newly constructed hospitals, sugar mills and cement factories. Under Zia, all this had been reversed. Once more Sindh was being discriminated against. The state held some of the best land in Sindh. Under Zia, it was parcelled out to army officers instead of to landless farmers. The Sindhis who had risen to management positions in industry were being replaced with retired army officers. Despite the fact that 65 per cent of the country's revenue came from the Sindhi port of Karachi, little of the revenue found its way back into the province. The economic woes of Sindh fuelled the fires of indignation which had begun burning with the assassination of my father. Many in the province felt that if he had not been a Sindhi, he would not have been hanged.

After the local bodies elections of 1979, the elected PPP Councillors of Badin and Hyderabad passed resolutions condemning the execution of my father and paying tribute to him. In retaliation, Zia had begun disqualification proceedings against PPP Councillors all over Sindh. Now Zia was seeking acceptance from the few remaining PPP Councillors, asking them to receive him on his tour of the province. To my horror, the newspapers seemed to imply that they were considering acquiescing to his wishes.

How could I get a message out? The servants were searched coming and going from 70 Clifton and were followed by Intelligence agents on motorcycles as they went about their errands. Finally I asked one of the servants to act ill in front of the guards and pretend to go on leave to his home in Larkana.

'I hope your son is not going to receive Zia,' was my verbal message to the Sindh PPP chief whose son was one of the Councillors. 'As you know, it's against party policy. Please pass the word along.'

I sent a message as well to the PPP Councillor in Larkana. 'You and the others can put yourselves in hospital or you can leave Larkana and not be traceable,' I told him. 'But don't go and meet Zia.'

I was helpless with fury when I turned on the television and saw that some of them had met Zia anyway. They had evidently decided in a meeting that the party couldn't take action against all of them. I was deeply disappointed. Once more, politicians were serving their individual ambitions at the expense of the unity of the party. Perhaps I was being too idealistic, but I expected more. I had no choice but to make a forbidden political phone call to a PPP President. 'I want you to expel the PPP Councillors who had a meeting with Zia. They have violated party discipline,' I said rapidly, knowing that with the phone being monitored I couldn't afford to waste any time. The phone immediately went dead. It was never reconnected.

I received no more calls from my relatives. The few visitors I had been allowed were stopped. The searchers at the gate cracked down on the household staff. As they passed in and out of the compound, they were made to take off their shoes and socks. Even their hair was searched. The packets of meat and vegetables the cook brought from the market were cut open. Even the rubbish was searched.

In total isolation again, I felt increasingly ill. The pain intensified in my ear. When I rubbed my left cheek, I felt little sensation. And the noises were getting worse again.

I was walking through the reception area at 70 Clifton one evening in April when the floor seemed to rise towards the ceiling. I gripped the arm of the sofa to steady myself, waiting for the attack of dizziness to pass. Instead a wall of darkness advanced towards me. I pitched forward onto the sofa, in a faint.

Luckily, one of the staff saw me collapse. 'Quick. Quick. Ms Sahiba needs a doctor,' he ran to tell the jailers. And, once again, it seemed as if God was protecting me. Instead of the usual bureaucratic routine of having to write to the Home Department for medical attention, then waiting for several days, sometimes two weeks for clearance, the police brought a doctor from the emergency room at MidEast hospital within hours. And, once again, the infection in my ear had burst outwards rather than inwards.

'Your condition is very dangerous,' the doctor said, after examining my ear. 'You must see an ear specialist.'

'If you don't specify that I need a specialist, then the regime will continue to claim I don't have an ear problem,' I told him.

The young doctor had the courage to write my need for an ear specialist on his records for the regime in very specific language. The regime sent the ear, nose and throat specialist who had operated on my sinuses three years before to see me. Preferring privacy, he does not want his name to be mentioned in this book. But he was to stabilise my health and perhaps even to save my life.

'There is a perforation in your ear,' this doctor told me, confirming my suspicions about the regime's doctor during my detention at Al-Murtaza four years before. 'The perforation has led to a middle-ear and mastoid-bone infection.' My current infection would have to be drained regularly to relieve some of the pressure on the facial nerve which was causing the numbness. When the infection was arrested, I'd need an operation. 'You'll have to go abroad for microscopic surgery,' he said. 'We don't have the technology here. We'd have to saw open your skull. This is a dangerous procedure. For your own safety, you'd be far, far better off to go abroad.'

I looked at him numbly. Was he implying something beyond the normal risks of this type of surgery in Pakistan? I knew that one of my doctors had been approached by the regime in 1980 to say that I had an inner-ear rather than a middle-ear problem and was in need of psychiatric treatment. 'We will form ten medical boards to back up your diagnosis,' he had been told. What a nice solution it would have been for the regime to dismiss me as a psychiatric case. But the doctor had refused. Now this doctor was adamant that I leave Pakistan. 'I can do the operation here, but I'm frightened they'll put pressure on me to do something under the anaesthetic,' he said. 'Even if I refuse, they'll get somebody else to do it. On all counts, it's much better for you to go abroad.'

I applied to the regime for permission to leave the country on medical grounds. At first, there was no response. But I needed the time anyway. 'You won't be strong enough to cope with a general anaesthetic for several months,' the doctor told me. 'You'll have to build up your system.' Like my mother, I was put on a high-protein diet of milk, steak, chicken and eggs.

But my ear did not improve. I began to lose feeling on the left side of my face. My head pounded steadily, the clicking in my ear making it almost impossible to hear anything else. The doctor obtained permission from the authorities to make weekly visits to try and drain the infection at 70 Clifton. And he was made to suffer for his medical concern for a Bhutto.

'You drive often to Hyderabad, don't you?' his neighbour, a Police Superintendent asked him shortly after he began his weekly visits. 'Have you seen "Death Wish"?' The next day a video of the film was delivered anonymously to his house. Threatening telephone calls followed, as well as a notice from the income tax authorities that he was being audited for tax evasion. His professional integrity was even called into question by the regime who served him a show-cause notice as to why he should not be dismissed from the hospital. Still, the doctor found the courage to go on treating me which I deeply appreciated. He was about the only human being from the outside world I had to talk to, though the regime, I later found out from Peter Galbraith, was claiming otherwise.

Peter Galbraith:

The Pakistani government finally responded at the end of June to the letter Senator Pell and the other Senators had submitted to Zia in December about the specific political prisoners being held in Pakistan. Echoing Zia's comments at the time, the letter said of Benazir's confinement:

'She is presently under detention at her residence in Karachi to prevent her from indulging in political activities which are banned. However, she is given all the comforts possible and doctors of her choice examine and treat her when required. She is allowed interviews with friends and relatives. Eight close relatives are allowed to stay with her in groups of three at a time. She is allowed to use twenty-four personal servants of her choice and has a telephone for her use.'

Soon afterwards I received a call from a cousin of Benazir's. I asked her about the facts in the letter.

'Not true,' she exploded. 'No friends have been able to visit her. Her sister Sanam has been able to see her only once in the previous three months. Her cousin Fakhri has also had a hard time seeing Benazir. She cannot even go out into the garden. She is lonely and ill. I am worried about her.'

I sent Senator Pell a memo. The timing was fortuitous. Yaqub Khan, Pakistan's Foreign Minister and former Ambassador to Washington, was in town. Yaqub had made many friends in Washington and had a reputation as a straight-shooter. I did not think Yaqub would be party to any duplicity on Benazir's treatment. When Senator Pell asked the Foreign Minister about the apparent discrepancy between the official account of Benazir's treatment and these new facts, Yaqub stiffened. He seemed genuinely shocked and promised to look into the matter when he returned to Pakistan.

June 21, 1983. The longest day of the year and my 30th birthday. Ever the optimist, I had written to the Home Secretary explaining that I had had no visitors for months and would like permission to see my school friends on my birthday. Much to my surprise and delight, the regime agreed.

In the evening, Samiya, her sister and Paree trooped in bearing a chocolate cake which Paree had spent hours baking. Under the watchful eye of the policewoman, we hugged and kissed each other. 'Thank God the cake is safe,' Samiya said. 'They searched everything else so thoroughly we were scared they'd cut into the cake before you could.'

Victoria Schofield and others of my friends in England had not forgotten me either. As my birthday approached, I found out later, Victoria had written to the current President of the Oxford Union, pointing out that this was my third birthday in detention. On June 21, the Oxford Union adjourned for a minute's silence, an honour normally afforded an ex-President only when he or she dies. Another old friend and former President of the Cambridge Union, David Johnson, was in the debating chamber of the Oxford Union at the time. He subsequently arranged for a prayer to be said for me the following Sunday at all the public services at Westminster Abbey and at St Paul's Cathedral in London. Both were lovely expressions of concern and friendship.

The expression of concern which arrived about the time of my birthday from a member of the regime was more suspect. 'Please be ready at 7.00 this evening,' one of the jail officials told me. 'We are taking you to a government rest house.'

'Why?' I asked him.

'Because the Martial Law Administrator wishes to see you,' he said almost triumphantly.

The Martial Law Administrator? 'I will not go to meet the General,' I said.

The jail official was shocked. 'But you have to go. You are a prisoner,' he said.

'I don't care,' I told him. 'I will not meet him. You'll have to drag me there, and even then I will shout and scream and make a scene. I will not go to my captors.'

The jail official scurried away, mumbling that I wasn't being sensible, that my refusal to meet General Abbasi would not be good for me. But I didn't care. To those of us opposing Zia, any contact with the hated military rulers was regarded as a sell-out. To go to them would be tantamount to accepting their authority and tacitly recognising them.

That night I began packing a suitcase, convinced that retaliation would come from the regime in the form of sending me back to jail. I collected what had become a familiar list of prison supplies – pens, diaries, insect repellent, lavatory paper – but no one came to take me to prison. Instead, to my absolute surprise, the Martial Law Administrator came to visit me at 70 Clifton.

It was unheard of for the arrogant military rulers so used to summoning and commanding to actually come and visit a leader of the opposition. I stared in disbelief at the white haired General sitting at 70 Clifton in his khaki uniform during the first of several visits. His message was always the same.

'I know you are ill,' he kept telling me. 'The fact that I'm in the army doesn't mean that I'm not concerned. Remember, our families have known each other for generations. I would like nothing better than to see you receiving medical treatment abroad. But we can't afford any political embarrassments.'

Remain polite, I willed myself. There is no point in showing your hand. I guessed that General Abbasi had come to gauge my morale and probe as to what I would do if allowed to go abroad. I gave him the impression that I was anxious to have my treatment and return home immediately. In a way this was true, because at the time I had no intention of staying in exile. I had every intention, however, of taking every opportunity I could to lambast the regime.

I didn't realise at the time what a bind the regime was in. The doctor had put on record that I needed medical treatment abroad and that if anything happened to me in detention the onus would be on the regime. There was the added pressure from Senator Pell and the Senate Foreign Relations Committee and possibly from Yaqub Khan. As the summer of

1983 dragged on, my detention had become not only an embarrassment to the regime but counter-productive. In my isolation at 70 Clifton, however, I knew none of this. Instead I was jeopardising my possible release by once more getting involved in politics.

The disturbances in Sindh during Zia's tour had not diminished. As August 14, Pakistan Independence Day and the date Zia had chosen to announce yet another bogus election schedule, drew nearer, the MRD launched its second mass movement to restore democracy. I followed the MRD call for agitation closely from 70 Clifton, reading the newspapers carefully and listening intently to the BBC. At great risk, I communicated by message with the PPP leaders who had organised a secret cell at the nearby MidEast Hospital and with my home district of Larkana, sending political instructions and helping to arrange funds.

This MRD movement developed differently from earlier movements. In the past, the mere mention of the words 'protest movement' would bring the regime sweeping down on political activists, arresting them in the thousands to pre-empt any action and to leave the people leaderless. Now the MRD leaders were being left free to court arrest – which they did. The police did not even prevent the crowds from gathering to cheer the MRD leaders on. The landlord class in Sindh threw themselves into the movement, providing tractors and trucks to transport party supporters and supplying better communication through their managers.

Some PPP leaders, however, showed initial hesitation in joining the movement. It was believed that the PPP leader Jatoi had had meetings with American officials and army officers and had received their backing to overthrow Zia; Jatoi would continue in power while the PPP would be out. I persuaded the PPP leadership to join the movement regardless, stressing that it was more important to unite at the time of an anti-Zia movement and to worry about the splintering off later, if necessary.

As the movement slowly grew, I smuggled out several letters to party officials, briefing them on what to tell foreign diplomats and what to tell the press, urging them to sustain the momentum and not give the regime the time to mop us up. If the messages were discovered, I knew that instead of being sent abroad I'd be sent back to prison. But the political emancipation of the people of Pakistan overrode anything else for me. To deflect the suspicions of the jail officials during their visits, I feigned more weakness than I felt. Normally, anger and defiance gave me temporary strength, however ill I was feeling, during these weekly visits. But during the Sindh Uprising of 1983, I consciously kept my eyes on the carpet so they couldn't see my spirit and would leave convinced that I was too ill to be thinking of anything else.

Meanwhile, Jatoi was putting pressure on me to get a message for the people from my mother. With great difficulty, somebody contacted her by phone. 'Tell Benazir to issue the statement in my name,' she relayed back. I sat before the electric typewriter and, in between bouts of power failures, typed like a demon, the words rushing through my fingers and filling the pages rapidly.

My patriotic and heroic Countrymen, my honourable Brothers and Sisters, my brave Sons and Daughters [I began my mother's call to the nation, which was translated into Urdu and Sindhi and distributed surreptitiously throughout the province]. . . . The aim of our movement is civil disobedience. For six long years we have been facing persecution and oppression. Our calls for resumption of democracy have been ignored, our workers have been imprisoned and sentenced to death. Enough is enough. We appeal to all the bus owners to take their buses off the roads, to all the railwaymen to stop plying the trains. To the policemen we say: follow the example of your brothers in Dadu and do not shoot innocent people who are your brothers. Do not be frightened of this movement. It is for our people, for our poor, for our children so that they do not live in poverty, hunger and disease. Struggle for your Parliament, for your Government, for your Constitution so that the decisions are taken for the poor people and not for the junta and its stooges. . . .

The movement exploded into an intense and very widespread expression of discontent against Zia ul-Haq. Railway stations were ransacked. Trucks and buses stopped running. Police stations were burned. Hundreds of people lost their lives. Zia himself was almost killed by a supposedly friendly crowd. The helicopter he was believed to be in was stormed shortly after it landed in Dadu and its occupants attacked. Actually, Zia was in a second helicopter which veered away to land somewhere else. When he was discovered in a rest house, he narrowly escaped being lynched.

The uprising in Sindh soon spilled over into the other provinces. The Bar Associations in Quetta, Baluchistan and Peshawar in the Frontier province defied the ban against political statements and called for elections. In Lahore, riot police sealed all the gates of the High Court to prevent the lawyers from taking out a protest procession, then pelted them with stones. A procession of lawyers went out anyway, led by one of my father's former lawyers, Talaat Yaqub. 'You who want to stay at home, take these bangles,' Talaat Yaqub shouted at the predominantly male Lahore Bar Association, throwing off her glass bangles and waving the Pakistani flag. 'I am calling for freedom.' Hundreds of lawyers joined her, chanting for democracy and marching defiantly into the clutches of the police.

The nationwide rebellion was not crushed by the guns and tanks of the Army until the second week in October, leaving particular bitterness in the hearts of the Sindhis. 800 people were reportedly killed. Whole villages were razed and crops burned. Women reportedly were molested by the Army, bringing back dark memories of the Army's rampage in Bangladesh twelve years before. In the ashes of fury, Sindhi nationalism was born. The move towards secession escalated in the other minority provinces as well. The fragile federation of Pakistan was strained to breaking point under the ruthlessness of Zia and six years of Martial Law.

The Reagan administration, however, stood by its man. 'Newsweek reported that Washington considers Zia its trump card in its global strategy,' I noted in my journals on October 22. 'One Western intelligence source is quoted as saying that the CIA has "substantially" expanded its operation in Pakistan. Last week Newsweek said the CIA was involved in holding up Zia's tottering regime. They want to make sure Zia does not become another Shah of Iran. Over the past year and a half, large numbers of American spooks operating in Egypt have moved from Cairo to Islamabad. The report concluded: "It has become clear that Zia will cede power only when he is forced to do so."' And I remained locked up at 70 Clifton, now in my fifth year of detention.

Darkness. Roaring in my head. Wave after wave of darkness. I woke up in my bedroom soon after the Sindh uprising to find the doctor's hand on my pulse and a great look of relief on his face. I had had a bad reaction to the local anaesthetic he'd used to drain my ear, he told me, but there was no way to summon emergency help. The phone lines at 70 Clifton were dead. A month later, I suffered a severe attack of vertigo, totally losing all sense of balance and becoming violently nauseous. Again, there was no way for the doctor to summon medical help.

For days after the treatments for my ear, I was feverish, coughing and sweating. After giving me an audiogram, the doctor determined that I had suffered a hearing loss of almost 40 decibels. 'I cannot take responsibility for the health of the patient if I continue to treat her in detention,' the doctor informed the Home Secretary in November, applying for permission to perform further treatments in the hospital. 'With the onset of winter months, even slight nose or throat infections will cause more damage to her hearing. Unless surgical measures are taken soon, possibility of complications like paralysis of the nerves of the face and loss of balance mechanism exist.' The permission for hospital treatment was finally approved and further treatments went more smoothly. But I still had to prepare myself physically and psychologically for the possibility of going abroad for surgery.

I held my head high when I was let out of Karachi Central
Prison in September of 1981 to attend my sister Sanam's
wedding. The next morning the police returned me to my
seventh month in solitary confinement.

Sanam took my mother to the airport on November 20, 1982, after the doctors on Zia's own medical board verified her need for cancer treatment abroad. 'There is nothing the matter with Begum Bhutto,' Zia insisted. 'If she wants to go abroad to do some sightseeing, then she can apply for that. . . .'

I was in sub-jail in Karachi in 1983 when lawyers defied Martial Law and called for elections (*above*). When women protested against Zia's Law of Evidence which reduced the worth of a woman's testimony to half that of a man's, they were tear-gassed and beaten.

Years of exile: In Washington (*below*), I thanked Peter Galbraith and Senator Pell for their efforts on my behalf. In Pakistan, General Zia confirmed the death sentences (*right*) of four other political prisoners ten days before his rubber-stamp court made the announcement public.

(*Opposite*) My brother Shah died in agony only hours after Sanam took this last photo of him in Cannes. Our grief was unfathomable when we took Shah home to be buried near my father in our ancestral family graveyard.

OFFICE OF THE CHIEF MARTIAL LAW ADMINISTRATOR

PAKISTAN

Confirmation minute in respect of accused
Muhammad Ayub Malik,Abdul Nasir Baluch,
Muhammad Essa and Saif Ullah Khalid of
Karachi.

    I do hereby confirm the sentence of death
awarded to -

    a. Accused Muhammad Ayub Malik s/o Ghulam
        Sarwar Malik,Karachi.

    b. Accused Abdul Nasir Baluch s/o Wali
        Muhammad Baluch,Karachi.

    c. Accused Muhammad Essa s/o Faiz Muhammad
        Baluch,Karachi.

    d. Accused Saif Ullah Khalid alias Sain
        Khalid s/o Muhammad Ali Jauhar,Karachi.

Rawalpindi.

                General
            (M.Zia-ul-Haq)

26 x 84

Return to Pakistan: Over a million people greeted me in Lahore in April, 1986. Supporters showered my jeep with rose petals as I toured the four provinces. *'Zia jahve!'* the crowds roared. 'Zia must go!'

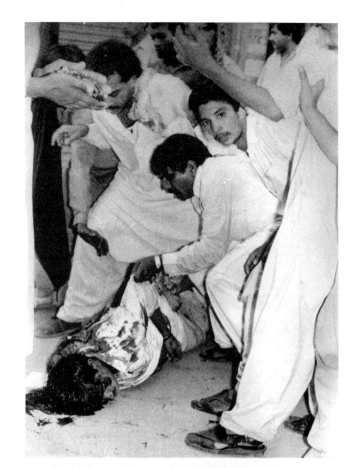

Shortly after President Reagan praised the regime for making great strides towards democracy', Zia's henchmen gunned down peaceful demonstrators marking Pakistan Independence Day. The police were just as brutal to those protesting at the attack on my Jeep in January, 1987.

My marriage to Asif Zardari on December 18, 1987, was 'arranged' by our families. 200,000 people danced and cheered at the People's Reception (*below*) in Lyari, giving Asif his first taste of the love and support of the masses for the Pakistan People's Party.

I had been in detention for so long that I was suspicious of everyone and everything. The thought of putting my life into a stranger's hands, even those of a British surgeon, made me apprehensive. To double-check whether or not I needed an operation, I smuggled my medical records to Dr Niazi in London. He concurred with the medical diagnosis.

Yet I still felt in deep conflict. Thousands of political prisoners remained in unspeakable conditions in jails throughout Pakistan, many facing death sentences. While I was incarcerated too, I felt I was a source of inspiration and comfort to them. I shared their suffering, their pain, their defiance. They were there for me, and I for them. Would they feel orphaned if I left them? Would they feel deserted?

As December passed, I felt sure the regime would have to release me soon. I had heard nothing from the authorities during the rebellion in Sindh. I knew they wouldn't release me at the height of the troubles, knowing I would take the news abroad. But now the rioting had subsided. They no longer had any excuse.

I was also strong enough now to make the journey. Though the doctor had planned to insert a drainage tube in my ear to allow me to fly, he now said I would be all right taking decongestants and chewing-gum during takeoff and landing. The stress and anxiety which had contributed to my bad reaction during my earlier ear treatments had lessened with the regime's decision to allow Sanam to visit me every day. The doctor had insisted to the authorities that it was impossible for me to regain my health if the regime continued to refuse me human contact.

Towards the end of December, the authorities asked Sanam and me for our passports, our visa forms, our foreign exchange forms. 'Make reservations,' we were told. But when the day came for our departure, no one would come for us. I spent the time tying up my personal affairs, arranging to have the houses managed in my absence, straightening out my taxes. Another flight came and went.

Our next scheduled flight was for the early hours of January 10, 1984. Without warning, the authorities arrived at 70 Clifton at 11.30 pm. 'You're leaving tonight,' they said. 'You have a few hours to pack.' I heard their words in disbelief. Hastily, I typed up a last message for the people. 'Brave Party Workers and Dear Countrymen,' I began. 'Before embarking on this journey in connection with ill health, I seek your leave, your prayers and your blessings. . . .' I felt numb as I gathered up my things, and put my cat in a travelling case. After all that had happened to me in the last seven years, even the good things seemed unreal.

Sanam was waiting for me in the courtyard in an unmarked car. There was no one on the roads as we were sped to the airport and put in a side room by ourselves. I didn't allow myself the slightest bit of excitement. I had just finished reading Oriana Fallaci's *The Man*. Air force planes had been sent to

213

bring the protagonist back to the airport after his flight had taken off.

We were taken out to the Swiss Air plane by the police. As I walked up the passenger stairs, I saw the smile on the stewardess's face. I'll never forget it. It wasn't the smile of a policeman or a Martial Law or prison official. It was the smile of a civilian, another human being. The door to the plane closed. At 2.30 am, Sanam and I took off for Switzerland. No planes came after us. I had no idea until I talked to Peter Galbraith later why, after seven years of Martial Law, Zia had chosen this moment to release me.

Peter Galbraith:

In late December, the Foreign Relations Committee asked me to travel to South Asia to prepare a report in connection with the Committee's review of regional security issues. I took a letter with me to Yaqub Khan signed by Committee Chairman Charles Percy and Senator Pell, reminding him of his government's statement that Benazir was permitted visits from friends. 'Mr Galbraith is a personal friend of Miss Benazir Bhutto dating back to their days as classmates at Harvard University,' their letter pointed out. The Senators asked that I be granted permission to visit her.

I planned my visit to Pakistan so as to make Karachi the last stop. This time the US Embassy was extremely helpful. The decision on whether I was to be granted permission to see Benazir, I was told, was being made by General Zia himself.

I arrived in Karachi late in the evening on January 9. Not having received any response to my request to see Benazir, I had made an arrangement to see Sanam the next day. I was very disappointed, and once more wrote Benazir a long letter.

Early the next morning I received a call from the US Consulate to come right over. When I arrived, the deputy Consul-General told me that Benazir had been taken to the airport shortly after midnight and put on a Swiss Air Flight. Sanam had gone with her.

I couldn't believe it. I had a Consulate car take me to 70 Clifton. The ever present police guards were gone. The house was all shut up. Benazir was free.

214

TAKING ON THE DICTATOR

11

THE YEARS OF EXILE

'Mummy!'

'Pinkie! You're free. How I've dreamed of this day!'

I look at the horizons, the unending space as we step out of Geneva airport. After three years of being constrained by walls, my eyes take time to adjust. I can't believe I'm free.

The telephone is already ringing when we arrive at my mother's flat. 'Yes, yes, she is really here,' my mother says over the phone to Mir and Shah. 'What you heard on the BBC about her release is correct.'

Mir. Shah Nawaz. My brothers' voices and mine interrupt each other in our excitement. 'How are you?' I shout over the line, pressing the receiver to my good ear. 'Thank God you're alive,' Mir shouts back. 'I'm coming to see you tomorrow.' 'Stay for a week, so I can come too,' Shah adds. 'Oh Shah, I can't,' I tell him. 'I have to go to London to see the doctor.' We make a promise to see each other as soon as possible.

The phone rings constantly from Los Angeles, London, Paris — my mother's friends and relatives calling to congratulate her on my release. I wasn't ready to talk to anyone yet, and only spoke to Yasmin and Dr Niazi in London. Ardeshir Zahedi, a friend of my parents and Iran's former Ambassador to the United States, arrived with caviare. Mummy, Sunny and I stayed up talking through the night. It all seemed so unbelievable. Yesterday I had been a prisoner. Today I was free, with my mother and sister. We were together. We were all alive.

Mir! A little brown-haired girl pulling at my coat! 'Meet your niece, Fathi,' Mir told me, standing in my mother's flat on my second day of freedom. Was my brother really standing in front of me? I saw his lips moving, heard my own voice responding. The noise of our reunion must have been deafening, but I can't remember a thing we said. At twenty-nine, Mir looked so handsome, his dark eyes flashing one minute, gentling the next as he lifted his eighteen-month-old daughter to give me a kiss. 'Wait till you see Shah,' Mir laughed. Shah had been eighteen the last time I'd seen him, just a boy. Now he was twenty-five with a longed-for moustache.

I watched the sun come up over the Alps, felt the cold clear air bathe my face. It felt wonderful although my ear was blocked and numb. Traffic was beginning to stir and I scanned the street below. There were no intelligence vans parked near the building, no agents that I could see hiding in doorways. Was it really true? Was I truly free? I rubbed my ear. My discomfort was a reminder of why I'd come abroad.

Meanwhile, word of my release was spreading among the Pakistani exile community scattered around Europe and highly concentrated among the 378,000 Pakistanis living in England. When Sunny and I flew on to London that afternoon, a crowd of Pakistanis had gathered to greet me at Heathrow airport. From the sound of political slogans in the air, I felt as if I were back in Karachi.

Yasmin Niazi, Heathrow Airport:

You can't imagine the number of people at the airport including the British press, all pushing and shoving to catch a glimpse of Benazir. It was as if she had come back from the dead. No one ever thought they'd see her again. 'Who is she, a film star or something?' an English policeman asked me as he and another policeman struggled to control the crowd. 'She's our political leader,' I told him. 'A politician?' he said in amazement.

'Have you come into exile?' the press asked Benazir when she finally came through the gate. Her answer was a great relief to the Pakistanis thronged at the airport as well as the millions who heard it later over the radio or read it in the newspapers. 'Exile? Why should I go into exile?,' she said. 'I am only in England for medical treatment. I was born in Pakistan and I'm going to die in Pakistan. My grandfather is buried there. My father is buried there. I will never leave my country.'

Her words brought great hope to all her countrymen, especially the poor. 'I am not giving up on you,' her message said. 'I will stay by your side until my last breath. The Bhuttos keep their promises.'

Flowers and fruit baskets filled up Auntie Behjat's small flat in London's Knightsbridge area where Sunny and I shared a guest bedroom. Journalists and old friends from Oxford called asking to see me, as did party leaders and supporters. London was the centre of political activity for PPP members in exile: my own brothers had lived here, and it was the base for many PPP leaders who had fled Pakistan after the coup. The phone rang constantly with their requests for appointments. 'I'll only take ten minutes of your time,' one after another said as they streamed in and out of the flat. Others among the large population of Pakistanis in England simply came to the front door, ringing the doorbell and clustering outside in the street. Auntie Behjat and her husband Uncle Karim were very gracious, but the situation was impossible. It grew more complicated when Auntie Behjat spotted a car full of Pakistani men parked all day outside the building. 'This is a free country. You don't have to put up with that,' Auntie Behjat told me when the car started following me wherever I went. She called Scotland Yard and, miraculously, the car disappeared. We felt a small triumph in being able to force Zia's agents to leave me alone. But my apprehension remained.

For all that I was free, I dreaded going out of the flat. Every time I stepped out of the front door my stomach, my neck and my shoulders tensed. I couldn't walk two steps without turning around to see if I was being followed. After all the years of living alone behind prison walls, even the crowded streets in London seemed threatening. I wasn't used to people, to voices, to noise. I leapt into the first taxi I saw instead of taking the tube to go to my doctors' appointments. When I reached my destination and was forced to get out in the street, even for a short distance, my heart would start pounding again and my breathing got shallow. Adjusting to real life was very difficult.

I put on a veneer of self-confidence and hid my anxieties from everyone. I had to. My years in detention and my family's treatment by the military regime had elevated me in the eyes of many Pakistanis to super-human status. The publicity surrounding my release and my arrival in England had catapulted me into being a public figure there as well. It would hardly have been seemly or inspiring for someone who had challenged Martial Law to suddenly succumb to an anxiety attack on Hyde Park Corner. Breathe deeply, I told myself whenever I was forced to go out. Move steadily. Don't panic.

A few days after I arrived in London, I received an unexpected visitor. Peter Galbraith had just arrived from Karachi and wanted to have lunch with me, Auntie Behjat told me. I had no idea of the role he had played in my release, and was merely excited to be able to see an old friend. Summoning my courage, I left the flat and took a taxi to the Ritz Hotel.

Peter Galbraith:

I wasn't altogether comfortable when I called her. It was one of those funny situations where you haven't seen someone in seven years, compounded by the very different experience she'd been through compared to my own. I waited for her somewhat nervously in the lobby of the Ritz where people gather for tea.

She looked surprisingly well when she arrived and we went into lunch. I didn't have any particular set of expectations, but she certainly seemed different. She had a new kind of self-confidence, a much more relaxed self-confidence than she'd had the last time I had seen her at Oxford in 1977.

She'd always been attractive, but now she seemed striking. And she was very focused. There was no aspect of 'I can't believe this is happening to me'. She picked up in mid-stride. I filled her in on developments in

Washington, and told about the efforts of Senator Pell and others on her behalf. I also brought her up to date on some of our mutual friends and showed her pictures of my son.

As we walked back to her aunt's apartment after lunch, I urged her as a friend to give up the dangerous life of politics. 'In Pakistan you risk imprisonment or even assassination,' I told her. 'Why not come to America and get on with your life? Perhaps you could get a fellowship at Harvard's Center for International Affairs.'

'I'd love the chance to read the books on the Bhutto years and on the years of Martial Law to see other peoples' interpretations,' she told me. 'But my first obligation is to the party. In political terms, it makes more sense for me to be here, where the Pakistani community is larger and less dispersed.'

She did, however, seem excited by my suggestion that she come to America for a working visit. She knew foreign influence and publicity could be important in securing the release of the political prisoners still in Pakistan. The only problem as we walked and talked was her ear. I kept forgetting which ear she was deaf in. I kept talking into the wrong ear.

My microscopic surgery in the last week of January took five hours. When I came round from the anaesthetic at University Hospital, my surgeon, Mr Graham, was there. 'Smile,' he said to me. I thought he was trying to cheer me up and groggily complied. Later he gave me a sip of juice. 'How does it taste?' he said. 'Delicious,' I said. He made notations on my chart. 'You came through the operation fine,' he said. 'The facial nerve on the left side of your face isn't damaged, and you haven't lost your sense of taste.'

I recovered slowly with my mother at a temporary flat she had taken in the pretty, tree-lined area of Collingham Gardens. For weeks I lay flat in bed, unable to sit up for more than ten minutes without my head pounding and being racked by bouts of nausea and dizziness. When I finally could sit up, it was difficult to bend my neck to read a book or to write without the pounding coming back. My head often felt as if it was going to explode. 'Your reaction isn't unusual,' Mr Graham assured me on my regular visits to have my ear examined and my hearing checked.

I was startled, though, by his news at my six-weeks check-up. 'There's the possibility you'll need another operation in nine months to a year's time,' he told me. Nine months to a year? I'd no intention of staying in London that long. I was already toying with the idea of going home to Pakistan, though my mother, Auntie Behjat, Sunny and Yasmin were all urging me to stay on in Europe.

'Take a break from politics and live with me for a while. Next time you go back Zia will put you in prison and you might not get out alive,' my mother argued.

'Even in prison I can be a rallying point against the regime,' I countered.

'Why not be a rallying point against the regime from here?' the others insisted. The doctor's words clinched their argument. But I still felt reluctant. Nine long months. How could I best spend my time?

As I recuperated, I decided to mount an international campaign to expose the regime's maltreatment of the 40,000 political prisoners still in jail in Pakistan. Though Pakistan was receiving financial aid from Western European countries as well as from the United States, the democratic countries were paying little or no attention to Zia's human rights violations. As a prominent and recently released political prisoner in exile, I was in a position to make known the details of what was happening in Pakistan. Perhaps then the democratic countries would use their leverage to help stop Zia from making arbitrary arrests and holding political prisoners for years without charge or hearings, and sentencing more and more innocent men to death just for their political opposition.

Eighteen political prisoners were about to be tried by a military court in Rawalpindi, accused of conspiring to overthrow the government. Fifty-four others were being held in Kot Lakhpat Jail in Lahore, charged with criminal conspiracy and sedition for their alleged involvement with Al-Zulfikar. The PPP labour leader at the Karachi Steel Mill, Nasser Baloach, was being tried with four co-defendants in Karachi on the false charges of complicity in the hijacking – a charge which could result in a sentence of death. Typical of Zia's military 'justice', few people inside or outside Pakistan even knew the trial was taking place, or what, if any, was the evidence against the accused.

I had only learned of the arrest of Nasser Baloach in 1981 from the jail superintendent at Sukkur Jail. It had taken two years for Nasser Baloach and his co-defendants to be brought before a military court. Surrounded by the secrecy of Presidential Order No. 4 which held not only that a man was guilty unless proven innocent, but forbade any disclosure of the court proceedings under the Official Secrets regulations, I had only found out about their trial when I received a note in Karachi Central Jail from Nasser Baloach, smuggled in by a sympathetic prison guard.

'The military court is so biased against us that we have already been told that we are as good as dead bodies lying in a grave,' he had written to me in May, 1983. 'During the eight-hour proceedings we cannot take notes, drink water, answer the call of nature or offer prayers. Our hands and feet are bar-fettered. When our defence lawyer could not attend, the proceedings continued with the remark "we need only the accused and the prosecutors".' By February, 1984, his trial had still not been concluded.

I was concerned too, about another labour leader, Ayaz Samoo, who had been arrested in December, 1983, and falsely implicated in the murder of a political supporter of General Zia's. His trial before a military court was about to get underway. Like Baloach, Samoo had been arrested in what the PPP saw as an attempt by the Zia regime to crush the labour movement in the industrial city of Karachi. As was the case in Baloach's trial, the charge against Samoo was punishable by death. We had to act, and act quickly.

When I could sit up in bed, I started to compile a list of other political persecutions with information from my own prison notes and reports coming from sympathisers in Pakistan. I learnt the value of providing Amnesty International with information when I saw how the human rights organisation could mobilise world opinion as they did in the case of Raza Kazim, a Pakistani international lawyer arrested at his home in Lahore in January and not heard from again. Amnesty's 'Urgent Call for Action' on Raza Kazim's behalf was taken up in the Western press.

'The recent disappearance of Raza Kazim of Lahore, Pakistan, is an alarming case in point,' ran a March article in *The Nation* about the numbing numbers of human rights offences worldwide. '. . . The United States, which supports Pakistan with $525 million annually in military and economic aid, has shown callous indifference to the case. . . . Apparently the Secretary of State has forgotten the letter of US law governing the disposition of foreign aid, which reads in part: "No assistance may be provided . . . to the government of any country which engages in a consistent pattern of gross violations of internationally recognized human rights, including torture, . . . prolonged detention without charges, or other flagrant denial of the right to life, liberty and the security of person."'

The timing of the article was perfect. I had been invited to speak to the Carnegie Endowment for International Peace in Washington in March. Armed with reams of material about the political prisoners and my old address book, Yasmin and I flew off to America.

Once more I found myself walking the long corridors of Congress. As a student at Harvard I'd taken advantage of the democratic process in America to come to Washington to protest about America's involvement in Vietnam. Now I was here to protest against the dead democracy in my own country. On that first visit I hadn't spoken out, anxious not to be deported as a foreigner engaged in political activity. Now I felt I couldn't talk enough.

For a week I talked incessantly about the need to end human rights abuses and restore democracy to Pakistan – with Senator Edward Kennedy; with Senator Claiborne Pell whom I thanked for his efforts towards my release; with anyone I could get to listen. Peter Galbraith helped me make other appointments on Capitol Hill. I had meetings with Senator Alan Cranston from California, Congressman Stephen Solarz from New York, members of the State Department and aides from the National Security Council. I spoke to former Attorney General Ramsey Clark who had come to Pakistan to observe my father's court proceedings, and with Senator McGovern whom I had supported as a student at Harvard. Now I hoped he would support me in my lobbying to bring human rights to Pakistan.

Pakistan was already very much on the minds of legislators in Washington. The 3.2 billion dollar US aid package voted to Pakistan in 1981 was in peril of being cut off because of Pakistan's unverifiable nuclear programme. The Senate had got around this point in the past by basing aid not on whether or not Pakistan had 'the bomb', but whether it had been tested. During my visit in 1984, this loophole was being plugged by Senators John Glenn and Alan Cranston in an amendment which precluded aid to Pakistan unless the President of the United States verified in writing that Pakistan neither had a 'nuclear explosive device' nor was acquiring material to manufacture or detonate one. On March 28, the Foreign Relations Committee unanimously adopted the amendment.

I hadn't come to Washington to debate the nuclear issue. I was therefore caught off guard during a meeting with the head of the Foreign Relations Committee Senator Charles Percy when he asked me if I favoured the cut-off of aid over the nuclear question. 'Senator, cutting off aid will only create misunderstandings between our two countries,' I said after a moment's hesitation. 'Both our countries would be better served if aid were linked to the restoration of human rights and democracy in Pakistan.' Senator Percy, who had known my father, smiled and thanked me for my views. And I went on to my next meeting.

In between appointments I walked the long corridors to Peter Galbraith's office at the Foreign Relations Committee. 'You speak too fast,' Peter coached me, helping me make the most of the short meetings common on Capitol Hill. 'Speak slowly, and stress one point.' I tried to follow his advice, though after years of isolation the words that had been suppressed during all the years in silence just kept spilling out. 'Benazir Bhutto talks as if making up for lost time,' Carla Hall wrote in a profile in the *Washington Post* in early April. '. . . Sentences shoot out in her vaguely British accent, well-ordered but racing off her tongue, accompanied by a flutter of hands, which are swathing her forehead, raking her hair.'

Carla Hall was right. I was making up for lost time. And I was very nervous. My memory, which had been excellent before the years of detention, was now failing me. Often I searched for dates and names, sometimes remembering them and sometimes not. And I was still uncomfortable around people. Though I pushed myself to meet as many government officials and members of the press as possible, I found I dreaded the interviews. While talking to Senator Cranston one day, I suddenly felt my cheeks go scarlet. The heat spread over my face until beads of perspiration broke out on my forehead. 'Are you all right?' he asked in concern. 'Yes, yes, I'm fine,' I told him with more composure than I felt.

The night of my speech to the Carnegie Endowment I felt especially nervous. The audience was filled with State and Defense Department officials, members of Congress, former Ambassadors and members of the press. The Western press was now consistently portraying Zia as a 'benign dictator' and the man who had brought 'stability' to Pakistan. It fell to me to expose his human rights violations and point to the long-term dangers to Pakistan's stability from centralised military rule. The influential members of the audience could help bring pressure to bear on Zia to free our political prisoners, to hold free elections, and to restore democracy to Pakistan. Their support was important.

'Calm down,' I admonished myself when I moved to the podium. 'Just pretend that you're at the Oxford Union.' But I couldn't. The debates at the Union had been intellectual games. Now I felt the weight of the lives of thousands of political prisoners and the political future of my country. 'We in Pakistan are confused and disappointed by the backing given to Zia's illegitimate regime,' I said to the distinguished audience. '. . . We do appreciate your strategic concerns, but ask you not to turn your back on the people of Pakistan.'

In the middle of the speech, I looked up at the audience – and lost my place. There was silence in the hall while I desperately scanned my papers. How could I have? I wanted the earth to open and swallow me up. With as much aplomb as I could muster, I found my place and continued, asking the members of the government present to link US aid to human rights. I felt better during the question and answer period, and sat down at the end of my talk to applause. I just wasn't my old self. But I had to press on.

From Washington Yasmin and I went to New York. To the consternation of the Pakistani Embassy, I had been granted a meeting with the top editors of *Time* magazine at the Time-Life building in New York, perhaps the first opposition leader in Pakistan to receive such an invitation. But I had an advantage. I had gone to Harvard with Walter Isaacson, now an editor at *Time*, and I had called him from Washington to see if he could fix up a meeting. My arrival at the Time-Life building with Yasmin caused quite a stir.

When we took the lift to the 47th floor and walked into the private dining room, the editors gathered there looked at us in shock. I didn't know what to do and thought perhaps that we had blundered into the wrong meeting room.

'Didn't Walter meet you in the lobby?' someone finally said into the silence. 'He is downstairs waiting for you.'

'I didn't see him,' I replied.

'But how did you get past the security guards?'

'In Zia's Pakistan you learn how to dodge security,' I smiled.

Over lunch the editors asked me so many questions that I didn't even have time to eat the delicious fruit salad and cottage cheese lunch they served, a favourite meal from my years at Harvard. 'US aid to Pakistan is seen by many Pakistanis as US aid to Zia,' I told them. 'You could all help clear up this misunderstanding by focusing media attention on human rights. For the political prisoners in Pakistan, publicity literally means the difference between life and death.'

I got publicity I didn't expect as Yasmin and I came to the end of our two weeks in America and prepared to return to London. On April 3, the Senate Foreign Relations Committee reversed its unanimous position on the tough anti-nuclear requirements for American aid. Instead they passed a new amendment allowing the continuation of aid to Pakistan with certification from the President that Pakistan did not have a nuclear bomb, and that American aid would 'reduce significantly the risk that Pakistan will possess a nuclear explosive device.' Though I suspected the real cause for the change was intense pressure from the Reagan administration, Senator Percy kindly gave me public credit for the reversal of his vote.

When I returned to London I took a flat in the Barbican, a fortress-like building close to St Paul's Cathedral. I felt safe there. There was a security desk in the lobby to announce all visitors to the building, and my tenth-floor flat, I noted with my usual security consciousness, was too high for Pakistani agents to break into or wire for sound. The building was home in exile, too, to Dr Niazi and Yasmin, and we were in and out of each other's flats all day.

Quickly, the Barbican became the de facto command centre of the PPP both for England and for the units abroad. The flat was soon overflowing with files on the branches of the PPP in the United States, France, Canada, Germany, Switzerland, Denmark, Sweden and Austria as well as those in Australia, Saudi Arabia, Bahrain and Abu Dhabi. A dedicated staff of Pakistani volunteers was soon in place. Sumblina, a young girl living in England, did the typing. Nahid, a student activist in exile, answered the telephone and helped Safdar Abbasi, a law student and the son of PPP Central Executive Committee member Dr Ashraf Abbasi, answer letters from Pakistan. Bashir Riaz, a journalist who had helped my brothers organise the campaign for my father's life, acted as our press spokesman and arranged press interviews. Dr Niazi joined forces with another exile, Safdar Hamdani, and with former Minister of Information Mr Naseem Ahmad to ensure that our information reached British Members of Parliament. As always, Yasmin did anything and everything to help. Together we turned out letters and reports on the human rights abuses in Pakistan from the spare bedroom we had converted into an office.

We sent photographs of political prisoners, their case histories and letter campaigns to the UN Secretary General, to Assistant US Secretary of State for Human Rights, Elliott Abrams, to foreign ministers, lawyers' syndicates and international trade organisations. We had meetings with British Members of Parliament, Amnesty International, and representatives of world leaders through their embassies. Nasser Baloach's life hung in the balance. So did the lives of many others. But we were losing the race.

In spite of protests by the bar associations all over Pakistan, three young men falsely accused of murdering a policeman were hanged in August, following a secret trial by a special military court. 'The recent murder of the three young men, who had been detained for three years in chains, might have been prevented if the political circles and media in Europe and North America had shown interest in their fate or that of the thousands of other prisoners being held,' I wrote to our growing mailing-list of members of governments and the press. 'The Western nations should assert their influence and raise their voices to save the lives of the political prisoners facing the gallows. . . . Please be so kind as to take urgent and effective action in response to this earnest appeal.'

Tony Benn, a Labour Member of Parliament, wrote a letter of protest to the Pakistan Embassy in London. He sent me a copy of his letter as well as the reply from the regime's spokesman, Information Minister Qutubuddin Aziz. 'Miss Bhutto's allegation that there are more than 40,000 prisoners in Pakistan jails and that they are held in miserable conditions, bears no relevance to facts,' wrote Qutubuddin Aziz. 'There are, no doubt, prisoners in Pakistani jails as in jails in any other country, but these prisoners are either convicted or suspected criminals. The conditions prevailing in our jails are certainly not worse than in most other developing countries. . . . While the government of Pakistan deals severely with those who commit acts of terrorism and murder, it adheres to the due process of law in every case.' The regime's spokesman made no mention of the continuing protests by the Pakistani bar associations over the lack of due legal process.

When we anticipated, or faced, another series of death sentences from one of Zia's military courts, all of us worked overtime. Envelopes, stamps and letters spilled out of the office into the living room as we spent day and night labelling, sealing and posting. The regular volunteers would be joined by others, including a former Major in the Pakistan Army and a Superintendent of Police now living in exile. We drank endless cups of tea and coffee to keep ourselves going. Zia wanted to hide his atrocities from the world simply by continuing to forbid any observers from the outside. We did our best to expose him and to appeal to the world's conscience on behalf of the prisoners.

It was essential to have specific information and documentation about the circumstances of a political prisoner's arrest and the conditions under which he had been held and tried. In Pakistan, where literacy rates were low and censorship extremely tight, such information was often hard to come by. Often the only people who had accurate and up-to-date details were the prisoners themselves.

With great difficulty, we set up a secret network of people who sent regular reports from inside the prisons, questionnaires filled out by the prisoners and smuggled back to us in London. We used sympathetic jail guards, mailings to safe houses, relatives of exiles flying in and out of Pakistan, sympathetic airline personnel and mail drops in Abu Dhabi and Saudi Arabia where our letters were posted with a different post-mark to get past the regime's censors. And the information began to flow in. The handwritten reply from Saifullah Khalid in Karachi Central Jail, a 23-year-old student from Larkana and one of Nasser Baloach's co-defendants, documented that he had been arrested in 1981 for his 'political views' and was 'brutally' interrogated to implicate the 'head of the Pakistan People's Party' in the hijacking. Like all political prisoners, he had been moved around from prison to prison and held incommunicado for months.

'I was held at Arazwali Fort for two days, three unknown places for a week, Fort Balahisar for four days, Warsak Cantonment for ten days, one day at Peshawar Central Prison, then FIA [Federal Investigation Agency] Centre at Karachi for six days, one month at CIA [Central Intelligence Agency] Centre Karachi, one month at Baldia torture cell in Karachi,' replied the student of political science, who three years after his arrest was still in prison and fearing the death sentence. Now imprisoned in Karachi Central Jail, he wrote that he 'was kept in the punishment ward for ten days, and beaten thrice a day. During interrogation bulbs of high voltage have weakened my eye sight, causing constant headache and pain in my eyes. I was kept in iron leg fetters which resulted in severe pain in my testicles. The prison doctor suggested I be shifted to Civil Hospital for treatment. Three months later I am now here for hernia operation.'

Like so many other political prisoners, Saifullah Khalid was at the mercy of the regime. 'My life and those of my co-accused are in danger as the prosecution demanded capital punishment,' the student added in a postscript. 'I appeal to Amnesty to intervene in the matter and save our lives.'

Nottingham. Glasgow. Manchester. Bradford. I travelled around England to speak to Pakistani communities, adding more supporters to promote our campaign. Germany. Denmark. Switzerland once a month to see my mother. I took the list of the prisoners with me everywhere; I had meetings with the former Prime Minister Ankur Jorgensen in Denmark who had known my father; with the Gaullists in France; with the Green Party in Germany. With a heavy heart I wrote 'martyred' by the names of the three young men hanged in August.

I was apprehensive every time I landed back in England, fearing that I would be turned away by the immigration authorities. At that time visas for Pakistanis were issued by British Immigration at the airport, and were valid for a single entry only. When I first arrived in England the immigration officials had questioned me for forty-five minutes on where I would be staying and what I would be doing. 'I'm just a tourist,' I assured them then and on every re-entry, feeling a flood of relief when the visa was finally stamped into my passport. But soon I had so many visas stamped there that my passport was running out of pages. I knew Zia would never issue me with a new one. I prayed every time I answered the immigration officials' questions and watched them look for my name in their huge black book that they wouldn't see the beating of my heart. We were making too much progress in our publicity campaign on behalf of the political prisoners to absorb such a setback.

'I intend using every Parliamentary and other opportunity to press the British government to call on the Pakistan government to cease its murderous campaign to eliminate political opposition, especially political opponents in the Pakistan People's Party,' Max Madden, a member of the House of Commons wrote to me in November. I received a response, too, from Elliott Abrams, the Assistant Secretary for Human Rights in America, to whom I had written about Nasser Baloach and Saifullah Khalid. 'I share your concern about the inherent unfairness of *in camera* military court proceedings against civilians, and in this case, the disquieting allegation that confessions were obtained through torture,' Mr Abrams wrote. '. . . Please be assured that our diplomats in Pakistan will continue to follow these cases closely.'

I was up every morning at 7.00 am at the Barbican to clean the flat, do the washing and get ahead on the meals for the day, preparing simple lentil dishes and leaving them to cook on the stove. Bashir Riaz brought *halal* meat and chickens that had been slaughtered in accordance with Muslim custom from London's Pakistani neighbourhoods. And then to work. The mailings were expensive. I budgeted as best I could, two-thirds of my money going to the rent, the rest for the telephone bill, postage and supplies. My mother had given me some money to decorate the flat. I bought a second-hand rug, a few pots and pans and some lamps with no shades. The money was better spent on the political work going on in the office.

We launched our own Urdu magazine, *Amal*, Action, with a few pages in English, and distributed it each month to international organisations, foreign embassies and the exile community to keep them up to date on events in Pakistan. *Amal* was produced on a shoestring budget, with Bashir Riaz working as both editor and advertising salesman, and Nahid buttonholing everyone she could for subscriptions. We smuggled the magazine into Pakistan, where activists photostated segments of it and distributed them to party supporters. Copies also reached the jails so that the political prisoners would know they were not forgotten. *Amal* proved to be invaluable for lifting morale. The prisoners loved it. The regime did not.

'I am not coming to work today,' our calligrapher suddenly phoned Bashir. 'Why?' Bashir asked in dismay. *Amal* couldn't be published without a calligrapher. Urdu printing is still done the old-fashioned way, with calligraphers writing out the text by hand on wax paper. 'The embassy has offered me more money not to work for you,' the calligrapher confessed. When the printer called to say that he, too, had had pressure put on him by the regime, we thought *Amal* was doomed. But the printer turned out to be a party sympathiser who not only refused to succumb to the regime's pressure, but agreed to hold his presses open for us at night. Bashir also convinced calligraphers who worked for the Pakistani newspapers in London to moonlight for us. Every time the regime bought one back, Bashir tenaciously found another. And *Amal* continued.

In Pakistan, Zia started to flex his Martial Law muscle again, to remind the people of his grip over them. While we ran articles about Nasser Baloach's unfair and cruel treatment in *Amal*, we began receiving ominous reports from Pakistan that he and his co-defendants were going to be sentenced to death. Our worst fears were confirmed on the chill and windy morning of November 5, 1984, when the military court in Karachi publicly announced its final verdict. Nasser Baloach and the others were sentenced to 'hang by the neck until dead'.

At the Barbican we all went back into emergency mode, circulating appeal after appeal for the lives of the condemned men in the international community. Our sense of outrage deepened after a party sympathiser in Pakistan managed miraculously to smuggle us secret documents suggesting that Zia had a direct role in the death sentences. The documents showed that originally the military court had sentenced only Nasser Baloach to death, and that the Martial Law Administrator of Sindh had been informed and did not object. But suddenly he had changed his mind and directed the military court to 'reconvene and reconsider' its original judgment. Only Zia, his immediate superior, could have got him to change his mind.

Moreover, we had Zia's signature on a piece of his Chief Martial Law Administrator stationery confirming the four death sentences on October 26, *a full ten days* before his kangaroo court had made its verdict public. The only avenue of appeal open to the condemned men was a mercy petition to Zia in his capacity as President. What a farce. They had to appeal to the man who had already confirmed their death sentences.

Many of the volunteers had tears in their eyes when they saw the documents, but I was too angry. For the first time, we had evidence confirming what we had always heard: military sentences in political cases went through Zia himself. We set to work editing and compiling the documents so they could be printed as quickly as possible. If anything could rally the international community and expose Zia's military courts as mere rubber stamps of the regime, these documents could. Lord Avebury, who had been so instrumental in my mother's release, now arranged a press conference for us to reveal the documents at the British Parliament. And our campaign intensified.

Again people of conscience responded, from the human rights organisations to labour leaders. 'Whilst we in this country are growing ever more conscious of the threat to our own trade union rights, we must be equally aware of the struggles being waged by our brothers and sisters in other countries,' wrote Nottingham trade union organiser Laurence Platt to the editor of the *T & G Record*, a major trade union magazine. 'There may still be time to save the lives of labour leader Nasser Baloach and his three co-defendants who are waiting execution and protests should be made to the government of Pakistan and its embassy here.'

Lawyers everywhere were shocked into action. 'These four men were tried and sentenced by a special military court set up under Martial Law Regulations in Pakistan,' read part of a statement signed by a group of prominent British lawyers. 'These courts are presided over by military officers who have no legal training, and the trials are held *in camera*. The burden of proof is shifted on to the accused, and it is upon them to prove their innocence. Furthermore they do not have proper access to lawyers to conduct their cases.

'We call upon the Government of Pakistan to stop such trials and executions. We especially appeal to General Zia ul-Haq not to confirm the death sentences passed on these four men and to spare their lives. We also call upon the British Government, which supplies economic and military aid to the Zia regime, to use their influence upon the Government of Pakistan to stop the execution of these four men and further trials of this kind.'

We were obsessed with saving the lives of the political prisoners. But, in the midst of our fight against death in Pakistan, others among the PPP leadership in exile were more interested in advancing their own special interests and power bases. The telephone rang incessantly at the Barbican with requests from these leaders, mostly ex-ministers from my father's government, for meetings with me. Mercifully the Barbican allowed only fifteen visitors a day, though I sometimes managed to squeeze in more by meeting groups of five or six at a time. I chafed and fidgeted throughout the meetings, thinking of all the important work there was to do.

The PPP had always been a multi-class party, a coalition of many different socio-economic groups: Marxists, feudal landowners, businessmen, religious minorities, women, the poor. Before my father's death, the conflicts of interests between all these different groups had been bridged by my father's strong personality and popular appeal. But in London, with the strain of exile and the political leaders' fears of being forgotten at home, self-interest took an upper hand to common goals. On top of everything else, there was an undeclared battle for party leadership. The old guard in London realised that if they accepted me once, they might have to accept me forever. 'It is not in my destiny to follow the father, then the mother, and now the daughter,' one of them was reported as saying when I'd first arrived in London.

'You must decide whose side you're on,' the various leaders had lectured me, each faction lobbying for greater importance in the PPP and probably preparing for an eventual takeover.

'I'm not on anybody's side,' I'd insisted. 'If the party presented a united front instead of the factions undercutting each other, we'd get more done.' I'd tried to sound as calm and reasonable as possible, anxious not to alienate the old 'uncles' and well aware of the weakness of my political position. Even though the Central Executive Committee of the party had re-affirmed my position as Acting Chairperson when I arrived in England, these men were old political hands. I was a young woman, the age of their daughters. These men had run the PPP in London since the time of the coup. I was newly arrived from Pakistan. They had spent years building up their own power bases. I believed in reconciling past differences, in balancing individual power bases for the greater good of the party. When I returned from my trip to America, the most vocal group, the Marxists, had attacked.

'You should never have gone to America,' the leader of the Marxists chided me, though he hadn't said a word before I'd gone. 'The Americans are friends of Zia's. We must join up with the Russians to put an end to him.'

'What makes you think the Americans or the Russians are friends of anybody?' I argued back. 'The Americans are supporting Zia because of their strategic considerations. The Soviets may want to support us today, but tomorrow, if their strategic concerns change, they'll ditch us. We must not get involved in these Superpower rivalries, but fight for our own national interests. We can't afford to fight global politics.'

The regionalists soon joined the fray. 'You are a Sindhi. You should stand up for Sindh over the other provinces, or they will never forgive you,' they warned.

'Why play into the hands of a Martial Law regime which uses the threat of division to project the Army as the unifying force in Pakistan,' I retorted. 'There are people who believe in democracy in all four provinces. Oppression does not know the meaning of provincial boundaries. Aren't our energies better spent fighting the common enemy instead of each other?'

The chauvinists, the establishment-oriented members of the PPP who had been wheeling and dealing and seeking compromises with Zia, added their voices of self-interest. My frustration grew and grew as the arguments wore on. Here were the volunteers in the next room doing the essential nitty-gritty work of the Party to save the lives of our supporters in Pakistan. And taking up my time were the old-guard politicians who insisted on putting their individual concerns above the concerns of the people.

I finally lost my temper when one of the old 'uncles' in exile arrived at the Barbican, sat calmly back on the sofa, and demanded that I name him President of the Punjab PPP along with a hand-picked team. 'I can't just appoint you,' I said in shock to this man who was not even popular among the Punjabi politicians at home and who had spent his entire time since the coup in safety in London. 'It will anger the party and undermine our policy of deciding on merit and by consensus.'

'You don't really have much choice,' he said to me patronisingly. 'The Marxists are angry at you. The regionalists have formed their own organisation. You can't afford to alienate me.'

'But it is against PPP principles,' I stuttered, still taken aback by his demands.

'Principles,' he scoffed. 'Principles are fine. But people are in politics for power. If you do not appoint me president along with my team, then I'm afraid I'll have to explore other options. I may even start my own party. I will be your biggest opposition.'

I felt my anger grow, a compendium of all the wasted hours I'd spent listening to the bickering of the special interest groups. And now this; a new ante raised. This was the old way of Pakistani politics. Angle for yourself. Throw your weight around. Grab every office you can. Blackmail. Threaten. I had had it with the old ways. And with him. 'Uncle,' I said, taking a deep breath and leaning forward in my chair. 'You know, if you leave the party, it will be hard for you even to win a seat in Parliament.'

'Really? Really?' he said, flicking his head back in surprise at my rude answer. And he stalked out of the room – and eventually, out of the party. More trouble, I mused before pushing the thought out of my mind. I was never happy when anyone left the party, but I came to realise that in politics nothing is permanent. People leave, people join, people reconcile. What is important is that a political party articulates the mood of a generation. Our work in London was boosting the morale of the people and energising the party in Pakistan. That was what counted. Especially by December, 1984, when it became clear that the PPP needed all the energy it could muster.

Under pressure from the United States, Zia decided to hold elections by March, 1985. But first, it was announced, he would hold a national referendum on December 20. The wording of the Islamic referendum, as it came to be called, would have been laughable if it hadn't been so clever. 'Whether the people of Pakistan endorse the process initiated by General Mohammed Zia ul-Haq, the President of Pakistan, for bringing the laws of Pakistan into conformity with the injunctions of Islam as laid down in the Holy Quran and Sunnah of the Holy Prophet (Peace Be Upon Him),' it read. How could anyone in a country that was 95 per cent Muslim vote against it? A 'no' vote was tantamount to voting against Islam. But politically, a vote of 'yes' would be just as dire. A positive vote, Zia announced, would constitute his 'election' as President for the next five years.

The whole set-up was nothing more than a smokescreen to give Zia the mandate he desperately needed. No other military dictator in the history of the sub-continent had ruled for so long without one. And Zia wasn't going to take any chances. Campaigning for a 'no' vote, he declared as extra insurance, would be a crime punishable by three years rigorous imprisonment and a fine of 35,000 dollars. Moreover, the ballots would be counted by the Army in secret and the results would not be challengeable before the civil courts. Did he really think he could pass the vote off as a fair and impartial one?

'Boycott,' we urged in *Amal*, in interviews, in speeches and press releases. 'Boycott,' the members of the MRD urged at home in Pakistan, where even two religious parties denounced the referendum as a 'political fraud in the name of Islam'. 'Vote! You don't even need an identity card,' countered the loudspeakers the regime set up on street corners in Karachi while the regime's agents hustled Afghan refugees on to buses heading for the polling stations in Baluchistan and brought whole villages by the busload to other polling places.

Predictably, the regime-controlled Pakistani press reported a turnout of 64 per cent, over twenty million people, 96 per cent of them voting 'yes'.

But the *Guardian*'s reporter in Islamabad calculated that the turnout was as low as 10 per cent, as did Reuters news service. Our call to boycott the farce had worked. 'Had General Zia frankly and courageously put himself to the test without the cover of "religion", he would in all probability, have lost,' read an editorial in *The* (London) *Times* on December 12. 'That no doubt was why he did not.'

I had been waiting for the right time to return to Pakistan with the PPP leaders in exile. Possibly this was it. 'Now is the time to launch a protest against Zia ul-Haq,' agreed one of the party barons in a meeting called in a former PPP minister's house in North London. 'The referendum has exposed Zia's unpopularity to the whole world.' Others disagreed. 'The country may not respond,' the counter-argument went. 'The people have been frozen into inertia for too long. We should work up to a showdown.' The discussion went back and forth until one of the 'uncles' turned to me. 'I know the answer,' he said. 'We should send Miss Benazir Bhutto back. That will fire up everybody.'

'All right,' I agreed. 'But if it is politically correct for me to go, then we should make a plan for all of us to go. Why don't we stagger our arrivals, one a day for ten days or so, to build up to a crescendo?'

There was silence in the room. 'Go back? I can't go back,' one after another protested, listing the charges, the prison sentences, the death sentences that were pending against each of them in Pakistan. I was astounded. They were perfectly willing to send me off, but were hardly sincere about mounting a common offensive at all. 'Either we do it properly or we don't do it at all,' I said. Silence.

All of us, however, were united in our gratification over Zia's setback in the referendum. Victory rallies were held by the PPP all over the world on the Day of Democracy, January 5, 1985, my father's birthday. Speaking in Sindhi, Urdu and English I led the meeting in London where we had organised a seminar and a *mushaira*, or poetry session. The atmosphere was electrifying, the crowds packed into the rented hall. I ended my remarks with the verses of a revolutionary poet. Waving their PPP banners, the entire audience joined in crying out the refrain to each verse: 'I am a rebel. I am a rebel. Do with me what you will.'

In the middle of the seminar I received a telephone call from my mother. Sanam had just had a baby girl. 'At Simla, the words "it's a girl" signalled bad news,' I announced joyfully to the assembled PPP supporters. 'Today, they bring the good news that my sister has given birth on Shaheed Bhutto's birthday. My new niece's name is Azadeh, which in Persian means freedom.' And the cheering rose. The seminar was video-taped and dozens of copies smuggled into Pakistan.

I was with my mother and Sanam myself three days later when Zia announced that the elections for the National and Provincial Assemblies would be held at the end of February. The issue of whether to boycott these elections was more problematic than the referendum had been. Martial Law was still in force and political parties banned. Our candidates would have to stand as individuals, not as party representatives for seats in the re-activated National Assembly. Still, these were the first national elections Zia had held since the coup in 1977. Should we participate?

'Boycott,' the members of the PPP in London and Pakistan had argued in anticipation of Zia's announcement. But I was torn. Never leave a field open, my father had said again and again. I didn't know what to do, nor did I know what the members of the MRD in Pakistan were planning to do. It was so frustrating sitting in Europe while there was so much going on at home. And Zia, as usual, kept changing the rules. On January 12, he announced in a nationwide broadcast that the leading members of the PPP and the MRD would be disqualified from the elections altogether, thereby eliminating them as candidates. Three days later he changed his tune and said most of them could participate after all. I couldn't stand it.

'I think I should go back home,' I told my mother while Sunny's baby cried in the background. 'I need to talk with the Central Executive Committee about the elections. We need to decide whether a political win will be best achieved by staying out − or going in.'

I expected her to be against my decision to return. Who knew what Zia would have in store for me. But she thought for a minute, then agreed with me. 'You're right,' she said. 'This is the time to talk the matter over with the party leaders in Pakistan.' Taking turns, my mother and I placed and re-placed calls to the party Deputy in Pakistan, a process that took hours. We couldn't get through to him. I did, however, get hold of my cousin Fakhri. 'Tell the staff to open up 70 Clifton,' I told her. 'I'll be there in three or four days time.' I had just come back from enquiring about flight schedules when the telephone rang.

'70 Clifton is surrounded by the army,' Dr Niazi said. 'I've just heard from Karachi that detention orders have been issued for you and your mother. The airports have been cordoned off all over the country and every woman arriving from London and France in a *burqa* is being searched.'

There was no use going back if I was going to be immediately thrown into detention and unable to take part in the discussions on whether or not to stand in the elections. At least in Europe I could telephone. I continued to try to get through to Pakistan. I had become convinced that we should mount an opposition to Zia at the polls and wanted to represent that opinion in meetings with the MRD.

'Is that Miss Benazir Bhutto speaking?' said the astonished voice in Abbotabad when one of my calls finally got through.

'Yes, yes, yes,' I said impatiently. 'Has the MRD taken a decision on the elections?'

'Yes,' he said.

'What is it?' I asked with bated breath.

'To boycott,' he said.

If that was the consensus of the party and the combined opposition, so be it. I returned to London and recorded another tape in Sindhi and Urdu calling for the masses to boycott the polls. It, too, was smuggled into Pakistan, and distributed by the thousand in the interior of Sindh, Punjab and other parts of the country.

On February 25, I sat glued to the television in London for the coverage of the voting for the National Assembly and, three days later, for the Provincial Assemblies. Elections are normally boisterous affairs in Pakistan, conducted in a carnival air. The streets throng with people, food pedlars pushing their carts among them to sell cold drinks, ice lollies, sweetmeats, *samosas* and *pakoras*. People gather in huge crowds in front of the polling stations and jostle each other for a turn to vote: Pakistanis have never bothered with orderly lines. But the voters I saw on television, probably government servants trotted out for the television crews, stood at attention in pathetically thin lines, one behind the other, with no food carts in sight.

The fact that Zia called it an election at all was an anathema. 'In the absence of political parties,' *Time* magazine's Asia/Pacific edition reported, 'there were no campaign themes, no platforms, no debate about national issues. Candidates were not permitted to hold outdoor meetings or rallies, to use loudspeakers or microphones or to go on radio or television. The most the regime allowed was for a candidate to go from house to house – and then he or she was allowed to speak only to the number of people who could comfortably fit into a single room. A few hopefuls tried to use mosques as a forum: they were quickly disqualified.'

The regime announced a turnout of 53 per cent. We estimated it at between 10 per cent and 24 per cent, depending on the region. The MRD's call for a boycott had worked again, although not as successfully as it had with the referendum. This time Zia had taken insurance against a successful boycott by issuing a Martial Law Regulation making a call for boycott punishable by rigorous imprisonment. In the end, there weren't any political leaders around to even call for a boycott. 'In the final days before the election,' *Time* reported, 'the regime rounded up an estimated 3,000 political opponents, including virtually every major political figure in the country, and held them in jail or under house arrest until after the balloting was over.'

Even so, the voting was a resounding rejection of Martial Law and Zia's policy of Islamisation. Six of his nine Cabinet Ministers who ran for the National Assembly were defeated, as were many of his other associates. The candidates backed by fundamentalist religious parties in the provincial elections also fared badly, only six out of sixty-one candidates of the *Jamaat-e-Islami* winning seats. In contrast, candidates who had claimed association with the PPP in spite of our boycott did remarkably well, winning fifty out of fifty-two seats. 'The PPP, which is led by Bhutto's daughter Benazir, 31, now in exile in London, is still the strongest party in the country despite its having been outlawed for nearly eight years,' *Time* said flatly.

Any hopes that Zia was truly moving towards a democracy were dashed less than a week after the elections. Before the newly elected National Assembly even met, Zia announced wide-ranging changes in the constitution. His amendments reconfirmed his presidency for five years and not only gave him the sweeping power to personally appoint his own Prime Minister, the chiefs of the armed forces and the four provincial Governors, but also to dismiss the National and Provincial Assemblies at will.

What was different about his new government? Nothing. Though Zia was ostensibly creating a 'civilian' government under pressure from Western governments, Martial Law was still in effect. Though he had given himself the more acceptable title of 'President', he was still Chief Martial Law Administrator and Army Chief-of-Staff, which ensured that the National Assembly stayed under the thumb of the Army. Zia would lift Martial Law, he said in an interview with *Time*, 'several months' after he had assumed the presidency and would resign at the same time as Army Chief-of-Staff. 'When I am sworn in on March 23 as President, I think I should have a civilian exterior,' he said, as if he could fool people with a change of clothes. He couldn't. Martial Law would not be lifted for another year. Zia is still Army Chief-of-Staff. And dressing occasionally in a long tunic instead of a uniform does not change his stripes.

On March 1, four days after the elections, Ayaz Samoo was sentenced to death.

On March 5, Nasser Baloach was hanged.

We were all extremely sad when we heard the news of Nasser Baloach's death. Zia had even turned a deaf ear to the petitions for clemency from nine of the newly elected members of the Provincial and National Assemblies. Several of the other political prisoners in Karachi Central Jail had managed to sneak out last-minute mercy petitions for Nasser Baloach themselves, but Zia had responded by transferring them to other jails. After our disclosure of the secret documents, he had been compelled by international pressure to commute the death sentences of the other three defendants. But Nasser Baloach was issued a 'black warrant'. The labour leader had gone to the gallows, the *Guardian* reported from Islamabad, 'shouting anti-military slogans, including "long live Bhutto".'

Sadly I went through the thick file of correspondence we had sent out and received on Nasser Baloach's behalf, reading and re-reading the letter he had written to me on the back of the foil from a cigarette packet and smuggled out of his death cell in Karachi Central Jail. 'May God give you and Begum Sahiba health and long life so that the poor people of Pakistan can get guidance from you,' his note began. 'We are passing our days with great bravery and courage in our cells like Chairman Shaheed [Martyr] Butto who did not bow his head in front of the military junta. We will never beg for life from this Military regime. . . . We prefer the honour of the Party to our own lives. We pray for your success. May God help you.'

I had prayed for Nasser Baloach for months. Now, with great pain, I prayed for his soul in private and at the religious ceremony we held for him at the home of one of the party leaders in exile. I felt I'd lost a brother. He had lived in Malir, one of the most poverty-stricken areas in Karachi where he and his wife and children shared their small home with his parents and his brother and family. Nasser Baloach was particularly proud of his daughters and talked about them often. One had married while I was in sub-jail at 70 Clifton in 1983 and I had helped as best I could by asking Fakhri to give the family some money to help with the expenses of the wedding. As I sat down now to write his family a condolence letter, I felt their anguish as my own. So reportedly did many other people. Extra police, I read in the British papers, had to be called in to control the crowds that gathered outside Karachi Central Jail the night of his hanging. When the family took his body for burial, the crowds were so large the police fired tear gas to disperse the mourners. Zia's new civilian government had begun with bloodstained hands. Would Ayaz Samoo be their next victim?

'I am writing to seek your help in saving the life of Ayaz Samoo, the labour representative at Naya Daur Motors who has been sentenced to death by a military court after an *in camera* trial on March 1, 1985,' started a letter to those on our mailing list signed by Dr Niazi for the Human Rights Committee of the Pakistan People's Party. 'Dear Members/Officeholders,' wrote Safdar Hamdani, our exile coordinator who corresponded with overseas units and who lived in the Central YMCA. 'In light of the important details regarding the Ayaz Samoo case, please redouble your efforts in: (a) meeting with your local MP/Parliamentarian; (b) arranging delegations to meet their MPs/Parliamentarians; (c) getting signatures on a Petition: (d) contacting Human Rights Organisations; (e) contacting the press.'

The details of the trumped-up case against Ayaz Samoo became clear after a sympathiser in Pakistan smuggled us out the Police report on the case. Samoo had been charged and sentenced to death for the murder of one Zahoor ul-Hasan Bhopali, a supporter of the regime, in his offices in Karachi in 1982. One assailant had been killed on the spot. According to the police reports, witnesses described the other as being between twenty-five and thirty, tall, muscular, and of wheatish complexion. He had been bleeding heavily from a shoulder wound, the witnesses reported, when he drove away from the scene in a car.

Ayaz Samoo fitted none of the descriptions. He was dark in colour, slight, and five-foot-four-inches high. He was twenty-two years of age and had had no wound when he was arrested. But the regime didn't bother itself with such details. They were so eager to convict Bhopali's killer that not one but three different military courts were trying or had tried three different defendants — and found them all guilty of committing the same crime!

But we needed proof of Samoo's innocence. Real proof. It came on a piece of cloth, smuggled out of Samoo's death cell by his lawyer. On it was a sample of Samoo's blood. The police in Pakistan had made a big show of the blood found in the get-away car, recovered after the murder. The blood in the car had been analysed by one Dr Sherwani, and included in the police report. Samoo's blood had never been tested to see whether it matched that of the assailant. We found a pathologist in London to identify Samoo's blood type. We had the proof, which we circulated among our mailing list: Samoo's blood type was not the same as that found in the car. But the death sentence was not lifted.

'My dear Sister,' Ayaz Samoo wrote from Karachi Central Jail on March 23. 'I am grateful that I have the opportunity to write to you. Our determination is stronger than mountains and taller than the Himalayas. Revolutionaries never, never, yield to the dictators. Life is given by Allah, not Zia.

'I will prefer to be hanged than live under the oppressor. To give in is not our principle. We are not ready to call a donkey a horse, or black, white, out of fear of Martial Law. My dear sister, your brother, Ayaz Samoo, assures you that the terrorist Zia ul-Haq can sever my neck, but he cannot bend it. . . . We the martyrs will keep shedding our blood. One day the dawn will bring the news of our blood to the people, In-sha'allah. . . . We will live and live forever. Your brother, Ayaz Samoo.'

I took the information about Ayaz Samoo's case with me everywhere, back to America in April where I was invited to deliver the Rama Mehta Lecture at Harvard, then to speak to the Council on Foreign Relations in New York, then on to Strasbourg in June where I addressed the members of the European Parliament. 'Ayaz Samoo, a labour leader and supporter of the Party, languishes today in a death cell, accused of a crime he did not commit, uncertain of his fate, knowing that his blood group does not even match the blood group of the assailant in the incident which he is accused of being involved in,' I said in a press conference in Strasbourg. 'When the conscience of the world is justly aroused against apartheid and against human rights violation elsewhere, then that conscience ought not to close its eyes to the murder by military courts which takes place in a country which receives substantial aid from the West itself.'

Just before I left for America in the spring of 1985, all fifty-four prisoners held in Lahore because of their alleged involvement in Al-Zulfikar were sentenced to life imprisonment, along with forty others *in absentia*, including my brothers, Mir and Shah. Once again the regime was using the buzzword of terrorism for its political ends. 'Amnesty International has been concerned over the years that the blanket charge of association with Al-Zulfikar may be used to imprison some people involved in non-violent political dissent,' Amnesty's 1985 report charged. Over seventy prisoners had been executed, more than one hundred sentenced to death.

Pakistan People's Party
111 Lauderdale Towers
Barbican
London EC2
June 18th

SAVE THE LIFE OF AYAZ SAMOO

Dear Member, you must act quickly and do your best to save the life of this innocent 22 year old son of Pakistan . . . Contact everyone on your lists. The mercy petition of Ayaz Samoo is to be filed today. Please act fast as there is very little time.

Letters were sent to Zia. Telegrams. Diplomatic pleas. Foreign pressure. Ayaz Samoo was hanged on June 26, 1985.

Crash! What was going on in the kitchen? Someone must have left the window open, I thought, going into my kitchen at the Barbican to pick up the things knocked off the wall by the wind. Everything was in place.

Could it be Ayaz Samoo's spirit, I wondered? I said a prayer to bless his soul.

The next morning I was back at work with Nahid, Bashir Riaz, Safdar, Sumblina, Yasmin and Mrs Niazi, writing letters to all the people who had taken an interest in Ayaz Samoo's case and answering condolence letters from such varied sources as Lord Avebury in the House of Lords, Elliott Abrams in the United States, and Karel Van Miert in Brussels who along with the Socialist Group of the European Parliament was advancing a motion to cancel the economic cooperation agreement about to be signed with Pakistan.

'I was very sad to learn of the execution of Mr Ayaz Samoo, though not altogether surprised,' Lord Avebury had written. 'It does show that Zia is completely impervious to humanitarian appeals, and I'm afraid he knows that, whatever he does, it will not affect the largesse from the US, or the Reagan administration's determination to see Pakistan as part of the "free world".'

We were working quietly in our sadness when suddenly there was a loud thud in the hall where we had stacks of papers and files and manilla envelopes. Startled, we all looked up at each other.

'One of the files must have fallen off the table,' Bashir said, going into the hall.

'Nothing has fallen,' I said, remembering the night before.

'You're right,' he said, returning.

'Do you think it's Ayaz Samoo's soul?' I asked the others.

'Oh God bless him,' said Mrs Niazi, who is a deeply religious person. 'We should have a *Quran Khani* for him here in the flat. It will give his soul peace so he can rest.'

Nahid quickly organised a group of Pakistani women to come to the flat that afternoon. We all read verses from the Holy Quran aloud, hour after hour, until we had completed several complete readings of the Holy Book. Ayaz Samoo's spirit never caused a noise again.

I was supposed to leave for the south of France on July 1 to have a holiday with my mother and the rest of the family. But one thing after another kept interfering; political meetings, visits from PPP leaders coming in from Pakistan who couldn't change their plans and so on.

My mother called to tell me how sorry Shah Nawaz was that I was missing the barbecue he had planned for me, as did Shah himself. We'd only been together a few times since my release. I was looking forward very much to seeing them all – Mir, Shah, their little girls Fathi and Sassi, their Afghan wives Fauzia and Rehana. But it wasn't until the middle of the month that I was able to join them.

On the morning of July 17, I threw my clothes into a suitcase and rushed for the airport. Ahead lay two weeks of much needed peace in Cannes after the strain and tragedies of the last month. I couldn't wait. I had had enough of death.

12

THE DEATH OF MY BROTHER

Where were they? Had they forgotten to meet me? My eyes scanned the busy Nice airport as I walked past immigration.

'Surprise!' Shah Nawaz said, leaping out from behind a column at the airport. He embraced me, his eyes twinkling with mischief.

'It was his idea to hide,' Mummy came up, smiling as she kissed me.

Shah picked up my suitcase and immediately set it down with a mock grimace. 'Oof. What have you got in there? Gold?' We laughed as we walked out of the airport. The fronds of the palm trees on the French Riviera moved lazily in the slow wind. After the tension of the past few months, it was lovely seeing the family again, and being with my mischievous younger brother, always full of laughter and light-heartedness. He was my favourite amongst the children and we had a special bond, he the youngest and I the eldest. I shook my head, smiling as I caught the female glances and the heads turned to look at Shah. He was slim and athletic and I could never walk with him without noticing the admiring glances from passers-by.

Shah and my mother sat in the front seat of the car and I in the back while we drove at speed into Cannes. Shah talked non-stop, looking as often at me through the rear-view mirror as at the road, his eyes sparkling under his long, thick eyelashes, his hair glistening with golden highlights from water-skiing. Dressed in a crisp white shirt and white trousers, he'd never looked more handsome and fit.

I was relieved to see him looking so well. Shah had seemed very thin to me during our brief visits in the year and a half since I'd arrived in England. For the first time I could see that he was putting on some weight, as was I. He was no longer worried about my detentions in Pakistan, nor was I especially worried about him or Mir. There had been no actions committed or claimed by Al-Zulfikar for a long time and I felt there was no immediate danger to the family. Zia was a long way away from the sunwashed beaches of Cannes where Shah was now living with his wife, Rehana, and our conversation in the car was not about politics, but about mangoes.

'So what sort of mangoes did you bring us?' Shah said into the rear-view mirror. 'We have been waiting for them for two weeks.'

'Sindhris,' I said, 'though I prefer Chaucers. They're smaller and sweeter.'

'A Sindhi who doesn't prefer Sindhris?' Shah said in mock horror. 'Are you sure you're from Sindh, Madam? Do you often confess to such acts of high treason?'

I laughed. Shah always made me laugh, made everyone in the family laugh. My jet lag and general tiredness seemed to slip away. Shah's vitality and zest for life was contagious. How did he do it? He had been so young when the world of politics had engulfed us. When he was born, Papa had just become a Minister. My mother was busy accompanying him on official events and my grandparents had died. No one, it seemed, had been able to spoil Shah in the way the three of us had been. So Shah developed a special attachment to me. He wrote me many letters at Harvard in his childish scrawl. As he grew older, we would play squash together in the summers. He was more fond of sports than studies. He was a key player for his school basketball team and at home he lifted weights to build up his body. But sports didn't equate with studies for my father.

Shah was packed off to a military cadet school, Hassan Abdal, to instil some 'discipline' into him. There, to the surprise of the other students who thought the privileged son of the Prime Minister would be soft, he distinguished himself in the physical fitness and 'survival courses'. But he wasn't happy at Hassan Abdal and soon cajoled Mummy into talking Papa into calling him back to the Prime Minister's House and the International School at Islamabad.

Shah Nawaz. In Urdu, the King of Kindness. Shah was so generous you never knew what he would do. In Paris a year earlier, on two occasions he had got change to buy a *Herald Tribune* while I waited at a café. Both times he returned empty-handed, after giving the money to poor people holding hats in the street. He literally gave away the shirt off his back. 'Take it, take it,' he would insist if someone admired what he was wearing, once proffering the new blazer my mother had bought him. He had empathised with the poor since childhood. He had built a straw hut in the garden at 70 Clifton and slept in it for weeks, wanting to feel the deprivations of the poor.

He was the only one of us who didn't go to Harvard, but went instead to the American College in Leysin, Switzerland. There he fell in love with a beautiful Turkish girl and made lots of friends. Much to my father's consternation, his grades didn't improve. As often as not he and his friends would drive down to Paris for an evening at Régine's. In 1984, he insisted on taking Yasmin and me to the famous night spot. Although seven years had passed, Shah was received with recognition and gusto.

Yet, I always suspected he was the brightest of us all. He had the most political exposure, my father taking him to campaign meetings. He addressed his first press conference at twelve. He had a sharp political sense, a gut reaction to knowing what people were thinking, what they were feeling in their hearts, what made their blood pound. A person is born with such a talent, be it for music, ballet or art. And he had it for politics.

'Shah reminds me of myself when I was young,' my father often said to me.

This was our second family reunion in Cannes. 'Do whatever you want during the rest of the year, but for the month of July I want you all to be with me,' my mother had told all of us. The family holiday the year before at Auntie Behjat's house in Cannes had not been a great success. Our schedules conflicted and we hadn't been able to spend very much time together. And Mir and I had argued constantly about our differing approaches to unseating Zia.

'Zia has turned Pakistan into a state of armed terror,' Mir had insisted. 'Only violence can answer violence.'

'Violence only breeds violence,' I had retorted. 'That kind of struggle cannot deliver anything lasting to the people. Any permanent change must come peacefully and politically through elections, backed by the mandate of the people.'

'Elections? What elections? Zia will never give up. He will have to be forced out by armed struggle,' Mir countered.

'The army will always have more arms than any guerrilla forces,' I argued. 'The state's capability will always be greater than any group of dissidents. Armed struggle is not only impractical, but counterproductive.'

Back and forth our argument raged, our voices rising until Shah slipped away to go swimming, to go to a café, to go anywhere that we were not. 'I can't bear it when you guys argue like that,' he told me. This year, to Shah's relief, Mir and I had agreed to disagree and not to discuss politics at all.

Shah's interest in politics had expanded beyond Pakistan. Having lived in several Middle Eastern countries since he was forced to leave Pakistan, he had become interested in the complexities of the politics of the Lebanon, Libya and Syria. 'You have a soft corner in your heart for Mrs Thatcher,' he often teased me. 'That's not true, Shah. She's right wing and I'm not,' I'd protest, citing among other things, the high unemployment figures in Britain. He'd shake his head and wave his finger at me. 'No, I'm right,' he'd say. 'You're soft on her because she's a woman.'

Circumstance, not choice, had thrown him into the dangerous, shadowed world of Al-Zulfikar. In Kabul, it had been Shah's job to train the volunteers in Al-Zulfikar's forces. Like everything Shah did, he approached his task with great enthusiasm and mischief, once slipping through the midnight streets of Kabul during the curfew imposed by the Soviets to join his 'troops' for breakfast. Mir had panicked in the morning when he discovered Shah was missing. 'How else can I teach the men evasive tactics,' Shah faced the furious Mir with a smile when he was found.

Shah, like the rest of us, had had his future derailed by the coup and the assassination of our father. His long-time engagement to the Turkish girl had been broken off by her family when they learned of his involvement in Al-Zulfikar. He had had to postpone his dream of going into business as well, though recently he had been talking about raising the capital to build blocks of flats in France. 'You and Mir can do the politics. I'll make the money for the family,' he had said during one of our get-togethers.

He was also interested in intelligence systems, and read extensively on the subject. 'When you and Mir are back in Pakistan involved in politics, just remember you have a little brother who can help you if you give him a high post in intelligence,' he told us. 'Leaders cannot be accessible to all segments of society, no matter how much they might want to be. Modern societies are too large and complex. You'll need someone you can depend on to tell you what the trends are, what the moods are, what's happening at the grassroots. So both of you remember, when the time comes, I'm here.'

'How long are you in Cannes for?' Shah asked me now in the car.

'Until July 30,' I said.

'No. No. No!' he protested. 'You must stay longer. Mir is leaving on the 30th and I'm not going to let you go, too. You have to stay with me for a week at least.'

'I have to go to Australia,' I told him.

'You have to go nowhere,' he said. 'You're staying with me.'

'All right, all right,' I gave in.

I knew I couldn't stay. But I didn't want to dampen Shah's enthusiasm. Of all the family, he had made the most effort to see me, even flying in to Paris unannounced in the spring of 1984 when I had gone on political business. 'The editor of the *Red Star* wants to interview you,' read one message after another from the receptionist at the hotel I was staying in. The *Red Star*? I'd never heard of it, but then I got many requests from people and organisations I'd never heard of. The third time the editor of the *Red Star* phoned, I took the call. 'Heads of State are easier to contact than you,' Shah had laughed. 'It's easier to get through to Walid Jumblatt at Druze headquarters in Beirut than it is to get hold of Ms Benazir Bhutto.'

Every morning in Paris, Shah called my hotel room at 6.00 am. 'You're still sleeping?' he'd say in mock amazement. 'Get up. Let's have breakfast together.' Political dinners weren't a problem to Shah either. 'What time will you be through?' he'd asked me my first night in Paris, when I was meeting Mr Nasim Ahmad, a former Minister of Information. At the appointed hour, I felt a stir in the dining room and looked up to see a tall, good-looking man moving gracefully towards us. My dinner partner blanched. Shah was not only the son of the former Prime Minister, but reputedly a terrorist. Lighting up a cigar, Shah soon had Mr Nasim Ahmad rocking with laughter at his stories. Later Yasmin, Shah and I walked the cobbled streets in the warm spring air, talking and drinking coffee in cafés until 3.00 am.

'I'll pick you all up at 7.00 pm,' Shah now said, dropping my mother and me at the two-bedroom flat in Croisette she had rented for the month. 'You'll come to see my new flat first, then we'll go for a barbecue on the beach. I've done all the preparations. All you have to do is enjoy yourselves.'

'Will Rehana be there?' I asked him.

'Yes,' he said, his expression giving no clue to the current state of his marriage. And he left to pick up last minute items for our picnic.

Sanam, her husband Nasser, their new baby Azadeh and I were all staying with my mother, along with a fifteen-year-old cousin from Los Angeles. Eastern families like to live on top of each other, so the lack of space was no problem. Mir, who was staying with his family at Shah's, joined us for a while with Fathi. I had brought Fathi a little present of plastic cut-outs and some books, which I read to her during the afternoon. There was no air-conditioning in the flat and it was very hot, so the family gathered on the little balcony. Together, we passed a nice, summer afternoon and looked forward to the evening. I barely knew the Afghan sisters my brothers had married four years ago in Kabul.

Mir seemed very happy with Fauzia. But the same was not true of Shah and Rehana.

'If I tell you something, will you promise not to argue with me?' Shah had asked me during our earlier visit in Paris.

'I'll try,' I replied.

'I'm going to divorce my wife,' he said.

My mouth dropped. 'Don't be crazy, Gogi,' I told him, calling him by his family nickname. 'You can't do that. There's never been a divorce in the family. Your marriage wasn't even an arranged one, so you don't have the excuse of saying it didn't work out. You chose to marry Rehana. You must live with it.'

'You're more concerned about the appearance of divorce than you are about me,' he said, quite rightly.

'What's gone wrong?' I asked, hoping I would be able to suggest a possible solution. But the stories he told me about his increasingly difficult marriage made it seem irreparable.

Rehana had changed radically after their marriage, he told me. Where at first she had been loving and attentive to him, preparing hot meals and a cool drink for him when he came home exhausted from working with his troops, she had suddenly refused even to bring him a cup of tea. Often he found her putting on her make-up when he arrived home. Then she would go out and leave him alone.

'I was so lonely,' Shah confessed. 'I had no home, no family. All I wanted was someone to talk to, to watch television with. But she was rarely there. I thought if we had a child we would have a better life, but things just got worse.'

Shah and Rehana had separated twice, Shah reconciling with her each time because of their daughter, Sassi, and because he hoped Rehana would revert to her original self. But in Paris he told me he wanted to end the marriage once and for all. And, like a fool, I talked him out of it.

'Perhaps she's just lonely and bored, Gogi,' I told my brother. 'Since your marriage you've lived in one Arab country after another. She's lived in countries where she had no friends or relatives, where she didn't understand the language, where she couldn't understand the television, where there was no shopping, no films, no theatre. She had no life. Add to that the emotional pressure of having a child at a young age.'

Shah seemed interested in my analysis of Rehana's problems. 'She wants me to do business in America and even claims she can get me off the American blacklist,' Shah said. 'But the life of an American immigrant is not for me.'

'What about living in Europe until you can return to Pakistan?' I pressed on. 'Look, if the two of you were in Europe, here in France for example, even if you weren't around Rehana could at least go out to the cinema or to see friends. This is not a conservative state where women are expected to remain at home and are stared at in public. With Mir living in Switzerland now, she'd be near her sister as well. If you put Rehana in the right circumstances, maybe she'd come out of her depression and go back to being the wife she was. If you like, I'll talk to some friends and see if I can get you French residence.'

Shah had looked definitely interested at that point. 'France is very dangerous,' he said. 'If I live here I'll have to get a gun permit.'

'I don't know about that,' I told him. 'But I could try.'

His mood had improved considerably after our talk. But mine had dampened somewhat when Shah took me with him to buy a bullet-proof jacket. 'I need it to wear in Europe,' he told me as he bought one for himself and a loose one for me in a security shop. 'You never know if Zia will be able to trace me.'

I tried to calm him because I myself was quite paranoid about safety. But he was insistent. 'I've got information that he wants to kill me,' Shah said.

'But, Gogi, Al-Zulfikar has left Kabul and hasn't done anything for years anyway,' I argued. He had just smiled at me. 'I have my information,' he'd said quietly.

When I was in jail in Sukkur, I had had a recurring fear for the lives of my brothers. They were wanted men, and as such, I always lived in fear that something might happen to them. The path of life they were treading was one in which the ominousness of death was very much present and they had taken that path out of free choice. But nonetheless, as a sister, I was very concerned. Having lost my father, I was even more concerned about the safety of the others who were near and dear to me. And the danger to my brothers was very real.

In Kabul, I learned on a later visit to Mir and Shah, one of their wives' old family retainers had tried to poison them. Fortunately for my brothers, but unfortunately for their dog, the dog had eaten the food first, and died. The servant had confessed to the crime, falling to his knees and begging their forgiveness. 'I was paid by the *mujahideen*,' he'd confessed. 'They wanted to please Zia.' My brothers had spared his life when Mir's wife Fauzia had intervened on the servant's behalf.

They had narrowly escaped another assassination attempt while sitting in the front seat of a car. Shah had dropped something and both of them bent down to retrieve it. In that instant, a bullet passed through the car right where their heads would have been.

The target may well have been Shah, not Mir. While my brothers were still in Kabul, a Pathan tribesman had come across from Pakistan to see Mir. 'It is Shah Nawaz's head that Zia wants first,' he had said. 'The order is to kill Shah first, then Murtaza.' That was very likely to be true, Mir explained to me. 'I'm more political, but it's Shah who spends all the time with guerrillas giving them physical training, Shah who has the military expertise, Shah who is more of an immediate threat.'

'I hope to God you and Mir never fly near Pakistan,' I said to Shah. 'If the plane were hijacked, Zia would get you.' Shah had laughed. 'You can't escape death. If it is waiting for you, then no matter what you do, you can't escape it. But Zia will never get us or any of the names he wants out of us. We carry vials of poison with us wherever we go. I'll drink mine if Zia catches me. It works in seconds. I prefer death to dishonour or betrayal.'

The evening in Cannes was very pleasant, starting with our visit to Shah's new flat up a long hilly road in fashionable Californie, which he and

Rehana had moved into about six months before. He had been delighted when I succeeded in getting him a residence permit. Rehana and he had reconciled and then travelled around France; they considered settling in Monte Carlo before choosing Cannes. With great pride now he took me on a tour of his flat, pointing out Sassi's room with clown puppets on the wall and stuffed animals spilling out of the bookcase, the dining area and living room which led to a terrace and, beyond, the distant glint of the Mediterranean Sea. The flat was lovely, the whole atmosphere like a stunning film shot.

I greeted Rehana warmly, hoping on this trip to break through her reserve and form some sort of relationship with her. As usual, she was dressed in the latest fashion, though her clothes looked more suitable for a restaurant than a beach picnic. But then our family had always preferred the comfort of informal clothes. While Shah passed cold drinks to the family, I tried, unsuccessfully, to talk to Rehana. Whether she was shy or simply uninterested, I don't know. But she soon withdrew to join her sister at the far end of the room. They were physically beautiful, the sisters, but I had no sense of what they were like underneath.

I gave little Sassi her presents and played with her for a while. Shah went into the kitchen to pack the hamper for the picnic. Auntie Behjat and Uncle Karim joined us. I sat at Shah's desk, while my family swirled around the living room. On the table were photographs of the family and of Sassi. A red leather folder was neatly placed on the desk. A vase of fresh flowers sat on the glass coffee table. I was pleased at how orderly Shah's life had become. 'For the first time, I feel on top of the world,' Shah said to me, sitting down briefly on the edge of the desk. 'Everything is going very well for me.'

'Catch me, *Wadi*. Catch me!' my two little nieces called to me on the beach, running in and out of the edge of the sea. I ran after them, making a big pretence of not being able to catch them. Shah finally got the charcoal going and we were all very hungry by the time the chicken was cooked. 'You get the first piece,' he said, bringing me what appeared to be half a chicken. 'Oh Gogi, I can't,' I protested. 'No, no, no,' he insisted. 'You must eat it all.'

I looked around at the family, gossiping and laughing together. How many years it had been since we'd had picnics on the beach outside Karachi, trying to finish our food before the bold birds of prey swooped down and tried to steal it. Who could have foretold that we'd ever be together at another picnic far away on the beaches of the French Riviera? But the family reunion was going very well. There was far less tension among us than there had been the summer before. I looked for my sisters-in-law. Rehana and Fauzia were sitting apart, by themselves. With Mir living in Switzerland and Shah in France, the sisters didn't see each other that often and had as many memories to sift through as we did.

'Let's go to the Casino,' Uncle Karim suggested.

I was feeling tired, but Shah turned to me with an expectant smile. 'We can *gup shup* all night. You must come, Pinkie.'

'Okay, I'll come,' I told him. I couldn't refuse this brother of mine.

'Great. And don't forget about tomorrow,' he said, reminding me of our plan to go shopping for my birthday present of luggage from my mother. 'I'm the expert on Louis Vuitton. Tomorrow, whenever we wake up, I'll take you shopping in Nice.'

Plans. So many nice plans. Shah and Rehana left the beach for their flat with the picnic hamper to unload. Sanam and Nasser were given a lift by Auntie Behjat and Uncle Karim. Mir and Fauzia dropped off my mother, my cousin and me at our flat before going back to Shah's to put Fathi to bed. 'Shah and I will be back to pick you up in half an hour,' Mir called as he left.

He came back alone.

Instead of the cheerful Shah we had left at the beach, Mir told us, Shah had looked very angry when he arrived at the flat. 'I asked him what was going on,' Mir said. 'But before Shah could answer, Rehana screamed "Get out! Get out! This is my flat!" she kept yelling. She was hysterical. "Don't go," Gogi said to me, but I didn't want to stand between them. I thought maybe she'd calm down if Fauzia and I packed up and left.'

'Then where's Fauzia?' asked my mother.

'She's downstairs in the car and very upset,' Mir said. 'She wants to go home to Geneva right now. It's the middle of the night, I told her, and besides, my sister has just arrived. She's demanding that we stay in a hotel but I told her no, that I didn't see my family often and I wanted to stay with you all. But let's not ruin the whole evening. Let's go out the way we planned.'

'You all go,' I told Sanam, Nasser and Mir. 'I've had a long day.'

'Read to me, *Wadi*, read to me,' Fathi pestered me the next day. Sanam, Nasser and Mir hadn't come in until almost 6.00 am and we had all slept late. I was still lounging about in my night clothes just after 1.00 pm when I heard the doorbell.

'*Wadi*'s got to get dressed now to go shopping,' I said to Fathi, thinking Shah had arrived to take me to Nice.

Instead Sanam rushed into the bedroom. 'Quickly! We've got to go quickly!' she said, handing me her baby while I stood there, half-dressed.

'What's the matter?' I asked her.

'Rehana says Gogi's taken something,' Sanam said, turning to rush back out of the room.

My legs started to shake. I took a deep breath to give myself strength.

'Is he ill? Is it serious?' I called as she hurried down the hall.

'We don't know. We're going to see,' she called back and was gone.

I stood there alone with Fathi and the baby.

The police. Get the police. Juggling the baby on my hip, I looked at the emergency number on the phone. I dialled it and got a recording in French. I grabbed the phone book to look up hospitals just as my mother and Sanam rushed back in. Mir and Nasser had raced ahead with Rehana to Shah's flat. Unable to get a cab on the streets, my mother and Sanam had come back to call one.

'Mummy, you know French better than me. If we can't get the police, get a hospital,' I said to her rapidly.

'Why don't we just go there and see if he's all right,' she said.

'No, Mummy, it's better to be safe. Remember Toni,' I said, reminding her of the case of a girl we knew who had taken an overdose of pills and had been taken too late to the hospital to be saved. I had learned a similar lesson myself when the police surrounded 70 Clifton. That was not the moment to ask why the police had come. First burn all the papers. Then ask.

My mother took the telephone book. She tried one hospital. They told her to call another. She called that hospital. Ring somebody else, they responded. She was ringing a third hospital when Mir came in.

He looked broken, beaten. Silently saying what his voice could not, I saw him mouth the words, 'He's dead.'

'No!' I screamed. 'No!'

The phone dropped from my mother's hand.

'It's true, Mummy,' Mir whispered in agony. 'I've seen dead men. Shah's body is cold.'

Mummy began to wail.

'Call an ambulance!' I said. 'For God's sake, ring the hospital. He may still be alive. He can be resuscitated!' I didn't know what to do with the baby in my arms. Fathi was clinging to my leg, staring up at me.

My mother picked the telephone up off the floor. The third hospital was still on the line. 'Just tell us where to go,' the operator said, having heard our screams. We ran out of the door.

Shah Nawaz was lying on the carpet in the living room beside the coffee table. He was still wearing the white trousers he had worn the night before. His hand was outstretched, a beautiful brown hand. He looked like a sleeping Adonis. 'Gogi!' I shouted, trying to wake him up. But then I saw his nose. It was white as chalk, standing out in sharp contrast to his tan.

'Give him oxygen!' I screamed at the ambulance crew who were taking his pulse. 'Massage his heart!'

'He's dead,' one of the crew said quietly.

'No! Try! Try!' I shouted.

'Pinkie, he's cold,' Mir said. 'He's been dead for hours.'

I looked around the room. The coffee table was askew. A saucer of brownish liquid sat on a side table. The cushion was half off the couch and the vase of flowers had fallen. My eyes lifted to his desk. The leather file folder was gone. I looked out on the terrace. His papers were there. The folder was open.

Something was terribly wrong. His body was cold. God knows how long Shah had lain there, dying. But no one had been alerted. And someone had taken the time to go through his papers.

I looked up to see Rehana. She hardly looked like someone who had just lost a husband or who had rushed to get help. She was dressed immaculately, her white linen jacket without a wrinkle, her hair all done up, not one strand out of place. How many hours had she spent grooming herself while my brother lay dead on the floor? She looked back at me with eyes that held no tears.

Her lips moved. I couldn't hear what she was saying.

'Poison,' her sister Fauzia said for her. 'He took poison.'

I didn't believe her. None of us believed her. Why would Shah take poison? He had been happier the night before than we'd ever seen him. He was enthusiastic about his plans for the future, including a return to Afghanistan in August. Was that it? Had Zia caught wind of Shah's plan and pre-empted it? Or had the CIA killed him as a friendly gesture towards their favourite dictator?

'For God's sake, at least cover Shah's body,' Sanam said, Someone fetched a piece of white plastic.

'*Wadi, Wadi*, what's the matter?' little Fathi kept saying to me, pulling on my shirt. 'Nothing's the matter, darling,' I absently soothed the three-year-old. Sassi, too, looked upset and confused, wandering through the living-room to sit by her father's body. 'Get the children out of here,' my mother said. I took them into Sassi's bedroom and left them with a book.

When the police came to take Shah's body away, Mir made me go into the kitchen. 'You don't want to see it,' he said. I looked at the half-cut tomato and the cooked egg still in the frying pan on the stove. Who had cooked it and for whom? A bottle of milk stood on the counter. It was a very hot day and the milk had curdled. Why had it been left out of the fridge? 'They've taken Shah,' Mir said, returning to the kitchen. 'The police said it looks like a heart attack.'

He turned away, wiping the tears from his face. When he dropped the tissue into the kitchen waste-bin, he saw something shining. It was the empty vial of poison.

The French authorities didn't release Shah's body for weeks. The wait was agonising for all of us crowded into my mother's flat. As Muslims, we bury our dead within twenty-four hours, but Shah's body was undergoing test after test. We didn't know what to do with ourselves. Alternately we cried or just sat and stared. No one was interested in food or drink or anything. We had Sanam's baby, Mir's daughter, and often Sassi whom Fauzia would drop off every time Rehana was called to the police station during the inquiry. 'Take us to the *jhoolas*,' the little girls begged me and I would take them to the swings in a near-by park. Sometimes Mir joined me. While the girls played, Mir and I sat on a bench, staring silently out to sea.

My heart ached for Sassi. She had been very close to her father. Shah was the one to get her up in the morning, to get her breakfast, to put her on the potty. On some three-year-old level, Sassi knew she'd lost him. 'My Papa,' she'd insist when Mir came to pick up Fathi. When the car passed La Napoule, the beach where we'd had the barbecue, Sassi would shout 'Papa Shah. Papa Shah.' The police had cut out the section of carpet on which Shah's body was found. When Rehana had the carpet replaced, Sassi pointed at the spot where she'd last seen her father. 'Papa Shah, Papa Shah,' she kept repeating. She took to clinging to us whenever Mir and I returned her to Fauzia. She didn't want to go into the house and wound her arms tightly around our necks. 'Go, little baby,' I'd whisper, while Fauzia pulled at her. But Sassi only clung harder. We had to prise her hands apart to break her grip.

It was awful sitting in Cannes, waiting for Shah's body to be released. Everything reminded me of him. I saw Shah everywhere, sitting at the Carlton Hotel, walking on the Croisette. The pain of his loss was heightened by the constant slandering of him in the Pakistani press. The regime-controlled papers reported that Shah had been a depressive, a gambler and suicidal. He had been drunk the night he died, they claimed. Lab reports refuted the claim, but our denial based on the reports received little play in the Pakistani press. Now that Shah had lost his life, our enemies were doing everything they could to destroy his honour. And the agonising wait for my brother's body to be released dragged on.

'I'm going to take Shah home to Pakistan to be buried,' I said to the family one afternoon.

My mother became hysterical. 'Oh Pinkie, you can't go back,' she cried. 'I've lost my son. I don't want to lose my daughter.'

'Shah did everything for me, but he never asked me to do anything for him,' I said. 'He longed to return to Larkana. Often he asked exactly where Papa was buried so he could picture it. I have to take him home.'

'Mir, tell her she can't go back,' my mother begged my brother. What could he do?

'If you go back, I'll go back, too,' he said, trying to frighten me into not going because we all knew Zia was certain to kill him.

'You don't go. I'll go,' Auntie Behjat said.

'I'll go,' Sanam said.

'I'll go,' Nasser said.

'Fine. We'll go together. But I'm going,' I said. 'I don't want Shah to have a small and hidden burial. I want him to have all the respect and honour that he deserves.'

As the autopsy dragged on, I flew back to London for a few days to take care of business at the Barbican. Hundreds of people came to call on me for condolence at the party office. The grief for Shah was real and shared amongst the Pakistani community as was the wide-spread suspicion that Zia was somehow involved in my brother's death. The grief in Pakistan, I was told by friends, was even more wide-spread. Prayer meetings were being held all over the country for Shah's soul, while thousands were coming to pray at 70 Clifton. Newspapers carrying the false charges that Shah had died of alcohol and drug abuse were being burned. In Sindh, most businesses had closed out of respect. Despite the July heat, people had been flooding into Larkana for two weeks. Every hotel was solidly booked and people were now camping on the railway station platform.

When I returned to Cannes, I had to control my own anguish suf-ficiently to communicate with London and Karachi about the arrangements for our departure after the autopsy was completed, as many Pakistanis wanted to accompany the family on Shah's final journey. To counter the confusion the restricted Pakistani press was creating about both the re-lease of Shah's body and the probable timing of our return, I organised the release of regular bulletins to keep our supporters informed.

There was no surcease to our sorrow. For no apparent reason, my mother's car was broken into, the only one among many on the street. Only the mail I had brought back with me and left briefly on the back seat was stolen. Our apprehension heightened and we felt unsafe. There was a strong possibility, if not probability, that Shah had been killed by agents of the regime. There was no guarantee they had left Cannes. We communicated our concern and our need for protection to the French government and they responded positively.

When Shah's body was finally released, we went to say prayers over his body. I thought I'd see my little brother as I remembered him, bronzed from the sun, slim and handsome in the white suit we had taken to the undertakers because he was so fond of white. But the body lying in the coffin was almost that of a stranger. Shah's face was powder-white and puffy. The morticians had had to chalk his face to cover the many incisions of the autopsies. The sight was heart-breaking.

Oh, my poor Gogi. What have they done to you? The room filled with wailing. Without knowing it, I started hitting myself in the face, sobbing in huge silent gasps where the breath was caught in my chest. We had to be taken out of the room. We forced some control over ourselves and walked to the car where press photographers were waiting.

I took Shah home to Pakistan on August 21, 1985. The regime had reluctantly agreed to allow his burial in Larkana, swayed perhaps by the people's outrage that, contrary to Muslim ritual, neither my mother and I nor they had been permitted to witness my father's burial. Yet the regime was once again making every effort to keep the burial of another Bhutto quiet.

Fearing an emotional mass turn-out, the Martial Law authorities made arrangements for us to fly Shah's body straight on from Karachi to Moenjodaro, then on to our family graveyard by helicopter where they had already built a helipad. The regime wanted Shah to be buried quickly and secretly, out of the sight and minds of the people.

I refused. Shah had longed to return to the home of his birth for eight years. I was determined to make his final journey as meaningful to him as it would be to us, to pass him by the doorways that had sheltered him: 70 Clifton in Karachi, Al-Murtaza in Larkana. I wanted to take him past the lands where he had hunted with Papa and Mir, past our fields and ponds, past the people he had tried to defend in his own way. The people, too, deserved the chance to honour this brave son of Pakistan before he was laid to rest near his father in Garhi Khuda Bakhsh.

'Tell the Martial Law authorities that they can do whatever they want to me, but I will not allow my brother to be denied the Muslim right of return to his own home for his final bath by his own family and members of his household,' I told Dr Ashraf Abbasi who was coordinating the arrangements with the local administration in Larkana. A compromise had been reached with the regime. We were not to be permitted to take Shah home to 70 Clifton, but we could take him to Al-Murtaza. Our home in Larkana was so remote and difficult to get to, the local authorities noted in their reports, that the crowds would be sparse, especially in the inferno of August.

To make sure, the Army set up roadblocks on all the roads leading into the province of Sindh. Buses, trucks, trains and cars were stopped and searched. The Army was put on alert in Sindh and PPP leaders were detained under house arrest. Karachi airport was cordoned off and trucks filled with soldiers and automatic weapons pulled across the main thoroughfares of the city. As further insurance against any outburst, the regime tried to placate the people by finally setting a date for the lifting of Martial Law. On the eve of my departure from Zurich to Pakistan with my brother's body, Zia's appointed Prime Minister Mohammed Khan Junejo announced that Martial Law would be lifted in December.

Black. Black armbands. Black *shalwar khameez* and *dupattas*. We stopped briefly at Karachi and transferred from Singapore Airlines to a smaller chartered Fokker for the final journey to Moenjodaro. As Shah's coffin, draped with an outlawed PPP flag, was unloaded onto a trolley, several of our servants who had come from 70 Clifton threw themselves on it, weeping. There was much weeping too, among the relatives who joined us in Karachi, as well as Paree, Samiya and her sister. And we flew on towards the most tumultuous funeral Pakistan had ever witnessed.

'Let's go. Let's go. Let's go to Larkana. Don't you know they are bringing Shah Nawaz today? Shah Nawaz, who is the son of Zulfikar Ali Bhutto, Shah Nawaz who is a warrior, Shah Nawaz, who has given his life for you and for me. Come on, come on. Let us go. Let us go and receive a hero today.' The beautiful song written for my brother was being sung all over Pakistan. In spite of the regime's threats, the people had been flooding towards Larkana for weeks, camping in the fields, sleeping on footpaths.

Black. More black. As the Fokker came in to land soon after 10.00 am at Moenjodaro, there was a mass of black ringing the airport, lining the roads for miles. The regime's roadblocks could not stop the mourners who had travelled through the searing heat to express their grief for this fallen son of the land. Even where there is enmity, it is incumbent on Muslims to express sorrow at death and to take part in the grief. But no one had anticipated these multitudes. The press reported the crowds at well over a million.

'Allahu Akbar! God is Great!' the people shouted as Shah's coffin was placed in a waiting ambulance and packed with the ice I'd asked for. After all the post mortems and autopsies he'd been through, I didn't want anything else to happen to him. *'Inna li Allah, wa inna ilayhi raji'un* — To God we belong and to Him we must return,' the people chanted as the ambulance passed, holding their arms out and their palms up in their recitation of the Muslim prayer for the dead.

I don't think many state presidents have been given as honourable and magnificent farewell as Shah was receiving at the age of twenty-seven. Two thousand vehicles of every sort, cars, motorcycles, trucks and animal-drawn carts draped in black, followed his coffin, a motorcade stretching ten miles. The people showered the ambulance bearing his body with rose petals in the loving gesture of farewell all along the twenty-eight kilometres from the airport to Larkana. As his coffin passed, many men in the crowd saluted, their heads topped with embroidered caps or wrapped in the turbans of their tribes.

Pictures of Shah rimmed in black. Shah Nawaz *Shaheed*. Shah Nawaz the Martyr. There were pictures of me, of my mother, one unforgettable one of Shah silhouetted against Papa. *Shaheed ka beta Shaheed*, the legend read – the Martyr's son has been martyred. The pent-up grief the people had not been allowed to express for my father, for their own suffering and for ours welled over. Wailing and striking their breasts, the grieving masses threw themselves at our motorcade, rocking the cars in their frenzy to touch the vehicle bearing Shah in the gesture of farewell.

The sun was high in the sky and there was still much to be done before the afternoon prayers: the ritual washing of the body, the viewing of the face by the family, the prayers for the dead read at home by women who do not accompany the body to the graveyard, the prayer service for men which had been organised on a nearby football field. Shah had to be buried before sundown. And Sanam and I still had to pick out the site for his grave. We hadn't been able to do that for my father. This time I wanted to be able to plan the space, to place Shah far enough away from my father so there would be room later to build mausoleums for both of them. As we neared Al-Murtaza, however, the crowds became a solid wall.

'Go straight on to Garhi,' I told the driver of our car. Somehow he got us out of the crush as the ambulance bearing Shah's body pulled into the courtyard of Al-Murtaza. The crowds were only slightly less dense at our family graveyard fifteen miles away, but they stayed outside the walls. Together Sanam and I chose a site in the far left-hand corner of the graveyard, quite a distance away from my father, who is buried behind my grandfather. After saying a brief prayer at my father's grave, we hurried back to Al-Murtaza.

Crying. Wailing. In the fever of their grief, the people had broken down the walls of Al-Murtaza and flooded not only into the courtyard but into the house. The house was packed not only with them, but with all our female relatives, with women party workers, and the household staff. Shah's coffin was in the drawing room still unopened because of the pandemonium. 'Please give us room,' I beseeched the people with folded hands as they pushed over each other. All discipline had simply been overwhelmed.

I had wanted to show Shah's face to the relatives but, when the staff started to move the coffin towards my grandfather's room where the *maulvi* was waiting to bathe the body, emotions reached fever pitch. The women, even the household staff became overpowered with grief and started hitting their heads on the coffin. Blood started to flow from men's heads, women's heads. 'For God's sake, move them all away before they harm themselves any more,' I cried. 'Move Shah quickly into my grandfather's room.'

Finally, quietly and tenderly, Shah was bathed by our *maulvi* and the household staff, and placed in a *Kaffan*, the unstitched Muslim burial shroud. The heat was suffocating, well over 110 degrees, and I was increasingly anxious to get on with the burial. 'Oh Baba, he had cuts all over his body,' one of the shocked staff said, returning from the washing. 'Don't tell me,' I said to him. But he couldn't stop. 'His nose was cut, his chin, his . . .' 'Stop!' I shouted. 'Enough. He is now home, back where he belongs.' My brother-in-law, Nasser Hussein came up to me. 'It's getting late,' he said. 'We must hurry.' Given the crowd, we decided it was best to take Shah to the graveyard in the strong wooden coffin rather than carrying him in the *Kaffan*.

I asked the servants to bring Shah's body back into the drawing room so the relatives could pray. Then, suddenly, Shah's coffin was being carried through the heaving crowd to the ambulance. Nasser Hussein hurried behind. In the chaos, I almost missed the departure myself. Hearing the chant of the prayers, I ran to follow the coffin to the door.

Good-bye, Shah Nawaz. Good-bye. The parting was so quick, so painful. As the ambulance started, I wanted to run out, to stop it, to bring Shah back somehow. I didn't want to let my little brother go. Oh, Gogi. Stay with me. A single moan rose from the five hundred women praying in the garden as the ambulance moved through the gates and out of sight. My brother was gone for ever.

In every generation, Shiite Muslims believe, there is a Karbala, a re-enactment of the tragedy that befell the family of the Prophet Mohammed, PBUH, after his death in 640 AD.

Many in Pakistan have come to believe that the victimisation of the Bhutto family and our supporters was the Karbala of our generation. The father was not spared. The mother was not spared. The brothers were not spared. The daughter was not spared. The band of followers were not spared. Yet, like the followers of the Prophet's grandson, our resolve never faltered.

As I stood now in the doorway of Al-Murtaza, a woman's voice rose above the moans in the courtyard, re-enacting the tragedy at Karbala. 'See, see Benazir,' the woman keened in the cadence of the subcontinent. 'She has come with the body of her brother. How young he is, how handsome, how innocent. He has been slain by the tyrant's hand. Feel the grief of the sister. Remember Zeinab, going to the court of Yazid. Remember Zeinab as she sees Yazid playing with her brother's head.

'Think of the heart of Begum Bhutto, how it bursts as she sees the child she gave birth to, who she played with as a baby. He grew before her eyes. Nusrat sees his first steps. The mother that made him grow with such love. Think of her.

'Think of Murtaza. He has lost his right hand. He has lost half of himself. He will never be the same . . .'

Cries echoed off the walls of Al-Murtaza as the women wailed and beat their chests. 'A-i-i-e-e-e!' It was a massive, heaving cry of farewell. I slowly backed into the house. My brother was being buried in the graveyard of our ancestors. I could do no more.

Nasser Hussein, Garhi Khuda Bakhsh:

When we arrived at the Bhutto family graveyard from the prayer service, the crowd was impenetrable. As the coffin came out of the ambulance, I shouldered the front corner. I have no idea who was behind me or what happened to them. I just clung to my position as the crowd pushed forward to try to carry the coffin even for a moment, to relieve our burden and share in the task.

There was no one to guide us toward the gravesite and we couldn't see where we were going. The coffin seemed twice as heavy because we couldn't coordinate our actions. It rocked like a rudderless ship on our shoulders as the sea of bodies pushed and shoved. Where our feet ended, somebody else's began. Our progress was so circuitous, it took us forty-five minutes, maybe longer, to blindly move the ten yards from the ambulance to the entrance of the graveyard.

Suddenly, an upturned, beckoning hand came out of the crowd in front of me. I caught a glimpse of the son of one of the staff at Al-Murtaza, and I followed his hand while he backed towards the gravesite. The crowd helped by pushing the coffin in his direction. I willed myself not to faint in the heat and hysteria. Yet, miraculously in all the crush, no one trod on the other Bhutto graves.

When we reached Shah's grave, I collapsed, my legs in the excavation. A villager brought me water in a rusty cup and I gulped it down. There was no room to take Shah's body out of the coffin. We had to tilt the coffin and slide it into the grave. The people were calling out to be shown Shah's face in the last viewing, but Benazir had asked me not to. The last quick prayer was said, and the mourners joined in the Fateha, the hand-raising act of prayer and submission. The elders were coming forward for the long recital of 24 prayers when I left. My sad duty was over. We had brought Shah Nawaz to his final resting place.

I was arrested by the Martial Law regime five days later in Karachi. I was not surprised. Though Zia had given assurances to the press that I would not be arrested on my return with Shah's body, and the Chief Minister of Sindh had also issued a statement saying that I would be free to come and go, the masses of mourners who had swept by the Army's barricades in Larkana to express solidarity with the family had badly shaken the regime. As the mourners continued to mass in the fields across from Al-Murtaza and in the street outside the house for the other religious rites surrounding death, the regime, I'm sure, feared an uprising.

Though my brother's death had forced them to announce the date for the ending of Martial Law, neither his death nor the suffering of thousands of others had been avenged. 'We should take the initiative now when emotions are running so high to oust Zia,' several PPP leaders suggested at an evening meeting after Shah's burial. Others argued that we should not give the regime the pretext for not lifting Martial Law. Even in grief, it seemed, politics could not be forgotten. 'Martial Law is the curse of the country and we must ensure that it is lifted,' I argued wearily in favour of restraint. 'Shah has given his life for it. If we mount an agitation now, then they can say that they wanted to lift Martial Law, but were forced not to. We must consider this aspect.'

Nonetheless, I took precautions against repercussions from the regime. The *soyem* ceremony for the dead is held on the third day following burial, the *chehlum* forty days afterwards. I was not at all sure I'd be free in forty days, so after great debate with religious leaders, we decided to count the forty days from the time of Shah's death in France in July rather than from his August burial. That way the *soyem* and the *chehlum* almost coincided.

Another Bhutto grave. Another mound of fresh mud. I took flowers with me to add to the masses already on Shah's grave. 'In the name of God, most gracious, most merciful,' I prayed along with hundreds of others crowded into the sweltering graveyard. It was heart-rending to see all that fresh mud. Shah Nawaz.

Sanam had to go back to Karachi the night after the *soyem*. So did Fakhri. I didn't want to be alone in my grief at Al-Murtaza and decided to go with them. It was some sort of consolation that at least Sanam and I were together, a little something of the family. But once more politics overrode our personal mourning.

Thousands greeted us at Karachi airport. We couldn't get through the crowds to reach the car. Members of the party finally forced a passageway of sorts, linking their arms around us to make a flying wedge. It took several hours for the car to make its way through the people to 70 Clifton. Some people in the jeeps and motorcycles accompanying us made the victory sign but there was no shouting of political slogans. Slogans are a sign of happiness and everyone was in mourning for Shah.

The garden at 70 Clifton was just as packed. I walked out to thank the people for taking part in our grief and for showing their solidarity. Many faces were familiar: men and women who had been to jail several times for their political beliefs. 'Whether we agreed with my brother's methods or not, he was a man who opposed tyranny,' I said to them. 'His conscience did not allow him to keep silent at a time when Pakistan was suffering.'

Nasser Baloach. Ayaz Samoo. Two other young men who had given their lives for the cause of democracy and were victims of military terror. They, too, had been my brothers, rallying round me, protecting me, thinking of me as their sister. The next day I contacted their families. Just as mourners were pouring in to 70 Clifton to condole with us, I wanted to pay condolence calls to their families, to share the grief of other mothers and sisters who had lost their brothers. I never got there.

The police surrounded 70 Clifton in the early hours of August 27. Once more 70 Clifton was declared a sub-jail and guarded by police and army units armed with tear gas. I was served a ninety-day detention order, the regime later claiming that I had ignored their warnings not to visit 'terrorists' in 'sensitive areas'. I had received no such warnings. The areas deemed 'sensitive' by the regime were Malir and Lyari, impoverished areas of Karachi, whose inhabitants including the families of Nasser Baloach and Ayaz Samoo had suffered the most under Zia. No wonder he considered the areas 'sensitive'. And Zia was no one to use the excuse of terrorism. If terrorism is defined as the use of force by a minority to impose its views on the majority, then Zia and his army had defined themselves.

In Washington, the Reagan administration expressed 'dismay' over my detention. 'Pakistan has taken encouraging steps towards the restoration of constitutional government ... putting Ms Bhutto under house arrest would appear to be inconsistent with this process,' a State Department spokesman was quoted as saying. The reaction from British parliamentarians was stronger, both MP Max Madden and Lord Avebury contacting Zia on my behalf. But I remained locked up, once more without a telephone or any contact with the outside world. Sanam and Nasser were with me for the first few days, as was my cousin Laleh who had been staying for the night and was inadvertently caught in the regime's net. But on September 2, the regime forced my family to leave and I was left at 70 Clifton, utterly alone in my grief.

The days dragged into weeks while I tried to reconcile myself to Shah's death. I read and re-read every old magazine in the house, wrote in my journals and tuned in to every BBC news report. It was frustrating being immobilised again. As much as I was burdened by my sorrow, I wanted to take advantage of the time I had in Pakistan. With Martial Law due to be lifted in less than three months, political opposition to Zia had to be organised and in place. Before my arrest I had scheduled meetings with the party leaders from the four provinces. Now they had been cancelled.

Though there was much trumpeting in the regime-controlled press about the lifting of Martial Law now announced for December 31, Zia's hand remained as cold and repressive as ever. Meetings scheduled in Lahore to propose my release were banned. MRD leaders heading towards a meeting in Karachi on October 21 were either externed or barred from entering the city. On the eve of the meeting, several MRD leaders were jailed. Still Zia claimed to represent the people of Pakistan.

Politics. Politics. Politics. The mantle of leadership felt heavy in my detention at 70 Clifton. How often politics had kept me from my family, especially Shah Nawaz, now lying under the dust of Larkana. 'Make time to see me. Why can't you make time?' he had phoned me in London time and again, only to mimic my inevitable reply. 'Oh Gogi, I have to go to America, to Denmark. I have important meetings in Bradford, Birmingham, Glasgow. . . .' If I had just paused, thought, given him more time. But then, no one can change destiny. His fate had been written. Still, it was very hard for me to accept that he was gone.

His room in the annexe across the courtyard was just the way he'd left it eight years ago, his yearbook from his high school in Islamabad still on the bookshelf next to the adventure novels he had loved and the Holy Quran my father had given him. Mir's room was the same as well, his poster of Che Guevara on the wall and his Harvard yearbook in the desk drawer. My brothers' rooms were locked now, as were the rooms of my sister and mother and father. The only light in the house in the few hours the electricity was uninterrupted by the regime, was in my room, one room in a whole, huge house.

I yearned to see Sassi, to bring Shah's daughter to see her family home and learn her heritage. She should never forget her father, but be taught what he stood for and what he had given for his country. Her heritage was a proud one, interrupted by tragedy. Perhaps it was all pre-ordained. 'Why does Shah want to call her Sassi?' Dr Abbasi had asked me one day as we drove together to Hyderabad. 'It's such a sad name. You remember the legend of Sassi who fell in love with Pannu, but they were separated. Sassi walked across deserts and mountains in search of him. "Sassi, Sassi," she heard Pannu call to her from one spot in the desert. But when she reached it, the earth opened, swallowing her up.' But Shah loved the name Sassi as much as he loved his daughter and the name stuck.

Would we ever know who was behind Shah's murder? Locked up at 70 Clifton, I kept coming back to the story Samiya told me on the plane flight with Shah's body to Moenjodaro. A man had visited several newspaper offices in Karachi the month before the murder, she told me, asking for current pictures of Shah. Had someone been looking for a picture to identify Shah as he looked at twenty-seven?

I was listening to the early morning BBC report on October 22 when my body went rigid. The police had arrested Rehana in Cannes, the broad-caster said, and charged her under French law for 'failing to assist a person in danger'. There were no details.

A few days after I heard the announcement about Rehana on the BBC, I read in the local newspapers that I had received a summons to attend the inquiry into Shah's death, but had responded that I did not want to go. What summons? I had never received a summons. 'It's not true that I do not want to attend the inquiry,' I wrote in a letter to the Home Department. 'I do want to attend, but it is in your hands, not mine. Please advise the French court that I wish to attend, but that you are preventing me.'

I was released on November 3. 'Today I begin a difficult journey, a sad journey which will take me into the court-rooms of a foreign land to inquire into the death of my beloved brother, Shah Nawaz,' I began a statement to our supporters. I had to type it on a manual typewriter. This time the regime had turned off all the electricity to 70 Clifton, as well as the separate electrical system in the annexe. 'I am determined to return as soon as possible,' I concluded the statement. 'God willing, I hope to be back in three months . . . no matter what the consequences.'

The air was light in France when I arrived to give my deposition, but my heart was heavy. It was to get heavier as I learned the details of Shah's death and Rehana's arrest.

Rehana had gone to the police station to pick up her passport on October 22, her passport having been confiscated by the French police shortly after Shah's death. After months of inconclusive questioning, during which Rehana had repeated her claims to both Interpol and the French police that she had neither seen nor heard anything while my brother was dying, her lawyer had argued successfully that her passport should be returned. Rehana had been all set to leave France when she called at the police station. Instead, she had dropped a bomb-shell.

Reversing her earlier claims, Rehana had confirmed what so far the police only knew from the autopsy report – that Shah had not died instantaneously. The police had questioned her further, charged her with failing to assist a person in danger and sent her before a magistrate. Instead of receiving her passport, Rehana had received an arrest warrant and had been sent to Nice Central Jail.

The family was devastated at the disclosure about Shah's death. The poison which both my brothers carried, Shah had told me, worked in-stantaneously. Mir's vial of poison had been examined by both the French and Swiss police, confirming Shah's claim – if taken undiluted, the poison worked immediately. That Shah had died quickly and painlessly had been a source of comfort to all of us. Our grief deepened greatly with the news that he did not.

For a week, I had nightmares. 'Help me!' Shah called to me. 'Help me!' In other dreams, he was shivering with cold and I would try to bring him blankets. During the day, I ran frequently to the bathroom to throw up. The unanswered questions surrounding Shah's horrible death plagued us. Why hadn't Rehana gone for help? And why was she continuing to claim that Shah had committed suicide, a particularly painful accusation for Muslims who believe that God alone should give and take life? We knew Shah's strength and joie de vivre. He would never have committed suicide. And no one would voluntarily have chosen the prolonged, painful death he had apparently experienced.

We were convinced as a family that Shah had been killed and filed charges of murder against unknown persons. At the Carlton, I met unofficially with one of the police officers investigating the case. The police, too, were stymied. 'Can you find out more about the poison?' he asked me. 'There wasn't a trace of it left in the body.' I followed up every lead I had, finally obtaining the details of the poison on a confidential basis. The description still haunts me.

'The poison works instantaneously if taken undiluted,' the report stated. 'If diluted, its nature changes completely. After thirty minutes the victim loses stability and is afflicted with a headache, a feeling of exhaustion and severe thirst. Within an hour the body starts shaking uncontrollably, accompanied by pain around the heart and stomach, then cramps throughout the body. Rigor mortis sets in before death, leaving the victim conscious during the onset of paralysis. Phlegm fills the throat, making breathing laboured and speech difficult. Still conscious, the victim feels cold. The time of death varies, between four and sixteen hours.'

The agony of Shah's death spread through the whole family, starting with the break-up of Mir's marriage to Fauzia. Sassi, too, was lost to us. When I arrived in Nice for the deposition, Rehana was in jail and Sassi was with Fauzia who refused to let us have access to her. Our pain seemed unending. Sassi was our blood. Sassi was our flesh. She looked just like Shah, especially her eyes. Sassi was all we had left of him. And we were losing her.

We had tried to work out a legal family settlement with Rehana. Sassi would live with her for nine months of the year and with us for three months, while we paid for all her expenses and education. But Rehana hadn't been interested. We were forced to turn once again to the court, though the legal procedings did nothing to relieve our feeling of loss.

In February, 1988, the court awarded my mother the right to see Sassi at weekends, but the judgment could not be implemented. Rehana had sent Sassi to California to stay with her grandparents. Who knows where she is now or how she is? I get a physical pain in my heart when I think of her. If only we could be assured that she is all right, that she is healthy, that she is happy. But we are told nothing. In the meantime, I cling to the dream that someday Sassi will come to us. Like her namesake, she will cross the deserts and the mountains to find the family who loves her. We will wait for her always.

In June of 1988, after more than two years of legal proceedings, the French Court ruled that Rehana would have to stand trial for failing to assist a person in danger, a charge punishable by one to five years in prison. To our disappointment, the court also ruled that there was insufficient evidence to uphold our charge of murder against unknown persons. But the stigma of suicide, at least, was removed from Shah's name. Shortly after the court's decision, the BBC reported Rehana's lawyer as saying that Rehana, too, now accepted that Shah had been murdered.

Sassi, like the rest of us, may never learn the truth of how her father died. In July, 1988, we learned that Rehana had left France to join her family and Sassi in America. The French authorities, it turned out, had returned Rehana's passport to her for 'humanitarian reasons'. It seemed that Rehana had no difficulty, our lawyers told us, in obtaining a visa from the American consulate in Marseilles. Her trial, we are advised, will not take place before 1989, if it takes place at all. In any case, our lawyers doubt that Rehana will return to France to be present at the proceedings.

Another Bhutto dead for his political beliefs. Another activist silenced. We go on, of course. Grief will not drive us from the political field or from our pursuit of democracy.

We believe in God and leave justice to Him.

13

RETURN TO LAHORE
AND THE AUGUST 1986 MASSACRE

Martial Law was lifted on December 30, 1985. I was still in Europe and saw the news on a hotel wire service. But what should have been a moment of great relief was not. The ending of Martial Law was nothing more than a publicity stunt for the West. It was not a return to true civilian rule, for Zia still retained the offices of both Army Chief-of-Staff and President, making it impossible to say that the Army had disengaged itself from the political process. The role political parties could play in elections was left unresolved, underlining the regime's fear of returning Pakistan to a true democracy.

Zia's new 'civilian government' was in fact a charade. Shortly before the lifting of Martial Law, Zia's puppet Parliament had rubber-stamped the scandalous Eighth Amendment Act which indemnified members of the regime not only for their past actions under Martial Law, but also for any actions taken in the three remaining months of Martial Law. Thus guaranteed that no judicial review could take place to determine the fairness of their actions, the military courts had rushed to sentence hundreds of people to long terms in prison so that as many political dissidents as possible would be safely behind bars – and remain there – when Martial Law was lifted.

The end of Martial Law did nothing to erase its legacy. Since 1977, Zia had been systematically destroying the institutions my father's government had installed – an independent judiciary, a structured economy, a parliamentary form of government, a free press, religious freedom, the guarantee of civil rights to all under the 1973 Constitution. Because of the lack of any legal order and the sense of impermanence in everything, life in Pakistan had become a free-for-all.

Bribery and crime had become nationwide industries. Under Martial Law, the most sought after jobs among the brightest young people were in customs, because the pay-offs were highest. A new class of 'entrepreneurs' was – and is – smuggling in everything from air-conditioners to video equipment, paying their way through customs, and then selling the items on the black market. A recent report from the State Bank revealed that nearly one-sixth of Pakistan's economic growth was due to smuggling. The country receives no tax revenues from the black economy.

The Soviet move into Afghanistan had cast an even longer and more ominous shadow. US arms destined for the *mujahideen* ended up in new and flourishing Pakistani arms markets. Kalashnikovs from the Soviets found their way into the hands of Pakistani craftsmen who copied them and sold them for as little as forty dollars on the black market. It was said that one could even rent a Kalashnikov by the hour in Karachi. In parts of interior Sindh people no longer travelled after dark, because the roads were taken over by gangs of bandits armed with automatic weapons and rocket launchers. Large landowners and industrialists all over Pakistan began to maintain private armies to protect themselves, and sometimes to launch attacks on their competitors. At times the regime raised these armies too, providing arms, uniforms and salaries to 'soldiers' recruited for them by tribal lords. In return, these forces intimidated PPP supporters, at times razing entire villages. Not even the mosques where the villagers took refuge were spared.

Drug trafficking had also become a by-product of the invasion of Afghanistan. Where Pakistan had been drug free before the build-up of Afghan refugees, now more than a million Pakistanis were thought to be addicted, while millions if not billions of dollars worth of heroin and opium rumbled down the roads from the refugee camps in the north to be shipped out of Karachi in the south. By 1983, Pakistan had become the major supplier of heroin to the rest of the world. Huge gaudy mansions paid for with drug money sprang up in Karachi, Lahore and the tribal territories. Again the regime turned a blind eye or took its cut. Many of the shipments, it was said, were transported to Karachi in the army trucks which had gone to the Khyber pass filled with weapons for the *mujahideen*.

Relatives of high-ranking regime officials, including the son of a military cabinet minister, were intercepted and arrested for drug trafficking by Interpol in America and other Western countries. But, in Pakistan, not one major government figure was arrested. Though he denies it, it was widely rumoured that the kingpin of the drug trade was the Military Governor of the Frontier province, who retained his position for more than seven years while Zia removed and replaced the other Military Governors at will. Almost as notorious was the case of Abdullah Bhatti, one of the two drug bosses the regime did actually arrest in the eight years of Martial Law. After being sentenced by a military court, Bhatti 'escaped'. Several years later, when bad weather caused his plane to divert to Karachi, Bhatti was rearrested. General Zia used his powers of Presidential pardon to set him free, a power he had never used for any political prisoner.

Zia's policies of 'Islamisation' had also divided and demoralised the country. Where under my father there had been religious tolerance, under Zia's 'Islamisation' there was persecution of all our religious minorities. Most Pakistanis followed the Hanafi school of Sunni Islam, a moderate interpretation of our religious beliefs. Our country had been founded on the Islamic principles of unity, mutual support, and tolerance for our religious minorities: the Ahmadis who had their own religious leadership in England, the Hindus, the Christians, and a small but united population of Parsis, Zoroastrians who worshipped fire. 'You are free to go to your temples, you are free to go to your mosques or to any other places of worship in this state of Pakistan. You may belong to any religion or caste or creed – that has nothing to do with the business of the State,' the founder of our country Mohammed Ali Jinnah had declared on the day he was elected President of the Constituent Assembly of Pakistan in 1947.

Zia, however, was backing the Wahabbis, a sect close to the reformists in Saudi Arabia who formed the right-wing groups like the *Jamaat-e-Islami* and believed in a much harsher, less tolerant interpretation of Islam. From the moment of the coup in 1977, the regime had preached Islamisation while the fundamentalists had tried to impose their bigoted minority views on the rest of the country. Christians, Hindus and Parsis woke up to find mimeographed letters slipped under their doors: 'Get out. We don't need you here.' Very quietly, many minorities had sold their holdings and left the country which had been their home for generations. Those who had stayed behind had adopted a lower profile – the Parsi women who in my father's time often wore jeans, for example, adopting the *shalwar khameez* out of fear of drawing the wrath of fundamentalist *mullahs*.

Under Zia, the *mullahs* became the sword of Islamisation. They provided his repressive rule with the cover of Islam to make it palatable, and he in turn introduced an Islamic tax – two and a half per cent of all income – which he distributed through them. Far more of Zia's tax went into the *mullahs'* pockets than into the hands of the needy for whom it was supposedly collected.

The *fatwa*, or judgment as to what was right and what was wrong, proclaimed by the *mullahs* in their Friday sermons at the mosques, took on deep significance. One almost comical *fatwa* in 1984 concerned the actors in a television film who, in real life, were married to each other. In the film, the male actor repudiated his 'wife', saying 'I divorce you', three times. The resulting *fatwa* from the *mullahs* declared that the married couple was now not only divorced, but that the 'wife' was subject to *rajm*, the practice of stoning a woman to death for adultery. A mob actually attacked the house of the couple in the middle of the night. But the public had become so anaesthetised by the unchecked and unchallenged fundamentalist view of Islam that the incident went virtually unnoticed.

Zia had consistently used Islamic rhetoric to justify his repressive measures and terrorise certain segments of society. Two weeks after Khomeni's return to Iran in 1979, Zia's *Shariat* Courts had issued the infamous *Hudood*

Ordinances, which punished crimes such as stealing, adultery and rape using the strictest interpretation of *Shariah*, the law set down in the Holy Quran and the Hadith, or sayings of the Prophet (PBUH). Under the *Hudood* Ordinances, four Muslim men were now required as witnesses to prove a woman's charge of rape. Without such evidence, which was obviously almost impossible to come by, the woman bringing the charges could be charged with adultery. The case of Safia Bibi, a blind servant-girl who bore a child after she was raped by her employer and his son became a classic case of fundamentalist injustice. Because neither man confessed and Safia Bibi couldn't provide four eyewitnesses to the attack — rape rarely being conducted in public — the two men went free while the young woman was charged with adultery and sentenced to a public lashing and three years' imprisonment.

Safia Bibi was saved by a campaign mounted by outraged women who gave the incident international publicity. Embarrassed, the regime hurriedly acquitted the young woman. A thirteen-year-old girl who became pregnant after being raped by her uncle was not so fortunate. Unable to convince the court of the rape, she, too, was sentenced to three years imprisonment and ten lashes. The court suspended her sentence until her newly-born child reached the age of two.

The 1973 Constitution framed by my father specifically barred discrimination against women: '. . . there shall be no discrimination on the basis of sex alone,' read Article 25 (2). Zia's political policies of Islamisation not only sanctioned discrimination, but promoted it. At Karachi University, where the mosque had been converted into a weapons depot for the students' wing of the *Jamaat-e-Islami*, the fundamentalist students began to agitate for campuses segregated by sex. 'Women are not safe with men,' the male students insisted. To prove their point they began to harass the female students who chose not to cover themselves in *burqas*, dousing a few of them with acid which burned through their clothes. The acid-throwing students were not punished.

Women were singled out for exclusion in all aspects of society. At some official functions, the guests began to be divided by sex, even the highest ranking women being separated from their male colleagues. On television, female newscasters were required to cover their head with *dupattas*, and those that refused were dismissed. The athletes on Pakistan's crack women's hockey teams were required to keep their legs covered on the field, effectively eliminating them from taking part in international competitions. The regime's Islamic zeal occasionally reached absurd proportions. 'This photograph shows a woman's bare legs,' a regime censor dressed down a newspaper editor, pointing to a picture accompanying a story on the conclusion of a World Cup tennis tournament. 'That is not a woman. That is Bjorn Borg,' the editor pointed out to the censor.

Women had fought back as other regime ordinances systematically diminished their influence and stature. When the regime's *Shariat* courts proclaimed in February, 1983, that a woman's testimony would be worth only half that of a man's, a coalition of professional women demonstrated in Lahore. The police charged the crowd of university professors, businesswomen and lawyers with *lathi* sticks and tear gas, dragging seventy to eighty of them off to jail by their plaits. As if that weren't enough, the fundamentalist *mullahs* then declared that all the protesters' marriages were dissolved as aggressive women were outside the parameters of Islam. The women could ignore the *mullahs*, but not the regime. Despite the protests, Zia's parliament passed the Law of Evidence in 1984. It remains in effect to this day.

Pending is a law disqualifying women as witnesses in murder cases, as well as one reducing the compensation to be paid to the relatives of a female murder victim. Going on the supposition that a woman's worth is only half that of a man, the woman's family would receive half the compensation paid for the murder of a male.

For all the talk of Martial Law being lifted, Zia's Pakistan continued to be repressive and divisive. The poor were demoralised. Women were demoralised. Instead of settling their differences peacefully, or just living with their differences, rival groups all over Pakistan were resorting to kidnappings and gun battles. Violence was especially pronounced in the minority provinces of Sindh, Baluchistan and the Frontier where Zia's divide-and-rule approach had led to ethnic polarisation and increased talk of secession.

From the beginning, Zia's ban on political parties had gone hand-in-hand with his patronage of secessionist leaders. Giving the secessionists' statements full play in the press, Zia had used them to build mistrust between the minority provinces and the Punjab, perpetuating the myth that military rule was needed to keep the country together. The non-party elections held by the regime had furthered the country's fragmentation. By banning political parties, the regime forced candidates to campaign not on a platform of political ideals which transcended ethnic and regional boundaries, but on the basis of individual identification. 'Vote for me, I'm a Shiite like you,' candidates in these elections told their constituents. 'Vote for me, I'm a Punjabi.'

The country was paying the price. Ethnic riots between Pathans and *muhajirs*, emigrants from India, had erupted for the first time in Karachi in 1985. More than fifty people were killed and more than a hundred wounded in the fighting which broke out after a bus driven by a Pathan accidentally ran over a *muhajir* girl. Angry mobs were soon burning hundreds of cars, scooters and buses. Fighting spread so rapidly that in many neighbourhoods the regime had been forced to impose curfews lasting over a month, a move which eliminated the symptoms of the problem but did nothing to address its cause. Over the next three years, the injuries, the death toll, and the property destroyed in ethnic rioting would only intensify. New political parties based exclusively on ethnic affiliation would gain popularity and fan sectarian tensions higher. Pakistan's unity was on the verge of breaking down.

'I'm thinking of going home,' I told the PPP activists gathered in the Barbican flat in January, 1986, when I returned from France. They looked at me expectantly, not sure what I had in mind. 'I'll probably land in Lahore or Peshawar,' I continued. Their faces lit up. 'Home' didn't mean 70 Clifton. 'Home' meant the length and breadth of Pakistan. The PPP's challenge to Zia was about to begin.

'I'm going with you,' said Nahid and Safdar Abbasi. 'I'll go back too,' Bashir Riaz joined in. 'Don't make hasty decisions,' I warned them, knowing that Nahid and Bashir both had cases pending against them in Pakistan. But our small cadre of volunteers was resolved. We would return together.

The timing seemed right. With Zia's much vaunted lifting of Martial Law, we could force the regime's hand and put their claims of renewed freedom to the test. If Zia arrested me upon my return, the farce of his democracy would be blown wide open. If he didn't, I could freely carry the PPP message to the people of Pakistan for the first time in nine years. Psychologically, the timing seemed auspicious as well. Two dictators had recently fallen – Ferdinand Marcos in the Philippines and 'Papa Doc' Duvalier in Haiti. The time had come for a third.

It was a major decision. But was it the right one? After my years in detention and exile, I was unable to directly assess the political temperature in Pakistan. So I convened a meeting of the PPP Central Executive Committee in London. 'I think this is the moment to go back,' I said to them. 'But it is up to you. There is a good chance that something will happen to me or that I'll be arrested. What can the PPP do in that event? Is the time right for protests and pressure on Zia for full democracy, or should I delay my return? You all decide.'

'You must return now. We'll stand by you,' the leaders declared unanimously. 'If Zia takes an action against you, he will be taking an action against all of us.' I was very pleased as some of us sat around my small dining-room table at the Barbican, drawing up possible routes for my tours of Punjab, the Frontier and Sindh. As ever, our strategy was political, not violent: to work within the system to erode it and not give the regime any pretext to arrest us. By organising massive political demonstrations all over Pakistan, we hoped to force the regime to announce a date for early elections, possibly in the autumn of 1986.

I kept adding cities to the tour. Rather than planning simultaneous demonstrations in the major cities, I wanted the PPP to hold sequential demonstrations over a period of time in many different cities. That way the people's confidence could snowball, breaking the fear that Zia had inculcated in the country with his policy of hangings, lashings and whippings.

'Can you take so much?' the leaders asked. 'I can take it,' I told them over the dinner I'd cooked of chicken and *dhal*. We agreed that Lahore would be our point of entry into Pakistan. Lahore was the capital of the Punjab, the province from which the army hailed. It was also a bastion of PPP support.

After we had worked out the rest of the itinerary, the other PPP leaders returned to Pakistan to start organising everything, though the final date of my own return was kept a secret. By this time we'd learned not to give Zia a chance to make preparations. We got an unexpected bonus when this element of secrecy did our publicity work for us. All over Pakistan, people started a guessing game. 'She is coming on March 23, Pakistan Day,' one popular rumour ran. 'No, she is coming on April 4, the anniversary of her father's death,' others insisted. Even the press carried the latest speculations.

Threats on my life began. A PPP supporter in Pakistan forwarded a message from an army officer in Sindh. 'Tell her not to come,' the message said. 'They plan to kill her.' Other messages of the imminent threat to my life were coming in from Punjab, from the Frontier, from all over the country: 'A woman in politics is more vulnerable than you know. Don't come back.' My private telephone began ringing at odd hours, early in the morning and late at night. When I picked it up, there was no one there. A friend telephoned to tell me that a Pakistani Major carrying my picture had been intercepted at Heathrow Airport and turned back.

I didn't know whether the threats were real, or whether the regime was just trying to intimidate me into not returning. But there was one very ominous sign. Noor Mohammed, my father's old and trusted former valet, had been brutally murdered in Karachi in January. Before his death, I had received a letter from his young niece and ward, Shahnaz, telling me that Noor Mohammed was very anxious to speak to me and to please telephone him. The regime was after him, he'd told her, because he 'knew something'. I had called immediately from London, but it was too late. Not only Noor Mohammed but also Shahnaz, a young girl of eleven, was dead, brutally stabbed to death. Shortly thereafter, I received a letter from Noor Mohammed himself, posted before his death. Again, there was the urgent request for me to call him. What had Noor Mohammed not had the chance to tell me?

I flew to Washington, wanting to draw attention to our forthcoming test of the regime's will to democracy. The people of Pakistan had been waiting for nine years for elections and the reinstatement of a democratic government. Who knew what my return would trigger among them and what the response would be from the regime? Zia's Prime Minister Mohammed Khan Junejo had gone on record to assure me I would not be arrested. But who knew what Zia would do?

In Washington I had meetings with Senator Pell, Senator Kennedy and Congressman Stephen Solarz, the bright, energetic Representative who had monitored the recent elections in the Philippines which brought Corazón Aquino democratically into office and who had become a personal friend of mine. They were very supportive of my return to Pakistan. They, too, were pressing for free elections and the restoration of human rights to Pakistan and promised to monitor the situation there closely following my return. Mark Siegel, a political consultant whom I had met on my visit to Washington in 1984, was also very helpful, persuading elected officials and other influential people to write to Pakistani officials, warning them of grave consequences if I were mistreated. As an added precaution, Mark bought me a bullet-proof vest.

Members of the American press were intrigued by the similarities between my approaching battle with Zia and Corazón Aquino's challenge to Ferdinand Marcos in the Philippines. Their views of the similarities between Mrs Aquino and me were a bit romantic, however. Yes, we were both women from well-known land-owning families who had been educated in the US. Both of us had lost loved members of our families to dictators — Mrs Aquino her husband, and I, my father and brother. Mrs Aquino had fought Marcos with 'people power' to orchestrate a peaceful revolution just as I was hoping to do in Pakistan. But the similarities between us ended there.

In the Philippines, Corazón Aquino had enjoyed the support of both the military and the church in her move to oust the Marcos regime. I had neither in Pakistan. The Generals opposed me because I threatened the corrupt system by which they received discounts on land, free cars, and exemptions on customs duties. And while some of the religious establishment was with me, the fundamentalist *mullahs* supported Zia's dictatorship.

Most important of all, the Americans had served notice on Marcos in the Philippines, and even provided transport out of the country for him, his family and entourage. The Reagan administration, however, was solidly behind Zia. Pending before Congress was a six year 4.2 billion dollar military and economic aid package to Pakistan, strongly supported by the

Reagan White House. I could expect little real help from America, except for the good wishes and moral support of various members of the US government and the press.

'We'll go with you,' several correspondents said to me. 'The Foreign press are the best insurance.' I thanked them, trying not to remind myself that opposition leader Benigno Aquino had also been accompanied back to the Philippines by the press when he was shot to death at the airport before he even set foot on Philippino soil. Someone had slipped a note under my door at the Barbican which read: 'Remember Aquino.'

I didn't know whether I would live or die when I returned to Pakistan. Nor did I want to think about it much. Whatever fate God had in store for me would await me no matter what I did or where I went. But nonetheless I wanted to fulfil a commitment I had made to my father to perform the Umrah, a religious pilgrimage, in his name. Almost immediately after I returned from Washington I flew to Mecca, accompanied by some friends. Every Muslim who is able must make the journey to Mecca once in his life to perform the greater pilgrimage during the month of Haj. The Umrah, which takes only a few hours rather than four days, can be made at any time of year.

I had had the intention of going on Umrah on behalf of my father since 1978. Twice Zia's so-called Islamic regime had denied me permission to travel to Mecca. Not knowing what lay ahead for me now, this was my last opportunity.

In Mecca my friends and I changed into the white, seamless robes of the pilgrims and began the rituals. 'Allah, You are the Peace and from You all Peace proceeds. Oh Lord of ours, greet us with Peace,' we prayed together in Arabic at the Gate of Peace, the entrance to the vast white marble courtyard of the Holy Mosque. Seven times we circled the Kaaba, the black structure fifty feet high and thirty-five feet long which Muslims believe marks the site where Abraham built the first house of worship dedicated to a single God. 'Allahu akbar – God is great,' we recited each time we passed the Black Stone set in the Kaaba's southeastern corner. The Prophet, Peace Be Upon Him, had kissed the small stone when he helped to place it in the Kaaba in the 7th century.

I felt my burdens lighten as we performed the rituals of the Umrah. At each stop, I prayed for my father, for the other martyrs struck down by the regime, for my brother Shah Nawaz, for the men and women still in prison. I felt uplifted by the religious experience, and stayed an extra day to perform the Umrah a second time for myself. Spiritually cleansed I returned to the world of politics and flew on to the Soviet Union where I had been invited by a women's group. Going to Russia, I hoped, would deflect the critics in the PPP who continued to accuse me of being too pro-American. I needed my return to Pakistan to have as solid a backing as possible.

On March 25, we sent out the word: I would return to Pakistan on April 10. The international press flocked to London in anticipation. Though we thought our cause was politically right and just, the press saw it more as a dramatic and poignant confrontation between a young woman and a military dictator, a modern and feminist version of David and Goliath. '60 Minutes' filmed me for CBS in America. *Vanity Fair* commissioned Lord Snowdon to do my portrait for a magazine profile. I was on breakfast television in London and by satellite in New York. The BBC recorded interviews with me in English for their world service broadcast and in Urdu for their Urdu-language news, and I was interviewed by Associated Press, UPI, Channel Four and the British press in Auntie Behjat's flat. Petula Clarke lived in the same building, and for the first time, Auntie Behjat noted drily, another flat had more attention than Petula's.

Anticipation of the PPP's successful challenge to Zia in the international press was enormous. But I had no idea what to expect in Pakistan. The years of repression might have sapped many of the people's will to resist. In *Prisoner Without a Name, Cell Without a Number*, Jacobo Timerman had observed the stages oppressed populations go through: anger, fear, apathy. Would the people respond to the PPP's call or had they been bludgeoned into a silence necessary for survival? A whole generation of Pakistanis had grown up under the shadow of Martial Law. A child of ten in July, 1977, had grown into a young adult of nineteen, unaware of his or her elementary rights. Would they want to recapture what they had never had?

We had put ourselves on the line by announcing our intention to return. The whole world would be watching. 'How many people do you think will meet us in Lahore?' I asked Jehangir Badir, President of the Punjab PPP, who was flying back just ahead of us.

'500,000,' he said.

'That's much too high a number,' I cautioned Jehangir.

'But there will be at least 500,000,' he protested. 'You haven't even left London and we have reports that people are already streaming into Lahore.'

'But we can't be sure,' I told him. 'If the press asks you, say that we expect 100,000, not 500,000. That way if the crowd is estimated at 470,000, no one can say it was smaller than expected.'

There was no flight from Europe to Lahore, so on April 9 I flew with Bashir Riaz, Nahid, Safdar, my schoolfriend Humaira and many others from London to Dhahran in Saudi Arabia to connect with a PIA flight to Lahore. The PIA crew was very co-operative and allowed the party supporters on the flight to festoon the aeroplane with PPP banners, flags and stickers that had been forbidden for nine years. I can't imagine what the other passengers felt. There were around thirty members of the PPP on the plane along with members of the press and the flight seemed more like a special charter.

The mood of celebration among us was infectious, though always tinged with the spectre of danger. During our stopover in Dhahran, the Saudi authorities took me to a special rest house and isolated the others in a waiting room alone. Later I found out that the Pakistani Ambassador had flown in to Dhahran at the same time and the Saudis were concerned with our security. The threats from Pakistan escalated as well. Nahid, Bashir and one other in our party received word in Dhahran that they were on the regime's list for immediate arrest. There were more entreaties for me not to return as well.

I tried to put the danger out of my mind and worked on my speech as we flew on through the dawn towards Lahore. The regime was reportedly stopping busloads of PPP supporters from crossing the borders of Baluchistan, Sindh and the Frontier. None of us had any idea what would greet us when we reached Pakistan.

Lahore, April 9. Amina Piracha:

The sight of Lahore the night before Benazir's arrival was like that of a giant carnival or festival. Mrs Niazi, my husband Salim and I came to Lahore from Islamabad to receive her and none of us had ever seen anything like it. Camps were set up all over the city with food and drink. There were food stalls as well along the road to the airport. The whole city was in the hands of the people. Students in Suzuki vans were moving through the streets, singing songs about the Bhuttos, one lovely one in Punjabi: 'Aaj te ho gai Bhutto, Bhutto – Today, today it's only Bhutto, Bhutto.' People kept arriving in cars, in buses, in bullock carts, in trucks, by foot. I saw a whole caravan of buses jammed with people, waving banners: 'This bus is from Badin, this bus is from Sanghar.' After all the long years of repression and ugliness and depression, there was excitement for the first time.

No one slept the whole night. We walked around the city and back and forth to the airport along with everyone else. One old man walked with us for a way, tears in his eyes. Another old lady joined us, crying bitterly at times, then smiling. No one had been able to grieve for Mr Bhutto. There had been no formal mourning period. Now people were finally able to express their grief as well as their joy over Benazir's return. Lahore that night was one of the most beautiful experiences of my life.

Dr Ashraf Abbasi:

It was like an *Eid*. Free meat and rice and fruit were being distributed to the people. People were singing and dancing everywhere and the air was filled with the sound of drums and clapping. Cassette players were blasting out songs about Mr Bhutto, about the PPP, about Benazir. The words were very catchy and were set to famous songs so everyone picked them up just like that. PPP flags suddenly fluttered from every balcony and lamp-post. People had gathered green, red and black fabric and had been making them secretly in preparation for Benazir's return. Even our fundamentalist opponents in the Jamaat-e-Islami were selling banners and pictures of Benazir in the street, taking advantage of our support to make money for themselves.

Mrs Niazi:

I so wished my husband and my daughter Yasmin could have seen Lahore, but the regime still had serious charges outstanding against them in Islamabad, and they couldn't return from London. Really, the celebration was a vindication of the suffering of the people. I kept being reminded of the lady who during the horrible period of persecution had told me that the Pakistan People's Party was finished, that Mr Bhutto's name would never be uttered in public again. No, I'd told her. The PPP will never be finished because the people are the party. The day will come when you will see Mr Bhutto's name printed freely. Now that day had come and everyone's emotions were pouring out.

Samiya:

The authorities were still putting huge iron bars and barbed wire barricades at the airport to keep the crowds back during Benazir's arrival. Even the airport's entry and departure routes had been restructured. At 4.00 am we all gathered at a rendezvous point. The administration was allowing only two hundred into the airport and we were given passes. They took us into the airport by a back way. I had a lump in my throat. We were all so happy we didn't know what was happening to us.

Dr Abbasi:

But our happiness mingled with fear. We were so afraid for Benazir's security that we all arranged to throng around her and form a human shield. There were so many people, so many, many people gathering in Lahore. Who knew who was among them?

*

The pilot's voice crackled over the public address system in the plane just before 7.00 am. 'We are beginning our descent into Lahore,' the pilot said. 'We welcome Miss Benazir Bhutto back to Pakistan.' A flight attendant came to my seat. 'The pilot has just received word from the ground that there are one million people waiting at the airport,' she said.

One million people. I looked out of the window, but could see nothing but the vibrant green fields of Punjab. 'Come up to the cockpit and see for yourself,' the flight attendant said. I peered out of the front of the plane, but could see nothing in the distance but the approaching runway. There were tiny stick figures all around the runway and on the tops of the airport buildings.

As we landed, I saw that they were security forces. The precautions were in fact so tight at the airport that all other flights were prevented from landing.

'Nahid, Bashir, Dara. Stay close to me,' I told those who had been warned that they would be arrested. It was ironic: my supporters crowded around me for my protection, and I kept them close to me for their protection. 'We're your security,' the members of the press said. But it was the crush of people outside the airport who turned out to be our security. The immigration authorities were so anxious to get us away from the airport that they conducted their formalities on the plane, quickly stamping all our passports.

Home. I was home. As I stepped onto Pakistani soil, I paused to feel the earth under my feet, to breathe the air of which I was a part. I had flown into Lahore many times. I had spent many happy times here. But it was also the city where my father had been condemned to death. Now I was coming back to challenge his murderer, the General who had committed high treason by overthrowing the Constitution.

Samiya! Amina! Dr Abbasi! 'I don't know how we're going to get out of here, there are so many people,' Samiya said in the terminal, adding to the garlands of roses around my neck. 'We're going by truck,' Jahangir said, leading me to a typically brightly-painted truck, its hand-wrought tin designs gleaming.

I gripped the notes for my speech as I looked at the rickety stair leading to the platform which had been built on the top of the truck for me to ride on. I sometimes had nightmares of a stairway I didn't want to climb, but had to. Suddenly that very stair was in front of me and hundreds of expectant eyes were waiting to watch me climb it. What could I do? We had agreed in London on this mode of transport to take me to the Minar-i-Pakistan, the monument my father had built in Lahore to commemorate the declaration which would lead to Pakistan's birth. I couldn't change the plan now. There were a million people waiting outside the gates. I put my foot on the first step and took a deep breath. *'Bismallah,'* I said to myself. 'In the name of God, I begin.'

There are moments in life which are not possible to describe. My return to Lahore was one of them. The sea of humanity lining the roads, jammed on balconies and roofs, wedged in trees and on lamp-posts, walking alongside the truck and stretching back across the fields, was more like an ocean. The eight mile drive from the airport to the Minar-i-Pakistan in Iqbal Park usually takes fifteen minutes. On the unbelievable day of April 10, 1986, it took us ten hours. The figure of one million people at the airport grew to two million then three million by the time we reached the Minar-i-Pakistan.

Hundreds of coloured balloons soared into the sky as the airport gates opened. Rose petals, not tear gas, filled the air, showering onto the truck until they rose above my ankles. Garlands of flowers flew through the air. I saw a girl whose brother had been hanged and threw a garland to her. More garlands were thrown onto the truck, as were hundreds of hand-made *dupattas* and shawls. I put one *dupatta* after another on my head and slung others on my shoulder. When we passed former political prisoners I recognised in the throng, I threw flowers and the embroidered cloths to them as well as to the families of those who had been hanged or tortured, and the young and very old women who lined the route.

The black, green and red colours of the PPP seemed the only colours in Lahore that day. PPP banners and flags billowed in the dry, hot breeze until they formed an almost continuous canopy. People were wearing red, green and black jackets, *dupattas, shalwar khameez,* hats. Donkeys and water buffalo had PPP ribbons braided into their manes and tails. The same colours rimmed photographs and posters of my father, my mother, my brothers and me.

'*Jeevay, jeevay,* Bhutto *Jeevay!* Live, Live-Bhutto Live!' the crowds roared in Punjabi, a sentiment that just three months before would have cost them rigorous imprisonment and lashes. '*Munjhe bhen, thunje bhen,* Benazir – My sister, your sister Benazir,' others called out in Sindhi. There were slogans in Urdu, in Pashtu, in every dialect of every region in Pakistan. '*Benazir, ay gi, inqilab ly gi* – Benazir will come, revolution will come,' our supporters had said before my return. Now they called out loudly: '*Benazir ay hai, inqilab ly hai* – Benazir has come, revolution has come.' When I waved, the crowds waved. When I clapped my hands over my head as my father had done, the crowds clapped back, their upraised arms undulating like ripples on a vast field of wheat.

There were times when I was in detention in Islamabad in that almost empty house that I would wake up in the morning, hearing the roar of a crowd. I would fight the mist in my mind, trying to identify the crowd.

Who were they shouting for? And what tone were they shouting in? Were they shouting in anger against Zia? Or were they shouting in joy at seeing the doors of Rawalpindi Jail swing open and my father step out? That was not to be. But I continued to hear the roar while I was in Sukkur Jail, in Karachi Central Prison, in detention at Al-Murtaza and 70 Clifton. I would search my mind to identify the sound, but it always eluded me. As I moved through the tunnel of sound in the streets of Lahore on April 10, I suddenly realised that this was the roar I had heard all those times before.

I stood on the top of the truck for all ten hours as we inched our way towards the Minar, past the Prime Minister's quarters at the Governor's house where our family occasionally stayed but where after my father's assassination General Zia reportedly wandered sleepless through the corridors with a lamp like Lady Macbeth. We went past the canopy where the statue of Queen Victoria once stood – the only representation left of her in Pakistan since fundamentalist strictures forbid figurative representations in art. Then past the Zamzama, Kim's gun immortalised by Rudyard Kipling. I felt lighter and lighter, sure that the martyrs who'd given their lives for democracy were walking happily together through the crowd. There was such an atmosphere of victory, of triumph, of vindication over our trials and suffering. 'Zia ul-Haq, we have not accepted you,' the crowds were crying out. 'We don't want your hand-picked assemblies. We don't want your bogus constitution. We don't want your dictatorship. Our spirit is greater than all your tear gas, lashing racks and bullets. We want elections.'

Though I was totally exposed on the truck, I felt no danger. Only someone who was willing to be torn apart by the crowd could harm me. There was no threat either from the police or the army. Overwhelmed by the crowds, some of our former enemies stayed behind the locked gates of their barracks, while many others came out to join in the celebration. My greatest concern was my voice, which was hoarse from a recent bout of 'flu. Along the route I kept flushing my throat with Disprin and warm water and drinking a glucose solution which my father's valet Urs had brought with him from Karachi.

The sun was beginning to set at the Minar-i-Pakistan by the time we arrived. There was not an inch of free space on the grounds for the hundreds of thousands who had come with us along the route. We barely made it to the stage ourselves. I had no security guards, as I did later, to move me through the crowds. We also had not yet devised the strategy of driving right up to the stage on the truck so that I only needed to step onto the platform. At the Minar, I dismounted with only four or five friends around me, struggling against the surge of the crowd.

The crowd meant no harm, but the excitement of the moment was nearing frenzy. The people surged towards me, pushing and shoving, trying to break into the circle around me. I thought we were going to die right there, either suffocated or trampled to death. Many seemed to have lost their senses, including a local party leader who was hurling himself against my battered cordon of friends. I had to give him a hard push to snap him out of it. Somehow we made it to the stage where the President of the Punjab PPP had collapsed in exhaustion. 'Perhaps we should discuss security,' I said, side-stepping him.

What a scene greeted me as I looked out over the grounds of Iqbal Park. Across the way, the red sandstone of the Badshahi Mosque, one of the largest mosques in the world, glowed as if on fire in the last rays of the sun. Looming out of the shadows to the right was the Lahore Fort, the Mogul fortress in whose dungeons our supporters had been tortured and had died. And everywhere, on all sides, were people welcoming me home. 'Some people advised me to leave politics,' I called out in Urdu. 'They warned that I could meet the fate of my father and brother. Some said the Pakistani political arena was not for women. My answer to all of them was that my party workers will protect me from danger. I have willingly taken the path of thorns and stepped into the valley of death.'

The loudspeaker system wasn't working well and certainly couldn't reach ten times the number of people we'd anticipated. But as if by tele-pathy the people fell quiet with one motion of my hand. 'Here and now, I vow I will make every sacrifice to secure people's rights,' I called out. 'Do you want freedom? Do you want democracy? Do you want revolution?' 'Yes,' the roar came back every time, three million voices shouting as one. 'I have returned because I want to serve the people, not to seek revenge,' I told them. 'I put an end to revenge. I don't have any such feelings in my heart. I want to build up Pakistan. But first I must take a referendum from you. Do you want Zia to stay?' 'No,' the sound wave roared. 'Do you want Zia to go?' 'Yes,' the roar mounted. 'Then the decision is Zia *jahve!*' I called out. 'Zia must go.' *'Jahve! Jahve! Jahve!'* millions of voices cried into the darkening sky.

There was not a single incident of violence during the entire day. Nor was there anything but a peaceful challenge to the regime. The crowd was so responsive that many felt the regime could have been brought down. With just a word, the crowd would have destroyed the Punjab Assembly, the Ministers' houses, the Lahore High Court where Zia's hand-picked bench had sentenced my father to death. But we didn't want to come to power through bloodshed. We wanted to bring about democracy through peaceful and legitimate elections. It was the regime that used violence to gain their ends, not us. And, that night, they struck again.

I was just sinking into the first sleep I'd had for forty-eight hours when someone knocked urgently on my bedroom door. For my own security, the local party officials had said I was staying at three different houses.

One of them, the house belonging to the family of Khalid Ahmed where earlier I had talked to the foreign press after returning from the Minar-i-Pakistan, had just been ransacked by an Army Major. What an ominous reminder that I was back in Zia's Pakistan. The Major had been looking for me.

Azra Khalid:

I was sleeping when one of the servants woke me. He was bleeding after being attacked in the servants' quarters by a contingent of army men. Fifteen or sixteen men had climbed over the compound walls, beaten the servants, and were coming to the house asking for Benazir, he told me. Our front door was locked, but the men broke down the door and threw flower pots through the front windows. 'Where is Benazir?' asked their leader, one Major Qayyum, who was waving a pistol. One of the servants who'd been sleeping outside crept up behind Major Qayyum and hit him on the head with his son's cricket bat. 'I'm an Intelligence officer, a Commando,' the Major cried out.

I called the police, although since Zia you never knew if they were your friends or your enemies. As the police car drew up, the other Army men ran. The police arrested Mayor Qayyum. In his car was a crate of beer and whisky which he was going to plant in our house. And in his diary were the phone numbers of many top Generals and Ministers in the regime.

Major Qayyum pretended to be mad. The regime, too, said he was mad and had been working on his own. But we knew Major Qayyum wasn't crazy. Benazir's reception that day in Lahore had been so incredible the regime didn't dare touch her. Instead they sent Major Qayyum to either kill her or scare her off from continuing her tour. He was in jail for only a short time. When he returned to his village, he was shot dead for no apparent reason. We think the regime killed him to destroy the evidence.

Gujranwala. Faisalabad. Sargodha. Jhelum. Rawalpindi. 'The reception in Lahore was unique,' our critics and even some of the newspapers declared. 'Benazir Bhutto won't find such welcomes in other cities.' They were wrong. We set off from Lahore on our tour of the Punjab at midday on April 12, planning to reach Gujranwala for a 5.00 pm rally. But the roads were so massed with people surrounding the truck for miles that we didn't reach Gujranwala until 5.00 am the next morning. 'There won't be anybody at the public meeting,' I said. 'They'll all be at home in bed.' Instead the meeting ground was packed. The people had waited all night long.

'We must try to move faster,' I said to our volunteer security guards. But it was impossible. There were so many people on the road between Gujranwala and Faisalabad, that the eighty kilometre journey took sixteen hours. A convey of trucks, buses, rickshaws and motorcycles surrounded us, forcing the on-coming traffic onto the side of the road. Thousands walked by the truck through the entire night, like a giant guard of honour. I stayed on the top of the truck, waving to the people. 'Throw flowers all over and put pearls on the paths because Benazir has arrived,' the people sang. 'Oh God, bring those days back when the poor suffering people have happy days!' It was a very humbling experience for me and the other PPP officials. 'Give us the courage and the wisdom to fulfil the people's expectations,' we prayed together on the truck as we inched along.

The sun was rising over Faisalabad when we finally arrived on the outskirts of the industrial city. Once again we were half a day late for the public meeting at the sports field where I had nervously delivered my first speech nine years before. Again I was sure that the grounds would be empty. But, as the truck pulled through the gates, a roar went up from hundreds of thousands of throats. '*Qawm ke takdir?* Benazir, Benazir! — Who is the fate of the people? Benazir, Benazir!' The excitement didn't subside when we left the sports field. The factory workers hadn't forgotten the party which had given them dignity and job security. Though many of the factory owners in Faisalabad had closed their factory gates, even locking them so the workers couldn't get out to show their support for the PPP, the men jumped over the walls to join us.

Jhelum, where many in the army were recruited. Rawalpindi, a city of government servants. Even in these cities where the people were more predisposed either to ignore or play down the PPP challenge to Zia, the turnouts were tumultuous. The foreign journalists and television crews could not believe the size of the crowds that they were recording for their countrymen. My countrymen would see nothing. Though Martial Law had supposedly been lifted, the regime had forbidden my image to appear on Pakistani television. Neither this tour, nor any other public political appearance I've made since my return to Pakistan, has ever been broadcast on television.

Press conferences. Condolence calls. Party meetings. I don't know where the energy came from. The people's reaction to my return acted as a tonic, but there were moments when I was engulfed in sadness. I kept picturing Shah's body lying on the carpet in Cannes, and my father in his death cell. How I wished they could come back for just one moment to see this vindication of their suffering. As children we had been taught that no price was too high to pay for our country. But the personal price to our family had been high.

To ease my sadness, I asked that the route into Rawalpindi be altered so I wouldn't have to pass Rawalpindi Central Jail where my father died. But I could not avoid the tragedies and sacrifices of others. At Gujranwala I visited the grave of Pervez Yaqoub, the first to immolate himself in protest over my father's death sentence. In Rawalpindi I paid a condolence call on the family of one of the three young boys hanged in August, 1984. So many lives lost, so much tragedy. This boy, like the others, had been only sixteen when he was arrested and nineteen when he died. 'Look at all these crowds,' his mother said to me. 'There was a time when people were too frightened to speak to us.'

We moved on to Peshawar in the Frontier province, the President of the PPP in Punjab handing me over to the Frontier PPP President at the border. Again the road was completely blocked by people, and we arrived at night. The regime had blacked out all the street lights so no one could see my arrival, but the people shone torches and home video lights at the truck to illuminate me.

My security chief was very apprehensive as we moved slowly through the narrow streets of this ancient trading city an hour east of the Khyber Pass and Afghanistan. There were three million Afghan refugees in Pakistan who were being supported by Zia and many of them lived in or near Peshawar. We had heard rumours that the regime was going to get the Afghan *mujahideen* to kill me. Though I didn't know it, the chief of security had asked the women on the truck, including his own wife, to cluster tightly around me so I would be less of a target. Bathed in the only light in the dark streets, however, I was absolutely vulnerable. But there was no attack.

'I salute the brave Pakhtoons just as my father did,' I said to the continually clapping crowd in a stadium flooded with lights run by our own generators. I was at a disadvantage in Peshawar, as one of my helpers had lost the notes to my speech. But it was important to reintroduce myself to this very conservative society whose threat to break away from Pakistan and form the independent nation of Pakhtoonistan was very real. It was also necessary to convince the male-dominated Pathan society that a woman could lead them.

'People think I am weak because I am a woman,' I called out to the crowds, 99 per cent of whom were men. 'Do they not know that I am a Muslim woman, and that Muslim women have a heritage to be proud of? I have the patience of Bibi Khadija, the wife of the Prophet, Peace Be Upon Him. I have the perseverance of Bibi Zeinab, the sister of Imam Hussein. And I have the courage of Bibi Aisha, the Prophet's favourite wife, who rode her own camel into battle at the head of the Muslims. I am the daughter of martyr Zulfikar Ali Bhutto, the sister of martyr Shah Nawaz Khan Bhutto and I am your sister as well. I challenge my opponents to come and meet me on the field of democratic elections.' The clapping turned into a cheer. 'Zia *za!*' I cried out, using the Pashtu word for 'go'. '*Za! Za!*' the people roared in response.

After addressing the Peshawar Bar Association the next day, we returned to Punjab to move on through Lahore, Okara, Pakpattan, Vehari and Multan where I paid tribute to the hundreds of workers massacred in the textile mills eight years before. Then home to Sindh and Karachi, where the residents of my own city did their best to outdo the crowds in Lahore, before moving on to Quetta in Baluchistan, and back into Sindh to tour Thatta, Badin, Hyderabad and finally Larkana during the fast of Ramazan. 'Maravee malir jee, Benazir, Benazir!' the crowds roared, calling me by the name of a Sindhi folk heroine who had refused to yield to the demands of a local tyrant. Though he locked her up in a fortress and kept her prisoner, the legend ran, he had never been able to break her spirit or her love for her people.

It was so hot in Larkana that I put ice cubes on my head and shoulders under my *dupatta* during the trip from the airport to the sports stadium where ten months before the men had massed in the final prayer ceremony for my brother Shah. The crowds were so thick we had to change our route to get to the stadium before sundown. I stood the whole time in the scalding heat, first through the sun-roof of my Pajero jeep and then on a truck, intermittently sucking on lemons and salt. The PPP President of Larkana succumbed to the heat. 'Don't let me faint,' I kept praying, knowing that all our foes would love me to collapse. And I managed to get through the public meeting.

Rumours of death threats and meeting disruptions preceded me everywhere on the nineteen-city tour, becoming particularly pressing in Baluchistan where my security guards spotted three Afghan *mujahideen* squatting on their haunches in the front of the crowd with automatic weapons concealed under them. It wasn't the weapons that were alarming. Most men in Baluchistan openly carried guns. It was the fact that these weapons were concealed. The guards told me nothing about the suspicious Afghanis and instead positioned themselves right in front of them during my speech so that they would take the bullets and not me.

I was concerned enough about getting dizzy on the revolving stage built for the occasion so that everyone in the enormous crowd would be able to see me. But, as I looked out over the masses of people, many of whom were poor and noticeably thin, I forgot my apprehension. Baluchistan was and is a poverty-stricken and quite backward province; the tribal chieftains resist any progress that would loosen their control over the people. Until my father's time, there were dirt tracks but no made-up roads in Baluchistan, no electricity, little fresh water, and limited crops from the unirrigated, unforgiving soil of the desert. For generations, the people had been exposed to nothing but hardship.

I had been in Baluchistan once with my mother when she had been surrounded by women and children whilst seeking shade under a tree. Her security guards tried to chase them away, but she told them to stop and let the women come to her. In wonder they began to touch my mother's hair which was smooth and clean while theirs was gnarled and dirty. They didn't know what combs were. My father's government had done much to improve the lot of the people in Baluchistan, in spite of the tribal heads who had launched an insurgency against the PPP government.

'The Pakistan People's Party believes that the well-being of the nation is in the well-being of the people,' I called out from the slowly revolving stage. 'If the man in the street has the security of work, if he has access to good health care and his children can get education and prosper, then the country will prosper. It is not the law of God that our people should live in poverty. The destiny of our nation is not slums. If we have the power to transform it through efficient use of our country's resources, then we must.' The people in the audience rose and started clapping, including the three Afghanis in the front row. My security guards heaved sighs of relief. The danger was over.

But it was not. In the rest of the country, it was just beginning. On May 30, less than two weeks after I returned to Karachi, the police entered a youth hostel in Hyderabad to ambush and kill Faqir Iqbal Hisbani, the PPP president of the Sindh Students' People's Federation and our chief of security for the whole province. His companion and fellow PPP member, Jahangir Pathan, was permanently paralysed in the attack, the policemen's bullets shattering his spine.

I felt the blood run out of me when Dost Mohammed woke me in the early hours of the morning with the news of Iqbal Hisbani's murder. More black armbands, more black headbands, black *dupattas*, black flags. Another funeral for a young man whom I'd trusted literally with my life. Another condolence call to a mother who'd lost her only son. She gave me a prayer she had written out for her son to replace the one he'd lost in the mêlée of my procession into Hyderabad. 'You take it,' his mother said to me. 'This is a present to you from Iqbal.' I still carry the prayer with me in my handbag. How many more good people were to die at the hands of the regime?

Peaceful demonstrations were held all over Pakistan to protest at Iqbal Hisbani's murder. But the regime remained intent on violence. At one protest meeting in Kashmor, a member of Zia's Provincial Assembly fired a Kalashnikov into the crowd to break it up. Luckily no one was killed, but it signalled a new and dangerous directive from the regime. Control your areas with bullets. Control it with injury and death. But control it.

Within weeks, two more members of the PPP were dead: the President of the Dokri PPP and a party worker shot down in Tando, Mohammed Khan. Another member of Zia's Provincial Assembly was suspected in the first death and, in the second, a police inspector using an automatic weapon not issued to the police. 'A Minister in the Sindh Cabinet gave it to me to kill the PPP dogs,' the inspector was reported by local people to have said at a tea shop. The regime was now arming lesser politicians and other subordinates to do their dirty work for them.

We were on a collision course with the regime. We knew it. And they knew it. No policy decisions were being taken, all the regime's energies being focused on the actions of the PPP. When the government released its budget in June we countered with the People's Budget. When they thought we were going to launch a movement in Sindh after the end of Ramazan, they declared a State of Emergency in the province. When we didn't in fact do this, they deferred their State of Emergency. With the regime off-balance, it was time to launch the second phase of our campaign to force Zia to hold elections in the autumn.

July 5, 1986. The ninth anniversary of the coup. We called it 'Black Day' and planned public meetings in all the district headquarters of Pakistan, from the Khunjrab Pass into China to the Arabian Sea. No one knew if the political structure of the PPP was strong enough yet to coordinate such simultaneous demonstrations. 'Black Day' was almost a rehearsal to see if the local and regional party officials were organised enough to manage the massive civil protests we were planning for the autumn to force the regime to hold early elections. To ensure the effectiveness of the autumn demonstrations, we needed to recruit over 100,000 'Doves of Democracy', PPP sympathisers who would be willing to court arrest by staging hunger strikes and sit-ins. Every detail had to be worked out in advance. As July 5 drew near, I criss-crossed the country to help with the organisational details. And 'Black Day' went remarkably well. 150,000 PPP supporters turned out in Karachi, more than 200,000 in Lahore.

August 14, the anniversary of Pakistan's independence, was the next important date on the calendar. Stung by the outpourings of support for the PPP during my tour of Pakistan, Zia's hand-picked Prime Minister, Mohammed Khan Junejo, announced that the regime's official Muslim League party would hold a rally on August 14 at the Minar-i-Pakistan in Lahore. As soon as Junejo announced his intentions, we announced that the PPP, too, would hold a rally in Lahore on Independence Day, knowing our crowds would be much bigger. The regime moved to pre-empt our crowds by reserving all the buses in Punjab to transport their own supporters. 'Go in the regime's buses,' we advised the PPP members. 'When you get to Lahore, walk over to our side.'

The MRD, too, joined the fray. Since my return to Pakistan, PPP leaders and I had been holding talks with members of the Movement to Restore Democracy, the coalition of political parties formed shortly before the hijacking in 1981, and had informally agreed to join forces again to put pressure on the regime. On August 10, the nine leaders of the MRD came to 70 Clifton for the first time in three years to cement our agreement. One of the leaders came wearing the white cloth of the *Haj* around him. The regime had stopped him at the airport on his way to make the pilgrimage.

Zia, on the other hand, was out of the country and on the run. In the face of his threatened humiliation and repudiation at the Independence Day rallies, he had left for Saudi Arabia on August 7, taking his whole family with him. A PPP sympathiser at the airport confided to us that Zia had also shipped out three airline containers of furniture, and a gold-plated Rolls Royce given to him in his capacity as President by an Arab head of state.

Once more the timing was critical. At the end of our meeting, the leaders of the MRD and I agreed on a basis for organising joint protest meetings within the framework of the law and to press for elections. The next day the MRD announced that the PPP and other opposition groups would hold joint rallies in Karachi and Lahore on Independence Day, and called on Zia to announce the date for elections by September 20. This time, it was Junejo's nerves which cracked.

I was having a meeting with several journalists and party workers on August 12 when I was told that Junejo was about to make an unscheduled announcement on radio and television. We watched as Junejo, citing possible 'confrontation' between supporters of the Muslim League and the opposition parties, announced he was cancelling the Muslim League's public meeting on Independence Day. He appealed to the opposition parties to cancel our meetings too. No administrative order was issued banning public meetings.

I wasn't surprised at Junejo's attempt to save face though I was very angry at his attempt to goad us into violence. The regime had consistently tried to provoke violence at our public meetings and processions, while we remained equally determined to bring about change peacefully through political means. My volunteer security guards didn't even carry arms. But Zia's puppet Minister had to create some pretext for curtailing all political expression in Pakistan a full eight months after Martial Law had supposedly been lifted. He couldn't risk exposing the true face of the regime. Junejo had just returned from the United States where President Reagan had praised Pakistan for making 'great strides in the transition towards democracy'. Junejo himself had boasted to *Time* magazine that he had solved the problems in Pakistan by lifting Martial Law and imposing democracy. 'We did it,' he claimed. 'Now what is left for elections?'

'This is a big victory for us,' I said to the party workers assembled in my office while we watched Junejo call off his own political rally. 'Junejo claims to be the democratic Prime Minister, but where is his support? He's cancelled his own meeting because he knows he'll be shown up by the PPP. The regime is running from the field.'

'Now we don't have to hold the August 14 demonstrations at all,' one person said. 'We've won already.'

'No, we should go ahead,' another offered. 'Why not hold the public meetings on the 15th.'

'The 15th is India Independence Day.'

'Then the 16th.'

'I'm going to a meeting of the PPP in Faisalabad tomorrow,' I told them. 'We'll take a decision then.'

I went right from the informal meeting at 70 Clifton to an emergency meeting called by the MRD. The mood there was very different. The MRD leaders were very angry at me for even suggesting that I consult with other leaders of the PPP about rescheduling the demonstrations. 'You don't know anything about politics,' they said. 'We must go ahead with the demonstrations on Independence Day. This is the time. We cannot backtrack now.'

I protested. I knew the PPP was not prepared for a showdown. We'd just had the massive meetings on 'Black Day' and there wasn't time or the organisation to prepare the people so quickly for another one. More important, our strategy was not to antagonise the regime directly, but to increase the tempo of political demonstrations over a period of time to erode the regime. With the government paralysed by strikes and sit-ins, business would be affected, the economy would be affected, the entire life of the country would be affected, breeding a greater discontent against the regime. Having a confrontation with the regime now would be counter-productive. The party leaders would probably be arrested. Many party sympathisers could be arrested. And the momentum would be stalled.

'We must go ahead,' the MRD leaders said.

I was caught on the horns of a dilemma. Either the coalition between the MRD and the PPP would be severed or I had to acquiesce. The consensus was that we should participate in the demonstrations. I was the only dissenting vote out of nine.

'All right then, we'll go ahead,' I said reluctantly. 'But for God's sake, don't announce the plans tonight. At least wait until tomorrow.' I needed time, if only a few hours, to tell the party leaders to go underground. If we were all arrested, then the plans for the autumn would come to nothing. The MRD made the announcement anyway.

August 13, 1986.

I go to the airport to fly as planned to the meeting of the PPP in Faisalabad. The police meet me at the gate. 'We have orders externing you from Punjab but, if you want to go, you can,' they tell me. They are using a new tactic, I realise, trying to provoke me into going despite their orders so that later they can claim I created trouble while they tried to prevent it. I refuse to play their game. Instead I consult hastily at the airport with the PPP members who are with me. I fully expect to find the police waiting for me when I return to 70 Clifton and give my companions last minute instructions, directing each of them to coordinate party activists in different parts of the country in the event of my arrest.

When I return to 70 Clifton, there are no police. Another peculiarity. But Radio India mistakenly announces my arrest and the telephone calls start coming in. There are riots in Lyari protesting against my arrest. The people gathered at the airport in Faisalabad to greet me are being teargassed and beaten by the police. So much for the regime's 'great strides . . . towards democracy'.

I continue to wait for the police. Nobody comes. Meanwhile every other PPP and MRD leader is being arrested. For the first time, they are all in and I am out. The regime wants to paralyse the party without touching me, I decide, and thus escape the opprobrium of the world – especially the United States where the new aid package will be voted on in the autumn. For my part, I see the externment as an opportunity to delay the PPP showdown with the regime to a time of our own choosing.

The press swarm to 70 Clifton: Ross Munro from *Time* magazine, a BBC television cameraman, Anne Fadiman from *Life* who is an old friend from Radcliffe and is in Karachi with photographer Mary Ellen Mark to do a story on my return to Pakistan, Mahmood Sham and Hazoor Shah, veteran correspondents from *Jang* and *Dawn*. By late afternoon, almost one thousand PPP and MRD leaders and workers are in detention. But not me.

A reporter arrives from the Karachi Press Club. He has just heard from one of the opposition leaders that the MRD meeting is still scheduled for tomorrow in Karachi and I will be attending it. I am taken aback. No one has consulted me about a change of plan. But the news spreads. That night the BBC announces three times in one broadcast that I'm going to the MRD meeting in Karachi on the 14th. I don't want to be forced into a provocative position by the regime or the MRD. But what can I do? If I don't go now, the opposition can claim I've lost my nerve.

I pass a message to one or two people in the lower echelons of the party to round up everyone who has managed to elude the police and ask them to come to 70 Clifton in the morning so that we can all go to the meeting in a procession.

August 14, 1986, Pakistan Independence Day.

'Jiye, Bhutto! My sister, your sister, Benazir!' When I wake up in the morning, I can hear the political slogans beginning to rise outside the walls of 70 Clifton. There are thousands of PPP supporters massed in front of the house, alerted to my appearance at the MRD rally by other party members and the BBC broadcasts. A message comes in which explains why I still haven't been arrested. Unable to make a decision, the regime had telexed Zia in Saudi Arabia after the MRD announcement the night before, asking him what to do about me. His answer didn't come back until 9.00 am Pakistani time. 'Arrest her,' Zia telexed back. But by that time the police don't dare. 'All those PPP supporters outside 70 Clifton? They would have lynched me,' a policeman tells me later. The police are also hesitant to fire into the crowd and start any disturbance around 70 Clifton. The Clifton area is home, too, to many diplomats, and the police do not not want enraged crowds to take out their anger by burning the embassies.

The police are also confused about my whereabouts. My friend Putchie had spent the night at 70 Clifton. She had left in a car early in the morning and the intelligence agents can't work out whether it was me. There is conjecture that I've slipped away to Faisalabad in spite of the travel ban. They have no idea whether I am even in the house. They soon find out, however.

'What time are you going?' an MRD representative phones me to ask. 'We'll be leaving at 2.00,' I tell him. Shortly thereafter, I receive word that the police are coming to arrest me at 2.00 pm, though they have no grounds. The Home Secretary hasn't announced a ban on the rally.

We decide to leave at 1.00 and the journalists gather. At Harvard, I remember ruefully, I used to occasionally read the column in *Life* called '*Life* Goes to the Movies'. Now *Life* is going to a confrontation with the Pakistani police and my certain arrest. I am worried about Anne Fadiman. Ross Munro, *Time*'s bureau chief in New Delhi, is used to politics on the sub-continent. No one knows what will happen when we leave 70 Clifton.

'*Qul Huwwa Allahu Ahad* – Say He is One God,' I read from the Holy Quran in the doorway of the house. Anne Fadiman, Ross Munro, the BBC television cameraman, a few members of the PPP and my friend Putchie get in one Pajero jeep. I get in my own one, covered with political stickers, with its public address system, cassettes of PPP songs, and PPP flags mounted on the bonnet. Samiya travels with me, as do a few other political workers and photographer Mary Ellen Mark. As the gates swing open, I stand up on the back seat through the sun-roof. '*Marain gai, mar*

291

jain gai, Benazir, *ko lahain gai* – We'll beat them, we'll die, but we'll bring Benazir,' the crowd chants in Urdu, crushing around the Pajero. My guard of honour has swelled to five thousand.

Whoosh. The police fire the first round of tear gas as we near MidEast Hospital, the first of 3,000 tear gas shells that will be fired that day in Karachi, 300 of them on the road to Clifton alone. The next barrage comes at the roundabout where the police on their way to arrest me at home, are sandwiched in the crowd. The police try to beat their way through the crowd to get to the Pajero, firing tear gas. Someone in the Pajero pulls me down and closes the sun-roof as we cough and choke. We put salt and lemons on our tongues, and cover our faces with the wet towels we've brought with us. I worry about the PPP officials and the journalists in the other van.

Anne Fadiman:

You could hardly see out the windows the clouds of tear gas were so thick. We tried to close the sun-roof in our Pajero as it filled with gas, but the sun-roof got stuck half-way. When we finally did get it closed, all the more complicated by the crowds scrambling onto the Pajero and reaching their hands through the sun-roof just to touch anyone close to Benazir, the situation was much worse. We were locked in with the tear gas, which we found out the next day, was made in America by Smith and Wesson.

Ross had been tear-gassed before and knew what to do. We cupped water in our hands and soaked our eyes, and held wet handkerchiefs to each other's eyes, but it was really bad. Putchie who had asthma had luckily gotten out of the Pajero as soon as the tear gas had started and gone home. But the rest of us suffered from the tear gas for weeks. I had steroid shots when I got home to ease what the doctor called a 'deep inhalation dose'. I was lucky. Bashir Riaz, I heard later, was ill for several months.

In the chaos of people, police and tear gas, the drivers of the Pajeros decide to leave the roundabout by two different roads to confuse the police. We each take off down back roads to get to the MRD rally in Lyari, the poorest section of Karachi and the stronghold of the PPP. But every time the police spot our cavalcade, now a long line of buses, trucks and cars, they radio ahead and we run into a roadblock. We meet up with the other Pajero and decide to head for the tomb of Mohammed Ali Jinnah. We are blocked from getting there as well. We are playing a deadly game of hide-and-seek with the police. We head back towards Lyari when we suddenly get a flat tyre. There isn't time to get out the jack and a crowd quickly gathers to hold up the side of the Pajero while the tyre is replaced. We're off again as the police close in.

Ross Munro:

A crowd of as many as ten thousand was seething around the motorcade when it arrived at Chakiwara Chowk, an expansive public square in Lyari. Benazir scored at least a symbolic victory by reaching the site and speaking for a few minutes. 'You are all my brothers and sisters,' she shouted in Urdu through her public address system. 'Zia must go.' This Independence Day had a particular irony, she said, because Pakistanis did not have enough political independence to demonstrate freely. Smoke billowed from a burning bus only two hundreds yards away as she spoke.

Anne Fadiman:

I didn't see a single act of violence committed by the PPP. All the violence was coming from the police who were beating the crowds to disperse them. The young men held up their arms to ward off the blows from the *lathi* sticks. When they saw Benazir's Pajero, they struggled to press their bloody forearms to the windows, showing Benazir that they were willing to sacrifice themselves for her. I suddenly saw the BBC Karachi correspondent Iqbal Jaffery, running along the edge of the crowd. 'There is such violence,' he called out to me. 'I just saw a ten-year-old boy beaten to the ground by the police for wearing a PPP sticker.' The police moved in with more tear gas in Lyari when they saw Benazir.

Duck! Duck! I hear someone shout. Someone pulls me down in the Pajero just as a tear gas shell hurtles by my head. It is just like the attack against my mother and me at Qadaffi stadium. The police are using the tear gas shells as weapons, not to disperse the crowd. More and more police cars are arriving. 'We can't allow the party leader to be arrested in the street,' one of the PPP activists shouts. The cry goes up. 'Stop the police. Stop the police!'

Barricades are thrown up. Tyres and piles of litter are set on fire. We whizz off again down the back alleyways of Lyari, our eyes and throats burning from the tear gas. The people pelt the pursuing police cars with stones. 'This way! This way!' the people shout, saving us from going down dead-end streets. When we momentarily lose the police, we flag down a taxi. There are clouds of smoke from the tear gas and the bonfires. People are screaming. Police sirens are wailing. My Pajero takes off again, Samiya sitting in the front seat with my *dupatta* on to draw the police. Our taxi driver is so terrified he starts to take off with the door open. 'What's the hurry?' I ask him.

He drives very fast through the narrow streets, but he can't lose the lone police motorcycle following us. I consult quickly with the PPP leaders in the car. We need to have a press conference, but where? Various sites are suggested, but I finally insist on returning to 70 Clifton. Though I will be walking right into the hands of the police, I want to address the press in my own home and if I have to, be arrested from there. But the motorcycle is still behind us. We have to lose it. 'Turn right,' I suddenly tell the driver as we pass the lane leading to the Metropole Hotel. He screeches in, around the hotel, and out the other side. We've lost the motorcycle.

As we near Clifton, there are police blockades and police everywhere. The driver panics and jams the car into reverse. 'Just drive ahead normally. Keep to a steady speed,' I tell him. 'The police are not looking for a yellow Toyota.' The poor man is quivering as we drive through the police lines. I have Samiya's *dupatta* over my face and the police don't spot me. We stop briefly at the house of a party official to wash away the tear gas.

'What's the fare?' I ask the driver, getting out my wallet. 'I'm not a taxi driver. This is my own car,' he says, still trembling. 'You're not a taxi driver?' I say to him in disbelief, remembering how I'd ordered him around. 'No. I'm just a PPP supporter,' he says. He refuses to take any money and leaves.

The press are already at 70 Clifton when we arrive. In the middle of the press conference, I get a message that the police have arrived. 'Let them in,' I say. Three policewomen sheepishly enter the room under the eyes of the foreign press and give me a thirty-day detention order, charging me with unlawful assembly. After I collect my clothes and toothbrush, I am taken to the police station in a huge convoy of police vehicles, followed by equally large numbers of PPP vehicles.

At the police station I learn that six people have been killed at the Independence Day rally in Lahore and scores wounded. Once more the regime has sent its henchmen to do their deadly work. The dead and wounded have been shot by sitting members of Parliament, firing Kalashnikovs into the crowd. The MPs were never charged. Nor, I learn later from a *Dawn* reporter in Lahore, were the police who stormed the emergency ward at the hospital and beat the wounded as they lay on stretchers and handcuffed to beds. A *maulvi* who was washing the tear gas out of the eyes of supporters in a mosque was also not spared. The police stormed the mosque and beat him.

The toll is high in Sindh as well: sixteen dead and hundreds wounded. There have been police attacks against peaceful demonstrators not only in Lyari, but in rural cities all over the province. In the Frontier, too, Zia's forces have attacked the demonstrators. And all for attending, on our part, peaceful rallies on the anniversary of the birth of independent Pakistan.

I was placed in solitary confinement at Landhi Borstal Jail, a prison for juveniles on the outskirts of Karachi. The police had arrested so many political prisoners, there wasn't room for me in Karachi Central Jail. Protests at my detention spread through the country, prompting the worst unrest since the MRD movement of 1983. Police stations were burned in Sindh, as were government offices and railway stations. In Lyari, PPP supporters battled against the guns and tear gas of the police for a week. The army joined the police in this violent suppression of the protesters, leaving more than thirty dead. Mary Ellen Mark's films of the rioting were confiscated.

International disapproval of the regime's brutal crackdown on political expression quickly followed from England and Germany. In the United States, Senators Kennedy and Pell expressed their concern, as did Congressman Solarz who was working particularly hard on my behalf. 'If the government continues to detain opposition leaders and refuses to allow peaceful political meetings, then friends of Pakistan will be hard pressed in Congress to seek additional US aid . . . in the months ahead,' warned Solarz, the head of a House subcommittee on Asian–Pacific affairs. But the Reagan administration stood by Zia and his 'civilian' Prime Minister Junejo. 'He [Junejo] had the courage to face down the opposition and ride out the foreign criticism,' said a member of the State Department.

Zia was quick to lend his voice to salve any criticisms from the all important US Congress when he returned from Mecca in late August. 'Miss Bhutto is not the problem,' he told *New York Times* correspondent Steven Weisman on August 26. 'It is Miss Bhutto's unnecessary, impractical ambitions and her attitude towards acquiring power which is objectionable.'

My case was to come up in the Sindh High Court on September 10. I was being held without charge. The Independence Day rally had been legal. And I hadn't broken any laws. As thousands of people trekked from Interior Sindh towards the court house on September 9 for my scheduled appearance the next day, the regime caved in. 'I've got a surprise for you. You're free,' the jail superintendent said, coming to my cell at 9.30 pm. But I wasn't surprised. I was already packed and ready to go.

Emotions ran high in the session the PPP held after my release to decide what to do next. Some were keen to push ahead with the movement, wanting to avenge the blood shed by the regime. For the first time, they pointed out, the regime had killed PPP demonstrators in the Punjab. The momentum to topple Zia had never been higher. We couldn't break it now.

'We have promised peaceful change through political means,' I argued successfully, urging restraint. 'But the regime has resorted to force. Continuing the protests now means more bloodshed, chaos, perhaps a loss of control to extremists. Let us take August as a moral victory, and stick to our commitment to peace.' Shortly after the meeting I began another tour of the country, taking the new message of cautious advance to the people.

I felt confident as 1987 dawned. I always feel that a new year will be better than the last year, and there were many optimistic signs. I was free in Pakistan for the first time in six years. And after the long ban on political activities we were increasing the strength of the PPP as a political institution. Launching a membership drive, we enrolled a million members in four months, a remarkable figure for Pakistan where the literacy rates are so low. We held party elections in the Punjab – an unheard of pheno- menon in the sub-continent – in which over four hundred thousand mem- bers voted. We opened a dialogue with the opponents of the Muslim League in Parliament and continued to highlight the human rights vio- lations of the regime.

Zia consistently claimed we were out for revenge, particularly in his talks to the army where he used that theme to spread fear of a PPP return. But our party was speaking out not for vengeance, but for nation building. And everybody knew it.

I called for Pakistan's need of a professional army disassociated from politics. I continued to criticise Zia's handling of the Siachin Glacier inci- dents with India, where Pakistan had lost more than 1400 square miles of territory over the last three years. The crowds we drew seemed more and more receptive. On a December visit I'd made to Lala Moosa to condole with the family of a PPP activist murdered on Independence Day, members of the army in this heartland of military recruitment had openly made the PPP's victory sign and waved to us as we passed. Once more, I was cutting too close to General Zia's quick.

'We have information that the regime is planning an action against you,' a PPP supporter and former Brigadier in the army told me when I went to Larkana on my father's birthday. 'We want to have a practice drill at Al-Murtaza to test your security.' Thousands had come to participate in my father's birthday on January 5, a day that had gone very smoothly, and I did not feel any more threatened than usual. 'The security at Al- Murtaza is fine,' I assured the Brigadier. 'It should be checked,' he cau- tioned. I was not alarmed. 'There is no need, Brigadier,' I told him.

Another warning came in from Rawalpindi. Then another from Lahore. 'The regime practised a mock assassination,' a sympathetic member of the administration told me. 'The "assassin" came right up to you, then reported back that it was simple, that anybody could get close to you.' I tried not to be alarmed. Though death was always a possibility, I did my best to focus on political issues instead.

The warnings escalated along with pleas from party sympathisers to increase my security. One man in the Frontier province wanted to give me six men armed with Kalashnikovs, but I refused. I had never liked the concept or display of guns, and had ordered my own volunteer guards not to carry weapons. I shortly began to doubt my decision.

Within one week in January, 1987, there were two attacks on people close to me. In the first, one of my security guards was fired on after the car he was riding in was forced into a dead-end lane in Karachi. It was only because he was accompanied by men with arms who drove off the attackers that Munawwar Suharwardy escaped with his life. An MRD leader, Fazil Rahu, was not as fortunate. On January 11, he was axed to death in his home village. At the same time, Bashir Riaz, my press officer and former editor of *Amal* in London, started getting threatening phone calls in the middle of the night. Were all these warnings from the regime for me? 'Get in touch with the authorities,' I told my lawyer. 'Let them know that if anything happens it is their responsibility. We are giving them advance warning.'

The attack came on January 30. I was planning to return to Larkana for a visit but my departure was delayed by a last minute appointment. I normally drove to Larkana in the Pajero, but I also made plane reservations as a fall-back position in case something came up. It was good security as well to have several different travel plans. I often made plane reservations which I didn't keep, sometimes even double-booking to cities I wasn't going to to keep Zia's intelligence agents in the dark. Often I didn't even tell my own staff my travel plans so there would be no inadvertent slip.

'Bibi Sahiba, it is getting late,' one of the staff said to me around noon. 'If you want to get to Larkana before dark, the cars should leave.'

'You all go ahead,' I told Urs. 'I have a meeting and will come later.' The cars never made it to Larkana.

I was in the middle of the meeting when one of the staff came in with an urgent note. I saw only two words – 'shots' and 'Pajero'. Ironically, I had just been talking about the attacks on my security guard and the murder of the MRD leader. The timing seemed almost staged. 'Excuse me for a moment,' I said to my guests. 'There has just been an attack on my car.' Quickly I gave instructions to the staff to call the police and my lawyers and, pulling my nerves together, went back into the meeting.

The story got uglier over the next few days as the facts unfolded. The two vehicles were proceeding along the road near Manjhand in broad daylight when a man waiting at the side of the road suddenly gave a signal. Four other men immediately appeared and started firing at the passenger side of my Pajero. Urs accelerated quickly and the Pajero, which was already going at 70 mph, sped through the hail of bullets. When the staff looked back, the men were still firing at my Pajero and had stopped the second car. The security guards and staff in the second car were taken away at gunpoint.

A cold-blooded assassination attempt. Though the regime claimed it was just a normal highway robbery, it was not. Nothing fitted the pattern. The attack occurred a full forty miles from the area frequented by dacoits or highway robbers. Dacoits usually attacked at night, not at 3.30 in the afternoon. And their intent was to stop a car to rob the occupants, not to riddle it with bullets.

Disturbances broke out again in the country as the news of the assassination attempt spread. The public outrage was so great that the regime made a great show of sending its own Inspector General of police to recover the kidnapped members of my staff. Meanwhile, more and more information filtered in. A man had been seen at the assassination site with a two-way radio around the time the Pajero had left 70 Clifton. Someone must have radioed ahead to say the Pajero was on its way, assuming I was inside the jeep which has darkened windows.

I totally discounted the regime's claim that the dacoits had launched the attack on their own. Their mode of activity was to stop a group of cars, not just one, and the car just ahead of the Pajero had passed the site without incident. The dacoits also considered it dishonourable to attack a woman. No. This was not a simple robbery attempt.

More stories came in. The night before, a car had reportedly approached the dacoits' secret headquarters and spoken to the chief. 'Tomorrow we have a very big job to do,' the leader had told the others when the car left. Other stories circulated about the threats the regime had used on the dacoits to make them do their dirty work for them. Meanwhile, whoever was holding the PPP staff members was not even asking for ransom. It was not a normal kidnapping.

The men were released some days later as suddenly as they were taken. They were unharmed, thank God. But what they had to say strengthened our suspicions about the involvement of the regime. 'We are on the staff of Miss Benazir,' the men had told their abductors, who had already seen my distinctive jeep with its PPP stickers, flags and loudspeakers on the roof. 'We are General Zia's men,' their kidnappers had responded. No 'dacoits' were ever arrested in connection with the crime.

Another gauntlet of violence thrown down by the regime in an increasingly violent society. The regime had armed the *mujahideen*, the fundamentalist students, the secessionists and the Muslim League. To try and retain credibility for his stance of heading a 'civilian' government, Zia had created private armies to gun down the political opposition for him. Before the first month of 1987 was over, a PPP activist was lashed in jail, in spite of the lifting of Martial Law, and more political dissidents were shot. It grew increasingly difficult for me to restrain the younger members of the PPP from resorting to violence themselves.

The situation in Pakistan was rapidly becoming chaotic, the London-based magazine *South* reported in an editorial in February, 1987. 'The military has exhausted its stock of credibility . . .' the editorial read. 'Now the government appears to be losing even its administrative presence. The institution of government, the army, the police force, the judiciary and the executive agencies are there, but they are all spinning like tops, each in its own orbit. . . . The country is in the grip of tension and strife, factional, parochial and ethnic. Law and order has virtually broken down and it is the narcotic and arms mafia which control the life of the people.'

Pakistan was verging on anarchy. Who needed an outside enemy? Zia was destroying the country from within. The minutes ticked by towards the promised national elections in 1990. But fewer and fewer believed that free and impartial elections would ever be held.

The local bodies elections held in the autumn of 1987 were a sorry case in point. Forty per cent of the candidates opposing the regime-backed Muslim League and chosen in a secret selection at grass-roots level to avoid disqualification, had their nomination papers rejected anyway by government servants who feared forced retirement. Shortly before announcing the elections, Zia had passed a law giving the provincial governments the power to retire any government servant after ten years of service, the length of time since the coup.

The contest, if one can call it that, for the remaining 60 per cent of the seats was even more manipulated by the regime. Polling lists we knew to be false were not only never corrected, but changed from day to day right up to the day before elections. Voting districts were gerrymandered, with constituencies ranging in size from 600 to 2600 people depending on what would give a victory to the regime-backed Muslim League. The rules changed constantly. The deadline for withdrawing candidates from the elections was announced for November 19. On the night of November 19, the deadline was extended to November 25. This gave the administration six more days to force and coerce other candidates into withdrawing and to declare the seat an 'unopposed' win for the Muslim League.

The voting itself was even further manipulated. Polling stations had always been set up in public places in the most populous villages and towns. In these elections, the regime announced at the last minute that the election sites would be in sparsely populated areas and even in the homes of Muslim Leaguers where people feared to go. On election day itself the regime changed the locations of some polling stations without informing the opposition, making it impossible for our supporters to cast their votes. Many couldn't get to the stations anyway. Two days before the polls, the Election Commission requisitioned the jeeps, cars and other vehicles of PPP supporters to transport the election staff. The vehicles belonging to members of the Muslim League were left untouched.

In spite of the regime's blatant stacking of the vote, the Muslim League did not always get the desired result. In our constituency in Larkana, which also happened to be home to Junejo's relatives, the Muslim League was anxious to claim that the Bhuttos couldn't even win an election in their home constituency. When their attempts to intimidate and bribe our candidate into withdrawing failed, they cut 600 solid PPP votes from a housing project built for the poor by my father. Yet we still won the seat.

The first tier elections in which councillors were elected were followed by second tier elections in which the councillors voted for the chairmen of the districts and municipalities. The second tier elections, too, were manipulated. When we had a majority, the regime through their hand-picked election machinery, disqualified our councillors to give the 'major-ity' to the Muslim League. When their mathematics failed, they changed the result anyway, as in the case of the second tier Larkana district election where the PPP-backed candidate was elected Chairman. After the count the District Commissioner serving as the Election officer left the room, and when he returned he demanded a recount. Several votes were mysteri-ously found to be 'spoilt', and the Muslim Leaguer was declared the winner. When the PPP councillors berated the District Commissioner he apologised, saying he was helpless.

In Shahadkot Municipality, the regime used a different tactic. On the eve of the elections for the Municipal Chairmanship, two PPP councillors were kidnapped. Members of a paramilitary group known as the Magsi Force broke into the homes of the other councillors and threatened them. 'If any of you file nominations against the Muslim League candidate tomor-row, you will also be kidnapped and Benazir cannot recover you,' they were told. Intimidated, the councillors did not file their nominations, and the Muslim League was declared the winner.

The regime trumpeted the 1987 local elections as a huge success for them. When we charged them with election manipulation, they replied 'sour grapes'.

'Realities keep changing,' my father argued at the United Nations in 1971 when Dacca was on the brink of falling to the Indian army in East Pakistan. Nazi forces were once at the gates of Moscow, he pointed out, France under German occupation, China under the occupation of Japan, Ethiopia under the domination of Fascists. But instead of accepting these 'realities', the people of these countries fought back and changed the course of history. His speech before the Security Council had had a pro-found effect on me as an eighteen-year-old university student and kept me going through all the ensuing years of tyranny and persecution under General Zia. 'Realities change,' I kept hearing my father say.

Visions can be dreams. Or they can be predictions. Nobody who loves Pakistan can help dreaming of a great and prosperous future for our country and for the people. But drastic steps must be taken to preserve that vision. By the year 2000, Pakistan's population is expected to grow to 155 million from the present count of 100 million. Fully 44 per cent of the projected population will be below the age of fifteen. With the ill-conceived policies of the current regime, it will be impossible to provide even the minimum facilities of health, housing and transport.

By conservative estimates, the urban population of Pakistan will be three times what it is today. Even now, 85–90 per cent of Pakistanis have no access to clean, hygienic water. The same percentage lives without proper sanitation or drainage in over-crowded temporary shacks or hut-ments in slums. In some areas of Baluchistan and the Northwest Frontier Province, people still live in caves. Yet only 0.5 per cent of the regime's annual budget is devoted to housing.

Instead of educating the people, the regime is ignoring them. According to one of the internationally accepted standards of literacy, 90 per cent of Pakistanis are illiterate. By another standard, which counts any person who can write his or her own name as literate, 73 per cent remain classifed as illiterate. Yet only 45 per cent of children between the ages of five and ten are enrolled in schools and, among these, four out of five are forced by economic exigencies to drop out before reaching the age of ten. The statistics are not only shocking but crippling. Pakistan is currently adding 1.5 million illiterates to its population every year. Under General Zia, the literacy rate is falling rather than increasing.

Our national priorities are tragically skewed. Under Zia's regime, defence spending has more than doubled, resulting in Pakistan having a higher per capita expenditure on the military than any other country in South Asia. Our per capita expenditure on education, housing and health is among the lowest. According to the United Nation's Children Fund, about 600,000 of the four million children born every year in Pakistan during the 1980s are destined to die before the age of one, another 750,000 before reaching the age of five. Compared to an equal number of births in the West, about 700,000 more children die annually in Pakistan. Yet the people have little or no voice in their future.

Free and impartial elections. We are still working towards the day de-mocracy will return to Pakistan. My father had dedicated his life to it, in giving constitutional equality to rich and poor, men and women, all ethnic groups and religious minorities. Through education and economic develop-ment he had benefited the whole country, and brought the voice of democracy to a population which cried out for it. He had paid the ultimate price for his vision.

'Tyranny, like hell, is not easily conquered; yet we have this consolation with us, that the harder the conflict, the more glorious the triumph,' wrote Thomas Paine in *The American Crisis* in 1776. We have been through the hell of Martial Law in Pakistan and are prepared to face any oppression that might still await us. We have suffered and sacrificed, seen members of our own families die and paid condolences to the children and parents in otner families. We may have to again. But, through it all, we have kept the flame of democracy alive. No victory will be more glorious than the day the dictator is finally vanquished and the dream of democracy once more becomes a reality in Pakistan.

EPILOGUE
MARRIED FROM MY FATHER'S HOME

My personal life took a dramatic turn on July 29, 1987, when I agreed to an arranged marriage on the prompting of my family. An arranged marriage was the price in personal choice I had to pay for the political path my life had taken. My high profile in Pakistan precluded the possibility of my meeting a man in the normal course of events, getting to know him, and then getting married. Even the most discreet relationship would have fuelled the gossip and rumour that already circulated around my every move.

To many Easterners, an arranged marriage is the norm rather than the exception. But my own parents had married for love, and I had grown up believing the day would come when I would fall in love and marry a man of my own choosing. Still, inquiries about my marriage plans and availability had begun while I was at Radcliffe. I came from one of the oldest and most well-known families in Pakistan and was, by then, the daughter of the Prime Minister.

As an undergraduate in America during the flowering of the Women's Movement, I was convinced that marriage and a career were compatible, that one didn't preclude the other. I believed then, and still do, that a woman can aim for and attain all: a satisfying professional life, a satisfying marriage, and the satisfaction of children. I looked forward to marriage with a man who would pursue his goals just as I pursued mine.

The military coup d'état changed all that. Although the inquiries continued during the first few years of Martial Law, I refused even to consider marriage at that time. How could I reconcile myself to the joy and happiness of marriage when my father was in jail and his life was in danger?

Marriage became even more remote after his assassination. Traditionally, when a senior or highly respected member of the Bhutto family dies, no one in the family marries for a year. But I was so traumatised by my father's death and thought of him as such a special person that, when the subject of marriage was again broached by my mother in 1980, I said no. I wanted to wait for two years. Not only did I want to pay my own tribute to my father, I couldn't think of marriage with happiness when I was so filled with pain.

So many of my father's childhood stories to us had revolved around our future weddings. 'I don't want you to get married, but of course you will,' my father used to say to Sanam and me. 'I'll be waiting for the day you come back and, if there's one tear in your eye or one crack in your voice, I'll go to your husband and beat him up and bring you home to me.' He was teasing, of course, but the subject of marriage would remind me of my childhood and fill me with sadness. I hadn't reconciled my grief.

By the time the two years had passed, I was in prison. Marriage then was obviously out of the question. When I was released three years later in 1984 and went into exile in England, the marriage probes resumed, but again I said no to my mother. I was too nervous, too tense after the years of solitary confinement to feel comfortable with people, let alone a husband. Conversations, even with my family, often made my heart pound and left me with a feeling of breathlessness. The smallest noise made me jump. 'I have to find myself before I am ready to marry,' I told my mother. 'I have to find a relative calm. I need time to recover.'

Slowly but steadily over the next year in England, I began to mend. Meanwhile the inquiries about marriage never stopped: different members of the family had their own candidates for me, and my friends had suggestions as well. Soon before the family was to gather in Cannes in July, 1985, my mother and Auntie Manna approached me with a proposal from the land-owning Zardari family on behalf of their son, Asif. Auntie Manna, I learned later, had done careful research into the prospective groom before passing on the request to Mummy, asking the Zardaris to answer such questions as Asif's academic qualifications (Petaro Cadet College, the London Centre of Economic and Political Studies), his profession (real-estate, agriculture and the family construction business), his hobbies (swimming, squash and his own polo team, the Zardari Four) and even whether he liked books!

'Well, he can't compete with Benazir, but he does like reading,' said his father Hakim Ali, a former member of the National Assembly and now vice-president of the Awami National Party, a member of the MRD. Auntie Manna, an old friend of Asif's family, wanted a personal inspection of the prospective groom as well. Asif was brought to her house where he evidently passed muster, appearing slim and smart in his polo outfit. Satisfied on all counts, Auntie Manna then contacted my mother in England. But once more tragedy intervened.

Within a month, my brother Shah Nawaz was murdered. I was shattered, as were we all. I told my mother and my aunt that I didn't want even to think of marriage for at least a year if not two. I didn't even ask the name of the intended groom from the Zardari clan.

Auntie Manna was determined, however, to pursue her candidate. When I returned to Pakistan in April, 1986, she kept badgering me to consider the Zardari son, heir to the chiefdom of the 100,000-strong Zardari tribe. Originally from Iranian Baluchistan, the Zardari clan had resettled in the Nawabshah district of Sindh several centuries ago where Asif now oversaw his family's farms. 'He's very nice. He's your sort of age. He comes from a landowning family. His family is political. Families from the business class in Lahore and Peshawar have approached me, but I don't think that's suitable for you. It's better for you to marry someone from Sindh who understands local customs and traditions . . .' On and on she went, but I wasn't interested. For the first time for nine years, I was enjoying my own country, free to go out and see my friends, to travel, to work. 'Just let me enjoy my freedom for a while,' I kept telling her.

But Auntie Manna didn't give up. Without telling me, she arranged for my cousin Fakhri to invite Asif to a dinner party in November of 1986, seven months after I'd returned to Pakistan. She even made him wear a suit so he'd make a good impression on me, instead of wearing the wild Baloachi robes he much prefers, even on the streets of London. Auntie Manna evidently waited at the dinner until there were only a few people around me to introduce him. When I heard the name Asif, nothing clicked. I had no idea who he was and remember only that we immediately got into an argument. Auntie Manna was more concerned that he was sitting by me for too long and that it would lead to conjecture. She sent someone to take him away which was a great relief to me. After spending all day listening to arguments within the party, I hardly wanted to spend the evening arguing as well.

At the same time, I wondered what future husband would be able to tolerate a life as demanding as mine. When I was at home, my political meetings often ran well into the night. And I was very often away from home, constantly travelling the length and breadth of Pakistan. What husband would accept that my time was not my own, so it could not be his? Was there a man in existence who could break with tradition enough to adjust to the fact that my first commitment would always be to the people of Pakistan and not to him?

I was concerned, as well, about the feelings of the people were I to marry. Because I was young, had spent so many years in prison and had had so much tragedy in my life, I had been told by friends that the people thought of me as some sort of saint. The sacrifices my family had made for a democratic Pakistan, leaving me to live alone without the protection of a father, a mother, or even my brothers, had also led the people to think of themselves as my family. A basic strength of the PPP lay in that sense of protectiveness people had towards me. If I married, would they think I no longer needed them?

On the other hand, I argued with myself, remaining single could work against me politically both inside and outside Pakistan. In the male chauvinist society we live in, little thought is given to a man who remains a bachelor. But a single woman is suspect. 'Why aren't you married?' journalists often asked me. Irritated, I wanted to ask if they would put the same question to a single man, but I restrained myself. The journalists were not used to dealing with single women in traditional Muslim societies, and the unusual circumstances dictated the unusual question.

Inherent in the question, and representative of a whole school of male thought, was the bias that there must be something wrong with a woman who wasn't married. Who knew if she would make a reliable leader? What would she do under pressure? Instead of considering my qualifications and the party platform, the unspoken reservations were that a single woman might be too neurotic to lead the country, or too aggressive, or too timid. This was especially true in a Muslim society, where marriage was regarded as the fruition of a man and a woman's life and children as its natural consequence.

Asif Zardari. Asif Zardari. Asif Zardari. Two years after his family's initial inquiry, neither he nor his family had given up. In the past, my tactic with other proposals had been to draw out the process for so long that the other person either lost interest or thought we were not interested. But not the Zardaris. In February, 1987, I went to London to take part in a television discussion on Afghanistan. Asif's stepmother unexpectedly turned up in London at the same time to pay a call on her old school friend, my Auntie Behjat. 'Asif's so kind, so courteous, so generous,' Auntie Behjat reported their conversation to me. 'Persuade Benazir to meet him.' Auntie Manna joined in the family persuasion. 'He's seen you. You're a real person to him, not just an image. He really wants to marry you.'

My mother added pressure of her own. 'We know the family,' she told me. 'He's thirty-four, your age. He's from Sindh, so he knows our customs and courtesies. He's not a rootless phenomenon like the urban professional people who can pack their bags and go anywhere. He's a rural, with commitments to his family and tribe, so he'll understand your commitments, too.'

Her lobbying only made me more sceptical. She usually promoted insipid characters, claiming they made devoted and caring husbands, while those who were more dashing and debonair would always be chased by other women and my marriage would never be peaceful. I knew I would be bored to tears with the insipids.

Auntie Behjat begged me to join her and Asif's stepmother for tea. I declined. Even a meeting could be seen as some kind of commitment and, though I was reconciling myself to the concept of getting married, the reality of it filled me with panic. 'Give me until June,' I pleaded with my relatives. 'I'm not ready yet.'

'How do you marry a perfect stranger?' I asked a friend in Lahore when I returned to Pakistan. 'Once you're married, you look at the person with different eyes,' she said. I asked another friend the same question. 'Even if you've never met him, you start to love him because he's your husband,' she said. 'You know the saying: first comes marriage, then comes love.'

I did some investigating on my own. Someone told me Asif had taken a bad fall from his polo pony and would limp for the rest of his life. That turned out not to be true, but even so it wouldn't have bothered me. A limp was not a character flaw. I spoke with someone close to Asif who told me he was generous to a fault, always giving money to his friends when they were in financial trouble. I liked generosity. Another mutual friend used an Urdu saying to describe Asif's strong will and loyalty: 'He's a friend's friend, and an enemy's enemy,' he told me. The description reminded me of my brothers and was appealing.

For all that I was inhumanly busy, I was lonely at times. 70 Clifton is a big house, built to contain several generations of Bhuttos at a time. Al-Murtaza, too, is large. Yet, often at night, the only room with lights on was mine. I felt a degree of insecurity about the houses as well. Neither property belonged to me. Mir would undoubtedly remarry and return to Pakistan as soon as it was possible. What would my position be in the home of my brother and his new wife? I needed my own home, I decided.

I needed my own family as well. My sister was married and had a child. My brothers, too, had had children. We, who had been the nuclear family, had given way to other nuclear families. Where did that leave me in the swirl of all these new families? Death, too, was weighing on my mind. Before Shah's murder I felt we were a big family but, when there were just three of us, the family seemed small. With only one brother, the balance was upset. The idea of having my own children seemed more and more appealing to me.

I had promised my relatives that I would meet Asif in June in England, but a meeting with the Parliamentary Opposition Group in Islamabad delayed my trip. When I returned from Islamabad to Karachi, I found a handwritten request to call on me from Asif's stepmother. 'Fakhri, Fakhri, what do I do?' I phoned my cousin. 'Meet her,' she urged. 'If you like, I'll stay with you. Besides, you can ask her about all those doubts you keep expressing to us.'

'It would be such an honour if you would consider Asif,' the impeccably dressed Cambridge graduate said to me in the living room at 70 Clifton. 'Marriage would give you a new dimension.' I restrained myself from saying that a woman doesn't need marriage to give herself a new dimension and instead proceeded to tell Asif's stepmother every reason why marriage to me would not, in fact, be an honour for a man, but a nightmare.

'My life in politics is not an ordinary one,' I told her. 'I don't have the luxury of calmly waiting for elections every five years. My politics are a commitment to freedom and the meaning of my life. How would a man feel, knowing that his wife's life does not revolve around him?'

'My dear, Asif is a very confident young man. He understands what he's in for,' Asif's stepmother assured me. I rushed on.

'I have to travel a lot, and I can't always take a husband with me.'

'Asif has his own work, my dear, and won't always be able to travel with you,' she countered.

'I hear he loves going out to parties and socialising,' I said. 'In the little private time I have, I prefer to stay at home with a few friends.'

'That's not a problem,' she said simply. 'When a man settles down he likes to stay at home with his wife and family.'

Feeling encouraged, I took a deep breath and broached the most difficult subject of all. 'In spite of custom, I cannot live with my in-laws,' I said. 'There are political workers and meetings in the house day and night, which take up the living room and the dining room. I will need my own house.'

'I agree, and so does Asif,' she said unbelievably. 'Asif's mother and sisters will need privacy, too.'

Who is this extraordinary man, I thought. And I rescheduled my trip to meet him in London, far away from the intelligence vans and the watchful eyes of the Zia regime.

Thank God for the political appointments which occupied my mind in London during the day of July 22, 1987. Not until evening did my stomach start to churn with anxiety as I realised that there was no escape from meeting Asif.

Auntie Manna sipped her coffee nervously as Asif and his stepmother rang the doorbell of my cousin Tariq's flat. From the security of an armchair in the drawing room, I tried to look casual, but my heart pounded harder and harder as each step of Asif's brought him nearer. They must have been excruciating steps for him, too, though he looked confident in the one glance I gave him. Everyone present talked politely of impersonal matters. No one mentioned marriage at all.

Asif and I didn't have a conversation by ourselves during the entire evening. He was wearing glasses, and I couldn't even see the expression in his eyes. I didn't have a single feeling about him at all after the evening ended, even when he sent me a dozen roses the next day. The crate of mangoes he sent me from Fortnum and Mason, however, along with a box of marrons glacés, my favourite sweet, were delicious. So was the crate of cherries he sent to Sunny.

'What's the answer, Pinkie?' asked my mother, Auntie Behjat and Auntie Manna that morning, and the next and the next. 'I don't know yet,' I said.

I felt torn apart. I knew my friends in the West would find it difficult to understand the peculiar cultural and political circumstances that were leading me towards an arranged marriage. Feminism in the West was also very different from that in the East, where religious and family obligations remained central. And there was also the personal side of the question. In my position as the leader of the largest opposition party in Pakistan, I could not risk the scandal of breaking any engagement or ever getting divorced, except in the most extreme circumstances. I was being asked to make up my mind about living the rest of my life with a man who I had met only three days before, and at that always in the company of our respective families.

I introduced him to a few of my friends from Oxford. They liked him. I introduced him to a Pakistani school friend. She found him charming and told me to marry him. Asif took my family out to dinner and I had to sit next to him. I kept my niece Fathi, who talks non-stop, on my other side for protection.

The next day my cousin Tariq and Asif had a man-to-man talk. 'If you marry Benazir, you'll be in the spotlight,' Tariq told him. 'The tiniest thing you do, even staying out late with friends, will reflect on her.' Asif won Tariq over, too. 'He understands the situation,' my cousin assured me later. 'He has wanted to marry you for years. He knows exactly what it means.'

'What's the answer, Pinkie?' Yasmin pressed. Every morning Sunny and Mummy rushed to my bedside and stared at me meaningfully. 'What's the problem? What's taking you so long to decide?'

'I don't know yet.'

Fate presented itself in the form of a bee. On the fourth day of the Zardari visit, I took Fathi to Windsor Park while Asif went to a polo match. A bee stung me in the hand. By dinner time, my hand was very swollen. The next morning, it was even more swollen. 'I'm taking you to hospital,' Asif told me when he arrived at the flat. He ignored my protests, calling for a car, arranging for the doctor, buying the prescribed medicine. 'For once I am not the one in charge,' I thought. 'I am the one being cared for.' It was a very nice and unaccustomed feeling.

Fate intervened again the following night during our search for an elusive Pakistani restaurant. My mother, Sanam, Asif and I piled into a car with some other Pakistani friends to go to dinner. We got lost. But instead of getting irritable or impatient Asif kept everybody laughing in the car. He was flexible and had a sense of humour, I noted, as well as being caring.

'What's the answer, Pinkie?' my mother asked the next morning.

I took a deep breath. 'All right, Mummy,' I said. Seven days after I met Asif, we were engaged.

'Conscious of my religious obligations and duty to my family, I am pleased to proceed with the marriage proposal accepted by my mother, Begum Nusrat Bhutto,' read the statement I released to the press. 'The impending marriage will not in any way affect my political commitment. . . . The people of Pakistan deserve a better, more secure future and I shall be with them seeking it.'

The reaction in Pakistan was mixed. In spite of my statement, the regime's agents lost no time in spreading rumours that I was giving up politics. Organised gangs began stopping buses on the highways and pulling my posters off them, saying they meant nothing now that I was getting married. 'Why have you still got the PPP flag up?' party workers were taunted. 'Benazir has given up and left you.' The fears of PPP supporters were further fuelled by a false interview with Asif's mother carried in the controlled press. 'I'm going to invite General Zia to the wedding,' she was alleged to have said.

But many in the country were happy that I was going to live a more normal life. The sweet shops in the cities were sold out for three days as the public celebrated the event. 'For ten years we've been mourning. Finally we can rejoice,' people were saying. Just as pleased were the Zardari tribe, fifteen thousand of whom gathered to welcome Asif on his lands in Nawabshah, singing and dancing and waving PPP flags.

When I returned to Pakistan, I travelled around the country, reassuring the people that I was their sister and would always be their sister, and that my marriage would have no bearing on my political career. Asif called me every night, wherever I was, and little by little, I got to know him over the phone. We had more in common than I thought. His family had suffered under Martial Law: his father Hakim Ali had been disqualified from politics for seven years by a military court and his crops on the family's 1800 acre farm in Hyderabad ruined after the regime cut off the water. Worse trouble came after the engagement when Hakim Ali's loans for construction projects were suddenly stopped by the nationalised banks. 'You are making a mistake,' people had told Hakim Ali when our engagement was made public. 'Your only son is marrying Benazir and the whole army and bureaucracy will be against you.' 'I don't care,' Hakim Ali had replied. 'My son's happiness means more to me.'

Asif, I knew, was not interested in party politics. 'One politician in a family is enough,' he had quipped to the press in London. But like many in families with a feudal past, he followed local politics, and had filed nomination papers for the 1985 elections. He later boycotted them on the call of the MRD. And he, too, had felt the sting of Martial Law.

He had been arrested from his house in the middle of the night, the army claiming that they had found him travelling on the road with an unlicensed weapon. Luckily for Asif, their false story didn't even hold up in a military court. 'I only spent two nights in jail. That was enough,' Asif told a friend of mine. 'I can only imagine what Benazir must have endured.'

He gave me a heart-shaped ring of sapphires and diamonds. He sent me roses every day. We talked and talked. Our marriage really wasn't between strangers, he told me. When we were teenagers, he'd watched me enter and leave the cinema his father owned. Two decades later, it had been his idea to marry me, not his parents'. 'If you want me to marry, then propose for Benazir,' he'd told his father five years before. He had waited patiently ever since. 'Are you in love with her?' a journalist asked him. 'Isn't everyone?' he replied.

We didn't really love each other yet, though my mother assured me that love would come later. Instead there was a mental commitment between us, a realisation that we were accepting each other as husband and wife totally and for always. In a way, I realised, that bond was stronger than love. Though I certainly did not – and do not – want to be seen as an advocate of arranged marriages, I realised there was something to a relationship based on acceptance. We were coming into our marriage with no preconceptions, no expectations of each other other than good will and respect. In love marriages, I imagined, the expectations were so high they were bound to be somewhat dashed. There must also be the fear that the love might die, and with it the marriage. Our love could only grow.

The crowds began gathering outside 70 Clifton a week before the wedding in December of 1987. Presents began to be delivered to the gate: simple hand-made *shalwar khameez* from Sindh, embroidered *dupattas* from Punjab, sweets, fruit and wedding dolls made to look like Asif and me. At times my relatives went out and joined the people dancing with happiness. Women and children came in and sat in the garden.

It is traditional for a prospective bride to remain in seclusion for one or two weeks before the wedding, wearing yellow clothes and no make-up so as not to attract the evil eye. But I didn't have time for this ancient custom called *mayoon*. I couldn't afford to take two weeks off from work before the wedding. We weren't even going to have a honeymoon.

We broke with more traditions as well, trying to set an example for the rest of the country. The wedding was to be dignified and simple, not the week-long lavish affairs many families in Pakistan feel compelled to hold, often draining their life savings and sending them into debt. Instead of the twenty-one to fifty-one elaborate sets of clothes traditionally presented to the bride by the groom's family, I set the limit at two, one for the wedding and one for the reception the Zardaris would give two days after the wedding. The bride's wedding clothes are usually sequinned and embroidered throughout with gold thread, but I requested that my dress have gold either on the top or bottom, but not both.

Presents of jewellery, too, are part of our tradition – the bride often wears seven sets of jewellery running from a choker around her neck to necklaces reaching her waist. I asked Asif to give me only two simple sets, one for the wedding ceremony and the other for the reception given by the groom's family. I don't live a life that calls for jewellery. How many diamond necklaces can you wear to the office? 'You have your whole life to give me jewellery,' I consoled Asif, who wanted to give me the best. I even eschewed the traditional gold bangles that brides wear on each arm from elbow to wrist, planning to wear a few of pure gold and the rest of glass. I wanted people to say that if Benazir can wear glass bangles on her wedding day, so can my daughter. I also chose to keep my own name. I had been Benazir Bhutto for thirty-four years and had no intention of changing my identity.

On my beloved's forehead, his hair is shining. On my beloved's forehead, his hair is shining. Bring, bring the henna, the henna which will colour my beloved's hands. For the three days before the henna ceremony on December 17, my sister, my cousins and my friends gathered at 71 Clifton, the annexe we use for receptions and offices, to practise for the friendly song and dance competition with the groom's family at the *Mehndi*. Samiya, Salma, Putchie and Amina were there, as was Yasmin who had flown in from London. Every day more friends arrived from England: Connie Seifert, who had been highly instrumental in pressurising Zia into letting my mother leave Pakistan on medical grounds, David Soskind, Keith Gregory and others from my Oxford days, Victoria Schofield whose visa was withheld by the regime until the very last moment. Anne Fadiman and my former roommate, Yolanda Kodrzycki came all the way from America, Anne to do a story on the wedding this time for *Life*. 'You came here to get tear-gassed in 1986,' I laughed with Anne. 'It's good that you've come here now to laugh and dance.'

It was a miraculous reunion of sorts, relationships that had not only endured but grown stronger through all the tyranny of Martial Law. My father's lawyers came, as did many former political prisoners. There was a stir when Dr Niazi arrived at 70 Clifton. Even though my father's dentist still faced serious charges in Islamabad, he had returned for my wedding after six lonely years in exile. He was safe enough in Karachi, but no one knew what would face him when he returned to Islamabad to try and resume his dental practice. Through it all moved my mother, anxiously checking on the details like any mother of a bride. She had not been in Pakistan since 1982 and, not surprisingly, was having difficulty sleeping.

While friends and family were gathering inside 70 Clifton, thousands were pressing towards Lyari in the centre of Karachi. We were going to have two weddings, one at home in the presence of family and friends, the other among the people in the poorest section of Karachi and a stronghold of the PPP. We had sent 15,000 invitations to party supporters who had been imprisoned during the years of Martial Law and to the families of the martyrs for the Awami or People's reception. The reception was to be held at Kakri Ground, the large sports field in Lyari where my father had been the first politician to speak to and for the underprivileged and where six people had been killed and others beaten and tear-gassed by the police in the demonstrations of August 14, 1986. Sections of Kakri Ground were also set aside for the public.

The night before the henna ceremony I slipped off to Lyari wearing a *burqa* to check on the preparations. Members of the Maritime Union and members of other unions were putting the finishing touches on the fifty by forty foot main stage at Kakri Ground, solidly constructed out of wood and eighty tons of steel. Emergency generators were in place to light the grounds if the regime decided to cut off the electricity, and twenty big-screen television sets were set up around the grounds to show the proceedings. Bowers of jasmine, marigolds and roses were being put up around the seating areas on either side of the carpeted stage for our two families, and chairs placed in between for Asif and me.

Hundreds of strings of lights, red and green in the PPP colours, and white, hung the length of the five-storey buildings surrounding the grounds, and spotlights shone on a huge painting of my father putting his hand on my head in blessing. We were expecting one hundred thousand people to come to Kakri Ground. At least ten thousand were already camped there, some having walked or bicycled from Interior Sindh. As my brothers and sisters, they felt they didn't need invitations. They had come to a family wedding.

The sound of drums and wooden sticks. Women singing. Ululations of greeting from my relatives. The groom's procession arrived at 70 Clifton on December 17, for the *Mehndi*, Asif's relatives bearing a platter of henna carved in the shape of a peacock, complete with real tail feathers. My female relatives placed garlands of roses around the necks of the Zardari entourage as they moved into the garden. Asif was in the middle of the procession, his sisters holding a shawl over his head. I was relieved that he had arrived on foot. He had threatened to ride in on his polo pony.

We sat together on a bench with a mirrored back and inlaid with mother-of-pearl at the top of the steps to 71 Clifton. I looked out through my veil at my family and friends clustered below me on one side of the carpeted steps, and Asif's family on the other. I doubt anyone had heard the likes of the lyrics from my side as the singing began. Asif must look after the children while I am out campaigning and not prevent me from going to jail, Yasmin, Sanam, Laleh and other friends sang. 'You must agree that Benazir will serve the nation,' they warbled in Urdu, then responded for Asif: 'That is all right with me, for I will serve the nation by serving my wife.'

The guests, two hundred of our closest friends, clapped and talked under the colourful tent set up in the garden before moving on to the buffet tables. I saw tears on Mummy's face. I didn't know whether they were tears of happiness or frustration over the number of foreign photographers who had somehow got past the security men and were crowding around Asif and me. The *Mehndi* was supposed to be a family affair, but the press billing of the two-day celebration as the wedding of the century on the sub-continent had brought press from the Arab states, Germany, France, India, the United States, and England as well as the wire services and, of course, members of the local press.

I so wished my brother Mir could be with us when we gathered in the garden the next night for the *Nikah*, the wedding ceremony. He hadn't been able to come to Sanam's wedding either, nor had any of our family been able to attend his wedding in Afghanistan. Mir had threatened to sneak into Pakistan for my wedding, in spite of the dangers of being caught by the regime and arrested. But my mother had forbidden him to take the risk.

'Don't walk so fast. You're not late for a public meeting,' Sunny whispered to me through the pink veil covering my face as she and Mummy led me to the wedding stage in the garden.

'Brides walk sedately,' echoed Auntie Behjat as she held the Holy Quran over my head and tried to keep up.

I tried to look demurely down at the ground as I took my place on the wedding dais. My cousin Shad came up, smiling.

'What's taking the men so long?' I asked, wondering what was happening on Asif's side, where the *maulvi* from our family mosque was reading the marriage vows.

'*Manzoor ah-hay?* Do you accept?' Shad asked me in Sindhi. I thought he was jokingly asking me if I was ready.

'*Ah-hay*,' I replied. 'Yes. But where are they?'

He only smiled and asked me the question twice more. '*Ah-hay. Ah-hay*,' I repeated. Before I realised it, I had said the customary 'yes' three times to the male witness, and was a married woman.

Seven items beginning with the letter 's' surrounded me, as well as plates of sweetmeats, nuts dipped in silver and gold, silver candles in silver candelabra. Thousands of white lights spangled the garden, the light dancing off the silver tinsel encrusting the dais. My female relatives held a green and gold diaphanous shawl over my head when Asif joined me. Together, we looked into the mirror placed in front of us, seeing each other as partners for the first time. Ululations filled the air as my mother and aunts ground sugar cones over our heads so that our lives together would be sweet, then knocked our heads together to signify our union.

Karachi went wild with celebration that night. Thousands pressed together outside 70 Clifton for a glimpse of Asif and me when we moved to Clifton Gardens for the private reception just a block away. PPP volunteer guards had to struggle to keep a path open for our guests who walked the few hundred yards from 70 Clifton. When we left for the Awami reception in Lyari an hour later, the streets on the way were just as crowded with well-wishers, jeeps blasting out the wedding songs which had popped up all over Pakistan to commemorate our marriage. There were strings of PPP lights everywhere, festooning the centre of the roundabout where so many had been tear-gassed the year before, and draped from buildings along the route.

The crowds at Kakri Ground swelled to over two hundred thousand, spilling into the streets. This was Asif's first taste of the love and support of the masses for the PPP and he looked worried as the security guards urged the crowds to open a passageway for the Pajero. There wasn't an inch of space on the sports field, nor room for one other person on the balconies on the buildings that rimmed the field. For days women members of the PPP had been wrapping wedding sweets into PPP-coloured boxes to distribute among the crowd at Lyari. Forty thousand were gone in an hour.

Jiye, Bhutto! *Jiye*, Bhutto! Folk music floated out over the crowd. People danced, cheered. Miniature hot-air balloons were released, trailing streamers of fire. A display of fireworks sent rockets soaring into the night air, while fountains of silver and gold erupted on the ground. I waved to the crowd. They waved back. It made no difference to their hopes and dreams whether I was married or single.

Zia's intelligence agents, I'm sure, were among the crowd at Lyari, hoping to be able to tell him that my marriage had diminished my support. But the regime's hopes were dashed. 'Now Zia won't call elections until Benazir starts a family,' Samiya joked with my relatives when we returned to 70 Clifton for a late-night supper. Everybody had a good laugh. Though Asif wanted a large family, we had decided to wait. We wanted the time to adjust to married life, and to each other. And my political priorities had not changed.

'Today, on an occasion so personal and solemn for me, I want to reaffirm my public pledge to the people of Pakistan, and restate my most solemn vow to devote my life towards the welfare of each citizen and the freedom of this great nation of ours from dictatorship,' I'd written in a statement released the morning of the wedding. 'I will not hesitate to make any sacrifice, be it large or small, as in the past. I will work shoulder to shoulder with my brothers and sisters – the people of Pakistan – to create an egalitarian society that is free from tyranny, from corruption and from violent tensions. This was my goal yesterday, this is the dream I share with you, and this will remain our unwavering commitment forever.'

POSTSCRIPT

On May 29, 1988, General Zia abruptly dissolved Parliament, dismissed his hand-picked Prime Minister, and called for elections. I was in a meeting at 70 Clifton with party members from Larkana when the startling message was passed to me. 'You must be mistaken,' I said. 'General Zia avoids elections. He doesn't hold them.' Even when the party official assured me that Zia had made the announcement at 7.15 pm on the radio and television, I still couldn't believe it. 'You must have confused it with some other country,' I said.

The congratulatory phone calls flooding into 70 Clifton and the clamouring of the press at the gate confirmed Zia's totally unexpected move. To some, the timing was suspect. Four days before, a Karachi newspaper had announced I was to become a mother. 'I told you if you started a family Zia would hold elections,' Samiya said triumphantly after I spoke with the press. Whether or not Zia's announcement was influenced by my condition I do not know, but it did follow the news confirming for the first time that I was expecting. Though Asif and I had wanted to wait before starting a family, we had been delighted with the unexpected news. Now with Zia's melodramatic announcement, 1988 promised to be a year for unexpected happenings all around.

No one knew of Zia's intent beforehand, including Prime Minister Junejo who had just returned from a trip to the Far East and at 6.00 pm was holding a press conference. Less than an hour later, a Junejo aide who had listened to Zia's broadcast informed Zia's prime minister that he had been sacked. Four reasons were given for the dissolution of the government: the failure of Prime Minister Junejo's government to introduce Islamic Law quickly enough; the mishandling of the investigation into the devastating Ojri munitions depot explosion in April which launched missiles and bombs into the civilian population; corruption in the administration, and the breakdown of law and order throughout the country.

Though I had little truck with Zia's hand-picked Prime Minister, I felt sorry for the petty manner in which Mr Junejo was dismissed. Junejo had served Zia well, rubber-stamping the Zia Constitution, indemnifying all actions of Martial Law, confirming Zia as President and Chief-of-Army-

317

Staff until 1990. But I quickly found that there was no echo of sympathy for him. 'When you lie with dogs, you get bitten,' ran one of the harsh responses. Junejo's epitaph, I heard several people remark, should read: 'the man who tumbled into history and tumbled out of it.'

Regardless, the mood throughout the country following Zia's announcement was ebullient. Zia's own constitution called for elections within ninety days of the dissolution of the government and to many, victory seemed near. 'No one can stop the PPP now,' said one supporter after another. I tried, unsuccessfully, to plead caution. Though publicly I issued a conditional positive response to the promise of elections — 'If fair, free and impartial party-based elections are held within ninety days, we will welcome it' — privately I had my doubts.

Free, fair elections meant the return of the PPP and the Bhuttos. Zia was already on record as saying he would 'not return power to those he had taken it from'. If he had found it difficult to co-habit with Mr Junejo, his own creation, how could he accept as Prime Minister the daughter of the man he had ordered to be executed? 'Zia hasn't dismissed Junejo to permit the PPP to capture Parliament,' I tempered the enthusiasm of our exultant supporters. Unfortunately but inevitably, Zia's subsequent actions confirmed my worst suspicions.

On June 15, Zia announced the installation of *Shariah*, or Islamic law as the supreme law of the land. Zia didn't define what it was or was not in his television address, and nobody was sure what it meant. Did this mean that currency notes with representations of Mohammed Ali Jinnah, the founder of Pakistan, would be withdrawn because some Islamic schools consider the portrayal of the human face unIslamic? Did this mean that government bonds, which carry a fixed rate of interest, would be declared usurious? No guidelines were offered. What it boiled down to was that any citizen could now challenge an existing law as 'unIslamic' before the High Courts. If the court found the law to be contrary to Islam, the judges could strike it down. But why had Zia waited until 1988 to implement *Shariah*?

Many thought that the timing of Zia's latest exploitation of Islam was directed at me. The Urdu press speculated that Zia could use the interpretation of Islamic bigots to try and prevent me, as a woman, from standing for election, or he could use it subsequently to try and disqualify me as the leader of the victorious party in the National Assembly. But I had my doubts as to whether he would succeed. The Constitution of 1973, which was approved by the country's religious parties, had declared women eligible to become head of government. Similarly, Zia's own Constitution of 1985 upheld a woman's eligibility for head of government. Zia's options were narrowing.

More than ever we doubted that the elections would be fair and impartial. Nonetheless, the PPP pressed ahead although we had no idea whether political parties would be allowed to field candidates or when the elections would take place. In spite of the fact that Zia had declared the date would be announced after Islamic Law was installed, no date was announced. Zia was up to his old tricks to avoid meeting the PPP at the polls. But this time we had ammunition of our own.

In February, we had gone to the Supreme Court to challenge Zia's 1985 Voter's Registration clause, which required all political parties to register with the regime. Under Zia's rules, all political parties wishing to take part in elective polls had to submit their accounts as well as their list of office holders to the administration's chosen Election Commissioner. Armed with that information, the Election Commissioner could then disallow any political party from participating in elections on such vague grounds as the party being against the ideology of Islam, regardless of the fact that the ideology was not defined. Just as incredibly, the Commissioner could also preclude the office bearers from standing for elections for fourteen years and even impose jail sentences of seven years!

Blatantly designed to keep the PPP out of the electoral field, the law not only violated the fundamental right of freedom of association to the citizenry, but gave Zia's nominee the right to recognise which party could operate and which could not. Fortunately for us, Mr Yahya Bakhtiar, the former Attorney General of Pakistan who had headed my father's appeal, consented to argue the case before the Supreme Court. Eleven judges heard the case, the largest bench ever convened in the history of the Court. Their unanimous decision, handed down on June 20, 1988, constituted a moral and legal victory for the people of Pakistan: Zia's Registration clause was struck down as 'void in its entirety'.

'Parliamentary government is a government of the party and a party government is a vital principle of a representative government,' the Chief Justice wrote in his statement. '. . . At a minimum an election provides a legal means for validating a claim to govern. It is a party system that converts the results of a Parliamentary election into a government.' Agreeing with the Chief Justice, another Supreme Court judge observed: 'Persons elected to the legislature in their personal capacities have hardly any importance. They just toss around on the political scene, rudderless and without a destination. It is only when they band themselves into a group as a party, that they become a force exercising some influence by their activities. Only as members of a political party and not as individual members of the legislature can they achieve their objectives.'

The intent of the Supreme Court in striking down Zia's 'registration clause' was clear: no party, registered or unregistered, could be prevented from participating in elections. The Court's verdict was also clear. Every citizen had the fundamental right to participate in elections through a political party of his or her choice. Elections had to be held on the basis of political parties. There was no other Constitutional option, even under Zia's own Constitution. But Zia, we all knew, was not one to hold himself accountable to the laws of Pakistan.

I continued to tour the country, travelling from Larkana to an enthusiastic welcome in Jacobabad, then on to Nawabshah where former members of the Muslim League joined ranks with the PPP. When I returned to Karachi, more Muslim League parliamentarians joined us. The momentum was building in favour of the PPP, starting a bandwagon effect. Potential candidates were all seeking the heavy party support that the PPP's symbol on the ballot would bring.

Wherever I went, the people turned out in thousands, in spite of the searing heat and the summer rains. At a speech in Lahore in July, the crowds were so huge that the press compared them to the crowds that had welcomed me home from exile in 1986. By the grace of God, I felt fit and filled with energy.

'Are you sure you're expecting?' asked a lady doctor before examining me. 'We all thought it was a political trick to get Zia to hold elections.' I was surprised to hear that many shared the rumour all over the country. 'People keep asking me how you can keep up such a hectic travel schedule if you're really in the family way,' Fakhri said to me in exasperation. But there was too much at stake to rest. If Zia upheld his own constitution, elections would be held by the end of August.

I was at a breakfast meeting with the Australian Ambassador at 70 Clifton on July 20 when another note was slipped to me. The elections, Zia had just announced, were to be held on November 16. Admitting that the Constitution provided that the elections should have been held within ninety days of the dissolution of the National Assembly, Zia said he had delayed the date in view of the coming monsoons, the Muslim month of mourning (*Muharram*) and the month of pilgrimage (the *Haj*). The tension that developed during *Muharram*, Zia maintained, would make elections impossible. Ninety thousand Pakistani pilgrims on *Haj* would be deprived of their right to vote, he claimed, if the elections were held during the constitutional period. And the rains had already caused flooding in many parts of the country. I took his excuses with a large grain of salt. The real reason he had postponed the elections, I felt, had more to do with my physical condition. Zia could not afford to have me on the campaign trail.

At least a date had been set, and we felt a sense of relief, though it was measured. Zia had already deviated from the constitution and we had no assurance he wouldn't deviate again in November and cancel the elections. We also didn't know yet if Zia planned to hold the elections on a party or non-party basis. All signs, however, pointed to panic in the Zia camp. The Muslim League had disintegrated following Zia's abrupt dismissal of

Prime Minister Junejo and the National Assembly in May. Zia had to woo back the very ministers he had accused of being corrupt and inept, including his own Prime Minister, to reunite the party against the PPP challenge.

In an effort to mend fences, Zia had already reappointed nine of Junejo's cabinet ministers to his interim caretaker government. Indeed, of the seventeen new cabinet ministers and one Minister of State, seven were sacked members of the Senate and ten ex-members of the National Assembly. Zia had even apologised profusely in public for 'hurting the feelings and sentiments' of the former legislators by accusing them of irregularities and corruption. This public apology was meant as a sop for Prime Minister Junejo himself. Ironically, just two months after dismissing him, Zia found he once again needed him.

In the face of the undiminished strength of the PPP, Zia's electoral staff was also running scared. When I sent a representative to get a list of voters from the Election Commission in Larkana he was told to come back the next day. He got the same answer on the next day and the next and the next. 'Why are you delaying matters?' my representative asked. The frightened official replied: 'We have sent a telegram to Islamabad to get permission. So far we have received no reply.'

Zia's fear of the PPP became blatantly clear on July 21. Claiming that party-based elections were against the spirit of Islam because party decisions often held sway over individual conscience and that the majority of people supported his view, Zia announced that the polls would be held on a party-less basis and the candidates deprived of political party symbols on the ballot. Once again, this would leave the vast majority of the population unable to identify whom them wished to vote for. Further, Zia's system would promote influential individuals at the cost of dedicated political cadres which could only win through party support.

Once more Zia had flouted the Constitution and the sentiments of the highest court in the land. A newspaper report on the 31st of July clarified why. Shortly before his latest anti-democratic announcement, Zia had summoned the Provincial Secretaries from all four provinces to Islamabad as well as other senior officials to discuss whether the polls should be held on a party or non-party basis. Because of the infighting in the Muslim League, the paper reported, the leaders from Baluchistan, from Sindh, from Punjab and from the Northwest Frontier Province all felt that the PPP would have little difficulty in sweeping the polls. The divided opposition, the leader of the Northwest Frontier Province was reported to have said, 'will make it comfortable for Ms Benazir Bhutto to earn enough seats to emerge as the single majority group.' Three days later, Zia announced the non-party elections.

Once again we turned to the courts, filing a petition before the Supreme

Court in early August which challenged the constitutionality of Zia's party-less elections. But would a victory at the Supreme Court really help us in light of the fact that Zia had held the Court's earlier judgment in such contempt? As a dictator, Zia holds vast powers. Even if the Supreme Court decides in our favour on the basis of the fundamental right of association, Zia can simply declare a state of emergency, thereby nullifying the decision. He may already be setting the stage. On August 4, the eve of the Muslim month of mourning, a Shiite leader was shot dead in Peshawar. In the opposition we speculated whether the regime was behind the assassination in order to create the strife which would justify a declaration of emergency.

As further protection for a Zia win, it is also being widely rumoured that new election laws are on the anvil whereby successful candidates can be disqualified on the pretext of having any support from political parties. Sources tell us that the law will be enacted during the first week of October, leaving Zia's opposition too short a time to challenge the law in court before the elections. That Zia is a dictator who has every intention of manipulating the election results through party-less polls, intimidation and stacked election laws is self-evident.

My mother is returning to Pakistan in mid-September to campaign and probably stand for a seat herself. In a party-less election, we will need every solid and well-known candidate possible. Regardless of the odds, we will continue to challenge Zia through peaceful, democratic means, using the legal framework that is the backbone of any civilised country. Bludgeoning the population into acquiescence with guns and tear gas may win capitulation and resignation, but not the soul. Zia knows he has never been able to win the hearts or the support of the people. Instead he has ruled by terror and threat.

As we approach the watershed of the November elections, Pakistan is at the crossroads of democracy and continued dictatorship. The people of Pakistan are crying out for self-determination. Their voice is the Pakistan People's Party. And Zia knows it. After eleven and a half years, Zia is still unable to hold free and impartial elections for fear that the PPP will sweep them.

Just as a flower cannot bloom in the desert, so political parties cannot flourish in a dictatorship. That the political parties have managed to survive and flourish despite the draconian measures taken against them is a tribute to those who gave their lives for democracy and to the people of the Pakistan who realise that their rights can be restored and protected only if they band together in a national party. We are the conscience of the country, the future and the hope. Our day, I know, will come.

Karachi
August, 1988

322

INDEX

INDEX

All references to members of the Bhutto family, including those who married into it, are listed under Bhutto; the relationships are given in each case, and the entries are marked with an asterisk.

Islamic names are listed under the penultimate name, e.g. Azra Ahmed. Where there are three names the same rule applies; e.g. Mohammed Khan Junejo appears as Khan Junejo, Mohammed, though there are cross references to assist the reader. The exception to this rule is for well-known people, e.g. Jinnah, Mohammed Ali.